GOD AND THE SCIENTIST

Ashgate Science and Religion Series

Series Editors:

Roger Trigg, *Emeritus Professor, University of Warwick, and Academic Director of the Centre for the Study of Religion in Public Life, Kellogg College, Oxford*

J. Wentzel van Huyssteen, *Princeton Theological Seminary, USA*

Science and religion have often been thought to be at loggerheads but much contemporary work in this flourishing interdisciplinary field suggests this is far from the case. The *Ashgate Science and Religion Series* presents exciting new work to advance interdisciplinary study, research and debate across key themes in science and religion, exploring the philosophical relations between the physical and social sciences on the one hand and religious belief on the other. Contemporary issues in philosophy and theology are debated, as are prevailing cultural assumptions arising from the 'post-modernist' distaste for many forms of reasoning. The series enables leading international authors from a range of different disciplinary perspectives to apply the insights of the various sciences, theology and philosophy and look at the relations between the different disciplines and the rational connections that can be made between them. These accessible, stimulating new contributions to key topics across science and religion will appeal particularly to individual academics and researchers, graduates, postgraduates and upper-undergraduate students.

Other titles in the series:

Cyborg Selves
A Theological Anthropology of the Posthuman
Jeanine Thweatt-Bates
978-1-4094-2141-2 (hbk)

The Cognitive Science of Religion
James A. Van Slyke
978-1-4094-2123-8 (hbk)

Science and Faith within Reason
Reality, Creation, Life and Design
Edited by Jaume Navarro
978-1-4094-2608-0 (hbk)

God and the Scientist
Exploring the Work of John Polkinghorne

Edited by

FRASER WATTS
University of Cambridge, UK

CHRISTOPHER C. KNIGHT
International Society for Science and Religion, UK

ASHGATE

Published by
Ashgate Publishing Limited
Wey Court East
Union Road
Farnham
Surrey, GU9 7PT
England

Ashgate Publishing Company
Suite 420
101 Cherry Street
Burlington
VT 05401-4405
USA

www.ashgate.com

British Library Cataloguing in Publication Data
God and the scientist : exploring the work of John
    Polkinghorne. -- (Ashgate science and religion series)
    1. Polkinghorne, J. C., 1930- 2. Religion and science.
    3. Providence and government of God--Christianity.
    I. Series II. Watts, Fraser N. III. Knight, Christopher C.,
    1952-
    215-dc23

Library of Congress Cataloging-in-Publication Data
God and the scientist : exploring the work of John Polkinghorne / edited by Fraser Watts and Christopher C. Knight.
        p. cm. -- (Ashgate science and religion series)
    Includes index.
    ISBN 978-1-4094-4569-2 (hardcover) -- ISBN 978-1-4094-4571-5 (ebook) 1. Religion and science. 2. Polkinghorne, J. C., 1930- I. Watts, Fraser N. II. Knight, Christopher C., 1952-
    BL240.3.G59 2012
    261.5'5--dc23

ISBN 9781409445692 (hbk)
ISBN 9781409445708 (pbk)
ISBN 9781409445715 (ebk)

Printed and bound in Great Britain by the
MPG Books Group, UK.

Contents

List of Figures

Notes on Contributors

Ian G. Barbour taught for many years at Carleton College in Minnesota, and his book *Issues in Science and Religion*, published in 1966, became a fundamental textbook for students of the science–theology dialogue. Other books followed, including two based on the Gifford Lectures that he gave in Aberdeen in 1989 and 1990. He was awarded the Templeton Prize for Progress in Religion in 1999 in recognition of his efforts to encourage the dialogue between scientists, philosophers and theologians.

Pat Bennett is a mature post-graduate student at Oxford Brookes University, where she is in the final stages of a PhD integrating theological insights with empirical data from cognitive neuroscience and psychoneuroimmunology. She is a member of the Iona Community.

Nancy Cartwright is Professor of Philosophy at the London School of Economics and at the University of California at San Diego, specializing in the philosophy of the natural and social sciences. In the first half of her career at Stanford University she focussed on philosophy of physics but since moving to LSE and UCSD she has concentrated on the social and economic sciences. She has written extensively about the laws of nature, scientific modelling and causation.

Philip Clayton, author of a number of influential books on the science–theology dialogue, is Dean of Claremont School of Theology and Provost of Claremont Lincoln University. He has taught at Williams College and the California State University, as well as holding guest professorships at the University of Munich, the University of Cambridge and Harvard University. He specializes in constructive theology, the religion–science debate, comparative theologies and the philosophy of religion.

Daniel W. Darg recently completed his DPhil degree in astrophysics at Oxford University, where he continues to work at a postdoctoral level on astrophysics and philosophical topics related to Cosmology and the Anthropic Principle. He previously studied physics at Imperial College London and Theology and Jewish Studies at Oxford.

Junghyung Kim is currently an associate pastor of the Presbyterian Church of the Lord, Seoul. Recently he completed his PhD degree at the Graduate Theological

Union, Berkeley, focusing in his research on Christian eschatology in dialogue with scientific cosmology.

Russell Re Manning is the Lord Gifford Fellow in the School of Divinity, History and Philosophy at the University of Aberdeen. He is President of the North American Paul Tillich Society and Co-convenor of the Boyle Lectures. Many of his recent publications have focused on the topic of natural theology.

Eric Martin studied Philosophy and Science Studies at the University of California, San Diego and is currently a postdoctoral researcher at the London School of Economics. He has written on the history and philosophy of science, the philosophy of biology, and science and religion.

John Polkinghorne was Professor of Mathematical Physics at the University of Cambridge before training for the ordained ministry of the Anglican Church and eventually returning to Cambridge, first as Dean and Chaplain of Trinity Hall and subsequently as President of Queens' College. He has written many books on the science–theology dialogue and in 2002 became the first President of the International Society for Science and Religion. In the same year he was awarded the Templeton Prize for Progress in Religion.

Robert John Russell is the Ian G. Barbour Professor of Theology and Science in Residence at the Graduate Theological Union, Berkeley, where he is the Founder and Director of the Center for Theology and the Natural Sciences. He is the author or editor of a number of books on the science–theology dialogue and is the co-founding editor of the journal *Theology and Science*.

Nicholas Saunders trained as a barrister after completing his doctorate at Cambridge University and publishing the results of his research in an influential book on divine action and modern science. He continues to work on the science–theology dialogue when his professional duties permit.

Keith Ward was formerly the Regius Professor of Divinity at Oxford University and is a Student of Christ Church, Oxford, and a Professorial Research Fellow at Heythrop College, London University. His interest in science owes much to John Polkinghorne and to fellow members of the Triangle Club (the triangle being science, philosophy and theology) at the University of Cambridge. He is a Fellow of the British Academy.

James M. Watkins is a PhD candidate in theology at the University of St Andrews. He also holds an MCS in Christianity and the Arts from Regent College, and a BA in Studio Art from Wheaton College, where he concentrated on painting. His research interests lie broadly within the relationship between theology, the visual arts and human creativity.

Fraser Watts is Reader in Theology and Science in the Faculty of Divinity at the University of Cambridge, and Director of the Psychology and Religion Research Group. His research focuses mainly on the interface between theology and psychology, and cognitive theories of religion.

Michael Welker is Chair for Systematic Theology at the Theological Faculty of the University of Heidelberg, a member of the Heidelberger Akademie der Wissenschaften and the Finnish Academy of Sciences and Letters, and Director of the Research-Center for International and Interdisciplinary Theology (FIIT Heidelberg).

Terry J. Wright is an Associate Research Fellow at Spurgeon's College (Baptist), and a tutor for both the Diocese of Rochester (Church of England) and the Barking, Dagenham and Ilford circuit (the Methodist Church of Great Britain). His main research interest is the Christian doctrine of God's providence.

Preface

John Polkinghorne – one of the most significant figures in the dialogue between science and theology over the past 30 years – was born in 1930. Most of his working life has been spent in the University of Cambridge, England, where as an undergraduate he read mathematics at Trinity College, remaining to work for his doctorate in mathematical physics in the group led by Paul Dirac. After relatively short periods elsewhere – as a Harkness fellow at the California Institute of Technology and as a lecturer at the University of Edinburgh – he returned to a lectureship in Cambridge in 1958, where he was promoted to a Readership in 1965 and to a Professorship in mathematical physics in 1968 – a position he held until 1979. During this period he became a key figure in particle physics, and he was elected a Fellow of the Royal Society.

In his undergraduate years, the distinctive evangelical approach of the (non-denominational) Christian Union played a significant role in Polkinghorne's religious development. Throughout his career in physics, his Christian commitment remained strong, although his theology became more broadly based. By his late forties, he felt that it would be appropriate to offer himself for the ordained ministry of the Anglican Church. Having been accepted for training for that ministry, he resigned his university chair and studied for two years at Westcott House, Cambridge. Ordained Deacon in 1981 and Priest in 1982, he worked first as an assistant curate in Bristol and subsequently as vicar of Blean, in Kent.

During this period of parish ministry, Polkinghorne's first book about the relationship between science and theology was published. This early book – *The Way the World Is* (1983) – was an indication that Polkinghorne was to play a significant part in the new phase of the dialogue between science and theology that had recently been inaugurated by books like Ian Barbour's *Issues in Science and Religion* (1966) and Arthur Peacocke's *Science and the Christian Experiment* (1971). This possibility was no doubt a factor in Polkinghorne's return to Cambridge in 1986 – first as Dean and Chaplain of Trinity Hall, and subsequently as President of Queens' College.

In the year of Polkinghorne's return to Cambridge, his book *One World* (1986) appeared, soon to be followed by two more volumes, *Science and Creation* (1988) and *Science and Providence* (1989). In this trilogy – still regarded by some as the best introduction to his thinking – Polkinghorne not only manifested the extraordinarily effective style of communication that was to characterise all his later work on the science–theology dialogue, but also set out the main outlines of the theology that he was to defend and expand in the more than 20 books that followed.

Polkinghorne's judgement is that the core elements of Christian belief are not threatened by scientific advance, although science has provided the resources for many of them to be reformulated in a more sophisticated and contemporary way. It is probably true to say that no one has championed the credibility of Christian faith in a scientific age more effectively than Polkinghorne, and his many books have attracted an impressively large readership. His core assumption has been that theology and science provide convergent approaches to the ultimate nature of reality, which is explored more effectively with the 'binocular' vision that is possible when both are used together, than by either on its own.

When the International Society for Science and Religion was formed in 2002, Polkinghorne was a natural choice as its first President. It was fitting, therefore, that eight years later, to mark his eightieth birthday, that Society decided to explore and celebrate his theological work by organising two events. The first was a competition for scholars not yet in permanent academic posts, who were invited to submit essays on any aspect of Polkinghorne's theology. The second was a major international conference to honour his lifetime's theological achievement. At this conference (held in association with the Ian Ramsey Centre in Oxford), Polkinghorne himself gave a summary of the theological perspectives that he had developed over his long and active career, and papers on aspects of his work were presented by many of the world's leading experts on the science–theology dialogue. Together with the five best competition entries (all but one of which of which were also presented at the conference), these invited conference papers form the main chapters of this book.

This book is far more, however, than a simple 'conference proceedings'. Invitations to present papers at the conference were given with the needs of the present volume in mind, and Polkinghorne himself has not only summarised his work in the conference presentation that forms the first chapter, but has also reflected on the other chapters of the book, and responded in what has now become its final chapter. This volume is, therefore, one that anyone interested in Polkinghorne's theology will find invaluable. The careful reader will find here not only an exploration and celebration of his understanding of the relationship between science and theology, but also the outlines of a debate that will go on, as part of his legacy, for many decades to come.

Fraser Watts (President) and Christopher C. Knight (Executive Secretary),
International Society for Science and Religion

Chapter 1

Reflections of a Bottom-up Thinker

John Polkinghorne

I spent more than 25 years of my life working as a theoretical elementary particle physicist. It happened to be a particularly interesting period in the subject, for it saw the discovery of the quark structure of matter. Being part of that community at that time was an enjoyable experience for which I am grateful. However, research in science is pretty hard work. As in all worthwhile activity, there is a good deal of somewhat wearisome routine to be got through and a fair share of occasional frustration to be endured, as the good ideas of the morning prove less convincing in the cold light of the afternoon. So why do we do it? I believe that the prime motivation for work in pure science is a deep desire to understand the world. The hard work involved receives its reward in the occasional experience of wonder as some new and beautiful aspect of the order of nature is revealed to our enquiry. Yet those imbued with a thirst for understanding will not find that it is quenched by science alone. The truth is that science has achieved its very considerable success partly by the modesty of its ambition. It does not seek to ask and answer every necessary and meaningful question, for science contents itself to limiting its enquiry to investigating the processes by which things happen, while bracketing out questions of whether there is purposeful meaning and value to be found in what is happening. The focus of science's attention is on events that are sufficiently impersonal in their character to lend themselves to repetition at will. This affords science its great secret weapon of experimental testing. I was a theorist – a paper-and-pencil chap – but I gladly acknowledge that during my time in particle physics the subject was largely experimentally driven by a wave of remarkable and unexpected empirical discoveries. However, there are many other kinds of human encounter with reality that are fundamentally personal in character and so are irreducibly unique and not open to manipulated repetition.

This single-minded concentration of scientific thought on the impersonal has been extremely effective methodologically, but taken as a metaphysical axiom it would be disastrously impoverishing. My favourite illustration of this fact appeals to our experience of music. The scientific account is that music is neural response to the impact of sound waves on the eardrum. Of course that is true, up to a point, and even worth knowing, but it scarcely begins to do justice to the rich character of music, that mysterious but undeniable way in which a temporal succession of sonic wave-packets evokes in us enjoyment of a timeless encounter with the realm of beauty. Science trawls experience with a coarse-grained net and many things of the greatest significance fall through its wide meshes. Many other forms of encounter with reality also need to be taken into serious account in our quest for understanding, including religion's encounter with the sacred reality of God.

My use of the word 'reality' will, of course, raise eyebrows in some quarters. Like most scientists, and indeed most participants in the field of science and religion – notably including my friends and valued colleagues, Ian Barbour and the late Arthur Peacocke, who have contributed so much to our field – I am a critical realist. The noun 'realism' indicates the conviction that our understanding is related to the way things actually are and what is involved is not just pleasant or convenient manners of speaking, which might be practically useful but not to be taken with ontological seriousness. However, the adjective 'critical' acknowledges that the defence of this realist position requires some subtlety of argument, for the character of our encounter with reality often lacks straightforward objectivity of the kind that the Enlightenment encouraged us to expect and which Albert Einstein so greatly longed for. My illustration this time will be drawn from quantum theory. The subatomic quantum world is cloudy and fitful, quite different in its character from the seemingly clear and reliable world of Newtonian thinking and everyday experience. Are those strange electrons, existing in states that are unpicturable mixtures of both 'here' and 'there', really to be taken to be ontological realities, or is the idea of them simply a handy means of correlating empirical data? Physicists believe in the reality of electrons because that belief enables them to understand a vast range of more directly observable phenomena, ranging from the whole of chemistry to unexpected physical properties such as superconductivity, as well as leading to the construction of many functionally effective devices, such as the electron microscope and the laser. Unless there really are electrons, these achievements are just a fantastic series of unbelievably lucky accidents. In other words, the physicists' belief in the reality of unseen entities such as electrons, and even in entities such as confined quarks that are in principle unseeable, rests on the *intelligibility* that this belief affords us. The philosopher of science whom I have found to be most helpful in thinking about these issues has been Michael Polanyi. He was, of course, a very distinguished physical chemist before he turned to philosophy and so he knew science from the inside. This enabled Polanyi to recognise the role played in science by personally exercised tacit skills, learned through apprenticeship in a truth-seeking community. The intuitive skill that enables an experimentalist to identify and control for unwanted background effects in an experiment, or a theorist to make an imaginative leap of understanding that goes beyond a plodding Baconian examination of common factors, is a task that cannot be delegated to a computer, for it requires personal acts of judgement that cannot be reduced to the following of a logically spelled out protocol. The delicate circular interplay between theory and experiment, in which theory is required to elucidate what is actually being measured in an experiment and experiments confirm or disconfirm theories, means that science is not only explanatorily highly successful but also logically somewhat precarious. Nevertheless, the depth and scope of the understanding that science attains in its investigation of a well-winnowed regime merit our commitment to its validity, even if we know that some revision may turn out to be necessary when one goes beyond that regime. Polanyi said that he wrote his great book *Personal Knowledge* to show how he could rationally commit himself to what he believed scientifically to be true, even though he knew that it might be false. I think that this is a stance necessary in all human quests for understanding.

The religious believer will find much resonance with these insights from scientific experience. Our belief in the unseen reality of God is supported by the way that belief in the Presence and Purpose of the Creator enables us to make sense of great swathes of spiritual experience, both our own and that recorded in the religious tradition to which we belong, as well as illuminating certain aspects of the universe that are revealed to us by science. (These latter are points to which I shall return.) The idea that intelligibility undergirds our belief in reality is one that is powerfully expressed in the theological writings of Bernard Lonergan. One of my favourite quotations from Lonergan is his statement that 'God is the all-sufficient explanation, the eternal rapture glimpsed in every Archimedean cry of "Eureka"'. That speaks to both the physicist and the religious believer in me.

Thoughts such as these form the basis of my belief – widely shared with others in the science and religion community – that science and religion are friends and not foes, 'cousins under the skin', since they both participate in the great human quest for truthful understanding, attainable through well-motivated belief. I believe it to be of the highest importance to emphasise and defend this cousinly connection. Today some strident atheist opponents of religion manifest their woeful ignorance of theological argument by claiming that religious beliefs are simply irrational assertions. Even unbelievers who are more balanced and open can sometimes fall into this trap. I have a number of scientific friends who are both wistful and wary about religion. They are wistful because they see that an honest science cannot claim to address or answer every meaningful and necessary question. They would like a broader and deeper view of reality and they realise that religion offers such a view. Yet they fear that it does so on unacceptable terms. Their picture of faith is that it requires unhesitating submission to the decrees of an unchallengeable authority, presented as non-negotiable and beyond question. Naturally they do not want to commit intellectual suicide, but neither do you and neither do I. I often find myself trying to show such friends that I have motivations for my religious beliefs, just as I have motivations for my scientific beliefs. Both sets of beliefs are the fruit of bottom-up searches for truth, seeking to move from experience to understanding. Neither set of beliefs is certain beyond the possibility of error, but both are sufficiently well-motivated to validate commitment to them. The scientist and the religious believer both walk by reasonable faith and not by incontrovertible sight.

This cousinly relation between science and religion means that each has some gifts to offer the other and that lessons learned in one field can often be translated into helpful guides to truth-seeking enquiry in the other. I have already pointed to the role of intelligibility as the grounding for ontology. Science discourages an Enlightenment assumption that there is a universal epistemology. Rather entities can only be known in ways that accord with their intrinsic natures. To demand to know the quantum world with the clarity of Newtonian epistemology is to aspire to something that is unattainable. The quantum world can only be known in accordance with its character of Heisenbergian uncertainty. Equally, we know persons in a different way to that in which we know things, since that encounter has to be based on mutual respect and trust and cannot properly depend upon manipulative testing. If I am always setting little traps to see if you are my friend, I will soon destroy the possibility of friendship between us. The transpersonal reality of God has to be known in yet another way, one that is open to the demands of awe and obedience.

Respect for the idiosyncrasy of what we are endeavouring to think about also implies that there is not a single form that rationality has to take. If science teaches us anything, it is that the world is surprising, often beyond human powers to anticipate. Once again, quantum theory makes the point clearly enough. Any philosopher in 1899 could have 'proved' that it is impossible that something should sometimes behave like a wave and sometimes like a particle. After all, a wave is spread out and flappy and a particle is like a little bullet. However, we all know that light has the strange property of wave/particle duality. This oxymoronic possibility arises from the fact that a different logic operates in the quantum world compared with that in familiar everyday experience. The latter is governed by Aristotle's law of the excluded middle, stating that there is no term intermediate between A and not-A. Yet a quantum entity can be in a state that is a mixture of 'here' (A) and 'there' (not-A), a middle term undreamed of in Aristotle's philosophy. It is quantum logic that allows light to have the property of wave/particle duality, a possibility that would never have been conceived of without the stubborn provocation of the way in which nature was actually found to behave.

Consequently, the natural question for a scientist to ask, within science and beyond it, is not 'Is it reasonable?', as if we know beforehand the shape that rationality has to take. Instead, the scientist asks a different question, at once more open and more demanding, 'What makes you think that might be the case?' No proposal is ruled out a priori, but if a counterintuitive suggestion is made, it will have to be backed up by motivating evidence. This is precisely the stance that the bottom-up thinker wishes to take in the search for truth. I wrote my Gifford Lectures to show how I believe a bottom-up thinker may defend and motivate the Christian beliefs expressed in the Nicene Creed.

Of course motivations for religious beliefs have a different detailed character from those for scientific beliefs because, as we have already seen, they relate to different dimensions of reality. Science's concern with the impersonal enables it to be impressively cumulative in its understanding. Any physicist today knows far more about the universe than Isaac Newton ever did, simply by living three centuries later than that great genius. In the realm of the personal there is no justified assumption of the superiority of present understanding over that of the past. Twenty-first-century music has no necessary superiority over that of Bach or Beethoven. In theology, we still need to engage with the insights of thinkers of earlier centuries. Augustine and Aquinas, Luther and Calvin remain participants in the diachronic conversation of theology. In particular, each faith tradition looks back to the witness of the persons and events that are foundational to it, seen as sources of transparent disclosure of the nature of sacred reality. Revelation is not the mysterious conveyance of disembodied and infallible propositions, but its focus lies in these disclosure events. The resulting 'scandal of particularity' is inescapable in the realm of the personal, where there is an irreducible uniqueness of insight and experience. The record of these foundational revelatory events is what we call scripture. For me as a Christian, it is the Hebrew Bible and the New Testament that play this scriptural role.

The Bible has been very important for me in my religious life and I would like to say something about its character. The first point is that it is not, in my opinion, a divinely dictated textbook in which we can look up all the answers. Instead, it is more like a laboratory notebook in which are recorded the prime ways in which I believe the divine will and nature have been disclosed to us, through the history of Israel and the life, death and resurrection of Jesus Christ. The Bible is not so much a book as a library, with many different kinds of writing in it. In an honest engagement with the Bible one has continually to be aware of the question of genre. It would certainly be a bad mistake to read poetry as if it were prose. The sad irony of a fundamentalist interpretation of Genesis 1 is that it abuses scripture by treating an assertion of the theological truth that nothing exists except through the will of God as if it were a quasi-scientific literal account of a hectic six days of divine activity. Its genre is theology and not science. The Bible was written over a period of about 1,000 years and in a variety of cultural settings, all different from our contemporary, science-informed, view of the world. Consequently, the Bible contains both timeless truths (such as the steadfast faithfulness of God) and time-bound cultural particularities no longer relevant to us (such as the injunction that women should wear hats in church). Moreover, the long time span of the biblical writings means that within the Bible there is a clearly discernible development of thinking about God, from the quite primitive to the much more profound. The stories of wars and genocide that figure so disturbingly in the Old Testament arise from a period in which faithfulness to the one God of Israel seemed to require the extermination of those who did not share that allegiance. By the time of the prophets of the Exile, such as Second Isaiah, a more just understanding had been gained of the love and mercy of God extended to all peoples. All these problems mean that reading the Bible requires care and sensitivity in interpretation. Yet without it we would know little of Israel and even less of Jesus Christ. For the Christian bottom-up thinker, the Bible remains an indispensable resource.

I am conscious that I have been speaking from the standpoint of a Christian believer. That is what I am and in honesty I cannot do otherwise. Yet I would not like it to be thought that I am in any way dismissive of other faith traditions. I feel sure that all preserve and propagate authentic experience of encounter with sacred reality. There are commonalities between the faiths, such as the value of compassion and the record of mystical experience, although there are also perplexing clashes of understanding. For example, is the human person of unique and abiding significance? Or is it transferable through reincarnation? Or is the individual self ultimately an illusion from which to seek release? These are not three culturally different ways of saying the same thing, but three conflicting assertions. I believe that the challenge of interfaith dialogue is one of the most important issues for us today and likely to be on the religious agenda for the third millennium, rather than simply the twenty-first century. One serious but not too mutually threatening context for this dialogue is provided by the faiths considering together how their traditional understandings relate to modern scientific discoveries. One reason that I welcomed the opportunity to play a role in the founding of the International Society for Science and Religion was that the Society has sought to be truly interfaith and to foster such dialogue.

I am a passionate believer in the unity of knowledge and aspire to have as integrated an understanding as possible of the rich and many-layered reality within which we live. I have pointed to the differences as well as the cousinly relationships that I see between science and religion. They certainly address different questions about the world, but I think it would be a bad mistake to think that those differences mean that they are 'non-overlapping magisteria' (in Stephen J. Gould's phrase) and have no real influence on each other. The questions may be different, but the answers have to display some consonance with one another. Who can doubt that theological discourse about creation has been influenced by scientific discoveries about cosmic and biological evolution, encouraging the concept of continuous creation unfolding through natural processes?

The elucidation of consonance between the insights of science and religion has been the dominant aim within our community during the 27 years that I have been an active member of it. In the earlier part of the period, the agenda was set principally by physics and by evolutionary biology. The universe has proved to be deeply transparent to scientific enquiry, so that we can understand not only the macroscopic world of everyday experience, but also the microscopic world of quantum physics, remote from direct impact upon us and requiring for its understanding counterintuitive modes of thought quite different from those that evolutionary necessity might be expected to have formed our brains to make. We also understand the vast cosmic realm of curved space–time, again quite different in its character from mundane expectation. Not only is the universe rationally transparent to the highest degree, but it is also rationally beautiful. It is an actual technique of discovery in fundamental physics to seek theories that can be expressed in terms of equations possessing the unmistakable character of mathematical beauty. One of my scientific heroes is Paul Dirac, who made his great discoveries through a relentless and highly successful lifelong quest for mathematical beauty. He once went so far as to say that it is more important to have mathematical beauty in your equations than to have them fit experiment! Of course, he did not mean that in the end empirical adequacy was unnecessary, but if at first it did not seem to be the case, this might be due to making an incorrect approximation in solving the equations, or even to the experiments being wrong.

There was, therefore, at least some residual hope that in the end all might be well. However, if your equations were ugly ... in Dirac's view there was no hope for them. The whole history of modern physics testifies that it is only beautiful equations that will display the long-term fruitfulness of explanation that persuades us that they are describing aspects of physical reality.

These scientifically discerned features of the universe are truly remarkable. They make physics possible and they reward physicists with a sense of wonder at the marvellous order that is disclosed to their enquiry. It would surely be intolerably intellectually lazy to see this as no more than an astonishing piece of luck. Cosmic intelligibility and beauty demand an explanation. If it is to be found, it will have to come from beyond science itself, since an honest science exploits these opportunities but the question of their origin is a metaphysical issue, beyond science's self-limited power to address. Setting science in a theistic context offers an answer that is coherent, and to me persuasive. The universe is shot through with signs of mind precisely because the Mind of its Creator lies behind it wonderful order.

Many scientist are not comfortable with the word 'metaphysics', but the fact is that no one can think at all deeply without adopting a metaphysics, for this simply means choosing a world view. We think metaphysics as naturally and inevitably as we speak prose. In Western thinking there have been two distinct metaphysical traditions. They differ in what they take as the assumed basis for their thinking. Nothing comes of nothing, and no world view can be totally self-explanatory, for it will require an unexplained foundation for the edifice of its thought. In the metaphysical tradition of materialism, the defining brute fact is taken to be the properties of matter as described by the laws of nature. In the metaphysical tradition of theism, the defining brute fact is taken to be the existence of a divine Creator. It seems to me that the laws of nature have been found to have a character that is such that they seem irresistibly to point beyond themselves, making it unsatisfactory to treat them as simply given brute fact. In affirming that judgement, I am influenced not only by cosmic intelligibility, but also by the anthropic fine-tuning of the quantitative detail of the laws of nature which we know was essential for our universe to be able to evolve the rich complexity of carbon-based life. For example, we know that a small change in the laws of nuclear physics would have meant that no carbon could be made in the nuclear furnaces of the stars, the only source of that vital element. We are people of stardust, made from the ashes of dead stars. All scientists agree about the remarkable and unexpected fact of cosmic fine-tuning, and many acknowledge that it calls for some metascientific explanation. Those who resist the theistic option that fine-tuning is an expression of the purpose of its Creator, are driven to the rather desperate expedient of invoking the existence of a truly vast portfolio of other universes, all with different laws of nature and all unobservable by us. Our universe would then simply be the one that by chance turned out to have the winning ticket in this immense multiversial lottery. Not only is this metaphysical guess ontologically extravagant – William of Ockham must be turning in his grave – but it is not even clear without much more specific discussion that it would actually achieve its object of explaining, or explaining away, the fine-tuning of our universe. Mere infinity does not guarantee the presence of all desirable properties. After all, there are an infinite number of even integers, but none of them has the property of oddness.

Intelligibility and fine-tuning have provided the basis for a revival of natural theology, something that I have been keen to develop. It is also a *revised* natural theology, different from the old style of John Ray and William Paley in two important respects. First, it appeals not to occurrences within nature, such as the development of the eye, but to the laws of nature themselves which are the given in terms of which science seeks to understand particular occurrences. The new natural theology seeks to complement science, rather than rival it on its own ground, by setting its insights in the broader and deeper context of intelligibility that theistic belief affords. Secondly, the new natural theology is modest in its claims. Its discourse is not in terms of 'proofs' of God's existence, but it offers insights that provide coherent and intellectually satisfying answers to metascientific questions, such as why deep science is possible and why our finely tuned universe is so fruitfully specific. Like science itself, its achievement is to be understood as persuasive best explanation rather than indubitable proof.

Biological evolution, although so often wrongly assumed to be a battle ground on which the forces of religion received a decisive defeat, in fact offers theology an insightful gift. As soon as Darwin published the *Origin of Species* in 1859, there were some theologians who welcomed his ideas. His clergyman friend, Charles Kingsley, coined the phrase that aptly summarises how one should think theologically about the scientific fact of an evolving world. Kingsley recognised that creation was something more profound than a ready-made world would have been, for it is so endowed with God-given potentiality that creatures can be allowed to 'make themselves' through the shuffling exploration of that fertile potentiality. If God is, as Christians believe, a God of love, the creation cannot simply be a divine puppet theatre with the Creator pulling every string. As every parent knows, the gift of love is always the gift of a due degree of freedom to the objects of love, allowed to be themselves and to make themselves. A world of this kind, made fertile by the evolutionary exploration of potentiality, is a great good, but it has a necessary cost. There is an inevitable shadow side to the evolutionary process, which not only gives rise to great fruitfulness, but also has ragged edges and blind alleys. Genetic mutation has not only been the engine driving the three and a half billion year history of the increasing complexity of terrestrial life, but it is also a source of malignancy. One cannot have the one without the other. This insight offers theology some help as it wrestles with its greatest perplexity, the natural evil of disease and disaster present in the creation of a good and powerful God. The more science helps us to understand the nature of the world, the more clearly we see its inextricable entanglement of fertility and wastefulness. I have suggested that there is a free-process defence in relation to natural evil, parallel to the familiar free-will defence in relation to moral evil. Natural evil is not gratuitous, something that a Creator who was a bit more competent or a bit less callous could easily have eliminated. Created nature is a package deal, with the emergence of new forms of life and the shadow side of malformation and extinction necessarily intertwined. I do not pretend that these considerations remove all the anguish and anger we sometimes feel at the spectacle of suffering, but I think that the insights of science are mildly helpful to theology in this way.

Evolutionary process highlights the importance of deep time. In a universe of unfolding emergent novelty, time is not simply the index of when things happen, but a category of fundamental significance, with the present constituted by its origin in the past. Since I believe that God knows things as they really are, I believe that this implies that the Creator of the temporal universe will know it in its temporality. That is to say, God does not simply know that events are successive, but knows them as they are, in their succession. There must then be a temporal pole in the divine nature, complementary to the eternal pole of unchanging faithfulness. Such a dipolar concept of deity is also entertained by process theology, but the latter sees divine engagement with time as a matter of metaphysical necessity imposed upon God. In contrast, I believe that divine dipolarity is freely accepted by the Creator, consequent upon bringing into being a temporal creation. This understanding corresponds to an important element in much twentieth-century theological thinking, which sees the act of creation as being a freely embraced act of divine kenosis, the self-limiting of deity that permits creatures to be themselves and to make themselves. Contrary to classical theology's atemporal view of God, who from an unqualified eternity knows the whole of created history *totum simul*, all at once, I believe that divine dipolarity implies a kenotic acceptance of the status of a current omniscience, knowing all that can be known now, but not yet all that could ever be known. This is no divine imperfection, because in a world of true becoming, the unformed future is not yet there to be known.

Much of what I have been saying so far would be as consistent with the spectatorial God of deism, distantly watching it all happen, as it is with the God of theism, in whom I believe, who is providentially interactive within the open grain of creation's history. In the 1990s, much effort was made in the science and religion community to understand how a belief in special divine action of this sort could be consistent with what science has to tell us about the causal structure of the world. A series of conferences organised by the Center for Theology and the Natural Sciences and the Vatican Observatory played an important role in this endeavour. Much of the discussion hinged on the recognition that physics has discovered the existence of intrinsic unpredictabilities present in nature, discerned first at the subatomic level of quantum physics and later at the macroscopic level of chaos theory. Of course, the word 'intrinsic' is crucial here. These are not unpredictabilities that could be resolved by more exact measurement or more precise calculation. Unpredictability is an epistemological property, relating to what can or cannot be known about future behaviour. The relation of epistemology to ontology is a philosophical issue that is certainly not decided by science, but requires an act of metaphysical decision. The fact that Niels Bohr and David Bohm could offer interpretations of quantum physics of equal empirical adequacy but differing in that one is indeterministic and the other deterministic makes it clear that the nature of causality, while constrained by physics, is not settled simply by science alone.

Those of a realist cast of philosophical inclination will naturally seek to align epistemology and ontology as closely as possible, believing that what is known is a reliable guide to what is the case. Such a strategy leads to interpretation of the presence of intrinsic unpredictabilities as signs of causal openness. This openness does not mean that future behaviour is some sort of random lottery, but that the causes that bring it about need not be simply the exchange of energy between constituents, which is the traditional account given by physics. It seems entirely reasonable to expect that the additional causal principles involved should be such as to accommodate the willed acts of agents, both human and divine.

In the discussions of the 1990s, many different detailed attempts were made to exploit this perceived openness in order to gain some understanding of the operation of divine providence. Some laid stress on the possible role of quantum theory, while I sought to emphasise the possible importance of the macroscopic openness offered by chaos theory. I was somewhat severely criticised by some for adopting this latter tactic. My critics seem to have been bewitched by the deterministic equations from which the mathematical theory of chaos is undoubtedly derived. However, from the physics point of view, these equations are known to be no more than approximations to reality and so are not to be taken with rigorous literalism. In fact, none of the approaches followed in the 1990s were free from difficulties, but this does not mean that the efforts were wasted. Agency is too complex a matter to expect a complete theory to be attainable through such simple approaches. Nevertheless, an important point was made by this decade of activity: physics has not established the causal closure of the world on its own reductionist terms. Taking science seriously does not require us to believe that we are automata or that God is excluded from specific actions within the open grain of created physical process. This point is reinforced by the recognition that the understanding of physics is distinctly patchy. Although frequently excellent within a well-winnowed domain, it often fails to explain how different domains relate to each other. The many unresolved perplexities about how the apparently clear and orderly everyday world emerges from its cloudy and fitful quantum substrate make this point. For example, quantum theory and chaos theory are incompatible with each other, since the former has a scale set by Planck's constant, while the latter's fractal character means that it is scale-free.

Wrestling with the issue of providential action is an example of the way in which in recent years the science and religion dialogue has come to have more of its agenda set by theological questions, so that it has become better balanced and less dominated by responding to issues raised primarily by science. I want to end what I have to say by briefly noting two other examples of this welcome trend.

The first is an engagement with Trinitarian thinking. One could write a history of science over the last 200 years as exemplifying an increasing recognition of the importance of relational thinking. Einstein's integration of space, time and matter, various unifications of the forces of nature starting with Maxwell's theory of electromagnetism, and the counterintuitive property of quantum entanglement are among the discoveries that point in this direction. Einstein thought that entanglement, by which two quantum entities that had once interacted could retain a power of instantaneous mutual influence even when widely spatially separated, was so 'spooky' that it must show there was something wrong with quantum theory. Nevertheless, as we all know, this has been abundantly shown to be a property of nature. Mere atomism is dead. It seems that nature fights back against a crude reductionism.

This scientific discovery that 'reality is relational' will come as no surprise to Trinitarian theologians who have long known about 'being as communion', including the case of the divine nature itself. Of course, quantum entanglement does not explain or necessitate Trinitarian theology, but it is strikingly consonant with the belief that the world's Creator is the triune God.

In the last 10 years, eschatology has been added to the list of topics to be discussed in the science and religion community. Every story that science has to tell ultimately ends in death and decay, owing to the second law of thermodynamics decreeing the relentless rise of the waters of chaos. However, the 'horizontal' story of science is not the only tale to tell. There is also the 'vertical' theological story of everlasting divine faithfulness that will ensure that nothing of good is lost. Famously Jesus appealed to this when, in response to the Sadducees' scepticism about a destiny beyond death, he reminded them that God is the God of Abraham, Isaac and Jacob, adding 'The God, not of the dead, but of the living'. The challenge for science and religion is to see if one can make sense of the idea of a life beyond death. One soon sees that this will require criteria both of continuity and discontinuity to be satisfied. It really must be the patriarchs who live again in the Kingdom of God and not just new characters given the old names for old times' sake. The issue is then what could be the carrier of human continuity? Many of us no longer take a dualist view of human nature, so that the soul, conceived of as a detachable spiritual component, freed at death for this role, is no longer available to us. Instead we have to reconceptualise the soul in a way consistent with belief in human psychosomatic unity. The soul is presumably 'the real me', whose nature is almost as perplexing to understand within this life as beyond it. The real me is certainly not simply the matter of my body, which is changing all the time through wear and tear and nourishment. I have suggested that the soul is the almost infinitely complex information-bearing pattern carried at any one time by the matter of the body. This pattern will decay at death, but I believe it is entirely coherent to believe that the faithful God will not allow it to be lost, but will preserve that individual pattern in the divine memory. For the continuation of a truly human life beyond death, that pattern must eventually be re-embodied in some new environment of God's choosing. The Christian hope is rightly resurrection, not merely spiritual survival.

Here the criterion of discontinuity has to come into play. The new creation, the environment of this re-embodiement, must not be subject to the thermodynamic drift to decay that characterises this world, otherwise we would live again simply to die again. It seems perfectly coherent to believe that the Creator can bring into being a new form of 'matter', so endowed with strong self-organising principles that the second law will no longer apply. This new creation will arise from the transformation of the old creation, not as a second act *ex nihilo* but as a redemptive act *ex vetere*. Inevitably, these are speculative thoughts, but I believe they are enough to indicate that the last word does not belong to death, but lies with our faithful Creator.

It has been an immense privilege to be part of the science and religion community over many years. I have learnt much from my friends and colleagues, and I am touched and grateful, more than I can say, by the generosity shown to me in this conference. Together we are all part of the great human quest for truthful understanding, attainable through the discovery of motivated beliefs.

Chapter 2
John Polkinghorne on Three Scientist–Theologians

Ian G. Barbour

In 1996 John Polkinghorne published *Scientists as Theologians: A Comparison of the Writings of Ian Barbour, Arthur Peacocke and John Polkinghorne.*[1] He continued the comparison of our views in several subsequent volumes.[2] In response, I will first examine the common ground the three of us share and then the differences among us. I will close by looking at the cultural and intellectual contexts within which we have been writing and offer some conclusions for the future of the science/religion dialogue.

It is regrettable that Arthur Peacocke did not live long enough to participate in the continuation of the three-way interaction among us that has been going on for 25 years. We particularly miss him because he was the founder and for many years the Director of the Ian Ramsey Centre, which is a co-sponsor of this celebration of Polkinghorne's eightieth birthday.

Similarities

Any comparison of authors is likely to focus on their differences, taking the similarities for granted. Let me note four important topics on which we agree, without quoting individual authors or citing particular passages.

Critical Realism

In *Issues in Science and Religion* (1966) and *Myths, Models and Paradigms* (1974), I defended critical realism in science and suggested parallels in the status of religious language.[3] I examined the role of analogies and models in both scientific and religious thought. I argued that statements about God are neither useful

---

[1]   John Polkinghorne, *Scientists as Theologians: A Comparison of the Writings of Ian Barbour, Arthur Peacocke and John Polkinghorne*, London, SPCK, 1996.

[2]   For example, John Polkinghorne, *Belief in God in an Age of Science*, New Haven, CT, Yale University Press, 1998, pp. 4–6; *Science and the Trinity*, London, SPCK, and New Haven, CT, Yale University Press, 2004, pp. 1–32.

[3]   Ian G. Barbour, *Issues in Science and Religion*, Englewood Cliifs, NJ, Prentice Hall

fictions nor literal descriptions. Peacocke advocated an identical epistemology in *Intimations of Reality* (1984).[4] Polkinghorne mentioned critical realism in science in *One World* (1986) and subsequently defended it in both science and religion.[5]

More recently, critical realism has come under attack by advocates of the "social construction" of both scientific theories and religious beliefs. However, the three of us have resisted such claims, holding that scientists are attempting to understand the world as it is, even though the observer influences what is observed, all data are theory-laden, and the concepts in which theories are expressed are culturally influenced and paradigm-dependent. Likewise religious experience is always interpreted with concepts drawn from particular religious traditions, but it does not have to be taken as a purely subjective phenomenon. I will not discuss this debate here, but only point out that our views on it are virtually identical.

Holism, Emergence and Levels of Organization

Very similar views on these topics are set forth in our respective Gifford Lectures.[6] We all maintained that organisms are organized in a hierarchy of levels, whether viewed successively in evolutionary history or simultaneously within any given organism. We defended ontological indeterminacy at the quantum level (and not just epistemological uncertainty reflecting the limitations of our knowledge). We all held that both law and chance are present in nature, a theme particularly prominent in Peacocke's writing. Polkinghorne and I emphasized the holism of quantum systems, such as the correlation of two particles, originating in a single event, striking two detectors many kilometers apart (the "nonlocality" and "entanglement" evident in Bell's Theorem experiments).

Peacocke drew more heavily from the literature on complexity and self-organization at higher levels as well as from recent work in systems theory. We have all opposed reductionism and supported the idea of emergence, highlighted in Peacocke's work. Events at higher levels must be analyzed using distinctive concepts irreducible to lower-level concepts (an epistemological assertion). We defended *top-down causality*: patterns of events at higher levels influence behavior at lower levels (an ontological assertion), not in violation of lower-

---

and London, SCM Press, 1966; *Myths, Models and Paradigms*, London, SCM and New York, Harper and Row, 1974.

[4]   Arthur Peacocke, *Intimations of Reality: Critical Realism in Science and Religion*, Notre Dame, IN, University of Notre Dame Press, 1984.

[5]   John Polkinghorne, *One World*, London, SPCK, 1986.

[6]   Our Gifford Lectures were: Ian G. Barbour, *Religion in an Age of Science*, Gifford Lectures vol. 1, San Francisco, CA, Harper and Row, 1990; Arthur Peacocke, *Theology for a Scientific Age*, enlarged edition, Minneapolis, MN, Fortress Press, 1993; John Polkinghorne, *Science and Christian Belief*, London, SPCK, 1994, published in the USA as *The Faith of a Physicist*, Princeton, NJ, Princeton University Press, 1994.

level laws but by the specification of boundary conditions and contexts within which those laws are exemplified.

Human Nature: A Multi-leveled Unity

A list of beliefs about human nature on which we agree would be long. Humanity is part of a continuous evolutionary history that goes back to primitive forms of life. Humans share many abilities with our hominid ancestors and with primates today, but we have distinctive capacities for abstract thought, language and culture. We reject the classical Christian dualism of body and soul and the Cartesian dualism of matter and mind, but we also question the adequacy of any purely biological account; we see intentionality and agency as important human characteristics. We acknowledge the limitations imposed by our genes, but do not accept genetic determinism; we hold that self-determination and choice are defensible concepts and prerequisites of social responsibility. We see a person as a multi-leveled psychosomatic unity, which Polkinghorne calls "a dual-aspect monism."[7] Peacocke gives a hierarchical table of scientific disciplines that study particular levels or the relationship between levels.[8]

On the theological side we have many points of agreement concerning human nature. None of us accepts the historicity of the story of Adam and Eve (Genesis 2:4 to 3:24) that portrays a paradise from which the first humans fell, with death as a punishment for sin. We now know that death was a necessary condition for evolution long before humanity was on the scene. Adam's story is Everyman's journey from innocence to responsibility. The idea that "original sin" was inherited by Adam's descendants can be reformulated as a recognition that we inherit unjust social structures that influence our individual actions. Sin can be understood today, not primarily as disobedience to a divine command, but as a violation of relationships. As Paul Tillich puts it, sin is estrangement from God, from other persons, and from our true selves. Genesis asserts that we are dust and will return to dust, but claims also that humanity is made "in the image of God." We see this image not just in our ability to reason, but also in our potential for creative relatedness.[9]

We find that recent science as well as biblical religion underscores the social character of selfhood. Children reared in isolation are incapable of acquiring language later in their lives. We are products of both culture and biological development. We are constituted by our relationships; we are who we are as fathers, children, members of a community. In short, each of us is multi-leveled, a biological organism and a responsible self. We are persons-in-community.

---

[7]   Polkinghorne, *Science and Christian Belief*, p. 7.

[8]   Peacocke, *Theology for a Scientific Age*, p. 217.

[9]   See Barbour, *Religion in an Age of Science*, pp. 205–209.

Limitations in God's Power

This topic requires more detailed discussion, although I think that in the end our similarities outweigh our differences. All three of us have questioned the classical doctrine that God is omniscient, omnipotent, unchanging and unaffected by the world. We believe that, if chance and human freedom are real, even God cannot know the open future. We have favored the "flowing time" interpretation of relativity rather than the "block universe" view. Space and time are united, but we see this as "the temporalization of space" rather than "the spatialization of time." (The latter has been sometimes been taken to support the theological claim that past, present and future are spread out in God's eternal gaze, which we also question.) We have rejected the attempt to distinguish divine foreknowledge from the predestination of events. Each of us has found the idea of omnipotence problematic also because it tends to make God responsible for evil and suffering in the world (despite the attempts of theologians for centuries to avoid such a conclusion).

Polkinghorne convened a memorable working group meeting in Cambridge and New York that resulted in a volume he edited, *The Work of Love: Creation as Kenosis*. In it Polkinghorne wrote that "the classic confrontation between the claims of divine love and the claims of divine power is resolved by maintaining God's total benevolence but qualifying, in a kenotic way, the operation of God's power."[10] He envisages a patient God who does not override the integrity of natural process and he cites Jürgen Moltmann's view of the Crucified God as well as W.H. Vanstone's emphasis on the vulnerability and costliness of love (human or divine). In the same volume Peacocke wrote that "God suffers in, with, and under the creative processes of the world with their costly unfolding in time."[11]

In my contribution I included sections on theodicy, the Cross and feminist authors, who have held that Western thought has emphasized divine power, control, independence and rationality (traditionally viewed as "masculine" virtues) rather than nurturance, cooperation, interdependence and emotional sensitivity (traditionally viewed as "feminine").[12] I also summarized process views that reflect more severe limitations in divine power. Alfred North Whitehead criticizes the monarchial model of God as "imperial ruler" and speaks instead of "the fellow sufferer who understands."[13] I cite the process philosopher Charles Hartshorne, who offers an extended critique of traditional concepts of divine immutability and impassibility, which he says were drawn more from Greek than biblical sources.[14]

---

[10]   John Polkinghorne, "Kenotic Creation and Divine Action," in John Polkinghorne, ed., *The Work of Love: Creation as Kenosis*, London, SPCK, 2001, p. 96.

[11]   Arthur Peacocke, "The Cost of New Life," in ibid., p. 37.

[12]   Ian G. Barbour, "God's Power: A Process View," in ibid., pp. 8–11.

[13]   Alfred North Whitehead, *Process and Reality*, New York, Macmillan, 1929, p. 352.

[14]   Charles Hartshorne, *The Divine Relativity*, New Haven, CT, Yale University Press, 1948.

Polkinghorne criticizes process thought for giving "an inadequate account of divine action which seems to be restricted to the role of a powerless pleading from the margins of occurrence."[15] I believe it would be more accurate to say that process thought points to a different form of power: not unilateral control over another, but response to and empowerment of another (as feminists have suggested)—which is neither omnipotence nor impotence. Process writers maintain that God's influence is *persuasive* rather than *coercive*, but also that God has the resources for the redemptive transformation of evil and suffering both in the world and in God's everlasting life.

Nevertheless, I find considerable validity in Polkinghorne's criticism. I have noted that there are two strands in almost all religious traditions, numinous experience of the holy (which suggests divine transcendence and power) and mystical experience of union (which suggests the immanence of the divine, participating in all things). The awe and reverence evoked in worship point to a more complex understanding of God than that presented by many process writers. This one of the points at which I try to adapt rather than adopt process thought. We must use a variety of models, none of which adequately represents ultimate reality.

Polkinghorne and Peacocke both maintain that divine self-limitation is *voluntary*, whereas I maintain that it is *necessary*. Here I am indebted to Hartshorne, who argues that all beings, including God, are inherently social and interactive. Every being has passive and receptive capabilities as well as active and causally effective ones. No being can have a monopoly of power or exercise unilateral control. However, this is not to say that God is limited by something external, as in Gnostic or Manichean dualism. If God's nature is loving and creative, it would be inconsistent to say that God might have chosen not to act lovingly and creatively. Moreover, the problem of theodicy remains acute if one believes that God was once omnipotent but chose to set aside such powers temporarily.[16] If for God there can be no distinction between "voluntary" and "necessary," I suggest that the three of us are really not far apart in our understanding of *kenosis*.

Differences

Let us now examine in greater detail five differences among us.

Diverse Classification Schemes

In 1990 I set forth a fourfold typology of ways in which science might be related to religion: Conflict, Independence, Dialogue and Integration. I wrote: "I will try to do justice to the Independence position, though I will be mainly developing the

---

15   Polkinghorne, *Scientists as Theologians*, p. 33.
16   Barbour, "God's Power: A Process View," in Polkinghorne, *The Work of Love*.

Dialogue position concerning methodology and the Integration thesis with respect to the doctrines of creation and human nature."[17]

In 1995 Polkinghorne was kind enough to send to me and to Peacocke a draft of *Scientists as Theologians* for our comments before it was submitted for publication. In it he repeatedly referred to his position as Consonance and mine as Assimilation, with Peacocke somewhere between us. He said that, in my writing, science assimilates religion. I replied citing a dictionary definition of *assimilate*: to consume or incorporate into the body (e.g. assimilation of food); to adopt the characteristics of another culture (e.g. assimilation of an immigrant group); to incorporate in one's understanding (e.g. assimilation of ideas). I pointed out that the first two definitions entail a loss of identity in the complete absorption of one entity by another, of which I did not think I was guilty. Peacocke also objected strenuously to the way his view was described. He pointed out that, in a book he edited in 1981, Ernan McMullin had used the term *consonance*, with which he had identified himself. He wrote to Polkinghorne: "I see myself as pursuing 'consonance' and certainly not 'assimilation,' for much the same reasons as Ian in his comments." He concluded: "I see myself as a veritable consonantist."[18] However Polkinghorne continued to use these terms to describe us when the volume was published and in several subsequent books.[19]

I was therefore delighted in 2004 when Polkinghorne introduced a new typology that he characterized as theological rather than methodological. The first category was *Deistic*, with the example of Paul Davies, who argues from the intelligibility and rational beauty of nature, in the tradition of natural theology. However, this approach, says Polkinghorne, can lead only to God the Cosmic Architect, a "diminished deity with no richness or depth," and no religious community in which a person might participate.[20]

The second category was *Theistic*, with Barbour as his example. "No one could fail to see that his thinking is contained within the envelope of Christian understanding. He makes use of a variety of biblical concepts and in particular he lays stress on the cross of Christ as the outstanding exemplification of the power of suffering love." However, Polkinghorne says that a theistic approach "does not come to grips with a fully articulated range of doctrinal issues, such as those that are laid out in the articles of the Nicene Creed."[21]

His third category is *Revisionary*, exemplified by Peacocke. Polkinghorne writes:

[17]   Barbour, *Religion in an Age of Science*, p. 30.
[18]   Peacocke, personal communication, 28 February 1985.
[19]   For example, Polkinghorne, *Belief in God in an Age of Science*, p. 86; *Science and Theology: An Introduction*, London, SPCK, 1998, pp. 117–18.
[20]   Polkinghorne, *Science and the Trinity*, pp. 11–13
[21]   Ibid., pp. 16, 17.

In an earlier survey of the thinking of scientist–theologians, I placed Peacocke between myself and Barbour in terms of the consonance–assimilation spectrum that I was then using. My judgment was that he appeared at times 'to operate in an assimilationist mode and at other times in a consonantist mode.' Since then in an article in *Zygon* that has a strongly programmatic tone to it, he has declared himself in terms that are much more unambiguously those of a radical revisionary.[22]

Polkinghorne holds that, in reacting to the emphasis on transcendence in classical Christianity, Peacocke moved too far in the direction of immanence, especially in subscribing to pan*en*theism, which he says blurs the distinction between Creator and creature.

Polkinghorne's fourth category is *Developmental*, as he calls his own position. He wants theology rather than science to shape the agenda, but he recognizes that theological ideas were developed in the Bible, and in later interpretations of it, within changing cultural contexts. I would argue that all three of us share a developmental understanding of the history of theology, but we differ in the extent to which we think *reformulations* are called for in the light of historical research and well-supported scientific theories. Polkinghorne states his own conclusion that "the Nicene Creed provides us with the outline of a rationally defensible theology which can be embraced with integrity as much today as when it was first formulated in the fourth century."[23] Peacocke and I see the fourth-century creeds as important in their own day as responses to several then-current "heresies," but we believe they provide little help in articulating a coherent theology for our own times. We maintain that the concepts used in the creeds (such as the "two natures" of Christ who was "of one substance with the Father," according to the Chalcedonian creed) were drawn more from Hellenistic than from biblical thought and are not effective in communicating to people today. So I conclude that neither Polkinghorne's earlier classification scheme nor his more recent one adequately represents the differences among us.

Trinitarian Theism, Panentheism or Dipolar Theism?

Polkinghorne acknowledges that the doctrine of the Trinity is not explicitly presented in the Bible, but he sees it as a well-grounded elaboration based on the ongoing experience of the Christian community. "After three centuries of intense reflection and struggle, the Church formulated and embraced the doctrine of the Trinity, expressing its belief that the one true God exists in the eternal interchange of love between the three divine Persons, Father, Son and Holy Spirit."[24] This was not an exercise in metaphysical speculation, he suggests, but an attempt to understand

---

[22]   Ibid., p. 23.

[23]   Ibid., p. 29.

[24]   Ibid., p. 99.

the transformation that had occurred in the lives of Christ's followers. To avoid the danger of tri-theism, the church fathers defended the unity of God, the three-in-one. Polkinghorne portrays a dynamic interaction within the Trinity, which has been a historic theme in Eastern Orthodoxy. He recognizes that Trinitarian thought is at odds with the strongly monotheistic convictions of Judaism and Islam, but he insists that in honest ecumenical dialogue our central convictions must not be watered down.

Peacocke identifies himself with *panentheism*. He quotes a dictionary definition: "The belief that the Being of God includes and penetrates the whole universe, so that every part of it exists in God, and (as against pantheism) that God's Being is more than, and not exhausted by, the universe."[25] He suggests that the panentheistic model "allows one to combine a strengthened emphasis on the immanence of God in the world with God's ultimate transcendence."[26] He notes that many panentheists speak of the world as God's body, and God as the world's mind, but he says that the analogy presupposes a dualist view of mind and body that is itself dubious. Moreover there are major dis-analogies: the world is not organismically unified the way the human body is, and God is not limited in understanding as humans are. God has no need for the cosmic equivalent of a nervous system, since God is omnipresent and knows all that can be known. God infinitely transcends the world and brought it into existence.

I have defended the *dipolar theism* of process thought. Whitehead holds that the "primordial nature" of God orders all potentialities relevant to particular events in the world, while God's "consequent nature" receives from and is influenced by events in the world. I cite Hartshorne, who says that God is eternal in character and purpose but temporal in responding to the world.[27] Similarly, John Cobb and David Griffin speak of God as "creative–responsive love"—creative as the source of order and novelty and responsive as temporal and affected by the world.[28] I have suggested that the basic analogy for God and the world in process thought is not the mind and body of one being but a society or community of beings of which a dipolar God is the dominant member.

In process thought *interiority* is postulated in integrated events at all levels. Whitehead and his followers have held that the basic constituents of reality are not two kinds of enduring entity (mind/matter dualism) or one kind of enduring

[25]   Philip Clayton and Arthur Peacocke, eds, *In Whom We Live and Mover and Have Our Being: Panentheistic Reflections on God's Presence in a Scientific World*, Grand Rapids, MI, William B. Eerdman's, 2004, p. xviii.

[26]   Arthur Peacocke, "Articulating God's Presence in and to the World Unveiled by the Sciences," in ibid., p. 151.

[27]   Charles Hartshorne, *Reality as Social Process*, Glencoe IL, Free Press, 1953.

[28]   John B. Cobb Jr and David Ray Griffin, *Process Theology: An Introductory Exposition*, Philadelphia, PA, Westminster, 1976, pp. 41–62. See also C. Robert Mesle, *Process-relational Philosophy: An Introduction to Alfred North Whitehead*, West Conshohocken, PA, Templeton Foundation Press, 2008.

entity (idealism or materialism), but rather one kind of event with two aspects or phases. Every momentary event is said to have an aspect in which it is receptive from the past, and an aspect in which it is at least minimally creative toward the future. However, events can be organized in many ways, leading to an *organizational pluralism* of many levels. All integrated entities at any level have an inner and an outer reality, but these take very diverse forms at differing levels. In simple organisms, interiority takes the form of rudimentary memory, sentience, responsiveness and anticipation. Viewed from within, interiority can be construed as a moment of experience, although conscious experience occurs only at higher levels of organization. Genuinely new activities and entities emerge in evolutionary history, but the basic metaphysical categories should be applicable to all events.[29]

Whitehead himself argued that an infinitesimal capacity for novelty could be postulated even at the level of separate atoms. I believe that he gave insufficient attention to the radically different ways in which universal categories might be exemplified at various levels. In this regard, Hartshorne and subsequent process philosophers have given greater recognition to diverse levels of organization. They said that stones are mere aggregates with no organization more complex than molecular attraction, so they have absolutely no unified experience. Invertebrates have elementary sentience, perception and capacity for action. The development of a nervous system made possible a far more complex unification of experience and new forms of memory, learning, anticipation and purposiveness, whereas consciousness and self-consciousness appear only at even higher levels.[30] Among the three of us there are thus significant differences in our concepts of God and our analyses of events in the world.

Laws of nature: Ordained by God, immanent in nature,
or "temporary habits of nature"?

Deists in the eighteenth century held that nature follows exact deterministic laws ordained by God, who could continue to act only by suspending the laws and intervening supernaturally. With increasing skepticism about such "miracles," it seemed that God could act only to establish a lawful system that would run on its own. All three of us believe that God can act in the world without violating the laws of nature, but we differ in our understanding of the status of such laws. Polkinghorne maintains that there is real indeterminism in nature, but he holds that the laws of nature are *ordained by God*:

> Certainly no one who holds a doctrine of creation will suppose that God and the laws of nature exclude each other, for the regularities of those laws will be understood by the theist to be reflections of the faithfulness of the Creator who

29 Barbour, *Religion in an Age of Science*, pp. 223–9.
30 Ibid., p. 169.

ordains them. The theist will also understand these laws not as being immutable necessities, but as holding simply for as long as the Creator determines that they should do so.[31]

We will see in the next section that for Polkinghorne the deterministic equations of chaos theory are only approximations of "a more subtle, supple, open-textured" underlying reality described by holistic laws that have not yet been discovered. Polkinghorne agrees with Robert Russell that God unilaterally determines the indeterminacies in the world, but he sees evidence of such openness in chaotic theory rather than quantum theory. We will see also that he holds that in Christ's resurrection there was a foretaste of an eschatological future in which God alone will bring in a new regime with a new set of laws differing from those he ordained for this world.

Peacocke envisions God acting through top-down causation or whole–part constraints, setting boundary conditions for lower-level laws without violating them. Moreover the laws are statistical, leading only to probabilistic predictions for individual events. In recent writing he stressed pan*en*theism in which laws are *immanent patterns* in events. Divine agency (and human agency) is *compatible* with natural laws, whether deterministic or indeterministic (although he defended the latter). This resembles the distinction in Neo-Thomist thought between primary and secondary causes that do not compete, because God is not a cause on the same plane with natural causes, but is rather their transcendent ground. If God is present throughout nature, we do not need to seek causal incompleteness or a "causal joint" across which God acts.[32]

For Whitehead the regularities of nature are *descriptive* rather than prescriptive, *contingent* rather than necessary, and *proposed* rather than imposed by God. He says: "People make the mistake of talking about 'natural laws.' There *are* no natural laws. There are only temporary habits of nature."[33] He is critical of classical Christian and later Deistic ideas of externally imposed laws that are prescriptive and unchanging, and permit no exceptions. He says that the world's order is immanent and expresses the social character of its components, which are constituted by their relationships. "The laws are the outcome of the character of

[31] John Polkinghorne, "Eschatological Credibility: Emergent and Teleological Processes," in Ted Peters, Robert John Russell and Michael Welker, eds, *Resurrection: Theological and Scientific Assessments*, Grand Rapids, MI, William B. Eerdmans, 2002, p. 46.
[32] The views of Polkinghorne and Peacocke are discussed in many chapters in Robert John Russell, Nancey Murphy and William Stoeger S.J., *Scientific Perspectives on Divine Action: Twenty Years of Challenge and Progress*, Vatican City State, Vatican Observatory, 2008.
[33] Lucien Price, *Dialogues of Alfred North Whitehead, as Recorded by Lucien Price*, Boston, MA, Little Brown, 1954, p. 367.

the behaving things; they are the communal customs observed."[34] In evolutionary history new regularities came into being along with the emergence of new kinds of relationship. Whitehead speculates that there may be other "cosmic epochs" having spatio-temporal regularities that differ from ours,[35] but he is also critical of Positivists, who see laws as merely descriptive of successions of observed phenomena, without seeking explanations for them in underlying structures.[36]

In the light of Whitehead's comment that there may be other "cosmic epochs" with regularities that differ from those with which we are familiar, a Whiteheadian today can be open to the possibility of multiple universes (multiverses) existing either in parallel or sequentially, with differing laws and constants—although their existence is highly speculative and direct observations are impossible. I note also that Whitehead's insistence that "there are no natural laws" is compatible with Nancy Cartwright's thesis that, instead of seeking universal laws, we should envisage a patchwork of behavioral and domain-specific regularities or tendencies of limited scope. She maintains that phenomena in controlled experiments in the laboratory may seem precisely ordered, but only because the effects of the wider context present in complex systems in the real world can be ignored.[37]

Whitehead holds that the order of nature has been *proposed* rather than *imposed* by God. It does not directly express God's will, for God presents options that can be realized only by entities in the world. God's "primordial nature" orders possibilities with relevance to the current situation in the world and offers the best of them as an "initial aim" for a new synthesis. God is thus the ground of order as well as creativity; so the world is not rigidly controlled, but it does not lapse into chaos. The regularities are not *necessary* but are *contingent* on God's ordering of possibilities and on the self-creative phase of every entity in nature. I am indebted here to Palmyre Oomen's analysis of Whitehead's understanding of the laws of nature.[38] These diverse views of the status of natural laws are particularly relevant to our interpretations of divine action.

Divine action: Information input, whole–part constraint, or two-way interaction?

In his discussion of divine action, Polkinghorne starts from *chaos theory*, in which an infinitesimal initial disturbance can be amplified enormously to trigger large-scale events distant in time and space (the "butterfly effect"). Because of this

---

[34] Alfred North Whitehead, *Adventures of Ideas*, New York, Macmillan, 1933, p. 147.

[35] Alfred North Whitehead, *Process and Reality*, corrected edn, ed. David Ray Griffin and Donald W. Sherburne, New York, Free Press, 1978, p. 91.

[36] Whitehead, *Adventures of Ideas*, pp. 159–64.

[37] Nancy Cartwright, *The Dappled World, a Study of the Boundaries of Science*, Cambridge, Cambridge University Press, 1999.

[38] Palmyre M.F. Oomen, "Immanence and Divine Persuasion: Whitehead's Provocative View on the Laws of Nature," in J.Y.G. Debrock, ed., *Process Pragmatism*, Amsterdam, Rodopi Press, 2003, pp. 87–102.

exquisite sensitivity and the impossibility of isolating any part of a system from its wider environment, the outcome of such a chain of events cannot be predicted, despite the fact that the equations of chaos theory are deterministic. Moreover, according to complexity theory, there are bifurcations in many types of pathway at which the outcome cannot be predicted. Polkinghorne holds that these theories point to actual indeterminacy in the world and not just the incompleteness of our knowledge. He argues that critical realism supports the claim that "epistemology models ontology."[39] He holds that this interpretation of chaos theory is similar to the Copenhagen interpretation of quantum theory in which the Heisenberg Uncertainty Principle is taken to reflect indeterminacy in nature rather than the limitations of our knowledge. Peacocke replies that the quantum case is different because the Uncertainty Principle quantifies the uncertainty and is consistent with a precise probability distribution and the formulation of statistical laws, which is not possible in chaos theory.[40]

Polkinghorne proposes that, if infinitesimal energy inputs can lead to divergent paths in chaos theory, we might imagine a limiting case in which God alters history with *zero* energy input through pure "*active information.*" (This would not be an inference from science, but a way in which a theologian might conceive of divine action that does not violate the scientific laws ordained by God.) He accepts the theorem in communication theory that the transfer of information within the world always requires some energy, even if only an infinitesimal amount. However, if God was omnipresent and was pure spirit without embodiment, this theorem would not be applicable. Moreover such a divine influence would not be scientifically detectable, even with any finite improvement in the sensitivity of instruments. In a study of recent proposals concerning Special Divine Action (SDA), Nicholas Saunders writes:

> By means of an application of 'epistemology models ontology', Polkinghorne appears to argue that the sensitivity of mathematical chaotic systems implies real-world indeterminism. However a better reading of his position is that this mathematical deterministic sensitivity is 'diagnostic' of the need for holistic treatment and of the existence of real-world systems as distinct from mathematical chaos being open in a sense suitable for SDA. Essentially what Pollkinghorne's scheme amounts to is the claim that mathematical chaos theory does not fully represent reality. Implicit in his understanding is an assertion about the reality of real-world indeterminsitic chaotic phenomena that operate in nature over and

[39]   John Polkinghorne, "The Metaphysics of Divine Action," in Robert J. Russell, Nancey Murphy and Arthur Peacocke, eds, *Chaos and Complexity: Scientific Perspectives on Divine Action*, Vatican City State, Vatican Observatory, and Berkeley, CA, Center for Theology and the Natural Sciences, 1995, pp. 147–56.

[40]   John Polkinghorne, "Creatio Continua and Divine Action," and Arthur Peacocke, "A Response to Polkinghorne," *Science and Christian Belief* 5 (1995), pp. 101–108 and 109–115.

above their mathematical representations. What he is essentially asserting is that the mathematical models used to study chaos are only an approximation of this character.[41]

For his part, Peacocke uses several vivid analogies to imagine divine action. God is like a choreographer for a creative dance troop, or the composer of an unfinished musical work for an orchestra that is improvising on a theme and variations. God's action is like a radar beam searching through diverse potentialities.[42] Peacocke at first suggested that the idea of *top-down causality* from higher to lower levels within an organism could be extended to include God's action from an even higher level (by providing the context and boundary conditions for lower-level laws rather than in violation of them). Later he preferred to extend the idea of *whole–part constraint* to God as the most inclusive whole. "Constraint" implies an influence but avoids the common assumption that an event might have a single cause, whereas we always have causal pluralism. God is conveyor of meaning through the pattern of events in the world as well as through human life and the person of Christ.[43]

Peacocke says that he once thought God could holistically affect the state of the world at all levels, but he now realizes:

[It] is perhaps more acceptable if the whole–part influence of God is understood to operate mainly at the level of the human person, the emergent reality of which can be located at the apex of the systems-based complexities of the world. God would then be thought of as acting in the world in a whole–part manner by influencing human personal experience, an influence that thereby affects events at the physical, biological and social levels … I am inclined to postulate a divine whole–part influence at all levels, but with an increasing intensity and manifestation of divine intention from the lowest physical levels up to the personal level, where it could be at its most concentrated and focused.[44]

He recognizes that whole–part analogies drawn from systems theory are "too impersonal to do justice to the personal character of the profoundest human experience."[45] He insists that a concept of personal agency is required in talking about either human or divine intentions.

In process thought, by contrast, God does not have to act as top-down or whole–part influence because God is already active at all levels as one factor in the

[41] Nicholas Saunders, *Divine Action and Modern Science*, Cambridge, Cambridge University Press, 2002, pp. 191–2.

[42] Peacocke, *Theology for a Scientific Age*, pp. 170–77.

[43] Ibid., pp. 157–60.

[44] Arthur Peacocke, *All That Is: A Naturalistic Faith for the Twenty-first Century*, ed. Philip Clayton, Minneapolis, MN, Fortress Press, 2007, pp. 46, 47.

[45] Ibid., p. 47.

unfolding of every integrated event. Every new occurrence is a present response (self-cause) to past events (efficient cause) in terms of potentialities grasped (final cause). God elicits the self-creation of individual entities, allowing for creativity as well as structure. By valuing particular potentialities to which particular creatures can respond, God influences the world without determining it. Every entity is the joint product of past causes, divine purposes and the entity's own activity.[46]

In the process view, God's influence for change is minimal at the atomic or molecular level, where order predominates over novelty, so it is not surprising that it took billions of years for life to emerge. At higher levels with more complex organization, the evolution of consciousness and then self-consciousness could occur more rapidly. In human life there is a much greater variety of possibilities for fulfilling divine purposes—or for failing to fulfill them.[47] Process thought thus ascribes to God a direct influence on the world in the earlier stages of evolutionary history, whereas Peacocke seems to rely on built-in potentialities or indirect whole–part influences prior to the emergence of higher life forms capable of more direct response to God.

Christ: Incarnate Son, New Emergent, or a Man Responsive to God's Call?

Polkinghorne holds that the pre-existent second person of the eternal Trinity was incarnate in the historical Jesus. He also defends an eternal–temporal polarity in God resembling that in process thought. He combines these ideas in a rather complex way: "Would it not be sufficient for Christian theology to suppose that it was *the temporal pole* of the Second Person that became incarnate in Jesus of Nazareth, while the eternal pole continued in the divine essence and governance?"[48] Polkinghorne adheres to the traditional doctrine of the *two natures* of Christ, holding that "it is necessary that Jesus be fully human, totally immersed in the life of humanity and so totally relevant to every aspect of our lives—he assumes all to redeem all, as Gregory of Nianzus stated so well— yet he must be truly divine so that it is the invincible life of God to which we have access through him."[49] Polkinghorne accepts the traditional doctrine of the Virgin Birth without a human father.

Polkinghorne also believes that the bodily resurrection of Christ is an anticipation of the resurrection of others in the future. He grants that science has almost nothing to say about life after death, which would be very different from life in this world, although with some continuity of personal identity. He suggests that the soul is an information-bearing pattern that might be re-embodied in a new kind of matter in a new kind of time. One cannot defend divine justice,

---

[46]   Ian G. Barbour, *When Science Meets Religion*, San Francisco, CA, Harper, 2000, p. 175.

[47]   Cobb and Griffin, *Process Theology*, pp. 63–79.

[48]   Polkinghorne, *Science and the Trinity*, p. 115.

[49]   Ibid., p. 114.

he says, unless there is a future life in which those who have suffered unjustly can be recompensed. Moreover, our sun will burn out in a few billion years, and eventually the universe will expand and cool off until life is impossible, or it will collapse and heat up dramatically ("freeze or fry"). We are left with cosmic futility unless we maintain the eschatological hope that all creation will be redeemed in an ultimate fulfillment beyond space and time as we know them.[50]

Peacocke, by contrast, holds that the Virgin Birth is legendary. It is mentioned in only two gospels and nowhere else in scripture. It should be seen today as an affirmation that God took the initiative in the whole of Christ's life, which is not really a biological question. The synoptic accounts of the empty tomb are inconsistent, and it is not mentioned in John's gospel or Paul's letters. Peacocke suggests that the disciples had a profound experience of Christ's continuing presence as an effective power in their lives; this was not a hallucination or a purely psychological phenomenon. They were convinced that Christ had been taken up into the fullness of God's life.[51]

Peacocke describes Christ as *a new emergent* in evolutionary history. What was distinctive was his radical openness and responsiveness to God. This was not a purely human accomplishment, but an expression of a human life transformed by the divine presence. It was Christ's relation to God, not "two natures" in one person, that marked him off from other persons, and this was a difference in degree, not in kind. In him was actualized what is a potentiality for all of us, for we are all called to such a relationship. Peacocke concludes:

> This encourages us now to understand the 'incarnation' which occurred in Jesus as exemplifying that emergence-from-continuity which characterizes the whole process whereby God is creating continuously through discontinuity. There is both continuity with all that preceded him, yet in him there appeared a new mode of human existence which, by virtue of its openness to God, is a new revelation of both God and of humanity.[52]

My own view of Christ has been close to Peacocke's. I wrote:

> I submit that in reformulating Christology today we should keep in mind the intent of classical doctrines but make use of categories of *relationship* and *history* rather than of substance. On *the human side* of the relationship, we can speak of Christ as a person who in his freedom was perfectly obedient to God. Through his own openness to God, his life reveals God's purposes to us. He identified himself with God and did not obstruct or distort God's will. He was inspired and empowered by God. On *the divine side*, we can speak of God as acting in and through the person of Christ. Christ is God's revelation to us. ... I

---

[50]   Ibid., pp. 143–69.

[51]   Peacocke, *All That Is*, pp. 33–4.

[52]   Peacocke, *Theology for a Scientific Age*, p. 307.

suggest, then, that in an *evolutionary perspective* we may view both the human and the divine activity in Christ as a continuation and intensification of what had been occurring previously. We can think of him as representing a new stage in evolution and a new stage in God's activity.[53]

In critiquing my view, Polkinghorne says it ends up with Christ as no more than an inspiring example: "Affording an example does not seem to be enough, for we stand in need of a source of grace that will enable human beings actually to follow that example."[54] I would reply by saying that I see Christ's life as an example, not just of what we can do, but of what God can do in our lives, which I think is what grace is all about. Christ's life is the supreme example of divine–human cooperation.

I see Christ as inspired and guided by the Holy Spirit, which I understand as God's activity in the world. According to the Bible, the Spirit is active in creation (Genesis 1:2), continuing creation (Psalms 104:30), the inspiration of the prophets (Isaiah 42:1), the worshipping community (Psalms 51:11), the baptism of Christ (Mark 1:10) and the experience of his followers at Pentecost (Acts 2). Reference to the Spirit thus ties together our understanding of creation and redemption, which are too often considered separately; they are two aspects of one activity involving both nature and history. The Spirit can be thought of as active also in other religious traditions, and perhaps on other planets on which intelligent life may exist.[55] I am particularly indebted to Geoffrey Lampe, who speaks of Christ as a man inspired by the Spirit.[56] Reference to the Spirit also seems to have much in common with the understanding of God in process thought.

Differing Contexts

John Brooke and Geoffrey Cantor,[57] and more recently Willem Drees,[58] have pointed to the dangers when we use oversimplified typologies or ignore the particular contexts of time, place and culture in comparing authors. In the case of the three scientist–theologians, this warning would not rule out comparisons, since we have read many of the same books, attended many of the same conferences, and written and spoken to the same or similar audiences. Nevertheless there are some

---

[53]   Barbour, *Religion in an Age of Science*, pp. 210, 211.

[54]   Polkinghorne, *Science and the Trinity*, p. 18.

[55]   Barbour, *Religion in an Age of Science*, pp. 236, 269.

[56]   G.W.H. Lampe, *God as Spirit*, Oxford, Clarendon Press, 1977.

[57]   John Hedley Brooke and Geoffrey Cantor, *Reconstructing Nature: The Engagement of Science and Religion*, Edinburgh, T & T Clarke, 1998.

[58]   Willem Drees, *Religion and Science in Context*, London and New York, Routledge, 2010.

points at which our differing disciplinary and intellectual contexts as recorded in our respective autobiographical accounts may be relevant.[59]

Scientific Disciplines

Polkinghorne and I were physicists and Peacocke was a biochemist. I have the impression that, although most physicists are totally engrossed in their scientific work, a significant minority is open to discussing philosophical questions arising from the Big Bang, the Anthropic Principle, multi-universe theories, quantum theory, relativity and the future of our solar system. In the eighteenth century, Newtonian physics was seen as an exciting and powerful intellectual advance, and it was tempting to think that it could explain everything. However, twentieth-century physics produced more enigmatic and counter-intuitive theories of whose limitations physicists are now more aware.

In recent decades molecular biology has provided immensely powerful tools for understanding organisms, and technologies for altering them, and some scientists expect it to give an exhaustive account of all phenomena in living things. Among biologists there is some interest in complexity, emergence vs reduction, evolutionary convergence, the evolution of embryonic development (Evo–Devo), and factors in evolution in addition to mutations and natural selection. However, awareness of the limitations of science seems rare among biologists. Perhaps in the future they will be more open to dialogue with philosophers and theologians. I might add that scientists carry considerable weight when they speak out in public, even on topics about which they have little expertise. It was undoubtedly our training in both science and religion that led to us receiving the Templeton Prize for Progress in Religion (myself in 1999, Peacocke in 2001 and Polkinghorne in 2002).

Theological Traditions

Polkinghorne and Peacocke have been deeply involved in the Anglican community, within which there is great diversity (high church and low church, liberal and conservative, diverse views on the ordination of women, gays and lesbians, etc.). However, sacraments are central throughout Anglicanism, as is evident in Polkinghorne's writing on the Eucharist and Peacocke's sacramental view of nature. I was exposed to Quakerism in school, college and summer work camps, but since 1955 I have felt at home in a local Congregational church (UCC) that is liberal theologically and very concerned about peace and social justice. Church membership figures are higher in the USA than in the UK, and fundamentalists and

---

[59]   Our autobiographical writings are: John Polkinghorne, *From Physicist to Priest*, Eugene, OR, Cascade Books 2007; Arthur Peacocke, *From Dean to DNA*, Harrisburg PA, Morehouse 1997; Ian Barbour, "A Personal Odyssey," in Robert John Russell, ed., *Fifty Years in Science and Religion: Ian Barbour and His Legacy*, Aldershot, Ashgate, 2004.

advocates of Intelligent Design have been more active. These cultural differences have no doubt influenced the way in which we have tried to defend our theological ideas. Process theology has only a small following in the USA and an even smaller one in the UK, although some of its themes have had a wider influence. It is for this reason that I try to convey process insights without relying on Whitehead's abstract terminology. Hartshorne's writing and that of process theologians such as John Cobb are more readily accessible.

I note with interest that more than half the contributors to this symposium show the influence of Whitehead on their thought. Polkinghorne acknowledges his indebtedness to Hartshorne for his own dipolar theism (God as temporal as well as eternal, the open future being unknowable even to God). Keith Ward's earlier writing was notably sympathetic to Whitehead, and even his presentation here portrays a more dynamic and interactive view of God than most versions of Platonism or Idealism. Michael Welker's early scholarship included detailed commentary on Whitehead, although his subsequent understanding of the dynamic character of God's Trinitarian life seems more indebted to theological than to philosophical sources. Phil Clayton has been a member of the Center for Process Studies and has defended many features of process metaphysics.

Academic Institutions

Colleges and universities throughout the world are plagued by departmental fragmentation that makes interdisciplinary exploration difficult. Academic advancement usually follows assessment by the criteria of individual departments. Polkinghorne established at Cambridge a program in science and theology that later included the Starbridge lectureship, held since its inception by Fraser Watts. Peacocke started the Ian Ramsey Centre in Oxford, which was later supplemented by the Idreos chair. They were probably influenced by their interaction with students and faculty through these programs. I am very grateful for my contacts with other scholars through the Center for Theology and the Natural Sciences in Berkeley, led by Robert Russell. I have appreciated the Center for Process Studies in Claremont, California, and especially the work of John Cobb. It was student interest at Carleton College in Minnesota, as well as my own ethical concerns, that led me to devote half my time for two decades to establishing and teaching in an interdisciplinary program on Technology, Ethics and Public Policy. Much of my subsequent writing, including my second series of Gifford Lectures,[60] was directed to ethical issues concerning the environment, pollution, energy, natural resources, computers and biotechnology.

---

[60]   Ian G. Barbour, *Ethics in an Age of Technology*, Gifford Lectures vol. 2, San Francisco, CA, Harper, 1993.

Conclusion

I have suggested that, in the context of the science–religion dialogue today, the similarities among the three of us far outweigh the differences. Three of the *similarities* explored were closely tied to our interpretations of science (critical realism, holism and emergent levels, and human nature), although not all scientists would agree with our interpretations. The fourth similarity (limitations in God's power) is shared by many theologians today, but by no means all of them. The five *differences* discussed (classification schemes, concepts of God, laws of nature, divine action and views of Christ) are primarily philosophical or theological; the contrasts would, of course, have been far greater if we had belonged to differing world religions. It is perhaps not surprising that the closer we are to science, the more we are in agreement, despite the fact that scientists also work in particular cultural settings.

I agree with Polkinghorne's assessment that the three of us who were trained in both scientific and theological disciplines were able to open up some space for a significant dialogue that subsequent authors have expanded and explored. At the same time any overall assessment of our work would have to look at our limitations. We did not consider Islam, Hinduism or Buddhism in sufficient depth, nor the variations within each of these traditions. Until the late 1990s we gave little attention to anthropology, psychology and neuroscience, all of which are crucial to any discussion of human nature. The growth of a truly global and interdisciplinary conversation is only just starting and remains a task for the future. However, I am profoundly grateful that interaction with Polkinghorne and Peacocke has been such an important part of my life. We have learned from each other, even when we disagreed. I join with others in gratitude for the life and work of John Polkinghorne.[61]

---

[61] A Powerpoint version of this chapter was presented in Oxford on July 10, 2010, at the celebration of John Polkinghorne's 80th birthday. The version offered here is adapted from Ian G. Barbour, 'John Polkinghorne on Three Scientist–Theologians', *Theology and Science* 8 (2010), 247–64, by permission of the editors.

Chapter 3

Is Informational Causality Primary Causality? A Study of an Aspect of John Polkinghorne's Account of Divine Action

Terry J. Wright

Introduction

A commonplace of Christian theological tradition is to contend that God, as primary or first cause, acts in the world by means of creaturely secondary causes.[1] The conceptuality is employed to affirm God's continuing action in a world that seems not to require it,[2] while ensuring that God is not reduced to the level of mundane causation.[3] As such, God transcends the world as its sovereign, while remaining immanently present in and to all that transpires.

This framework for divine action holds wide, but not universal, assent. Of those who critique the notion of primary causality, John Polkinghorne is especially scathing of what he believes is "an unintelligible kind of theological doublespeak,"[4] the "imposition of a mysterious theological gloss on natural process."[5] Instead of

---

[1]   This conceptuality especially prevails in the Thomist and Reformed traditions.

[2]   Cf. Colin E. Gunton, *The Triune Creator: A Historical and Systematic Study.* Edinburgh Studies in Constructive Theology (Edinburgh: Edinburgh University Press, 1998), 152 n. 16: "It is surely significant that the concept of secondary causality was introduced in order to establish some form of limited autonomy in the creature."

[3]   A reduction of God to the level of mundane causation, where God is no more than a cause among causes, is generally considered a violation of the God–world distinction that is fundamental to mainstream Christian belief. An essential feature of this distinction is that God and the world occupy two intrinsically dissimilar ontological orders that God transcends through the immanent working of the Holy Spirit. The Christian doctrine of creation is an attempt to maintain this delicate balance, lest God's immanence is stressed at the expense of divine transcendence (pantheism), or divine transcendence overemphasized so that God cannot be said to play any meaningful role in the world (deism).

[4]   John Polkinghorne, *Science and Christian Belief: Theological Reflections of a Bottom-up Thinker. The Gifford Lectures for 1993–4* (London: SPCK, 1994), 81–2.

[5]   John Polkinghorne, *Scientists as Theologians: A Comparison of the Writings of Ian Barbour, Arthur Peacocke and John Polkinghorne* (London: SPCK, 1996), 31.

primary causality, Polkinghorne proposes that God acts through "informational causality,"[6] that is, a holistic form of causality that organizes the world's patterns of behavior at the structural level.[7] On this account, God seems to act not so much by *causing* things to happen, but by influencing the context *within which*, or the conditions *under which*, things happen. It is an idea that appears to hold some promise for those seeking to offer a cogent account of divine action that stays true to mainstream Christian belief.[8]

Given that primary causality and informational causality both refer to God's action, the question must be asked: *is informational causality no more than an interpretation of primary causality for a scientific age?* Is it not possible that primary causality *is* God's shaping of all things through the input of so-called "active information"?[9] My intention in this paper is to probe this possibility.

Analyzing Primary Causality

Although found in the thought of Plato and Augustine,[10] the first systematic arrangement of God's providence around the conceptuality of primary and secondary causality is found in Thomas Aquinas. According to Aquinas, God governs all things by willing to act through inferior or secondary causes, which nonetheless retain genuine powers of causal efficacy.[11] On this account, an action or an effect issues *fully* from both the primary cause *and* the secondary cause.[12] Such a claim suggests that actions and effects issue from two sufficient causes, which poses a challenge to the conceptuality's intelligibility: divine causality,

---

[6]   John Polkinghorne, "Chaos Theory and Divine Action," in *Religion and Science: History, Method, Dialogue*, edited by W. Mark Richardson and Wesley J. Wildman (New York: Routledge), 247; *Faith, Science and Understanding* (London: SPCK, 2000), 122; "Kenotic Creation and Divine Action," in *The Work of Love: Creation as Kenosis*, edited by John Polkinghorne (Grand Rapids, MI: Eerdmans, 2001), 99.

[7]   John Polkinghorne, "The Laws of Nature and the Laws of Physics," in *Quantum Cosmology and the Laws of Nature: Scientific Perspectives on Divine Action*, edited by Robert John Russell, Nancey Murphy and C.J. Isham (Vatican City State: Vatican Observatory Publications, 1993, 1996), 434; "*Creatio Continua* and Divine Action," *Science and Christian Belief* 7 (1995): 105; *Scientists as Theologians*, 36; *Science and Theology: An Introduction* (London: SPCK, 1998), 42–3.

[8]   Cf. David Fergusson, "Darwin and Providence," in *Theology After Darwin*, edited by Michael S. Northcott and R.J. Berry (Milton Keynes: Paternoster, 2009), 82: "Polkinghorne's account of divine action seems to me attractive and possibly under-rated within the theological community."

[9]   Polkinghorne, "*Creatio Continua*," 105; *Scientists as Theologians*, 36; "Chaos Theory," 247.

[10]   Plato, *Timaeus*, 46cd, 68e; Augustine, *On the Trinity*, 3.2.7–3.4.9.

[11]   Thomas Aquinas, *Summa Theologiae*, 1a.19.8; 1a.22.3.

[12]   Thomas Aquinas, *Summa Contra Gentiles*, 3.70.8.

if *sufficient* to ensure that an action or effect occurs, should render secondary causality redundant (or vice versa). However, it is important to recognize that, for Aquinas, the Creator–creation distinction means that God acts as the primary cause from an entirely different ontological order to creaturely secondary causes. Consequently, there is no reason to suppose that an action or an effect cannot be caused by two sufficient causes each operating from its particular ontological order.[13]

The implication of Aquinas' position is that God's action, divine causality, is unique, having no analogue in the world.[14] As a concept, primary causality, especially as it is described in relation to secondary causality, warrants careful exposition. Secondary causality is rooted in primary causality; primary causality ensures that secondary causes are genuinely efficacious; primary causality is sufficient to initiate and execute actions and effects in the world of secondary causes *through* secondary causes, and does so while remaining ontologically distinct from the created causal nexus. Primary causality does not act differently from secondary causes in producing particular actions or effects;[15] and secondary causes do not influence primary causality, unless God has already determined secondary causes to do so in certain instances.[16] Thus God is not a cause among causes, but rather founds, empowers and upholds secondary causes in such a way that God may also be said to enact what secondary causes themselves enact.[17]

As noted earlier, the conceptuality of primary and secondary causality is employed to affirm God's continuing action in a world of mundane causation, while preserving God's ontological distinctiveness. However, its logic is not as incontrovertible as its champions appear to suppose; its intelligibility may be queried at certain points. Is it really feasible, for example, to claim that an action

---

[13] Aquinas, *Summa Theologiae*, 1a.2.3; 1a.103.6; 1a.105.5 ad 2.

[14] Cf. Polkinghorne, *Faith, Science and Understanding*, 123; Karl Barth, *Church Dogmatics* (13 vols), edited by G.W. Bromiley and T.F. Torrance (Edinburgh: T&T Clark, 1957–1975), III/3, 136.

[15] William Stoeger's use of the concept of primary causality dissents from the norm at this point. His point is that primary causality is *necessary* for an action or an effect to occur in the world, but not sufficient; that is, primary causality must ensure that an action or an effect *can* occur, but it does not ensure *that* it happens. According to Stoeger, God surrenders divine causal sufficiency to allow secondary causes to flourish. See William R. Stoeger, S.J., "Describing God's Action in the World in Light of Scientific Knowledge of Reality," in *Chaos and Complexity: Scientific Perspectives on Divine Action*, 2nd edn, edited by Robert John Russell, Nancey Murphy and Arthur R. Peacocke (Vatican City State: Vatican Observatory Publications, 1997/2000; 1st edn 1995), 254–5.

[16] See Kathryn Tanner, *God and Creation in Christian Theology: Tyranny or Empowerment?* (Minneapolis, MN: Fortress Press, 1988), 90–98, for further discussion of these points.

[17] Cf. Charles M. Wood, *The Question of Providence* (Louisville, KY: Westminster John Knox Press, 2008), 84.

issues *fully* from two *sufficient* causes?[18] Aristotle demonstrated that actions may occur through a plurality of causes,[19] but primary causality and secondary causes do not fit neatly into Aristotelian categories, given the emphasis on the ontological disparity between each level of causality. Moreover, if the decision is made to reclassify primary causality as a *necessary* condition for secondary causality, as does William Stoeger,[20] then the likelihood of there being *actual* divine action in the world is lessened. Conversely, if primary causality is simply the necessary condition for secondary causes to obtain genuine causal efficacy, the possibility of incorporating primary causality within the nexus of secondary causes is increased.

Perhaps, though, the underlying issue is that human language is inadequate to capture all the nuances of the mechanics of divine action in precise detail. The need conceptually to attend to ontologically distinct causal orders indicates that any description of primary causality and secondary causality as belonging to the same causal order is, in fact, a category mistake.[21] Aquinas suggests that it is impossible adequately to speak of God using terms that more naturally apply to creatures; terms must acquire analogous meaning when applied to God.[22] However, such analogous predication straddles a chasm between using terms comparatively (univocation) and using them so obliquely (equivocation) that even the *possibility* of uttering a meaningful statement about God is jeopardized.[23]

Thus the relation between primary and secondary causality demands further clarification. Conventional accounts of God's providence fail to do justice to the mechanics of primary causality—so much so, that the notion appears easily to be no more than "mere fideistic assertion, compatible with any known facts about the way things happen and so lacking any interpretative force in relation to the way things happen."[24] Given this danger, John Polkinghorne insists that the search for

---

[18]   Cf. Paul Helm's discussion in *The Providence of God*. Contours of Christian Theology (Leicester: IVP, 1993), 177–82.

[19]   Aristotle, *Physics*, 2.3.194^{b}24–2.3.195^{b}30; *Metaphysics*, 5.2.1013^{a}24–5.2.1014^{a}25.

[20]   See n. 15 above.

[21]   Wood, *The Question of Providence*, 81. Cf. Taede A. Smedes, *Chaos, Complexity, and God: Divine Action and Scientism*. Studies in Philosophical Theology 26 (Leuven: Peeters, 2004), 178–9.

[22]   Aquinas, *Summa Theologiae*, 1a.13.5.

[23]   The doctrine of revelation surely presupposes the adequacy of language to convey divine truth, propositional or otherwise, even if it does not imprison or exhaust that truth. It is beyond the scope of this paper further to defend this claim. Cf. n. 59 below.

[24]   Polkinghorne, *Science and Theology*, 86. This quotation, encapsulating Polkinghorne's most significant objection to the concept of primary causality, perhaps reflects a physicist's concern with the intricacies of physical reality. That said, Polkinghorne is not slow to recognize that an insistence on God's involvement through primary causality in all that happens, good or bad, stumbles into a theodicean pit; that given the uniqueness of God's action, there can be no possibility of an analogy between divine and human action; and that the conceptuality employed casts science and theology as two irreconcilable language games that endorse claims that the natural order has no need for the God-hypothesis.

a "causal joint,"[25] a location or *the* location(s) where God interacts with the world, is not as impossible or as impious as some would contend.[26] This is no failure to distinguish between two absolutely distinct causal orders, for Polkinghorne maintains that God is not merely a cause among causes.[27] Instead, the motivation for Polkinghorne's question comes through his need to find consonance between science and theology.[28] Scientific discussions about physical process and human agency must have some influence on accounts of divine action.[29] "Conjectures concerning a causal joint are attempts to take both matter and providence seriously."[30] Polkinghorne recognizes that any claim to have discerned a causal joint must of necessity be "tentative and provisional";[31] but appealing to mystery is the final option for those attempting to describe the mechanics of God's action in the world—*not* the first.[32]

Polkinghorne's main criticism of primary causality lies in the notion's essential inscrutability. As a means of accounting for divine action, the concept of primary and secondary causality in practice has little "explanatory power"[33] and is potentially no more than "double talk."[34] The task that Polkinghorne has commissioned for himself is straightforward: he must locate a causal joint where God acts in the world, and offer an explanation for how divine action operates, all

---

See *Scientists as Theologians*, 86; *Faith, Science and Understanding*, 115–17; "Kenotic Creation," 97–8. Cf. the distinction between "two storeys" and "two stories" in Paul S. Fiddes, *Participating in God: A Pastoral Doctrine of the Trinity* (London: DLT, 2000), 120.

25   Austin Farrer, *Faith and Speculation: An Essay in Philosophical Theology* (London: A&C Black, 1967), 65.

26   John Polkinghorne, *Belief in God in an Age of Science. The Terry Lectures* (New Haven, CT: Yale University Press, 1998), 58–9; *Faith, Science and Understanding*, 115. Throughout his writings, Polkinghorne often refers to Austin Farrer's notion of "double agency" (Farrer, *Faith and Speculation*, v), a modern restatement of Aquinas' account of primary and secondary causality.

27   John Polkinghorne, *One World: The Interaction of Science and Theology* (London: SPCK, 1986), 66; "The Laws of Nature," 438; John C. Polkinghorne, "Creation and the Structure of the Physical World," *Theology Today* 44 (1987): 54.

28   Polkinghorne, *Scientists as Theologians*, 7. Consonance between science and theology means that each discipline retains its autonomy, but that whatever statements they make about reality must be reconcilable. See *Science and Theology*, 22.

29   Polkinghorne, *Scientists as Theologians*, 38.

30   Ibid., 41.

31   Polkinghorne, *Belief in God*, 59.

32   Polkinghorne, "Chaos Theory," 244; "The Metaphysics of Divine Action," in *Chaos and Complexity: Scientific Perspectives on Divine Action*, 2nd edn, edited by Robert John Russell, Nancey Murphy, and Arthur R. Peacocke (Vatican City State: Vatican Observatory Publications, 1997/2000; 1st edn 1995), 150–51.

33   Polkinghorne, *Scientists as Theologians*, 31.

34   Polkinghorne, *Faith, Science and Understanding*, 116.

the while avoiding the reduction of God to the level of mundane causation and the diminishment of creaturely causal efficacy and freedom.

Chaotic Systems and the Openness of Physical Process

Polkinghorne self-consciously locates himself within mainstream Christian tradition.[35] This is not to claim that dogmatics assumes priority over all else; as a physicist and an ordained minister in the Church of England, Polkinghorne strives for consonance between the tasks of science and theology, so that the doctrine of creation in particular must recognize and adopt insights from scientific engagement with the natural order.[36] Thus it is possible for Polkinghorne still to affirm certain basic tenets of Christian belief. God is the Creator of all that is not God, the *continual* source or origin of all that exists.[37] Moreover, such a statement indicates a fundamental ontological distinction between God and the universe,[38] a distinction that avoids becoming an unbridgeable dualism through God's ceaseless interaction with all things.[39] The theological conviction that God the Creator continually interacts with all things can only be contradicted by scientific investigation if the latter is already shaped by *metaphysical* commitments hostile to the interpretation of the world as God's creation.[40]

One consequence arising from these foundational principles is Polkinghorne's contention that the universe must be an open system to allow for God's interaction. The world, as God's creation, has "a generous measure of independence" and evolves according to the laws that God has granted it.[41] This independence—not autonomy, note—is granted to the world precisely because its Creator is the God

---

[35]   Polkinghorne, *Scientists as Theologians*, 9, 17; "The Life and Works of a Bottom-Up Thinker," *Zygon* 35 (2000): 957–8.

[36]   Lyndon F. Harris, "Divine Action: An Interview with John Polkinghorne," *Cross Currents* 48 (1998): 13; *Scientists as Theologians*, 83; *Science and Theology*, 22.

[37]   Polkinghorne, *One World*, 66; *Science and Creation: The Search for Understanding* (London: SPCK, 1988), 54.

[38]   Polkinghorne, *Science and Christian Belief*, 73; "Kenotic Creation," 94–5.

[39]   John Polkinghorne, *Science and Providence: God's Interaction with the World* (London: SPCK, 1989), 6; *"Creatio Continua,"* 108.

[40]   Cf. Polkinghorne's fleeting comments on science and the place of metaphysical decisions in "Metaphysics," 147, and *Theology in the Context of Science* (London: SPCK, 2008), 25, 60.

[41]   Polkinghorne, *Science and Creation*, 52. Cf. "Creation and Structure," 66; *Science and Christian Belief*, 76. Polkinghorne usually interprets the regularities of the world and its laws of nature as "pale reflections" or signs of God's faithfulness. See "Creation and Structure," 54; *Science and Creation*, 52; *Science and Providence*, 6. Elsewhere, Polkinghorne describes natural processes as "expressions of the divine will." See *Encountering Scripture: A Scientist Explores the Bible* (London: SPCK, 2010), 98.

who loves to ensure its prosperity. In doing so, God limits and empties Godself—"a kenosis, as the theologians say"[42]—so that the world has space to be itself.[43] In its freedom, the physical world may be characterized as "subtle and supple" and so "open to the future."[44]

Nowhere is this physical openness more apparent than in complex dynamical systems. Such systems are so sensitive to circumstance that they are "inherently unpredictable."[45] Classical Newtonian physics offered a mechanical, predictable interpretation of the world, a world capably illustrated by the image of one billiard ball hitting another.[46] However, so-called chaos theory demonstrates that even the most infinitesimal change to the initial conditions under which the balls collide could radically alter their paths. Even if all the initial conditions are known, the future directions of the balls can be accurately predicted only to a certain degree.[47] That said, the unpredictability of chaotic systems is not a manifestation of totally *random* behavior. The behavior of chaotic systems develops according to a range of future possibilities limited by its strange attractor.[48] Polkinghorne concludes,

> The general picture resulting from these considerations is that of deterministic equations giving rise to random behaviour; of order and disorder interlacing each other; of unlimited complexity being generated by simple specification; of precise equations having unpredictable consequences.[49]

These observations encourage Polkinghorne to suppose that the unpredictability of chaotic systems (an epistemological concern) is a strong indication that the world of physical process is *ontologically* open.[50] This conjecture is permissible for Polkinghorne, for he believes that there is an unassailable connection between scientific knowledge of the world and the world's physical structure, between epistemology and ontology, whereby the former models the latter.[51] Chaotic

---

[42]   Polkinghorne, *One World*, 34. Cf. the analysis of *kenosis* in Smedes, *Chaos, Complexity, and God*, 187–204. I do not believe that Smedes's critique deals a fatal blow to Polkinghorne's application of *kenosis* to divine action.

[43]   Polkinghorne, *Science and Creation*, 61.

[44]   Polkinghorne, *Science and Christian Belief*, 25. Cf. "Chaos Theory," 247.

[45]   Polkinghorne, *Science and Providence*, 2.

[46]   Cf. David Hume, *An Enquiry Concerning Human Understanding*, 4.8. Polkinghorne's use of this billiard ball imagery is found in *Science and Providence*, 28.

[47]   Cf. John Polkinghorne, *Reason and Reality: The Relationship Between Science and Theology* (London: SPCK, 1991), 36.

[48]   Polkinghorne, *Reason and Reality*, 36; *Science and Theology*, 41.

[49]   Polkinghorne, *Reason and Reality*, 37.

[50]   Polkinghorne, *Reason and Reality*, 42. Cf. *Belief in God*, 59; *Faith, Science and Understanding*, 147; *Theology in Context*, 78–9.

[51]   It is almost axiomatic for Polkinghorne that "epistemology models ontology." See,

systems are "the sign of a true openness to the future,"[52] an openness that allows for a variety of causal principles, both energetic and non-energetic,[53] to operate in the world.[54]

This openness in physical process suggests that there are "gaps" in physical process that allow for free action, both divine and human.[55] Moreover, this openness permits Polkinghorne boldly to state that *the causal joint allowing God to act in the world is to be located in chaotic dynamics.*[56] God acts in the world through the "gaps" in physical process, as do humans.[57] Thus the way is prepared for depicting divine action in a manner that does justice to the reality of God's action in a world hospitable to energetic and non-energetic causality.

---

for example, *"Creatio Continua,"* 104; *Scientists as Theologians*, 14; *Faith, Science and Understanding*, 113.

[52]   Polkinghorne, "Chaos Theory," 247.

[53]   Cf. Polkinghorne, *Science and Theology*, 42; "Metaphysics," 153.

[54]   Polkinghorne has been criticized for his intuition that epistemology models ontology, particularly in so far as this intuition persuades him to develop an indeterministic interpretation of physical process from chaos theory, which itself is very much a deterministic account of certain phenomena. However, throughout his writings, Polkinghorne emphasizes the *provisionality* of this move from epistemology to ontology. See the careful phrasing adopted in, for example, *Reason and Reality*, 42; "Chaos Theory," 247; and *Science and Christian Belief*, 53; all of which foreshadow Polkinghorne's acknowledgement that his move is essentially a metaphysical choice between equally plausible alternatives (*"Creatio Continua,"* 104; *Scientists as Theologians*, 34). Epistemology *models* ontology; even in this slogan, the choice of words is deliberate, for Polkinghorne is simply attempting to describe a relationship between epistemology and ontology that defies precise categorization.

It is beyond the scope of this paper to assess the viability of Polkinghorne's metaphysical move from epistemology to ontology, but I shall regard it as feasible. See Nicholas Saunders, *Divine Action and Modern Science* (Cambridge: Cambridge University Press, 2002), 186–96, and Smedes, *Chaos, Complexity, and God*, 70–96, for further discussion.

[55]   Polkinghorne, *Science and Providence*, 34. It is not immediately clear what status Polkinghorne assigns to these "gaps." Certainly, it seems that he is not positing the existence of actual breaks in created ontology; rather, the term "gaps" appears metaphorically to elucidate the open nature of physical process. Regardless of the exact meaning of "gaps," it is certain that the world for Polkinghorne is not some closed, deterministic order. There is scope for genuinely free action on the part of humanity and of God.

[56]   Polkinghorne, *Belief in God*, 63. Cf. *Science and Providence*, 2, 34; *"Creatio Continua,"* 106.

[57]   Elsewhere, Polkinghorne observes that accounts of agency, divine and human, must recognize the complexity of the issues involved. This means that it is inadequate simply to describe such agency by reference to God or humans exploiting ontological "gaps" in physical process. See *Theology in Context*, 78.

Informational Causality and Divine Action

The issue that Polkinghorne now needs to address is that of *how* God acts in the world. According to Polkinghorne, God acts in the world through the "gaps" in physical process, most readily apparent in the openness of complex dynamical systems. However, it is not God alone who exploits these "gaps"; humans, too, if they are genuinely to act through a variety of causal principles must take advantage of the ontological room provided by physical process. Thus Polkinghorne builds on a commonly held assumption that it is permissible to interpret human action as an analogue for God's action.[58] Polkinghorne is aware that such a move is speculative and must be made carefully; but this is more due to current ignorance about the mechanics of intentional human action than it is a flaw discernible in the use of analogy per se.[59]

This point acknowledged, Polkinghorne attempts to offer an explanation of how a human person—and so God—acts in the world. In the case of a human action, such as raising an arm, it is supposed that the mental somehow impresses on the body the requirement to channel its powers into lifting the appropriate limb.[60] Polkinghorne is careful to avoid any dualistic suggestion that the mental and the physical are independent realms, with the former arbitrarily prioritized over the latter. Instead, he argues for a dual-aspect monism, in which the human person is constituted as a psychosomatic unity. Somehow the human mind initiates physical action, but this interaction between mind and body is not to be interpreted

---

[58] Polkinghorne, "The Laws of Nature," 437; "Chaos Theory," 245. Cf. Philip D. Clayton, *God and Contemporary Science*. Edinburgh Studies in Constructive Theology (Edinburgh: Edinburgh University Press, 1997), 201: "Historically, most thinkers have utilized some form of analogy to human agency in order to conceive divine agency."

[59] Polkinghorne, "Chaos Theory," 246. It is wise to recall that Aquinas' use of analogy renders it difficult to describe how God acts. Analogical predication is a linguistic pendulum swinging between the alternatives of univocation and equivocation. God is wise (univocation), but God's wisdom is totally unlike human wisdom (equivocation)— so how can an account of God's wisdom be given that is not open to the charge of irrelevance? Similarly, God loves (univocation), but God's love is totally unlike human love (equivocation)—so again, how can an account of God's love be given that does not leave the average person scratching his or her head in bewilderment at what is being predicated of God?

In my view, Polkinghorne avoids this problem because he does not see analogy as a *tertium quid* interceding between univocation and equivocation. While God is totally unlike the world, divine condescension allows for the accurate, although not exhaustive, description of God's attributes and actions. Whereas Aquinas' use of analogy suggests a certain apophatic approach to God that refuses the attempt to depict God in human language, Polkinghorne's use means that something positive can be said about God, even if the language employed is always in need of refinement. See *Science and Creation*, 52; *Faith, Science and Understanding*, 125.

[60] Polkinghorne, *Science and Theology*, 88; *Belief in God*, 57; "*Chaos Theory*," 248.

as a Cartesian mind–body dualism simply because the mental and the material are dual aspects of the same created reality.[61] Consequently, for Polkinghorne, it is the *whole* person who initiates and executes physical action.[62] Humans are "total beings"; it is "the 'whole me' that wills the localized action of raising my arm."[63] Moreover, such *intentional* action appears to suggest causal behavior that cannot easily be accounted for in terms of energetic causality alone. Mental causation ought to some extent be characterized as "active information,"[64] a "vague but suggestive phrase"[65] that points to the supplementation of energetic causality by "holistic causal principles of a pattern-forming kind."[66] The action of raising an arm is thus a combination of energetic causality and so-called "top-down causality,"[67] interpreted as non-energetic active information.

All this leads Polkinghorne to speculate that God acts similarly to humans. "If we have some purchase on what happens in the world, may not God enjoy analogous room for manoeuvre?"[68] Polkinghorne locates this room in complex dynamical systems,[69] for, as noted earlier, the openness in physical process suggested by chaotic systems allows for a variety of causal principles, energetic and non-energetic. This is illustrated by a bead perched atop "a vertical smooth U-shaped wire."[70] The bead's eventual slide is settled by a combination of energetic causality and non-energetic informational causality. While there is no "energy barrier" to determine the *precise* path taken by the falling bead,[71] it is the "fine detail of the disturbance" that acts as information-input to shepherd the bead in a particular direction.[72] A similar combination of energetic and non-

---

[61]   Polkinghorne, *Science and Creation*, 71; *Science and Providence*, 33; *Science and Christian Belief*, 21.

[62]   Polkinghorne, *Science and Christian Belief*, 23.

[63]   Polkinghorne, *Belief in God*, 57.

[64]   Polkinghorne, "The Laws of Nature," 434; "*Creatio Continua*," 105; *Science and Theology*, 42–3. Cf. "Chaos Theory," 248.

[65]   Polkinghorne, "Metaphysics," 154.

[66]   Polkinghorne, *Scientists as Theologians*, 36. In my view, Polkinghorne has never offered a definitive account of active information. By his own admission, the concept remains elusive and difficult to describe. See *Exploring Reality: The Intertwining of Science and Religion* (London: SPCK, 2005), 32, 48.

[67]   Polkinghorne, *Science and Theology*, 88.

[68]   Polkinghorne, *Science and Providence*, 23.

[69]   Polkinghorne, *Belief in God*, 63.

[70]   Polkinghorne, *Science and Providence*, 32. Cf. *Exploring Reality*, 21.

[71]   Polkinghorne, *Science and Providence*, 32.

[72]   Polkinghorne, *Exploring Reality*, 21. Cf. Smedes, *Chaos, Complexity, and God*, 100–102.

energetic causality is presumably discernible in a person's intentional action, such as raising an arm.[73]

Polkinghorne's point is that if human actions, intentional or otherwise, occur by means of a combination of energetic causality and informational causality, then *it is possible to depict God acting by pure active information*.[74] This account of divine action is desirable for at least two important reasons. First, informational causality is "perfectly consonant with the activity of the Spirit," immanent within the world.[75] Secondly, informational causality ensures that descriptions of divine action avoid casting God as merely an agent among agents, a cause among causes.[76] God acts by pure active information, rather than by a combination of energetic and non-energetic causality, as do creatures;[77] the fact that God acts in this manner points to the *uniqueness* of divine action. However, as noted earlier, primary causality is also uniquely divine action. Given this observation, the question must be asked once more: is informational causality no more than an interpretation of primary causality for a scientific age?

Primary Causality and Informational Causality: A Comparison

Ostensibly, primary causality and informational causality are similar to the point of strict identity. God acts in the world by primary causality; God acts in the world by pure informational causality. Each of these causalities is properly attributed to God; God acts uniquely. Creatures are either secondary causes, or actors who interact with their surroundings through a combination of energetic and non-energetic causal principles. The issue is not that God is not the causal agent at play, but that these two forms of causality—primary and informational—may be indistinguishable. Is it not conceivable to contend that primary causality founds, empowers and upholds a particular instance of human arm-raising *precisely by* information-input in order to "make" that person raise her arm? On this interpretation, the concept of active information has ascribed content to primary causality that was previously absent.

Clearly, Polkinghorne himself does not equate primary causality with informational causality:

---

[73] According to Polkinghorne, the concept of information-input could help to explain how the mind acts causally on the body. See *Reason and Reality*, 45; "Chaos Theory," 248.

[74] Polkinghorne, *Science and Providence*, 32–3; *Reason and Reality*, 45; "The Laws of Nature," 437–8; *Scientists as Theologians*, 40; *Science and Theology*, 89.

[75] Polkinghorne, *Science and Christian Belief*, 150. Cf. "*Creatio Continua*," 105; *Science and Theology*, 89.

[76] Polkinghorne, *Science and Providence*, 34; *Reason and Reality*, 45; "The Laws of Nature," 438.

[77] Polkinghorne, *Belief in God*, 63.

It appears that there are certain theological concepts, which though not logically locked together, tend to constellate in association with each other. In one group are atemporality, *primary causality*, divine impassibility, an inclination towards determinism, and an emphasis on divine control. In the other group are temporality, *top-down causality*, divine vulnerability, an inclination towards openness, and a recognition of creaturely self-making.[78]

The second association of theological concepts oppose those in the first, meaning that Polkinghorne contrasts top-down causality—and so, the concept of active information—with primary causality. It is fair to say that Polkinghorne himself does not offer an especially nuanced account of how primary causality and informational causality differ from one another—indeed, if they really *do* differ. There are, in fact, at least seven points that can be made about the differences—*and* similarities—between these two forms of causality.

It must first be noted that *primary causality equates to God's will*, whereas *informational causality is consonant with the action of God's Holy Spirit*. According to Polkinghorne, active information is useful terminology that moves beyond language that threatens to reduce God to a cause among causes.[79] While talk of God *willing* to act in the world necessarily distances God from this undesirable possibility, the phrasing of divine action in voluntaristic terms has an equally unwelcome corollary, that of failing to address how divine action is to be depicted as the action of the triune God of Christian confession. The advantage of active information is that it appears to encourage an explicitly pneumatological interpretation of divine action that the language of will ignores.

Secondly, as God acts through information-input into chaotic systems, *God's action cannot be differentiated from creaturely actions*. "There will be an inextricable entanglement—it will not be possible to itemise occurrences, saying that God did this and nature did that."[80] Polkinghorne supports this point by attending to the apparent indistinguishability of God's action and natural process found in Genesis 1:24–5.[81] That said, divine action may still be discerned, although not demonstrated or proved, through faith. This is a trait that active information surely shares with primary causality. God's action through primary causality cannot be detected, but "the eye of faith"[82] (to employ John Calvin's memorable phrase) may peer into the mysteries of the God–world relation and perceive God acting through secondary causes. The significant difference between primary causality and informational causality at this point lies in the scope of God's

78   Polkinghorne, *Belief in God*, 74, emphasis added.

79   Polkinghorne, *Belief in God*, 72.

80   Polkinghorne, *Belief in God*, 72.

81   John Polkinghorne, "Scripture and an Evolving Creation," *Science and Christian Belief* 21 (2009): 165.

82   John Calvin, *Concerning the Eternal Predestination of God*, trans. J.K.S. Reid (Cambridge: James Clarke, 1961), 168.

action. Primary causality indicates God's constant presence in all occurrences; informational causality does not appear to guarantee the same comprehensiveness of involvement, for the causal joint between God and the world is found in chaotic systems alone.

Perhaps this ambiguity is not especially disturbing, for Polkinghorne argues, thirdly, that *the regularities inherent in physical process are manifestations or signs of God's faithfulness.*[83] Does this mean that God acts in chaotic systems because God has no need to act at those levels of the world that already mirror the divine nature? If so, this appears to suggest that God's ceaseless interaction with all things through the regularities of physical process continually sustains the world in existence[84]—a statement consistent with an affirmation of primary causality. The wider point that must be made is that the conceptualities of informational causality and primary causality each attribute the reliability of physical process to God.

This means, fourthly, that *God's action is not restricted by these regularities.* Although "in comparable circumstances God will act in comparable ways," Polkinghorne is certain that God remains free to act "in totally novel and unexpected ways."[85] The resurrection of Jesus Christ is the most obvious example of this, although curiously Polkinghorne also recognizes that the resurrection is an instance of divine action that cannot be elucidated by attending to God's exploitation of the "gaps" in physical process.[86] However, the conceptuality of primary causality also finds a place for God's freedom, for secondary causes are what they are only through the divine primary causality that founds, empowers and upholds them. Indeed, God can act in the world without using secondary causes if necessary.[87]

Fifthly, *both primary causality and informational causality connote determinism.* Within the conceptuality of primary causality, secondary causes "incarnate" God's voluntaristic action. The notion of secondary causes is thus employed to dignify creatures with a semblance of genuine freedom.[88] Active

---

[83]   Polkinghorne, "Creation and Structure," 63; *Science and Creation*, 52; *Belief in God*, 73. As noted earlier (in n. 41 above), Polkinghorne also describes natural processes as "expressions of the divine will." See *Encountering Scripture*, 98.

[84]   Cf. Polkinghorne, "Creation and Structure," 55; "Evolving Creation," 165; "God and Physics," in *God is Great, God is Good: Why Believing in God is Reasonable and Responsible*, edited by William Lane Craig and Chad Meister (Downers Grove, IL: IVP, 2009), 75.

[85]   Polkinghorne, *Belief in God*, 73.

[86]   Polkinghorne, "Chaos Theory," 251.

[87]   John Calvin, *Institutes of the Christian Religion*, 1.17.1.

[88]   Admittedly, this concern is more pressing for incompatibilists such as Polkinghorne than it is for those who see no contradiction between determinism and human freedom. It is beyond the scope of this paper to address the issue of compatibilism and incompatibilism in matters concerning human freedom, but a useful introduction is Roy C. Weatherford,

information does not lead *necessarily* to determinism, but the fact that God acts through information-input, which is action that effects within the constraints of physical process, suggests that God does intend certain outcomes to occur at specific times,[89] along with the possibility that God's intentions may be thwarted by creaturely intentions and actions.[90]

It must be noted, however—and this is the sixth point—that, despite the lingering stench of determinism, *informational causality is better able conceptually to respect the integrity of physical process than primary causality.* An assertion that God acts as primary cause through created secondary causes is ambiguous, in so far as such a claim posits God's action and a creature's action as two sufficient causes somehow operating from two ontologically distinct causal orders. Whatever it may prove to be,[91] active information acts *at the level of energetic causality.* This is an important point, for primary causality appears not to influence physical process through energetic causality. However, the problem that remains for the notion of active information lies in the ever-present need for the ontological distinction between God and the world to be bridged. The ontological space here is not that between God and the world as such, but that between God and the active information that God inputs into the world at the level of physical process. Polkinghorne's contention that active information is consonant with the work of the Holy Spirit means that the issue can at least be addressed from a pneumatological perspective.

It is this pneumatological orientation coupled with the contention that active information operates within physical process that offers conceptual distance between informational causality and primary causality. There is no strict identification of the two forms of causality, although it must also be recognized that the two are not as contrasting as Polkinghorne perhaps supposes. However, a comparatively late development in Polkinghorne's reflections offers further ammunition against a potential conflation. Polkinghorne has always insisted that God cannot be reduced to the level of mundane causation; God cannot be a cause among causes. At the same time, Polkinghorne has emphasized the notion of *kenosis*, the idea that God limits Godself for the good of the world.[92] This *kenosis* applies not only to God's self-limitation of divine *omnipotence*, as is often assumed

---

"Freedom and Determinism," in *The Oxford Companion to Philosophy*, 2nd edn, edited by Ted Honderich (Oxford: Oxford University Press, 2005).

[89]   Indeed, the analogue by which (intentional) human action is said to complement (intentional) divine action appears to support this contention.

[90]   Polkinghorne accepts that God may fulfill the divine purposes for the world "along contingent paths, as God responds to the free actions of others". See *Faith, Science and Understanding*, 128.

[91]   Polkinghorne expects that a thorough account of active information will be developed by the end of the twenty-first century. See "God and Physics," 73–4.

[92]   Polkinghorne, *One World*, 34; *Science and Christian Belief*, 81.

in matters of Christology,[93] but also potentially to matters of divine *agency*: "God may have, in his freedom, accepted a self-limitation which circumscribes his *mode* of action."[94] The idea contained in the notion of a *kenosis* of divine action appears to militate against the claim that God is not a cause among causes—and now, within the last decade or so, Polkinghorne is confident to dissect the various theological assumptions here at play using Christological tools:

> If we believe that Jesus is God incarnate then, there in first-century Palestine, God submitted in the most drastic way to being a cause among causes.[95]

God's action may be conceived as a cause among causes—the seventh and final point. This is not to suggest that divine *kenosis* sets boundaries to God's absolute governance of the universe, but that Christology should determine precisely what is meant by such governance.[96] Moreover, the uniqueness of divine action persists: God continues to sustain all things in existence; God continues to act in unforeseen ways; God *will* fulfill God's purposes for the world.[97] However, Polkinghorne also recalls that the uniqueness of God's action lies in the notion that, unlike humans, God acts by *pure* information.[98] Given his increased emphasis on God's (incarnate) action as being a cause among causes, this is a curious point for Polkinghorne to restate. Implicit in the wider claim about causality is now a recognition that divine action can be exercised informationally *and* energetically.[99] Does this mean that divine action in fact *would* lose its distinctiveness? There is a tension here that I am not convinced Polkinghorne has noticed.

Informational Causality as Divine Presence

It should be clear that Polkinghorne conceptually distances informational causality from primary causality by attending to the former's potential for pneumatological and Christological elaboration. In the remainder of this paper, I attempt to assemble Polkinghorne's insights about informational causality into a brief proposal for divine action that can be explicated from within an explicitly theological framework of divine presence.

---

[93] Cf. Donald Macleod, *The Person of Christ*. Contours of Christian Theology (Leicester: IVP, 1998), 205–220.

[94] Polkinghorne, *One World*, 71, emphasis added.

[95] Polkinghorne, *Faith, Science and Understanding*, 126.

[96] Polkinghorne, *Faith, Science and Understanding*, 126. Cf. *Science and the Trinity: The Christian Encounter with Reality* (London: SPCK, 2004), 114–16.

[97] Polkinghorne, *Faith, Science and Understanding*, 127–8.

[98] Polkinghorne, *Faith, Science and Understanding*, 124; "Kenotic Creation," 101.

[99] Polkinghorne, "Kenotic Creation," 105.

Active information is an insufficiently defined holistic causal principle that is claimed to organize behavioral patterns in physical process. However, it seems theologically appropriate to interpret active information as an instance of divine self-communication.[100] Such an approach has a Christological foundation: the universe is "held in being solely by the *Logos*, the Word and Reason of God, eternally uttered."[101] It is the Word of God eternally *uttered* that is crucial here: the world does not exist until the Word *ascribes* structure to a formless void already receptive to the immanent presence of God's Spirit (Genesis 1:2–3). While in a world of energetic causality, sound is a physical phenomenon capable of interpretation as speech, music, explosions, birdsong, and so on;[102] in this instance, the Word uttered is *non-energetic* but *energetically effects*. At some point between the Word's *speaking* and the world's *hearing*, the Spirit is present to communicate the divine life in such a way that non-divine life becomes possible—and not only possible, but able to accommodate the life that births it. Through the action of God's Word and Spirit, the world welcomes communicative interaction with its triune Creator; and through the incarnating action of the Spirit, the Word is made flesh and acts as a cause among causes in a world of physical process.

Thus God acts in the world through pure information-input and a combination of energetic and informational causality. While God acts uniquely on certain occasions (the resurrection of Jesus and God's continual sustaining of all things are two obvious examples of God's unique action),[103] more typical are those instances of divine action where God communicatively interacts with creatures, especially in the particularities of history made possible through various acts of divine *kenosis*.[104] Polkinghorne links God's particular action to the concept of active information: "These are the actions to which the concept of active information might have some bearing through the supposition of the divine exercise of top-down causality."[105] Moreover, by connecting the concept of *pure* active information specifically to the (work of the) Holy Spirit,[106] Polkinghorne contributes to the explicitly theological project of attempting to define divine action in terms of the particular action of the triune God of Christian confession in the world's physical process. The Spirit communicates the Father's Word to the world in order to sustain it in being and to

---

[100]   Arthur Peacocke has already made use of this concept. See, for example, "A Response to Polkinghorne," *Science and Christian Belief* 7 (1995): 113.

[101]   Polkinghorne, "Creation and Structure," 55.

[102]   Cf. Polkinghorne, *Scientists as Theologians*, 12.

[103]   Polkinghorne, "Chaos Theory," 251; *Faith, Science and Understanding*, 123.

[104]   Thus it should be noted that acts of divine *kenosis* must also count as God's unique action.

[105]   Polkinghorne, *Faith, Science and Understanding*, 124.

[106]   Polkinghorne, *Faith, Science and Understanding*, 124. Does Polkinghorne equate the *inputting* of information with the *work* of the Spirit (so that the task of the Spirit is to input active information), or does he posit a strict identification of pure information and the Spirit?

act in the world's history, the most important instance of which is the incarnation, resurrection and exaltation of the sustaining Word, the man Jesus of Nazareth.[107]

The connection between divine action and ideas of communication has been noted before. Kevin Vanhoozer argues that the Christian doctrine of providence ought to be depicted not in causal terms, but in language focused on divine communicative agency. "Speech is a form of action," Vanhoozer observes, "but not the sort of action that can by itself deprive another of his freedom."[108] Accordingly, the God–world relation is best pictured as "a communicative interaction that respects the integrity of the creature in addressing itself specifically to its rational and spiritual nature."[109] Vanhoozer's proposal is attractive and complements the idea that God acts through active information. However, in my view, more should be claimed. In the communicative act, if this is to be interpreted as having affinities with active information, God must be said not only to *interact* with the world but, through Word and Spirit, *communicate Godself* to all things. This is an important implication of portraying divine action as communicative agency or information-input, for Polkinghorne's near-strict identification of pure information with the Spirit means that this is best understood as God increasingly giving Godself to the world[110]—and this is fundamentally a matter of divine presence rather than one of communication, which, unless carefully qualified, could be a stage removed from the actual being of the triune God.

Taking my lead from Polkinghorne, I submit that *informational causality may be interpreted feasibly as active divine presence*. Informational causality understood as God's active presence provides a useful framework for explicating divine action. The promise of active information lies in its potential for *suggesting* how God acts; that is, God acts through infusing God's life into the world. As with any suggestion, this theoretical construct is subject to the possibility of future revision as new models and theories are proposed. Moreover, it must be remembered that what is being suggested by appropriation of the idea of active information is a model for *how* God acts. It does not have any bearing on the theological conviction *that* God acts in the world, for the primary basis for this lies in God's self-revelation in Jesus Christ, communicated or mediated throughout

---

[107] See Polkinghorne's Christology in *Science and Christian Belief*, 88–145.

[108] Kevin J. Vanhoozer, "Providence," in *Dictionary for Theological Interpretation of the Bible*, edited by Kevin J. Vanhoozer (Grand Rapids, MI: Baker Academic, 2005), 645. Cf. Kevin J. Vanhoozer, "Effectual Call or Causal Effect? Summons, Sovereignty and Supervenient Grace," *Tyndale Bulletin* 49 (1998): 242–51. I am aware that Vanhoozer has recently published *Remythologizing Theology: Divine Action, Passion, and Authorship*. Cambridge Studies in Christian Doctrine 18 (Cambridge: Cambridge University Press, 2010), but have not yet had the opportunity to read it.

[109] Vanhoozer, "Providence," 645.

[110] Polkinghorne's eschatological panentheism complements this idea. See, for example, *The God of Hope and the End of the World* (London: SPCK, 2002), 114–15, 132–6.

the world by the Holy Spirit's enablement of the faithful testimony of God's people. On this account, God's people enact God's presence in the world. This is, of course, a discussion well beyond the scope of this paper, but the movement from describing divine action in terms of active information to ecclesiology surely indicates strength and creativity in Polkinghorne's speculations.

Conclusion

In this paper, I raised the possibility that, despite his evident dissatisfaction with the notion of primary causality, John Polkinghorne's use of the concept of informational causality is no more than an interpretation of primary causality for a scientific age. My conclusion is that informational causality is sufficiently, although not overwhelmingly, nuanced to be distinguished from primary causality, as the former fits more easily with the contention that God communicates Godself to the world. Primary causality remains nebulous, but informational causality scientifically grounded and theologically interpreted has the potential to do justice to the physicality of a world God created good. It is to Polkinghorne's credit that his scientifically motivated insights inspire such theological interpretation.

Chapter 4

Polkinghorne on Mathematics and Chaos Theory

Nicholas Saunders

One of the most remarkable aspects of mathematics is its ability to apply to the natural world. Why should an abstract mental creation be so astoundingly successful in underpinning the laws of nature as we understand them? Eugene Wigner once famously remarked that 'the miracle of the appropriateness of the language of mathematics for the formulation of the laws of physics is a wonderful gift that we neither understand nor deserve'.[1] What underpinned Wigner's comment is the widely held belief amongst mathematicians that mathematical constructs have a far wider domain of application than the setting in which they were originally developed. Indeed some scientists, such as Max Tegmark, have gone as far as to argue that there is such a degree of 'unreasonable' mathematical order in the universe that there can be no other explanation than that the physical world is completely mathematical.[2]

This notion that mathematics is 'unreasonably effective' in describing the physical world has, of course, also drawn the attention of theologians. What is the extent to which pure mathematics (or perhaps more accurately the availability of certain mathematical tools and methods developed for their own sake) reflects and shapes our understanding of God's creation? As Pope Benedict XVI has put it,

> Was it not the Pisan scientist who maintained that God wrote the book of nature in the language of mathematics? Yet the human mind invented mathematics in order to understand creation; but if nature is really structured with a mathematical language and mathematics invented by man can manage to understand it, this demonstrates something extraordinary. The objective structure of the universe and the intellectual structure of the human being coincide; the subjective reason and the objectified reason in nature are identical.[3]

[1] Wigner, E. 1960. 'The Unreasonable Effectiveness of Mathematics in the Natural Sciences'. *Communications in Pure and Applied Mathematics* 13(1) (February).

[2] Tegmark, M. 2008. 'The Mathematical Universe'. *Foundations of Physics* 38: 101–50.

[3] Benedict, HH Pope. 2009. Message of His Holiness Benedict XVI to Archbishop Rino Fisichella on the Occasion of the International Congress 'From Galileo's Telescope to Evolutionary Cosmology. Science, Philosophy and Theology in Dialogue'. http://www.

It would perhaps be fair to say that, taken as a whole, there has been relatively little rigorous engagement with the philosophy of mathematics by the science and religion community. Yet establishing a dialogue in this area remains a fruitful area for future work – not least because of the extent to which mathematical methods seem so remarkably able to describe some aspects of creation and yet remarkably ineffective in relation to others. There are, of course, a number of central questions that could be asked about mathematics that have important ramifications for theology. Firstly, there is the question of essentiality – to what extent is it possible for physics to be carried out in any meaningful way without mathematics? This issue has raised a lively debate between proponents of the approach that mathematics is indispensable to physics following the work of Quine and Putnam, and nominalists such as Field who say that it is merely a convenient shortcut but not formally essential.[4]

However, a second question is of more fundamental interest to theologians – to what extent does mathematics engage with the ontology of the world and to what extent are mathematical structures such as fields and superpositions a description of what is really out there? Does mathematics represent or merely describe the natural world and is there a domain of applicability in which mathematical modelling breaks down? The answer is in part dependent on what approach is adopted to the ontological status of laws of nature more generally.[5] This second question is of interest not least because physicists have a tendency to adopt different positions on the realism of mathematics depending on whether they find the consequences palatable. For example, many physicists balk at saying that the concurrent superimposed worlds implied by quantum mechanics actually exist and there remains a feeling that the indeterminism inherent at the point of measurement in the Copenhagen interpretation of quantum mechanics is unfortunate and unrealistic. Similar interpretative issues, of course, also arise in relation to chaos theory and the remainder of this chapter sets out the background to chaos theory and looks at detail at John Polkinghorne's work in relation to it with reference to this second question.

What is 'Chaos Theory'?

The recent 'discovery' of chaos theory is essentially a product of the development of modern computers. It is in essence a mathematical phenomenon the

---

vatican.va/holy_father/benedict_xvi/messages/pont-messages/2009/documents/hf_ben-xvi_mes_20091126_fisichella-telescopio_en.html.

[4]   A useful collection of essays on mathematical indispensability can be found in Hart, W., ed. 1996. *The Philosophy of Mathematics*. Oxford: Oxford University Press.

[5]   There is a considerable literature on the ontological status of laws of nature – see for example the review in Saunders, N. 2002. *Divine Action and Modern Science*. Cambridge: Cambridge University Press.

underpinnings of which had been known for around a century.[6] Unlike quantum mechanics and relativity theory, which are each in part a result of the introduction of fundamental new postulates about the workings of nature, chaos theory is essentially a consequence of classical mechanics. This point has been well drawn out by Theodor Lieber:

> Physical chaos research does, however, not constitute a new research programme, or a novel theory of physics: the theoretical core (or negative heuristic) is still constituted by the axioms and theorems of classical mechanics ... [this] has led to a certain 'renaissance' of classical mechanics by emphasizing the (general and possibly unifying) question of (algorithmic, effective) computability of dynamic systems.[7]

Lieber's comment focuses on the extent to which dynamic systems are computable, but his premise is correct – chaotic behaviour can be observed in some of the most basic applications of classical physics. Chaos theory is usually considered to be the study of non-linear deterministic mathematical systems that exhibit unstable behaviour.[8] These systems are generally bounded (i.e. isolated from their surrounding environment) and accordingly capable of having their 'state' recorded at a particular moment. However the non-linear and unstable nature of the underlying mathematical models has certain consequences, including the following, which is alluded to by James Gleick:

> Watch two bits of foam flowing side by side at the bottom of a waterfall. What can you guess about how close they were at the top? Nothing. As far as standard physics was concerned, God might just as well have taken all those water molecules under the table and shuffled them personally.[9]

Gleick's point is not one about the extent to which God might be able to 'shuffle' deterministic systems, but that there are limits to our ability to predict physical phenomena in chaotic systems. There are constraints on our knowledge – for all *we*

---

[6]   In particular Henri Poincaré was responsible for the development of much of the formalism. A popular account of the theory can be found in Gleick, J. 1998. *Chaos: Making a New Science*. London: Vintage.

[7]   Leiber, T. 1998. 'On the Actual Impact of Deterministic Chaos'. *Synthese* 113: 357–79.

[8]   Kellert, for example, defines chaos as 'the qualitative study of unstable aperiodic behaviour in deterministic non-linear systems' (Kellert, S. 1993. *In the Wake of Chaos: Unpredictable Order in Dynamical Systems*. Chicago: University of Chicago Press, 2f). However there remains considerable debate as to exactly what properties constitute mathematical chaos – see, for example, Peitgen, H., Jürgens, H. and Saupe, D. 1994. *Chaos – Bausteine der Ordnung*. Berlin: Springer., chap. 1.

[9]   Gleick, J. 1998. *Chaos: Making a New Science*. London: Vintage, 8.

know, God *might* have 'shuffled' the water molecules personally – because long-term epistemological prediction in chaotic systems is extraordinarily difficult. Nevertheless, the underlying physics remains necessarily deterministic.

Before we go any further it is important to be clear about what we mean by determinism. Although there are many different approaches to the concept, some of which are more rigorous than others, one of the most intuitive high-level descriptions of what determinism is can be found in a lecture given by William James in an address to the Harvard Divinity Students of 1884:

> [determinism] professes that those parts of the universe already laid down absolutely point and decree what the other parts shall be. The future has no ambiguous possibilities hidden in its womb: the part we call the present is compatible with only one totality. Any other future complement than the one fixed from eternity is impossible. The whole is in each and every part, and welds it to an absolute unity, an iron block in which there can be no equivocation or shadow of turning …
>
> Indeterminism, on the contrary, says that the parts have a certain amount of loose play on one another, so that the laying down of one of them does not necessarily determine what the others shall be.[10]

James continues by associating determinism with a denial of the ontological status of alternatives and indeterminism with the existence of open possibility, features which resonate with contemporary discussions of divine action in the science and theology literature.

One of the points made by John Earman in his important book *A Primer on Determinism* is that boundary conditions are a necessary feature in making physical systems deterministic.[11] Earman establishes persuasively that even Newton's laws of motion taken on their own do not lead to a deterministic system unless one seals the systems described by them off from any external causally active influences – what Earman calls 'space invaders'. Certain closed classical systems can therefore be deterministic in the sense, as James put it, that there exist no ambiguous possibilities. However, the converse does not hold – merely because a particular system is unpredictable this does not necessarily imply that it is indeterministic. Unpredictability can be both a symptom of our lack of knowledge of the system under study (i.e. epistemological constraints) and a result of there being true ontological indeterminism. Both deterministic and indeterministic systems can be unpredicatable and it is precisely this unpredictability that rears its head when studying even the most simplistic chaotic systems.

---

[10]   James, W. 1979. *The Will to Believe and other Essays in Popular Philosophy.* Cambridge, MA: Harvard University Press, 117–18.

[11]   Earman, J. 1986. *A Primer on Determinism.* Boston: D. Reidel.

The meteorologist Edward Lorenz was at the forefront of identifying that difficulty in the 1960s when he examined the Navier–Stokes equations for viscous fluid flow. Those equations have no general solution, and Lorenz therefore simplified them slightly and then reduced them to a set of three very simple ordinary differential equations:

$$\dot{x} = \sigma\,(y - x)$$
$$\dot{y} = -xz + rx - y$$
$$\dot{z} = xy - bz$$

In these equations x is proportional to the intensity of convection, y is dependent on temperature difference between ascending and descending currents and z is a representation of the change in the temperature profile of the air.[12] The rate of change of each variable is dependent on the other two and on a number of constants relating to viscosity and temperature of the convecting air and other things. These are a very difficult set of equations to solve analytically so Lorenz investigated them on a 1960s computer at MIT.

The story goes that the machine Lorenz was using calculated the various parameters with an accuracy of six decimal places. Once his program had run he printed out the results to three decimal places. One day Lorenz decided to put the data from the print out back into the computer to more closely investigate some interesting phenomena he had identified. However the difference between the computer's internal accuracy and that of the data that Lorenz fed back into it made a big difference to the output he obtained.[13] His conclusion was that

> … two states differing by imperceptible amounts may eventually evolve into two considerably different states. If then, there is any error whatsoever in observing the present state – and in any such system such errors seem inevitable – an acceptable prediction of an instantaneous state in the distant future may well be impossible.[14]

This was, no doubt, a profoundly depressing thing for a professional meteorologist to have written. The 'imperceptible amount' Lorenz refers to is actually far smaller than even Lorenz could have realised with the computing technology available to him in the 1960s. His model as commonly implemented

---

[12]   Lorenz, E. 1963. 'Deterministic Nonperiodic Flow'. *Journal of the Atmospheric Sciences* 20: 130–41.

[13]   There appears to be disagreement in accounts of the story of Lorenz's discovery as to whether the computer was accurate to 6 or 9 decimal places, but the principle remains the same. An interesting discussion of the circumstances of his research is given in Gleick, J. 1998. *Chaos: Making a New Science*. London: Vintage.

[14]   Lorenz, E. 1963. 'Deterministic Nonperiodic Flow'. *Journal of the Atmospheric Sciences* 20: 130–41.

is in fact so sensitive that if one wants to be able to predict something as simple whether a particular air current will be convecting in a clockwise or anti-clockwise direction after 100 seconds you need to know the initial position of the air molecules to approximately 40 decimal places. This idea of sensitive dependence on initial conditions has been widely described and is commonly called the butterfly effect – a flap of the wings in south America can influence the weather in the UK. Lorenz himself originally used a seagull for the metaphor but it wasn't long before the seagull was replaced with a rather more delicate butterfly.[15] Every time you sneeze, the metaphor goes, you affect the weather in China.

One little appreciated implication of sensitive dependence on initial conditions is that it raises significant problems for the practical study of chaos because any computer only represents numbers to a particular given precision (say fifteen to twenty decimal places). Small errors in computation therefore become magnified as the system evolves – just as the lack of precision in Lorenz's printout led to a different future evolution of the system to that which he had previously studied. So, even though we think that we are 'following' the trajectory of a particular air molecule by applying Lorenz's equations, the sensitive dependence of his equations, in conjunction with the errors induced by the fact that our computer is only accurate to, say, 20 decimal places, means that we are not necessarily following the trajectory we thought we were. This difficulty in the computer study of chaotic systems was alluded to by Lorenz himself,

> In phase space a numerical solution … [of the Lorenz equations] must be represented by a jumping particle, rather than a continuously moving particle. Moreover, if a digital computer is instructed to represent each number in its memory by a pre-assigned fixed number of bits, only certain discrete points in phase space will ever be occupied.[16]

The problem is that if we follow the trajectory of a particular particle using computer modelling the errors get compounded over time and we are no longer following the original trajectory that we thought we were. Our plot of the trajectory of an air particle is therefore actually a combined plot of a number of different other possible trajectories for different particles. The consequences of this are not as bleak as they might appear, for our computer modelling still gives us points of genuine trajectories resulting from other possible initial conditions.

Another feature of importance in connection with chaotic systems is the existence of what are commonly called chaotic attractors. Lorenz's model is based upon a three-dimensional space in which air particles move. There are a huge number of possible trajectories in Lorenz's model, but the underlying equations are

---

[15]   Hilborn, R.C. 1994. *Chaos and Nonlinear Dynamics: An Introduction for Scientists and Engineers*. Oxford: Oxford University Press, 40.

[16]   Lorenz, E. 1963. 'Deterministic Nonperiodic Flow'. *Journal of the Atmospheric Sciences* 20: 130–41, 134.

deterministic - the implication of this determinism being that none of the possible trajectories in the three dimensional space of Lorenz's model of air convection can cross or intersect with each other or themselves. This is a crucial consequence of using deterministic models. If there are any joins between the potential trajectories then at the point of the join the particle in question can evolve from that intersection in two or more different ways and accordingly there is a choice for the future evolution of that particle – its future is not 'decreed' as William James' approach to determinism would suggest.

Attractors are a common feature of dissipative systems such as those which lose energy to the environment. Consider the example of a pendulum comprised of a string tied to a weight and swung circularly: if we plot out the motion of the weight in two dimensions, we would obtain a spiral. As air resistance slows the pendulum to rest, the pendulum dissipates energy, the size of the oscillations decreases, and the trajectory closes in on an equilibrium point where the string is hanging vertically. There are of course a number of different potential trajectories which correspond to how hard we pushed the pendulum and the precise direction of our push. Each of them, however, terminates at the common point of this equilibrium or 'attractor' where the pendulum has come to rest.

Until Lorenz plotted the numerical solutions to his equations on a computer only three forms of attractors were known – the fixed point, limit cycle and torus. Lorenz discovered a fourth, the so-called 'strange' attractor. The reason why these strange attractors are so fundamentally unlike anything previously studied is that they combine the two features of chaos theory we have already discussed – determinism and sensitive dependence on initial conditions – and yet still 'funnel' the potential trajectories to a particular point. The way this occurs is by a complex folding of phase space which curves trajectories in on each other, without letting them touch (recall the determinism) in an infinitely complex way. In the attractors in Lorenz's model the potential trajectories are focussed towards these strange attractors and as they get closer and closer to the attractor, they become more and more intricately wound up. At no point do the separate trajectories cross or join because the equations are deterministic, and the only place where they actually touch is at the infinite limit of the strange attractor itself. This is where the link between chaos theory and 'fractals' arises. This object of infinite complexity is known as a fractal, a term coined by Benoit Mandelbrot from the Latin *fractus*.[17] The strange attractors have what Mandelbrot called a fractal structure – they are areas of infinite complexity in which, as you approach the infinite limit, the energy differences between different possible trajectories become vanishingly small. Given the difficulties of extremely sensitive dependence on initial conditions, the difficulty with computer simulation, and the existence of these strange attractors, one might be forgiven for wondering whether dissipative chaotic models were of any use whatsoever. Returning to the Lorenz model as an example there are, however, at least two different ways in which meaningful study can be made: as a

---

[17]   Mandelbrot, B. 1983. *The Fractal Geometry of Nature*. New York: W.H. Freeman.

very short-term model for predicting the precise behaviour of a trajectory in phase space given suitably accurate initial conditions; or as a model describing the 'bulk' behaviour of the entire system if the constants in the equations are altered and the behaviour of 'typical' trajectories is studied under these different conditions. It is in this second sense that most of the qualitative predictive power of the Lorenz equations (and in general any chaotic system) resides. What Lorenz himself did was to alter the values of the constants in his equations and see what qualitative effects this had on the typical evolution of his convection model.

Polkinghorne on Chaos Theory

The starting point in relation to Polkinghorne's work on chaos theory is his approach to reductionism more generally. Biology, to take an example, has its own concepts and explanations that are not reducible to complicated descriptions in physics and chemistry. Yet Polkinghorne acknowledges that it is hard to dispel from one's thinking in general a reductivist tendency: when you begin to consider elementary particle physics the question becomes one of emergence – how within physics itself, and beyond, new properties arise, such as the power of classical measuring apparatus to determine the outcome of otherwise uncertain quantum mechanical experiments, and the development of consciousness and self-consciousness. It is a fact that we understand very little of how these different levels of description interrelate with each other – this could either be a problem in the way that the we describe the phenomena of one level at another (that is to say an epistemological problem), or more generally it could be a symptom of an ontological disconnect between the various underlying laws – a dappled world as Nancy Cartwright has called it.[18]

The central point that Polkinghorne makes is that it is equally possible that, if it is true that subatomic particles are not in some sense more real than cells or persons, they are not ontologically more fundamental either. It is therefore possible that emergence is a two-way process – it is conceptually valid to climb the ladder of complexity in both directions, not only looking from a bottom rung of particle physics to the higher rungs of cells and persons but also looking from higher rungs down towards the bottom rungs. Therefore the key to Polkinghorne's position in relation to chaos theory is to approach it from the context of his work on reductionism and being open to *both* downward and upward emergence. Polkinghorne emphasises that not only are theory descriptions at certain levels autonomous, but they are also reciprocally related both up and down the ladder of complexity.

As sensitive dependence is itself a direct result of the determinism of chaos theory, it is clear that Polkinghorne accepts that the theory is deterministic.

---

[18]   Cartwright, N. 1999. *The Dappled World: A Study of the Boundaries of Science.* Cambridge: Cambridge University Press.

Moreover, he argues that this sensitive dependence is constrained by the regions of phase space known as strange attractors, which he describes as implying a 'limited range of possibilities' in the evolution of a chaotic system.[19] Indeed attractors only become 'strange' in connection with dissipative deterministic systems in which the potential trajectories cannot cross or interact. He notes that 'real world' chaotic systems that show chaotic behaviour cannot easily be isolated from their environment and consequently that chaos theory suggests a holism or interconnectedness of nature. The following short quotation succinctly illustrates his position:

> The general picture resulting from these considerations [in relation to chaos theory] is that of deterministic equations giving rise to random behaviour; of order and disorder interlacing each other; of unlimited complexity being generated by simple specification; of precise equations having unpredictable consequences.[20]

The resulting worldview is certainly not one of tedious regularity, even though it is inspired by classical physics. The divine watchmaker of deism now works in a shop full of clocks each showing different times ticking with different intervals that are each dependent on each other in an astonishingly complex and unpredictable way.

Yet how open are chaotic systems really and is there any sense in which they are indeterministic? Polkinghorne acknowledges that they are certainly unpredictable, but that is as a result of the inexactitude of our knowledge of initial conditions, combined with chaotic system's exquisite sensitivity to the precise character of those conditions. He emphasises, however, that the underlying mathematics is deterministic. What we encounter is an epistemological limitation (an inability to be able to know the starting point with enough precision to be able to determine what will happen) as opposed to an ontological consequence. Therefore, chaos theory is deterministic; Polkinghorne expressly acknowledges this, but nevertheless he has appealed to it to provide a possible consonance with the notion of God acting in the world.

The key argument Polkinghorne makes is that there is a possibility of augmenting bottom-up thinking by traffic in the opposite direction. Therefore there is an possibility that some of the characteristics of a low-level description of the world – that of basic physics – may be regarded as being emergent at that low level so that they are not necessarily universally prescriptive for metaphysics. At the root of his argument is an implicit distinction that runs through Polkinghorne's work between deterministic mathematical chaos and indeterministic real-world chaotic-like phenomena. Polkinghorne introduces this distinction by questioning why there should be any metaphysical priority of one set of assumptions over another:

---

[19]   Polkinghorne, J. 1991. *Reason and Reality*. London: SPCK, 36.

[20]   Polkinghorne, J. 1991. *Reason and Reality*. London: SPCK, 37.

if apparently open behaviour is associated with underlying apparently deterministic equations, which is taken to have the greater ontological seriousness
– the behaviour or the equations? Which is the approximation and which is the
reality? It is conceivable that apparent determinism emerges at some lower
levels without its being a characteristic of reality overall.[21]

Polkinghorne's position is therefore that it is perfectly conceivable that determinism
emerges at lower levels without being a characteristic of reality overall. It might
arise from the approximation of treating systems as if they were isolatable from
the whole, when in fact they are not. He is a critical realist about science – his
epithet is that epistemology models ontology. It is therefore possible that intrinsic
unpredictability in so much physical process is indicative of there being ontological
openness in those processes.

This is of course a metaphysical position but it is bolstered by the delicate
sensitivity of complex dynamical systems to circumstances that are not only
unpredictable but also unisolatable. A favourite example of Polkinghorne's
to illustrate this point is to consider the collisions of gas molecules treated as
tiny classical billiard balls. So rapidly do the effects of the initial circumstances
propagate in a sequence of collisions that, at normal temperature and pressure,
the 50 or so collisions that take place for each molecule in the space of a milli-
microsecond would differ significantly in their outcome if an unconsidered
electron (the smallest particle) were on the other side of the observable universe
and interacting through the weakest known force – gravitational attraction – alone.
This, he argues, gives rise to the notion that an isolated set of basic entities is an
extremely abstract idea.

Accordingly Polkinghorne's approach to mathematical chaos is to view it as

emergent-downward approximations to the true, supple, physical reality. The
approximation involved is probably that of treating constituents as isolable ...
there is an essential holism built into the nature of chaotic dynamics.[22]

Polkinghorne's use of the term 'emergent-downward' is very important.
Essentially his position is that he postulates that there is a pervasive indeterminism
in the real world. This real-world indeterminism is modelled by the deterministic
mathematical chaos theory, but the determinism of mathematical chaos is
not applicable to this real-world chaos. What Polkinghorne does is to turn the
standard notion of ontological emergence on its head, and assert that, as one
moves down from this true supple indeterministic reality, one eventually meets
the deterministic equations of mathematical chaos. This metaphysical assertion
that nature is inherently flexible cannot be caught by any simplistic critique on
the basis that mathematical chaos theory is fundamentally deterministic. The

[21]   Polkinghorne, John. 1991. Reason and Reality. London: SPCK, 41.
[22]   Polkinghorne, John. 1994. *Science and Christian Belief*. London: SPCK, 26.

choice between these two metaphysical interpretations of nature is one which Polkinghorne elsewhere likens to the decision between adhering to Heisenberg or Bohm's interpretation of quantum mechanics.[23]

Therefore the picture that Polkinghorne builds up in his work on chaos theory is of a physical world that is far from being merely mechanical but retains those orderly elements that science has so successfully described. Such a world, he argues, is one in which intertwined order and novelty are consonant with God's gifts of reliability and freedom. In the context of chaos theory, in particular, that novelty can arise from the greatly differing trajectories that would result from initial conditions that differ only infinitesimally from each other. Because the differences between two trajectories are only infinitesimally different, Polkinghorne has suggested that there is no energetic discrimination between the possibilities. The choice of path, as it were, that is actually followed corresponds not to the result of some physically causal act (in the sense of an energy input), but rather to a simple 'selection' from options in the sense of an informational input.

This, he argues, opens up the possibility for two fundamentally different forms of causation – energetic and informational. The first is that which is a common part of any physicist's experience and involves interactions in a 'bottom-up' sense. The latter is the input of pattern formation that relates to the behaviour of the whole. It is crucial to appreciate that 'information' in this sense is not the same as 'information' stored on a piece of paper. The term is used in the sense of an ordering principle that operates without any input of energy into a system. Polkinghorne states that 'these higher-order principles act in a way corresponding to the input of information rather than energetic causation'.[24] The great advantage of the approach of information input understood as pattern organisation is, as we have already noted, that such assertions avoid potential interventions in the law of conservation of energy:

> since the paths through the strange attractor all correspond to the same energy, we are not concerned with a new kind of energetic causality. The energy content is unaffected whatever happens. What is different for the different paths through phase space is the unfolding pattern of dynamical development they represent. The discriminating factor is the structure of their future history, which we can understand as corresponding to different inputs of information that specify its character (this way, not that way).[25]

Typically those open options might be expressed in terms of bifurcating possibilities (this or that), whose particular realisations resemble bits of information (switches

---

[23]   Polkinghorne, J. 1996. *Beyond Science: The Wider Human Context*. Cambridge: Cambridge University Press.

[24]   Polkinghorne, J. 1994. *Science and Christian Belief*. London: SPCK, 77.

[25]   Polkinghorne, J. 1998. *Belief in God in an Age of Science*. New Haven: Harvard University Press, 62.

on or off). Polkinghorne argues that this type of information may provide a picture of how God could act in the world. Based on Polkinghorne's approach to chaos theory, God is not an interfering agent with a similar status to other agents (that would imply an energy input), but there is a possibility that God influences his own creation in a non-energetic way.

It is a pity that Polkinghorne's approach to divine action and the metaphysical implications of chaos theory has not been more positively received. His position has been subject to a considerable amount of misplaced criticism on the basis of the link between unpredictability and indeterminacy. What chaos theory shows, the critics claim, is not that there is genuine indeterminacy in the universe but that instead we need to make a more careful distinction between predictability (an epistemological concept) and determinism (an ontological concept). The reign of determinism is not broken, the critics claim – the non-linear equations describing chaotic systems specify exactly what each new state will be, given the immediately preceding state.

The problem is that these criticisms miss the point. The argument Polkinghorne deploys is more subtle and far-reaching than the simple parody that is approached by these arguments. In essence the criticisms commonly reduce Polkinghorne's argument to the following set of four propositions: (1) chaos theory arises from deterministic sets of non-linear equations; (2) the problem is that we cannot know the starting conditions accurately enough – therefore chaotic systems are unpredictable; (3) Polkinghorne says that epistemology models ontology – if something is unpredictable it must be ontologically indeterminate; and (4) that ontological indeterminacy gives flexibility and openness in nature. However, we know that 1 remains true and that therefore 4 (or perhaps the application of 3) cannot be correct as nothing has changed. However, this is not Polkinghorne's argument. His approach is much more fundamental – it is about the applicability of models in mathematics and a recognition not only that physics operates in certain domains of applicability but also that there is both upwards and downwards emergence at different hierarchies of explanation, as we have already seen. In essence what he says is that there is no ontological primacy of one form of explanation over another. Therefore, rather than look at these misplaced criticisms of Polkinghorne's position, we will look further at the notion of information input.

Mandelbrot, who has been widely dubbed the 'father of fractal geometry', has been very keen to assert a direct consonance between fractal mathematics and natural forms. It turns out that many mathematical structures have a form of underlying geometric regularity, known as scale invariance or self-similarity. If you examine these objects at different scales and magnifications, one repeatedly encounters the same fundamental elements. As Mandelbrot himself put it:

> [fractals] have the same degree of irregularity on all scales. A fractal object looks the same when examined from far away or nearby – it is self-similar ...

Nature provides many examples of fractals, for example, ferns, cauliflowers and broccoli and many other plants, because each branch and twig is like the whole.[26]

However, ferns and cauliflowers could never be said to be actual fractals – as we zoom in closer and closer on the fern leaf, we reach a point where the individual prongs are not themselves made from other prongs. There is no infinite complexity in nature – not least if we are right about atomic physics. The point has been well made by Peter Smith in his excellent book on the philosophy of chaos theory:

> given a merely surface-descriptive appeal to fractals, where it is claimed that some natural phenomenon has a fractal-like look to it, we can agree that there may well be similar measurement behaviour at course scales. But we really should be cautious about leaping to assert that some department of nature really has a fractal geometry. We always need to ask: won't a better surface description of nature in fact be provided by prefractals that lack the infinite detail? To which the answer seems invariably "yes".[27]

So while it is remarkable that, for example, a simple deterministic equation will produce something that looks like a fern at a particular scale, it is important to appreciate that those equations do not describe the fern any more satisfactorily than saying that the superposition of Schrodinger's cat as both dead and alive actually exists. Nature simply does not embody the infinite detail that comes as an albatross around the neck of chaos theory.[28]

We can see this even more clearly when one looks at aspects of nature that can be modelled using chaos theory. To take one example, Boris Belousov noticed by chance that a certain mixture of chemicals produced unusual changes in the concentration of bromide and cerium ions in solution. The result is spectacular – when the chemicals are mixed in a dish there is a series of colour oscillations between red and blue.[29] Now, it turns out that this aperiodic behaviour can be looked at through the telescope of chaos theory. The reaction has been studied in great detail and it turns out that, lo and behold, when it is modelled it gives rise to chaotic fractal attractors. The problem is that no one would really say that there is anything other than a finite number of atoms of any particular type in the beaker at

---

[26] Mandelbrot, B. 1991. 'Fractals – A Geometry of Nature'. In *The New Scientist Guide to Chaos*. London: Penguin, 123–4.

[27] Smith, P. 1998. *Explaining Chaos*. Cambridge University Press, 33. See also the more trenchant criticisms to be found in Shenker, O. 1994. 'Fractal Geometry is not the Geometry of Nature'. *Studies in History and Philosophy of Science* 25(6): 967–81.

[28] See Saunders, N. 2002. *Divine Action and Modern Science*. Cambridge: Cambridge University Press, chap. 7.

[29] There are many videos of the reaction available on the internet by, for example, searching for 'BZ Reaction' at www.youtube.com.

any moment in time. In short there is a point at which the fractal nature of chaos theory breaks down – it stops approximating to reality.

Therefore, deterministic chaos theory is both a blessing – there is more that is predictable in the world than we had hitherto thought – and a curse – an inevitable consequence of fractal mathematics is that nature does not, as far as we are aware, embody the infinite intricacies required.

There are at least two consequences of this – one for Polkinghorne's appeal to chaos theory and one for his critics. Firstly, it strongly suggests that we need to be wary about making realistic claims for fractal structures in nature. One aspect of Polkinghorne's approach to information input is to look at circumstances in which the energy differences between potential evolutions of a chaotic system are vanishingly small. This occurs in the infinite limit of the chaotic attractor – i.e. where the different trajectories are so tightly bound up that there is no energy difference. The problem is that there are serious difficulties relating this type of fractal mathematics to reality – the world is far more 'coarse grained' than the infinite levels of complexity would suggest.

However, this observation also has consequences for the detractors of John's appeal to chaos theory. At the very least the deterministic equations of chaos theory reach a point where, on a certain scale, they cease to adequately describe ontology. The situation is ironic given the basis of much of the criticism of his position – the very determinism that makes the theory so unattractive to John's critics is actually what leads to its limited sphere of application in support of his approach. So what we see here is a clear example of mathematical models having very discrete spheres of application – they have, as it were, boundary conditions in which those particular models inevitably break down not in terms of their ability to predict, but in terms of their fit with ontology. However, the infinite complexity remains part and parcel of the very model that in certain other circumstances provides a helpful qualitative way of looking at so many physical systems.

When we model nature using classical mechanics we typically make simplifying assumptions. Imagine the pendulum swinging on a string – we might assume that the string is inelastic so that we can ignore any effects of the string lengthening or shrinking, that the pendulum is a perfect sphere and that the air surrounding it is perfectly uniform, and so on. However, it turns out that there is a surprising complexifying effect – in order to be able to predict the position of the pendulum at a point in the future, it will be necessary to know the initial position of the pendulum with infinite precision. So to return to William James's approach to determinism – although it may be true to say that

> The future has no ambiguous possibilities hidden in its womb: the part we call
> the present is compatible with only one totality,

the issue is not just the practical issue of the difficulty of epistemological prediction, it is also the problem of aspects of what is otherwise a very successful model being unrealistic.

The practical epistemological problem is that we will never know the one totality because we can never know the initial conditions to a sufficient level of accuracy, and that is just in relation to a closed model – the epistemological problem becomes all the more acute when one considers the impact of other factors such as the wings of flapping seagulls and butterflies and the complexity of real systems.

This in my view gives support to John's more general approach – it would seem to suggest that this is another instance of theories being limited to certain spheres of application. We not only need boundary conditions for a chaos theory model to take effect, but we also need boundary conditions over our critical realist claims for the theory itself. Perhaps just such a flexible and downward and upward emergent account of nature is one in which a creator God can act and remain consistent with the regularity and intelligibility of his creation.

I would like to end on a personal note. I first met John when I was an undergraduate studying physics 18 years ago. What I found remarkable was that John was very happy to engage with my ideas no matter how misconceived or junior their proponent. This, I later found, was just one aspect of John's good-natured generosity and kindness to the science and theology community at large. It has been a privilege to be a minor part of that community in the relatively short period in which I have been involved with it, and I wish John the very best for the future.

Chapter 5

Queen Physics:
How Much of the Globe is Painted Red?

Nancy Cartwright and Eric Martin[1]

Prelude

This paper has two authors. We begin with Nancy Cartwright's account of the hodgepodge of nature. Much of this account is shared with John Polkinghorne, which is why we have the honor of contributing to this volume in tribute to him. In the next section Eric Martin explains some of Polkinghorne's ideas on order in nature and shows how Cartwright's ideas sometimes mesh with these but sometimes do not.

The Hodgepodge of Nature

Despite all of the apparent differences we see among the unlimited number of things that happen in the world, there is but one realm, we are told, and physics is its queen. I reject this claim. There is not one realm, as the ambassadors of physics maintain, nor two, as mind–body dualists proclaim, but many: cooperating, quarrelling and negotiating. I reject the universal rule of physics not because I dissent from her dictates but because I respect her strengths. What physics can do, she does exceedingly well. However, her very strengths suggest that she cannot rule everything with the same iron hand, nor can she do it alone.

I adopt this position as an empiricist. As an empiricist I maintain that our best guide to the structure of nature is how our sciences work when they work best. We do not use only physics to build a laser. So why suppose that Nature behaves differently? An empiricist stance maintains that the way to learn about the structure of nature is to look at it, and when it comes to the parts of the world studied by physics, our best lens for looking at them is through our most successful accounts in physics. When I look through that lens, I see a quite different world from one where physics reigns, supremely and by herself. I see a dappled world with a

[1] The authors would like to thank the Templeton Foundation for their support of the ongoing research project, "God's Order, Man's Order, and the Order of Nature."

hodgepodge of different kinds of features interacting in a variety of different ways.[2] This is true even for the effects that physics herself is supposed to control.

The sciences give us the best basis for our beliefs about nature. However, it is what the sciences need *as they are used to predict and manipulate the empirical world* that we have warrant for believing in. These uses in fact rely on an enormous number of concrete, diverse, complicated and particular laws—hardly just a few high-level fundamental principles of physics.

Consider French physicist, historian of physics and Catholic apologist, Pierre Duhem, writing in 1906 on *The Aim and Structure of Physical Theory*. Duhem argued that there are two kinds of minds: ample and deep. The ample mind "analyzes an enormous number of concrete, diverse, complicated, particular facts, and summarizes what is common and essential to them in a law, that is, a general proposition tying together abstract notions."[3] The deep mind "contemplates a whole group of laws; for this group it substitutes a very small number of extremely general judgements referring to some very abstract idea." This is the French mind. Duhem explained: "In every nation we find some men who have the ample type of mind, but there is one people in whom this ampleness of mind is endemic; namely, the English people."[4]

Writing in *How the Laws of Physics Lie*, in 1983 I urged that God has the mind of the English. If this is the way the English can do science, why should it not be the way nature does it too? However, today I think that, moreover, it is the mind of an English engineer! That is a thesis we shall come to later. For now let us consider just the substitution of a few abstract general principles for the myriad concrete detailed ones that we use on the ground to model and manipulate nature.

It is a mistake to think that the language of high theory can be a substitute for all those diverse concrete laws to which Duhem referred. In trying to fit the concrete laws into its own framework, the high theory substitution:

- distorts many of them;
- omits much of their information;
- ignores many of them; and
- overstretches its own abstract vocabulary.

Trying to fit so many laws into the high theory of abstract ideas is trying to pack too much into too little. High theory cannot accommodate the plenitude of concrete and particular principles that are necessary to get the details just right to get a laser to work or a superconducting quantum interference device (SQUID) to test whether a patient has had a stroke.

---

[2]   Nancy Cartwright, *Dappled World*, Cambridge, Cambridge University Press, 1999.

[3]   Pierre Duhem, *The Aim and Structure of Physical Theory*, Princeton, NJ, Princeton University Press, 1954 [1906], p. 55.

[4]   Ibid., p. 63.

While at Stanford University, I was enamored with quantum physics and, being a committed empiricist, particularly with the startling empirical successes that speak for its credibility, especially lasers and superconductors, which I made a special area of study. I was especially impressed simultaneously by how crucial quantum considerations are for understanding these devices and by how little they can do by themselves. They must be combined with huge amounts of classical physics, practical information, knowledge of materials and exceedingly careful and clever engineering before accurate predictions emerge, and none of this is described—or looks as if it is even in principle describ*able*—in the language of quantum physics.[5] Physics can measure, predict and manipulate the world in precise detail, but the knowledge that produces our extraordinarily precise predictions and our astounding devices—the very knowledge that gives us confidence in the laws of physics—is not all written in the language of physics, let alone in one single language of physics. Its wellspring is what I call "the scientific Babel."

I was clearly influenced in these views not only by what I saw in the building of lasers and the exploitation of SQIDS but also by my hero Otto Neurath. Neurath spearheaded the unity of science movement of the Vienna Circle. However, his idea of unity was not that physics—or anything else for that matter—could produce predictions by herself. He argued for unity *at the point of action*. His idea was that we must bring the requisite sciences together as best we can, each time anew, to achieve the projects we set ourselves, from building a laser or a radar to even—as Neurath believed we had the intellectual resources for—organizing and controlling the roller-coaster of the economy. Although he urged us to talk the same language wherever possible, he never believed that this language would stretch far or last long or capture much of what the separate users mean by its terms. Neurath advocated not a shared language but a "universal jargon."[6] This idea has recently been taken up and defended with a vengeance in Science Studies.

Consider the Massachusetts Institute of Technology World War II radar project. Designing the radar took the united efforts of mathematicians, physicists, engineers and technicians, each themselves expert in one small domain with a language of its own, put together by the urgency of war and often against their will. It took a year for them to be able to communicate well enough to build a usable device, and redesign the physical environment. The building used to be arranged floor-by-floor according to prestige, with mathematicians at the top. The radar project mixed researchers from the different disciplines at long tables on each floor, tables that reflected in their very geometry the five components of the radar to be built. Success was achieved not by constructing a single language nor by translation, but by face-to-face contact that allowed enough interchange to make a go of it.

---

[5] Nancy Cartwright, *How the Laws of Physics Lie*, Oxford, Clarendon Press, 1983.

[6] Nancy Cartwright, Jordi Cat, Lola Fleck and Thomas E. Eubel, *Otto Neurath: Philosophy Between Science and Politics*, Cambridge, Cambridge University Press, 1996.

Peter Galison calls this space of interchange the "trading zone."[7] Consider theoretical and experimental physicists treating what we like to think of as the very same phenomenon. Galison pictures this as very often like two tribes stuck in linguistic isolation. They trade in the "commerce" of vital "shared" concepts, but each group in this trade maintains its own understanding of these concepts within itself, and even these internal understandings may be out of kilter in various ways. Otherwise they would not be able to produce the detailed well-founded results needed for their own projects to succeed. They speak Neurath's universal jargon or what Peter Galison describes as a kind of pidgin, with each group maintaining different understandings of the terms they use in common. According to Galison this is often the case for theoretical and experimental physicists, even with respect to the very same claim, a claim the theoreticians derive and the experimentalists test.

Other scholars in Science Studies see the same thing. Sang Wook Yi's study of thermodynamics[8] rejects the usual story that it reduces to statistical mechanics. He argues that a more useful way of understanding the relationship is as collaboration and competition among alternative methodologies rather than reduction of one theory to another. The theme of cooperation and competition carries over from Yi's work on condensed matter physics, where he shows how it plays a crucial role in generating the right kind of models for systems with many bodies.

Marilena Di Bucchianico writes about the quarrelling camps in high-temperature superconductivity.[9] It seems that they do not share a common meaning for the same terms even in this single narrow domain. For example, the "kink" is an observed and unexpected spike in the dispersion curve during photoemission studies. Using the same word, different groups construct the kink differently from the same body of data. Or take the *phase diagram*, a type of chart that shows conditions under which thermodynamically distinct phases occur. Often, each camp builds and presents its own phase diagram, which contains only a selection of observed features, thus creating a vast series of almost incommensurable theorizations.

Hasok Chang's important study[10] of the long struggle to measure temperature makes it clear how essential were contributions from potters, experimentalists with specialisms from thermal physics to glassblowing, chemists, doctors, physicists from the most abstruse theoreticians to the most down-to-earth instrument builders, famous inventors, entrepreneurs, soldiers and myriad others.

---

[7]   Peter Galison, *Image and Logic: A Material Culture of Microphysics*, Chicago, IL, University of Chicago Press, 1997.

[8]   Sang Wook Yi, "Reduction of Thermodynamics: A Few Problems," *Philosophy of Science* 70(5) (2003), pp. 1028–38.

[9]   Marilena Di Bucchianico, *Modelling High Temperature Superconductivity: A Philosophical Inquiry into Theory, Experiment and Dissent*, PhD Dissertation, London School of Economics, 2009.

[10]   Hasok Chang, *Inventing Temperature*, Oxford, Oxford University Press, 2007.

Harry Collins in his study of gravity-wave experiments[11] concludes that gravity waves are "boundary objects"—understood and valued differently by the different cultural groups that share them. Alternatively, look at the study of the original BCS model of superconductivity by Cartwright, Tomar and Suarez.[12] This model was the first successful theoretical account of the phenomenon, a tour de force of quantum modelling, which still lies at the heart of our understanding of superconductivity. Although it has been tidied up considerably, it remains a hodgepodge of high quantum theory and ad hoc assumptions grounded in classical electromagnetic theory.

So science is conducted within a Babel of languages, drawing on expertise from different corners of research. Why suppose the Book of Nature is written in a single language when science is not? The problem is not unity at the "high" end—the grand unity in one mathematical theory that many physicists long for. Rather, the problem is unity at the "low" end—where physics finally engages with the empirical world. There, unity is a superstition.

If we are to extrapolate from our knowledge of science to an understanding of nature, the metaphysical significance of these considerations is novel and has not been sufficiently appreciated. To appreciate the consequences of this view it is helpful to recall some of the positions it might oppose. Take, for example, recent work from Lydia Jaeger,[13] which supposes that God's wisdom demands order and comprehensibility, that comprehensibility entails order and that order entails the immutable rule of law. I dispute all three claims.

The scientific world view articulated by Jaeger and a host of others is that science will slowly reveal, hidden within the all-too-apparent mess, a truer and more fundamental reality that is beautiful, clean and entirely orderly. This tidy image of nature is governed *thoroughly* by laws: essentially those of high theory physics. Physics, then, ends up as the ultimate arbiter of reality, her sparse laws pervading and ordering the natural world. This familiar image of nature dates at least to the scientific revolution and remains influential.[14] For all of our advances, the image of an orderly, deterministic, clockwork universe, with its roots in a particular vision of monarchical divine governance, has been surprisingly enduring.

I have not been alone in questioning that traditional world view. The abundance of recent scholarship in Science Studies constitutes a quiet revolution in terms of the received view of natural order. This scholarship is not about the standard philosophical question of realism and anti-realism in science. The questions at

---

[11] Harry Collins, *Gravity's Shadow*, Chicago, IL, University of Chicago Press, 2004.

[12] Nancy Cartwright, Towfic Shomar and Maricio Suarez, "The Tool Box of Science: Tools for the Building of Models with a Superconductivity Example," *Poznan Studies in the Philosophy of the Sciences and the Humanities* 44 (1995), pp. 137–49.

[13] Lydia Jaeger, *Einstein, Polanyi, and the Laws of Nature*, West Conshohocken, PA, Templeton Press, 2010.

[14] Stephen Weinberg, *Dreams of a Final Theory: The Search for the Fundamental Laws of Nature*, New York, Vintage Books, 1993.

hand are more precisely about *dominion*—how far the reach of physics' laws extends (or any laws for that matter)—and *autocracy*—whether physics reigns supreme and by herself, or is one part of a more motley assembly of sciences. The studies mentioned above suggest that physics is not even an autocrat in her own domain, much less autocratic across all of nature. The answer that physics might be just one among many sciences is a revolution in terms of our thinking about the relationship among the sciences and about the order of nature.[15]

If my story, or something like it, is true, and nature does not fit the old image of law-governed order, whither then order and comprehensibility? Is it still possible to speak intelligibly about the creator of such a world at all, much less a rational creator? I imagine God as an engineer, not as a mechanic, as the Mechanical Philosophy would have it, where those terms are intended in what Norton Wise picks out as their nineteenth-century sense.[16] For instance, the English mathematician and engineer Charles Babbage divided objects of machinery into *engines*, employed to produce power, and *mechanisms*, merely to transmit force and execute work. While engines implied productive power, "mechanism," in this more specific sense, referred to a device for executing a typically repetitive motion. Engineers use principles about how things behave in special circumstances to construct devices that give rise to regular behavior, where those principles are not necessarily universal laws. I suppose that God is like an engineer, not a mechanic, and order, where it exists in nature, results from clever engineering.

This metaphysical picture is in many ways more modest than the received scientific world view. It suggests only that the world is as our sciences are, and that order, where it exists, arises from good engineering, whether God's or our own. Such order need not be universal or necessary, and yet the world, or at least some parts of it, remains comprehensible.

A ready response can be made to this mass of evidence from Science Studies if you believe in the autocratic powers of physics, despite her repeated failure to rule by herself in even the best of circumstances: blame it on us, not her. This standard response draws a line between epistemology and metaphysics, and insists that, *really*, the world is totally ordered under the rule of universal law, and it is only our limited (post-lapsarian) knowledge that is failing. The world is totally ordered; it is just us weak intellects who have so far produced only an incomplete and inadequate approximation to what Queen Physics is really accomplishing.

Yet that is hardly the simplest or most natural conclusion to draw from the evidence. If we speculate about the structure of Nature, as empiricists we had better stick as close to the evidence as possible. Moreover, the standard response is an unattractive metaphysical conclusion, on several fronts. Nothing ever happens in a mechanical world under the universal rule of law; genuine novelty and creativity

---

[15]   Miriam Thalos, *Without Hierarchy: An Essay on the Scale of Freedom in the Universe*, forthcoming.

[16]   M.N. Wise, "The Gender of Automata in Victorian Britain," in Jessica Riskin, ed., *Genesis Redux*, Chicago, IL, Chicago University Press, 2007.

are nowhere found. A single time-slice contains all the information about the past and the future. Is God then a mechanic in this sense? As H.G. Wells's Time Traveller[17] teaches, "There is no intelligence where there is no change and no need to change." Why would the Deity create such a boring universe?

An engineered universe, on the other hand, suggests several fruitful and attractive alternatives. It provides a new aesthetic, a new view of nature, new questions about God, and new questions about the human role in nature. It suggests an aesthetic based on diversity and variety rather than uniformity. It suggests that nature is piecemeal and more like a hodgepodge than a solid color. Far from the austerity described by one set of fundamental laws dictating the motions of the world's machinery, this alternative is an abundant and plentiful universe, and in the tradition of natural theology, this could make for an important component in thinking about the character of the world's creator. It therefore contains new theological questions: what kind of God prefers a hodgepodge to hegemony? Further, there are new queries about us humans. Is it our job to build order? What kind of order? What counts as order, beauty or perfection?

Polkinghorne's Bottom-up Thinking

John Polkinghorne shares a commitment to empiricism and to bottom-up thinking; his Gifford Lectures were even subtitled *Reflections of a bottom-up thinker.*[18] This empirically motivated outlook has guided Polkinghorne's work on science and religion in several ways. Most generally, he insists that science be taken very seriously and incorporated into theological reflection, whose vision has too often been parochially restricted to humanity.[19] Polkinghorne urges that the deliverances of natural science become a part of that vision, a view congenial to any empiricist.

Secondly, while recognizing certain built-in limitations to its objectivizing epistemology, Polkinghorne believes that science is the best way to learn about the natural world. "[W]hy go to all the trouble involved in doing science if one does not believe that thereby we are learning what the physical world is actually like?"[20] Polkinghorne counts himself a "critical realist" who believes that the well-confirmed products of science can count as progress towards truth. Cartwright agrees.

Thirdly, Polkinghorne writes about how scientific knowledge informs important debates in epistemology and metaphysics. From his own study of quantum mechanics, Polkinghorne draws the conclusion that "there is no universal

---

[17]   H.G. Wells, *The Time Machine, an Invention.* London, William Heinemann, 1895.

[18]   John Polkinghorne, *The Faith of a Physicist; Reflections of a Bottom-up Thinker: the Gifford Lectures for 1993–4,* Princeton NJ, Princeton University Press, 1994.

[19]   Ibid., p. 5.

[20]   John Polkinghorne, *Science and the Trinity,* London, Yale University Press, 2004, p. 79.

epistemology, no single sovereign way in which we hope to gain knowledge."[21] This insight runs counter to the tradition which says that there is only one Scientific Method, whose application is definitive of science. Polkinghorne also calls this "epistemic specificity,"[22] arguing that physics alone does not suffice to tell us about the complete structure of reality. Polkinghorne points out the need for theology in addition to physics, but his argument holds equally well for the incorporation of other sciences. On top of Polkinghorne's detailed attention to physics and theology, Cartwright urges greater attention to the interstices in this space of knowledge. The picture becomes yet more rich and complex when chemistry, biology and social sciences are added into the jumble.

Like Cartwright, Polkinghorne resists drawing the sharp line between epistemology and metaphysics that allows the postulation of a simple or monolithic Nature in the face of our complex and fragmented knowledge. His motto that "epistemology models ontology" testifies to the close connections between scientific insight and warranted belief about what exists. "[I]n forming our account of reality we should be open to all aspects of our encounter with it. Tidy schemes, produced by selective oversimplification and resulting in a neglect of part of the data, are not of any value."[23] Again, Cartwright heartily agrees.

Two of Polkinghorne's favored descriptions of nature are "subtle" and "veiled"—metaphors that imply that nature is neither reducible to a small number of mathematical equations nor fully describable in grand theoretical syntheses. They imply further that there is more to reality than our simplest, highly controlled physics experiments tell about it. Cartwright agrees that there is no single complete picture of nature, much less one yielded directly by physics.

All the same, Polkinghorne retains a traditional physicist's aesthetic about the pervasiveness of natural laws, their connection with God's mind and the total comprehensibility of nature.[24] This is where the views of Cartwright and Polkinghorne depart most strongly. While Polkinghorne recognizes that much of our scientific knowledge is "patchy,"[25] he is more likely to identify the reason for such patchiness as the incompleteness of science, whereas Cartwright and fellow travelers (e.g. Dupre[26]) have sought to articulate the metaphysical underpinnings of our piecemeal knowledge. They argue that our knowledge may well be patchy because that is an accurate reflection of the world's own patchiness.

[21]   John Polkinghorne, *Quantum Theory: A Very Short Introduction*, Oxford, Oxford University Press, 2002, p. 87.

[22]   Polkinghorne, *Science and the Trinity*, p. 77.

[23]   John Polkinghorne, *Faith Science, and Understanding*, London, SPCK, 2000, p. 24.

[24]   Polkinghorne, *Science and the Trinity*, pp. 12–13.

[25]   John Polkinghorne, *Exploring Reality*, London, Yale University Press, 2005, p. xii.

[26]   John Dupre, *The Disorder of Things*, Cambridge, MA, Harvard University Press, 1993.

From the hints of pluralism in Polkinghorne's corpus come some surprising points of contact with Cartwright's work.[27] They both realize that the breakdown of the traditional view of natural order has not been sufficiently appreciated. Polkinghorne has given greater attention to the role of indeterminism and the in-principle limits to human knowledge suggested by chaotic and quantum phenomena, while Cartwright has utilized case studies from the practice of several sciences to argue for nature's dappled construction. Both are at pains to generate alternatives to the deterministic, mechanical world view promulgated for so long in the name of science.

---

[27]   Eric Martin, "Polkinghorne and Cartwright on Pluralisam and Metaphysics," *Theology and Science*, forthcoming.

Chapter 6

God and Time: A New Flowing Time Interpretation of Special Relativity and its Importance for Theology[1]

Robert John Russell

> Relativity physics is a puzzling case for my thesis, the most puzzling indeed of all … What is God's "frame of reference", if there is no objectively right frame of reference for the cut between past and future?
>
> Charles Hartshorne[2]

Most of us take it for granted that time flows. Time is a momentary, ever-changing universal present wedged fleetingly between an uncertain future coming at us and an irretrievable past vanishing behind us. Such a flowing view of time is presupposed not only in our daily lives but in all fields of study from the social sciences to historical sciences, psychological sciences, jurisprudence and the arts. Crucially, it is assumed by Christian theologians, for ours is an historical religion concerning God's "mighty acts" of creation and redemption, and not just a collection of timeless propositions.

Nevertheless this view is only held by a minority of philosophers of science in the Anglo-American tradition. Instead these scholars more often support a timeless view of nature—the so-called "block universe"—in which only tenseless "before and after" relations are admitted and the claim that the future is not real, or at best only potential, is dismissed. Moreover, in light of Einstein's Special Theory of Relativity (SR), the arguments in favor of a timeless "block universe" seem almost undeniable.

Hence for Christian scholars in the interaction between theology and science, a defense of flowing time in light of SR is essential. None have been more outspoken about the importance of a flowing-time interpretation of SR for the relation between God and creation than John Polkinghorne, to whom this volume is dedicated. It is my hope, then, to offer new support for a flowing-time interpretation of SR as a

[1] A much more extensive treatment of the themes of this chapter can be found in Robert John Russell, *Time in Eternity: Physics, Pannenberg and Eschatology* (Notre Dame, IN: University of Notre Dame Press, 2012). I want to thank Dr Joshua Moritz for creating Figures 6.7 and 6.8.

[2] Charles Hartshorne, *A Natural Theology for our Time* (La Salle, IL: Open Court, 1965), 93.

way to express my profound debt to John's pioneering leadership in theology and science and my personal appreciation for our lasting friendship.

Flowing Time vs Timelessness: New Philosophical Arguments for Flowing Time in the Pre-relativistic Arena via a Relational Ontology

Apparent Contradictions in Flowing Time: McTaggart's Paradox

> Past, present and future are incompatible determinations. Every event must be one or the other ... But every event has them all ... How is this consistent with their being incompatible?[3]

A classic example of a philosophical argument against flowing time is known as "McTaggart's Paradox."[4] To understand the paradox, consider Figure 6.1, where time *t* is treated as a continuous one-dimensional variable (e.g. the time axis, *t*).

Figure 6.1 Time as a one-dimensional continuous variable

Now let us add in events along *t*, represented by points on the timeline, and let us label them in relation to a single event chosen as the present. In Figure 6.2 the present event (denoted "pr") is B, with event A in the past of B ("p") and event C lying in B's future ("f").

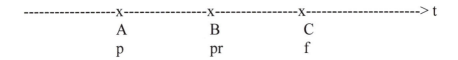

Figure 6.2 The present event B with a future event C and
a past event A relative to B

---

3   J.M.E. McTaggart, "The Unreality of Time," reprinted in Peter van Inwagen and Dean Zimmerman, eds, *Metaphysics: The Big Questions* (Malden, MA: Blackwell, 1998), 67–74.

4   Ibid.

Figure 6.3 helps us visualize the ontological contradictions that flowing time seems to raise, particularly as represented in McTaggart's Paradox: *As a future event becomes the present and then the past, the ontology assigned to this event changes. What was an event in the potential and indeterminate future becomes the actual and determinate present moment and then it becomes an actual, determinate but permanently unavailable past moment.* Paraphrasing the quote from McTaggart seen above, no event can simultaneously possess two or more incompatible temporal predicates. Every event must be either past, present or future. However, if flowing time were correct, every event would have all three incompatible predicates. This is the contradiction to which McTaggart's Pardox points.

To emphasize this change in the status of an event's predicates and the implied ontologies that flowing time seems to require, I will add the following notation to the figure:

pr, the present event, is real, actual and determinate—$R^{A, D}$;
p, the past event, is real, actual and determinate but unavailable—$R^{A, D, U}$;
f, the future event, is potentially real and indeterminate—$R^{P, I}$;

Now we can experience the paradox in its full force (Figure 6.3).

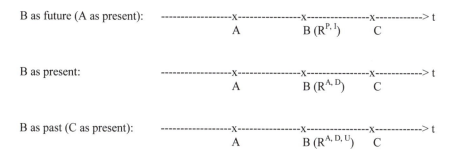

Figure 6.3 The paradox of flowing time:
         Which temporal ontology for event B is correct?

How can an event B have the ontological status of the "present" if it is also to have the ontological status of "past" when C is the present and the ontological status of "future" when A is the present? Which ontology should we assign to event B? And how can it change "in time"? I call this "the tangle of conflated ontological assignments." The conflation arises because we assert that the event B is somehow present (real, determinate), future (potential, indeterminate) and also past (irretrievable, determinate).

Resolving the Apparent Contradictions in the Paradox

> I cannot myself see that there is any contradiction to be avoided. When it is said
> that pastness, presentness, and futurity are incompatible predicates, this is true
> only in the sense that no one term could have two of them simultaneously or
> timelessly. ... (But) certain terms have them successively. (C.D. Broad)

In this quotation, C.D. Broad takes us a long way towards resolving McTaggart's
paradox. In Broad's view, McTaggart has run afoul in assigning incompatible
predicates—past, present and future—and their associated ontologies to the same
event *at the same time*. Flowing time theorists, however, do not assume that events
have incompatible predicates "simultaneously". Instead flowing time itself allows
these predicates to change as an event moves from the future into the present and
then to the past. In this sense the paradox is resolved.

I accept Broad's point, but I want to build on it. My concern is that Broad, like
McTaggart, assumes that tenses are Aristotelian-like predicates of temporal objects
(i.e. events). This in turn forces him to introduce a "meta-level" time, a point that
is clear in his use of the term "successively" in the preceding quotation. This could
easily beg the question of whether there is a "succession" of temporal events as
required by flowing time and whether this does not in turn lead to an endless
series of levels of temporality, the upper one in its successiveness explaining the
changing ontologies of the lower one. I do not believe that these ideas solve the
problem raised by McTaggart entirely.

In my view, the key to fully overcoming McTaggart's apparent contradictions,
building on Broad's crucial point, involves my proposal that past and future tenses
are not Aristotelian properties of events. Instead I will claim that they *are relations
between events* suggestive of Leibniz's philosophy. Moreover, these relations
carry an *ontological weight* in addition to the ontology of the events themselves.

A New Addition towards the Resolution of the Paradox: Tense as Relational

In order to explore the idea of tenses as relations let us return to Figure 6.3, take B
as present, and indicate how the past and the future are relations to B in Figure 6.4:

> pr—event B as present;
> p—ArB, event A as past to B is its relation to B as present;
> f—CrB, event C as future to B is its relation to B as present.

To say that A and C are past and future in relation to B as present is to name
their temporal relations to B and not refer to their intrinsic properties or varying
ontologies. Put another way, the terms "past" and "future" refer to the ontologies
of the abstract temporal relations between events A and C to event B as present.
Since these temporal relations of past and future lie outside of flowing time, we
should first redraw the timeline in Figure 6.4 as three successive times t_1, t_2 and t_3

```
------------------X----------------X----------------X--------------->t
                  A                B                C
              p: ArB             pr       f: CrB
```

pr: event B as present
p: ArB, event A as past to B is its relation to B as present
f: CrB, event C as future to B is its relation to B as present

Figure 6.4 Tensed relations to event B as present

in which first A, then B, and then C, are present (see Figure 6.5, and note that the "arrowhead" is removed from these timelines since the figure represents abstract temporal relations "outside" of time).

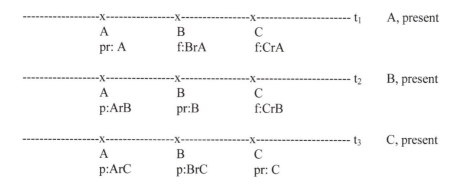

```
------------------X----------------X----------------X--------------------- t₁   A, present
                  A                B                C
                pr: A            f:BrA            f:CrA

------------------X----------------X----------------X--------------------- t₂   B, present
                  A                B                C
                p:ArB            pr:B             f:CrB

------------------X----------------X----------------X--------------------- t₃   C, present
                  A                B                C
                p:ArC            p:BrC            pr: C
```

Figure 6.5 The temporal relations for three events considered
           successively as present

Finally we can combine this with the inhomogeneous ontology mentioned above and add the axis of flowing time *t*, arriving at Figure 6.6 (below), in which this axis of flowing time crosses through the abstract structure of temporal relations and connects them as a set of "sequential" present events.

If we adopt this inhomogeneous and relational temporal ontology, I believe we have gone a long way in overcoming McTaggart's Paradox of assigning the properties of past, present and future to the same event. There is, of course, much else to say about the kind of conundrums which lie within the worldview of flowing time. However, we must turn now to the massive challenge rendered to flowing time by Einstein's special theory of relativity.

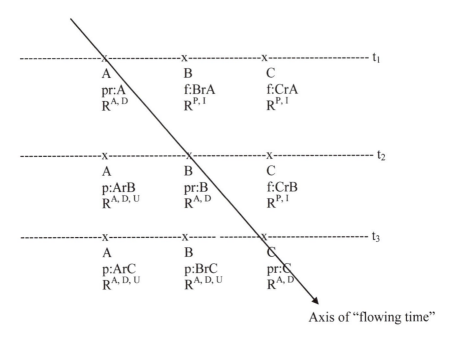

Figure 6.6 "Flowing time" as the axis connecting multiple present events
            in times t_1, t_2 and t_3

Note here that the ontologies indicated by $R^{P, I}$ and $R^{P, I}$ are relational ontologies between events while the ontology indicated by $R^{A, D}$ is the ontology of the present moment.

From Classical to Relativistic Physics: The Problem Thickens

> If the speed of light had been much smaller … we would never have fallen into
> the error of assuming that, at each moment of our experience, the whole universe
> divides into events that have not yet happened, and those that have.[5]

The Special Theory of Relativity constitutes a serious challenge to any tensed view that maintains that the future is not real.[6] Before proceeding with the problem SR poses to flowing time, I need to acknowledge a pedagogical challenge here: we need to probe into SR, but space will not permit a decent introduction to it. Luckily there will be some readers who already know SR. For those who do not,

---

[5]   Chris J. Isham and John C. Polkinghorne, "The Debate Over the Block Universe," in *Quantum Cosmology and the Laws of Nature: Scientific Perspectives on Divine Action*, edited by Robert J. Russell, Nancey C. Murphy and Chris J. Isham, Scientific Perspectives on Divine Action Series (Vatican City State/Berkeley, CA: Vatican Observatory Publications/ Center for Theology and the Natural Sciences, 1993), 137.

[6]   Michael Tooley, *Time, Tense & Causation* (Oxford: Clarendon Press, 1997), 373.

I recommend a brief tour through some very useful online materials[7]—or simply trust me to "get it right" in what I say about SR, especially about the famous "pole-in-the-barn" paradox.

The Problem of "The (Global) Present" in SR

In 1905 Albert Einstein published the Special Theory of Relativity.[8] Within three years Hermann Minkowski[9] had given the mathematics of SR a geometrical interpretation. Here three-dimensional space and one-dimensional time, which were entirely separate in ordinary experience and in classical physics, are combined into the radically new idea of a four-dimensional "spacetime" geometry. Minkowski's spacetime interpretation of SR has become more or less the standard one in physics today, and it leads, seemingly inevitably, to the "block universe" view of the world and thus the challenge to flowing time in the context of SR. To see this we turn to the role of the elsewhen in SR.

Recall that every event P in spacetime has an associated lightcone that divides spacetime into three regions around P: the causal future which P can influence, the causal past which can influence P, and the elsewhen, that volume of spacetime surrounding P which P can never influence and which can never influence P. The problem posed to flowing time lies with the multiplicity of physically equivalent global presents that lie within the elsewhen of P. If we insist that there be a unique global present in order to establish flowing time, how do we determine which one it is? Another way to state the problem is as follows: if events are only real when they are all simultaneous, which events in the elsewhen of P are simultaneous to P?

Consider Figure 6.7, a spacetime diagram for event P. Here observers A and B in relative motion coincide at event P. The axis of simultaneity, or global present, for A is x_A but for B it is x_B. This means that event T is present for A while event S is present for B. Yet that cannot be because event S can affect T since T is in the

---

[7]   Online introductory resources include: http://en.wikipedia.org/wiki/Introduction_ to_special_relativity; http://www.pbs.org/wgbh/nova/einstein/ and http://www.spacetime travel.org/ueberblick/ueberblick1.html.

[8]   A. Einstein, "Zur Elektrodynamik Bewegter Korper," *Annalen der Physic* 17 (1905): 891–921. There is a vast literature discussing the scientific and philosophical implications of SR. For a helpful guide, see Arthur I. Miller, *Albert Einstein's Special Theory of Relativity: Emergence (1905) and Early Interpretation (1905–1911)* (Reading, MA: Addison-Wesley, 1981). For an introductory text see Joseph and Michael McGuinness Schwartz, *Einstein for Beginners* (New York: Pantheon Books, 1979). For works more specifically treating philosophical issues see Lawrence Sklar, *Space, Time and Spacetime* (Berkeley, CA: University of California Press, 1974), and James T. Cushing, *Philosophical Concepts in Physics* (Cambridge: Cambridge University Press, 1998). For a very readable online overview of SR see: http://www.pbs.org/wgbh/nova/einstein/kaku.html.

[9]   See Miller, *Albert Einstein's Special Theory of Relativity*.

causal future of S. So is T present or future for P? And similarly for event S: is it present or past for P? For easy reference let us call this the "T, S" problem.

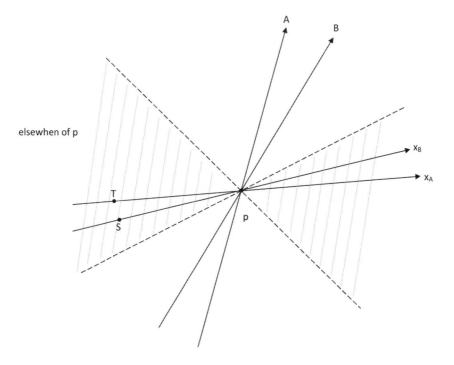

Figure 6.7 How can T and S both be real if T is in the causal future of S?

There are at Least Three Options for Responding to the Problem of the Global Present

The first, simplest and most intuitive is the Block Universe. Here all events in the elsewhen of P are equally present and real to P. Supporters include Chris Isham, Costa de Beauregaard, Edwin Taylor and J. A. Wheeler, and Albert Einstein after Minkowski published his spacetime interpretation of SR in 1908. The good news it that it solves the T, S problem, but at an enormous cost: it undermines our experience of time as real, it challenges free will and historical consciousness, and so on.

Taylor and Wheeler give compelling support of the block universe interpretation of spacetime.[10] Here I will paraphrase their argument for an analogy between spatial length in ordinary space with its three dimensions (x, y and z) and the

---

[10]   Edwin F. and John Archibald Wheeler Taylor, *Spacetime Physics* (San Francisco, CA: W.H. Freeman, 1963 (revised, 1992)). See Chapter 1, "The Geometry of Spacetime."

spacetime interval in SR's four dimensions (space x, y, z, plus time t). The analogy is as follows: the length of a ruler in space (which is invariant under the Euclidean metric) is analogous to the spacetime interval between two events in spacetime (which is invariant under the Lorentz metric).

$$r^2 = x^2 + y^2 + z^2$$ Length in Euclidean space

$$\tau^2 = t^2 - (x^2 + y^2 + z^2)/c^2$$ Length (interval) in Minkowskian spacetime

Now a length in space, r, presupposes that all events along it are present to each other. If a length in space is analogous to an interval, τ, in spacetime, then by analogy all events along it are present to each other. With this the argument by anaology is complete, and we arrive at the block universe.

The second option is to claim that only event P is present, that reality is reduced to the "I-Now." Milic Capek[11] can be read as a supporter of this view. It clearly solves the TS problem, but once again at an enormous cost. It undermines our everyday experience of a real, objective world and it challenges the validity of our inter-personal experiences, social world, etc.

The third option is flowing time. If we can affirm a unique, global present in light of SR, then the question of which events are present to P, T or S is solved. Supporters include Arthur Peacocke, Ian Barbour, Albert Einstein (at least in his original 1905 view of SR) and, notably for the occasion of this volume, John Polkinghorne. According to John, if scientific theories do not support flowing time, "so much the worse for scientific theories!"[12] The question, of course, is how do we know which is the real global present running through P? It is the task of this chapter to respond in a new way to this question.

Defending Flowing Time in Light of SR

Three Ways to Defend Flowing Time in Light of SR

First, the global present is an epistemic limit, but it is not ontologically significant. John makes this argument frequently. According to him, the relativity of simultaneity is merely a "retrospective construction" that we make after all the data is in. It represents an epistemological limit to what we can know about reality, but it does not have ontological significance. It is not clear to me, however, that

---

[11]   Milic Capek, "Time in Relativity Theory: Arguments for a Philosophy of Being," in J. T. Fraser, *The Voices of Time*, 434–54. For a detailed exposition see Milic Capek, *The Philosophical Impact of Contemporary Physics* (Princeton, NJ: Van Nostrand, 1961).

[12]   Isham and Polkinghorne, "The Block Universe," 139.

this position is entirely consistent with his overall support of critical realism, in which, to cite his famous saying, "epistemology models ontology."[13]

The second way is neo-Lorentzian: it turns out that we can, in fact, obtain a unique, global present within the context of SR. The way to do it mathematically is to abandon Einstein's assumption that the speed of light is the same in all directions. While this seems implausible, it is after all a fact that we can only measure the average round-trip speed of light. We do not know if the speed differs when light moves left to right versus right to left. The "neo-Lorentzian" view leads to the claim that dilation and Lorentz contraction are real effects in nature, and thus that they must be explained by real, if unknown, causes. Supporters include Michael Tooley[14] and William Lane Craig.[15]

The third means of defending time is inhomogeneous relational ontology. Earlier in this chapter I argued for a relational view of tenses like past and future, combined with an inhomogeneous ontology, to defend flowing time in the pre-relativistic literature. Now I claim that an inhomogeneous, relational ontology, when applied to spacetime, leads to a new flowing time view consistent with relativity. We shall next explore this via a famous spacetime paradox, the "pole-in-the-barn" paradox

Pole-in-the-barn Paradox: Will it Help us Defend Flowing Time?

Presentation of the paradox   Imagine a runner carrying a 10 meter pole and rapidly approaching a barn. Doors A and B are located on the left and right side of the barn, respectively, and they shut and close according to pre-programed instructions. From the barn's point of view the pole is Lorentz-contracted to 5 meters and, since the barn is 5 meters wide, the pole just fits inside the barn the instant both of its doors shut and open rapidly. From the pole's point of view, however, the barn is Lorentz contracted to 2.5 meters. How, then, can the pole fit inside the barn without its doors breaking the pole into pieces?

Combining the barn and the pole diagrams into a single, generalized spacetime diagram   Both perspectives are "true". In order to resolve the paradox we first construct two separate spacetime diagrams, one representing the barn's point of view and the other representing the pole's point of view. The crucial move,

---

[13]   Ibid., 139.

[14]   Michael Tooley, *Time, Tense & Causation* (Oxford: Clarendon Press, 1997).

[15]   William Lane Craig, *Time and Eternity: Exploring God's Relationship to Time* (Wheaton, IL: Crossway Books, 2001). Chapter 5 provides a helpful overview. For details see Craig's more technical works: William Lane Craig, *The Tensed Theory of Time: A Critical Examination* (Dordrecht: Kluwer Academic, 2000); *The Tenseless Theory of Time: A Critical Examination* (Dordrecht: Kluwer Academic, 2000); *Time and the Metaphysics of Relativity* (Dordrecht: Kluwer Academic, 2001); *God, Time, and Eternity* (Dordrecht: Kluwer Academic Publishers, 2001).

then, is to combine them what I call a "generalized spacetime diagram." Such a diagram incorporates the separate worldviews of the barn and the pole into a single worldview (Figure 6.8 below).

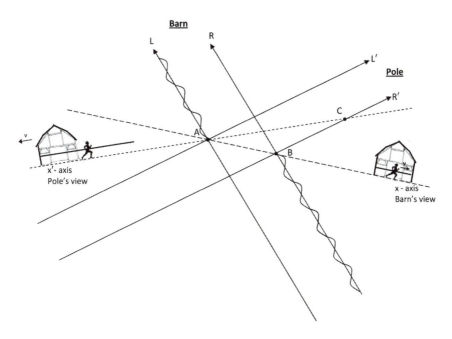

Figure 6.8 A generalized spacetime diagram that incorporates the previously distinct sequences of worldviews from the perspectives of the barn and the pole

Here we see events A and B lying along the barn's axis of simultaneity, and events A and C lying along the pole's axis of simultaneity. At event A the left door of the barn closes while at event B the right door opens. The pole is thus trapped for an instant entirely within the barn and this is to be expected from the barn's perspective since the pole, moving at rapid speeds towards the barn, is Lorentz-contracted. From the pole's perspective the pole is much too big to fit into the barn, but fortunately the barn doors are not synchronized. Instead when the left door closes (event A) the right door has long been opened and the pole sticks way out to the right with its right tip lying at event C. The paradox is resolved: Lorentz contraction from the barn's perspective and lack of synchronization from the pole's perspective are different physical phenomena, but they can be combined into a single overall representation of the essential physics: the pole is undamaged in being carried quickly through the barn whose doors do indeed shut and close.

Resolution of the "spacetime" version of McTaggart's paradox   The resolution of the "pole-in-the-barn" paradox also sheds light on how to resolve McTaggart's paradox in the context of spacetime. One might have thought that the problem would be intensified from what it posed in the context of classical physics and ordinary experience. Surprisingly, however, the same response I offered to it previously can be adopted here.

To see this consider triangle A–B–C triangle in Figure 6.8. We can state McTaggart's paradox in the spacetime context as follows: C is simultaneous to A according to the pole, and thus C and A are present in the pole's world. However, B is simultaneous to A according to the barn, and thus B and A are present in the barn's world. Finally C is in B's future according to the barn and the pole. Have we then not attributed conflicting properties to C: C is both present and future?

My response once again is to treat tenses such as future not as properties of an event but as relations between events, relations that carry ontological weight. In this approach, C as future to B as present is the relation f: CrB. B as past to C as present is the relation p: BrC. Since these relations are distinct, and since they carry different ontologies, there is no contradiction in asserting them both. Symbolically:

f: CrB $\neq$ p: BrC

In short, McTaggart's paradox is resolved even in the spacetime interpretation of SR.

The Inhomogeneous Relational Spacetime Ontology as a Response to Taylor and Wheeler

My response to Taylor and Wheeler is to point out that, while the Lorentz metric provides an invariant measure of the spacetime interval between B and C, this does not in itself determine the ontological status of events B and C, namely that they are identical as in the block universe. In particular, the invariant value of τ does not require that τ refers to an objective feature of spacetime with a uniform ontology the way the invariant measure of distance in space refers to an objective feature of space. Instead I offered a *relational spacetime* ontology for intervals in spacetime such as τ.

I can put this in a slightly different way. If intervals in spacetime are like objects in ordinary space, then we would expect there to be an analogy between the length of objects in space and the measure of intervals in spacetime, i.e., an analogy between the Euclidean metric and the Lorentz metric. However, the converse need not hold: an analogy between the Euclidean and Lorentz metrics does not necessitate that both are measures of extended objects, one in space and the other in spacetime.

Does Flowing Time Require a Unique Global Present?

Flowing time theorists typically assume the need for a single, physically meaningful definition of simultaneity—a global present—in order to demarcate the universal future from the universal past, and thus SR is a challenge to them. Atemporalists view the lack of a unique global simultaneity, because of SR, as a key argument against flowing time. However, is this the best way to understand the impact of SR on the meaning of simultaneity and thus the plausibility of flowing time?

Clearly SR shows us that simultaneity is observer-dependent. However, I believe the problem is not that, given SR, we cannot chose a single, observer-independent axis of simultaneity that corresponds to the classical present. *The problem is actually about why we believe we need to do so.* Suppose the implications of SR are correct: The region of the elsewhen surrounding a given event P is actually composed of an uncountably infinite number of equally valid axes of simultaneity. It is nevertheless true that for each observer moving along its worldline there is only one axis of simultaneity. Does construing "the world" using any of these axes lead to physical problems? My point is that it does not.

For example, no two events along any axis (say events A and B or A and C in Figure 6.7) are causally related: neither can physically affect the other. Alternatively, events that are causally related according to one observer (say events B and C) are causally related according to all observers regardless of their relative motion. We know this because causality is Lorentz-invariant. Therefore the causal portrayal of a series of events is observer-independent, even if the way this portrayal is described (e.g. barn doors synchronized or not) can differ radically. In addition, there are dozens of purported construals of "what happened" that are disallowed by SR: the pole missed the barn, the barn's doors sliced the pole into pieces, the pole poked through the barn doors, one of the barn's doors failed to close or to open, etc. In short, what I call the "essential physics"—that the pole was run through the barn without being scathed—is true for the perspective of both the pole and the barn. The loss of a universal "narrative" does not lead to a loss of objectivity—what happened regarding the pole and the barn together—and in this sense even the most ardent supporter of "critical realism" need not shy from the relativity and multiplicity of the global present in SR.

Why we Care Theologically: God and Time in Light of Physics

In this final section I turn to the broader concerns of this volume, God and physics, and thus the reasons why John and I care about physics and flowing time theologically. I follow that with a focus on the way John's dipolar theism and my Trinitarian theism provide resources for understanding this relation. In doing so I will use this section to lay out briefly what I believe are mainly areas of agreement between John and me, with a few points of relatively minor disagreement. I do so in hopes of pointing to fruitful directions for our future interactions and as an informative discussion of our views for other scholars in theology and science.

God and Time: Do John and I Agree or Differ on Key Theological Questions?

The first question is flowing time: is it essential for Christian theology? John and I both respond affirmatively: the historical character of the Christian witness and the Biblical understanding that God acts in nature and history commit us both to flowing time and lead us both to reject the block universe.

This shared commitment, in turn, leads us to affirm that the God who acts in time nevertheless remains eternal. It leads us to affirm that God can respond in time to prayers even while remaining eternal. Even more importantly, because Christianity is essentially and irreducibly an eschatological faith, John and I both affirm that God can act in time in a radically new way, starting at the Easter events, to transform the present universe into the New Creation.

Finally we come to a difference on a key issue: Does God know the future? John replies with an emphatic "no" whereas I will say "yes" if I define God's knowledge of the future not as predictive from the present (i.e. not as foreknowledge). Instead God knows the future directly in its state as present. This is related to my claim that the future is potentially real and not simply not real.

What are our Theological Sources?

While being quite close theologically, I take one difference of emphasis to be that John supports a form of dipolar theism within a Trinitarian framework, a form of theism whose distinctive claims include the following:

- Eternity and time are bound together in the divine nature.
- God is fully temporal since the world is one of "true becoming."
- God cannot know the future because the future is not real, i.e. it is not there to be known.
- The divine kenosis includes a self-emptying of God's omniscience consistent with the future not being real and therefore not knowable even by God.
- God is also "ready for the future," being able to bring about the eschatological fulfillment of the world via the New Creation beginning at the original Easter.

I work entirely within Trinitarian theism with these distinctive claims:

- The way God's eternity is more than timelessness or unending ordinary time is as "supratemporal" (Karl Barth's term), the source of creaturely time and its fulfillment in the New Creation.

- God's Trinitarian eternity is the basis for the eschatological unity of our experience of time even as now in this life we experience it as separated and broken into an irretrievable past and an unavailable future associated with every present moment. (I take this from Wolfhart Pannenberg.)
- God acts from the future to create and redeem events in time. This means that God acts retroactively from the immediate future on each present moment as Creator and God acts proleptically from the eschatological future on each moment as Redeemer (following both Pannenberg and Ted Peters).

Conclusion and Further Work

I hope to have offered the outline, at least, of a new approach to defending flowing time in light of the challenges raised by Einstein's Special Relativity. I do so because, like John, I am committed to a flowing-time view of nature and history, one that I believe is essential to the biblical witness, to ordinary daily experience and historical experience, to acts of moral conscience and the nurturing of virtue, and to the experiences of the presence of God in liturgy and personal prayer. I also do so because the conversations between theology and the natural sciences require that we reformulate a theology of both dipolar theism and of Trinitarian theism in light of the natural sciences. If we are to reformulate the doctrine of God, particularly God's attributes of eternity and omnipresence, in light of science, the challenge of SR must be met. In the process it is my hope that a reformulated theology in light of science can eventually offer novel suggestions for research directions both in the philosophy of science and in research science.[16]

Thus the stakes are high for us to take SR seriously as we theologize about God. No one has done so more eloquently than John Polkinghorne, to whom this volume is most deservedly dedicated. I hope that these brief comments will stimulate many years of continued discussions both personally between John and me and in the wider theology and science community.

---

[16]   Again please see *Time in Eternity*, where I take up this challenge in Chapters 5 and 6.

Chapter 7

Cosmic If-statements

Daniel W. Darg

Foreword

This paper discusses and proposes controversial ideas that will fall outside the comfort zone of some readers. Nevertheless, the arguments are logically sound and derive from much interaction with the works of John Polkinghorne and are consistent (as I shall argue) with his scientific and theological position. With that said, and since this paper is written in recognition of Polkinghorne's contributions to the field, it will be expedient to begin by appealing to his sense of open-mindedness:

> Metaphysical endeavour in general, and talk of agency in particular, will inevitably require a certain boldness of conjecture as part of the heuristic exploration of possibility. In our present state of ignorance, no one has access to a final and definitive proposal. The test of the enterprise will be the degree to which it can attain comprehensiveness of explanation and overall coherence, including an adequate degree of consonance with human experience.[1]

It is important to lay out the central conceptual scheme right from the start as it aims to establish clarity in the complex topic of God's relation to the world. From there, I can begin to interact with the works of Polkinghorne more directly, making points of contact between his ideas and the scheme at hand, before developing the final practical challenge that Polkinghorne and others can present to progressive creationists such as proponents of Intelligent Design.

---

[1] J.C. Polkinghorne, 'The Metaphysics of Divine Action', in *Chaos and Complexity: Scientific Perspectives on Divine Action*, edited by R.J. Russell, N. Murphy and A.R. Peacocke (Berkeley, CA: Vatican Observatory Publications and Berkeley University Press, 2000), 147.

The Cosmic Computer

Representing Universes

The observation that the physical world resembles a computer program goes back to the very early pioneers of information science.[2] The connection goes as follows. The Universe, viewed from the perspective of Newtonian physics, consists of objectively existing particles in motion having well-defined (even if unknown) positions and momenta with respect to some fixed coordinate. One of the most remarkable features of this (Newtonian) Universe[3] is that, somehow, it keeps track of a seemingly vast array of numbers[4] that get updated according to specific rules. As Laplace famously pointed out, in such a world the future state of the Universe is in principle discernible given perfect knowledge of the present state (that is, the values of each number in the cosmic array), the physical laws that relate the state of the Universe from one moment to the next, and unrestricted computational power.

Quantum Mechanics and General Relativity complicate the details, but the overall idea remains the same: the physical Universe can be effectively represented as an array of numbers[5] that get updated at each temporal slice by a set of rules that the physicist seeks to express through mathematical operators.[6, 7]

----

[2]   Such as von Neumann. For a masterful account of the history and development of this subject, I thoroughly recommend chapters 4–6 of Paul Davies's *The Mind of God*, first published 1992, Simon and Shuster Ltd.,UK.

[3]   I shall use universe with a capital 'U' in contexts where there is an intended sense of isolatability or uniqueness, otherwise with a small 'u' for those belonging to an ensemble of either putative universes or those belonging to a Multiverse. This distinction is *not* fundamental to the essay.

[4]   To be precise, six numbers for every particle and thus an infinity of numbers if the Universe has an infinite number of particles. This is commonly referred to as the 'phase space' of the physical system.

[5]   In these cases, namely, the amplitudes of wave-functions in Quantum Mechanics and the metric of the space–time manifold in General Relativity. The scheme works best if space–time is ultimately quantised but can still prove illustrative even if it is not.

[6]   If Quantum Mechanics is intrinsically probabilistic, then the rules would have to include a 'random number generator', and would mean that the future state is in principle unknowable given the present state, but this does not invalidate the conceptual scheme.

[7]   Some might argue that relativity invalidates the notion that you can carve up the world into temporal slices owing to the relativity of simultaneity. I do not believe that this is a major conceptual issue since, even in the Block Universe, there is a notion of causality that can used to relate hypersurfaces. See C.J. Isham and J.C. Polkinghorne, 'The Debate Over the Block Universe', in *Quantum Cosmology and the Laws of Nature*, edited by R.J. Russell, N. Murphy and C.J. Isham (Berkeley, CA: Vatican Observatory Publications & Berkeley, 1996), 139, for discussion.

This provides a useful scheme for conceptualising the physical form of possible worlds.[8] Any hypothetical universe that is logically possible can be physically represented by a particular array of numbers that gets updated by a particular set of rules. In the case of our Universe, these would correspond to boundary conditions and physical laws in ordinary scientific parlance.

An important notion in what follows is to speak of the complexity of any such representation. It seems conceptually feasible to formulate some measure[9] or, at the very least, some qualitative notion of the complexity of these representations of universes. It is not essential to determine whether there is a natural or unique way to construe such a measure for the purposes of this discussion. It is sufficient to point out that any such measure would need to do justice to intuitive notions such as 'information compressibility' (to what extent an array of numbers can be reduced to a non-redundant representation of its information content) and rules that make use of primitive mathematical operators, and so on. This is connected to the notion of 'algorithmic compressibility'. As Barrow explains,

> [Science is] predicated upon the belief that the Universe is algorithmically compressible and the modern search for a Theory of Everything is the ultimate expression of that belief, a belief that there is an abbreviated representation of the logic behind the Universe's properties that can be written down in finite form by human beings.[10]

Unfortunately, attempts to formalise physics in this way are fraught with practical and conceptual difficulties and so the notion of measuring the 'complexity' of the Universe remains a merely qualitative, although deeply illustrative, concept.

Assuming we had such a measure, one could categorise any possible world in relation to ours by its comparative complexity. For example, a world that is like ours in every way except that random macroscopic objects appear *ex nihilo* at different places and times is perfectly representable in this scheme, the only difference is that such a world is relatively *complex* compared with ours. Such a world would demand more 'disk space' in the cosmic hard drive and/or physical laws with sharp discontinuities and extra terms that are carefully weighted so as to be negligible except in particular locations in space and time. The reverse engineering (figuring out the rules) and expressing them mathematically would

---

[8]   Whether or not this scheme is adequate to describe all aspects of the non-physical world, such as the presence of consciousness amidst the particles that make up the human brain, will largely depend on the truth or falsity of mind–brain reductionism. Hence I qualify this scheme, stated thus far, as a representation only for the *physical* state of a universe.

[9]   That is, some way of mapping the array of numbers and algorithms ('physical laws') that update that array in any given representation of a universe onto the real number line whose value can be compared with others using the 'greater-than', 'less-than' or 'equal-to' operators.

[10]   J.D. Barrow, *Theories of Everything* (Oxford: Oxford University Press, 1991), 11.

be indescribably more difficult and probably impossible in practice. Nonetheless, there is nothing conceptually incoherent about such worlds.

The Computational Analogy

This representation of the physical Universe is strikingly analogous to the running of a program on a computer. A computer program in operation is, viewed from one perspective, an array of numbers corresponding to pixels on a screen that gets updated according to a set of rules specified in the computer code. Unlike the Universe though, whose numbers get updated by a set of very consistent physical laws that we cannot alter, computer code is, in general, only constrained by the loose requirement of self-consistency. The universal–computer analogy therefore leads to a powerful means of exploring the space of conceptual possibilities. As Stephen Wolfram explains,

> Executing a computer program is much like performing an experiment. Unlike the physical objects in a conventional experiment, however, the objects in a computer experiment are not bound by the laws of nature. Instead they follow the laws embodied in the computer program, which can be of any consistent form. Computation thus extends the realm of experimental science: it allows experiments to be performed in a hypothetical universe ... [as such]. Scientific laws are now being viewed as algorithms ... processing information much the way computers do. New aspects of natural phenomena have been made accessible to investigation. A new paradigm has been born.[11]

I wish to argue that this conceptual approach to the functioning of the world has much promise for understanding not just science, but also theology. In particular, it can shed light on the nature of miracles and God's interaction with the world. Before delving into details, I wish to make two comments regarding this conceptual scheme.

Firstly, it is metaphysically neutral.[12] A representation by itself says nothing about the origin of any given universe or why that universe complies with that

---

[11]   S. Wolfram, 'Computer Software in Science and Mathematics', *Scientific American*, 1984, accessed 29 March 2010, http://www.stephenwolfram.com/publications/articles/general/84-computer/2/text.html.

[12]   Or, at least, about as metaphysically neutral as you can get. Modern science owes much of its success to its eschewal of metaphysical presuppositions (such as Aristotle's notion that Nature strives towards 'the Good') in ascertaining the evolution of physical systems. Instead, the (classical) scientific method proceeds by representing physical systems at different moments in time by numbers (quantifying the position/density of a particle/substance) as (would be) measured by experimentation and then linking these sets of numbers with the simplest mathematical relationships (represented by the single-width arrows in the diagram). The scheme is therefore not entirely metaphysically neutral since

particular representation rather than some other. The representation merely *describes* – it does not *explain*. Secondly, and of particular relevance to theism, a universe in which apparent miracles occur (say, those akin to macroscopic appearances *ex nihilo*) are those having relatively complicated representations in terms of information content and evolutionary laws. That is, in some sense, a miraculous world is equivalent to (or perhaps indistinguishable from) a complicated world; miracles in this perspective are the *complication* rather than the *contravention* of physical law.

How then does the computational–universe analogy link in with God's interaction with the world? From the perspective of the software engineer, the array of numbers corresponding to the pixels on a computer screen gets updated according to a set of abstract rules that are decided, ultimately, by the will of the programmer. The patterns on the screen thus express the character, propensities and desires of the programmer as well as any external constraints that he/she might be subject to. In this analogy then, the screen is to the programmer what the Universe is to God – a canvas on which one's creative will can be expressed. By choosing the right initial array of numbers (the 'state' vector) and appropriate laws with which to evolve the vector, God can actualise any self-consistent universe.[13] The form and contents of the Universe thereby reflect the character, nature and desires of the Creator[14] as well as any constraints he might be subject to.

---

it constantly imposes a preference for mathematical simplicity upon Nature that, time and time again, has eventually proved inadequate to save all the phenomena. Moreover, since this method can work *only* by assuming the tractability of Nature, the scientific method has developed so as to turn this need around and treat it as axiomatic (e.g. by insisting on the 'smoothness' (differentiability) of space–time and amplitudes in (quantum) field theory). This essentially pragmatic approach to the functioning of Nature means that discontinuities (e.g. the Big Bang singularity, collapse of the wave function, etc.), when encountered, are taken to be non-physical artefacts of mathematical representations that approximate a deeper, more unified theory. As such, mathematical simplicity and tractability have tacitly become the metaphysical presuppositions that govern the practice of (hard) science.

$$\begin{bmatrix} 1 \\ 2 \\ 3 \\ \dots \\ 8 \end{bmatrix} \rightarrow \begin{bmatrix} 2 \\ 3 \\ 4 \\ \dots \\ 9 \end{bmatrix} \Rightarrow \text{abstract the patterns} \Rightarrow \psi \rightarrow \psi'$$

[13] Of course, God is not just a software engineer, but a hardware engineer as well; once he has decided what abstract rules are to govern the evolution of the Universe, he can then actualise whatever metaphysical substances would be needed to reflect (or behave according to) those abstract relationships.

[14] For example, God might find a Universe that evolves its state vector using a random number generator (*viz.* quantum mechanics) more interesting than a strictly deterministic world.

What might these constraints be? When humans program, they are constrained by the speed of their computer, the limits of their memory and the fact that, in order to attain a certain degree of complexity with respect to the image on the screen, there will always be a minimal amount of corresponding complexity in the code (a rough measure of this complexity would be the number of lines of code required to achieve the desired pattern on the screen). A human will thus attempt a trade-off between these various constraints in order to minimise memory usage and produce code that is elegant and easy to decipher whilst achieving the intended screen pattern. There is most definitely an art to programming[15] and one of the key aesthetic practices is to use, generally speaking, as few lines of code as possible, eliminating redundancies whenever they crop up.

It is of particular importance to this discussion to point out that the programmer cannot compress the code to an arbitrary degree *and* retain full functionality in the desired screen pattern. For any non-trivial program expressed in some language, there is always a minimal complexity required in the code, as well as a minimal amount of memory space used at any one time beyond which no compressibility is possible without compromising full functionality.[16]

The programmer of the Universe is constrained for different, although analogous, reasons. A God who desires free-willed and intentionalistic creatures to function rationally within the Universe is constrained to make the operation of its natural processes consistent enough to allow for sound inductive reasoning. This places an *upper limit* on the complexity of the physical laws that govern the Universe. If there are too many discontinuities and apparently uncorrelated events, the deciphering of any pattern becomes too difficult and all sense of moral responsibility gets obscured in the unpredictable chaos that ensues.

At the same time, there is a minimal degree of complexity required by the Creator to make the world sufficiently interesting. A Newtonian universe consisting of two particles would be simple enough for physically grounded creatures to figure out, but not complex enough to furnish their existence. There is thus an anthropic *lower limit* on the complexity of the Universe corresponding to some minimal size of array of numbers representing the physical state of the cosmos

---

[15]   It is difficult to convey this aesthetic sense to those without much background in programming; it is akin to the elegance that mathematicians speak of, as Polkinghorne himself says, 'This is a concept not all will find accessible, but among those of who speak the language of mathematics, mathematical beauty is a recognizable quality', J.C. Polkinghorne, *Beyond Science* (Cambridge: Cambridge University Press, 1998), 79.

[16]   Imagine challenging a programmer to write an adventure game using only 10 lines of code – the fact that this is impossible in no way reflects a deficiency in the programmer; it is simply too great a constraint. Similarly, the fact that God cannot beat Gary Kasparov at chess just starting with a king and a pawn hardly calls into question his omniscience, it would simply be a constraint such that no possible combinations of moves would be available to God that could beat Kasparov.

and/or a minimal degree of complexity in the laws that evolve one temporal slice of the world to the next.[17]

Thus we find that the (weak) anthropic principle[18] – the fact that Universe must be such as to allow us (who observe it) to exist – calls into question the long-held assumption of science that continued thought and research will simplify our physical theories to an arbitrarily great extent whilst saving the phenomena. If we have not already essentially reached this 'complexity limit' with our current state of knowledge, we will do so eventually. Consideration of this minimal complexity and the computer analogy that gave rise to it therefore motivates us to consider how it is that complexity is most efficiently encoded in computer science.

If-statements

An invaluable concept found in virtually all programming languages is an 'if-statement'. These control the execution of a program by asking whether a particular condition has been met and act thereby as 'switches' between different regimes of behaviour. It is difficult to overestimate how important if-statements are in computer science. They simplify programming to such an extent that it would be safe to say that computer software would be inefficient to the point of uselessness without them. This is because they allow a degree of non-linearity in the complexity of the code that would otherwise require copious amounts of memory and/or computational power.

One can readily see that this is the case by considering a simple step-function $f(x)$ involving an if-statement, such as

$$f(x) = \begin{cases} 1, & \text{if } |x| < 1 \\ 0, & \text{otherwise.} \end{cases} \qquad (1)$$

---

[17]   Elsewhere Barrow makes a point along similar lines, 'Just as the most expert computer programmer is the one who can write the shortest program to effect a particular task, so we might expect the Architect of the ultimate program that we call the laws of nature to be elegantly economical on logic and raw materials. It is a common tendency to think that it would be a hallmark of the universe's profundity if it were unfathomably complicated, but this is a strange prejudice. This view is motivated by the idea that the Creator needs to be superhuman – and what better way to assert that superiority than by incomprehensibility? But why should that be so? Anyone can explain how to assemble a model aircraft in 500 pages of instructions; it is not so easy to do it in 10 lines. Profound simplicity is far more impressive than profound complexity.' J.D. Barrow, *Impossibility: the limits of science and the science of limits*, (London: Vintage Press, 2005), 76–7.

[18]   See J.D. Barrow and F.J. Tipler, *The Anthropic Cosmological Principle* (New York: Oxford University Press, 1996), 16, for definition and discussion.

An equivalent mathematical representation of the same function can be found by taking the Fourier transform. In this case, the same function takes the form

$$f(x) = \sum_{n=1}^{\infty} a_n \sin(nx + \phi) \qquad (2)$$

This does away with the (sharp/discontinuous) if-statement but requires an *infinite* number of (smooth/continuous) terms to precisely reproduce the same graph. Thus, it is far simpler and more efficient, computationally speaking, to use an if-statement here. This is a general result. The functionality achieved by using an if-statement can *always* be achieved in principle without it by complicating one's code and so, in some sense, the effects of if-statements are connected to (or perhaps indistinguishable from) complexity. In the case of human programming, given the constraints of computing power available to us, it would be impossible, practically speaking, to achieve much non-linear complexity without them (we cannot carry out an infinite number of calculations).

Given the close analogy then between the physical laws of the Universe and the functioning of a computer program noted previously, the question naturally presents itself as to whether or not the physical laws of the Universe possess if-statements (or laws so complex so as to be indistinguishable from if-statements). If so, where and to what extent do they occur? Perhaps it is the case that the minimal complexity of the Universe necessitated by the Anthropic Principle is such that if-statements (or effects that are indistinguishable from if-statements) are required to write down its representation in its most compact form. Their effects could even give rise to phenomena that appear to be genuinely emergent from the view point of contemporary science that tries to reduce everything to 'fundamental laws' like the Schrödinger equation.[19] Such if-statements could thus form a sort of 'biotonic law' – a term coined by the biologist Walter Elsasser, who believed that regularities persist in biological phenomena that cannot be derived from the (fundamental) laws of physics.[20] *A priori*, there is no way to know if the most compact representation of the Universe would need to involve if-statements. From the theistic perspective, it may be that God *had* to use them, not because of any deficit in his capabilities, but because it is the simplest way to encode the necessary

---

[19]   Note that, in this essay, I shall treat Schrödinger's equation as an archetype for a fundamental law of physics from which scientists typically try to explain higher-level physical phenomena such as biochemistry. One could of course point to even more fundamental equations such as Dirac's, but my purpose here is merely illustrative.

[20]   By 'genuinely emergent' effects I mean effects/properties that would not be predictable or determinable from their underlying constituents *in principle.* By contrast I do *not* mean statements of epistemological limitation or convenience. It is debatable whether Elsasser understood biotonic laws in this 'genuinely emergent' way. I will assume he did in this essay in making reference to such laws.

complexity for life to arise in the Universe. Just as God cannot make carbon-based life in a Newtonian world with only two particles left to run their own course, so perhaps it is not possible for a world like ours to incur self-organised complexity to the extent observed without emergent behaviour that 'switches on' in certain regimes of physics. One can then go one step further and ask whether there is the philosophical–theological possibility that *mental*, *spiritual* or *moral* states of affairs control these 'phase changes', to borrow Polkinghorne's analogy, in the laws of nature.

To summarise so far, I have laid out a scheme for representing universes and pointed out that a universe where miracles appear to happen can be construed as a universe that follows consistent laws provided that it is recognised that these laws are *complicated* (probably to the point of being intractable). I also pointed out that there is a connection between complexity and the implementation of if-statements in programming. This leads to the question as to whether the minimal complexity required by the Anthropic Principle could require the implementation of if-statements in the most concise representation of the laws of nature. It also raises the prospect of understanding miracles as phenomena where apparent departures from the laws of physics are not actual departures, but the fulfilment of conditions operated on by cosmic if-statements.

In the remainder of the essay, I shall explore these connections between complexity, divine interaction and the Anthropic Principle in their conceptual relationship to if-statements in representations of the world in analogy to a computer program, examining both the theological motivation and scientific motivation to suppose that such 'phase changes' might actually be embedded in the structure of the world.

Theological Motivation for Cosmic If-statements

Matter's Bias and the Reductionist Stance

The antithesis of the scheme presented in this essay is reductionism – particularly with respect to biological complexity – and so a short exposition on this subject will prove useful. In *Science and Providence*, Polkinghorne reflects on the following excerpt by Montefiore:

> Although there is no external force imposed on species, and in particular on their genetic systems, mutations occur which would not be expected by random mutation. This is not because of external pressure, but because of the bias implanted in matter. Such bias is not, of course, to be detected by scientific measurement (and so the hypothesis is not testable) since there is no possibility

of setting alongside it matter which is not implanted by the bias towards complexity and integration.[21]

What is the essence of this 'bias' to which Montefiore refers? According to him, there is an intuitive sense in which the propensities of physical systems to generate biological complexity go against our *a priori* expectations, but how well founded are these expectations? Is this essentially a statement of our ignorance of the physical structure of the world? In scientific inference, outcomes of measurements of systems that we know little (or nothing) about are usually treated with a flat probability distribution, that is, they are assumed to be equally likely. For example, the probability of getting a particular roll of a die is usually treated as 1/6 until there is reason to believe that the die is sufficiently irregular so as to break the physical symmetry and result in some preferred configuration. In virtue of this extra information (that the die is loaded), we are then no longer surprised by the bias it exhibits.[22] As Polkinghorne comments,

> Another way of describing the "bias" would be ... simply to call it "scientific law" ... There is no absolute expectation of randomness; the odds of chance events are to be calculated in relation to some lawful expectation. If I know the die is loaded I shall do my calculations differently from the way I would if I thought the die were true.[23]

The 'unexpected' is thus connected, sometimes at least, with one's ignorance of all the facts. We do not know how matter operates in all its intricacies, so our imaginations conjure up some notion of impotent and unreactive matter with a flat-prior 'not implanted by the bias'. However, as Polkinghorne points out, matter without the bias would not be matter – matter is not structureless but does what it does because of the fundamental laws of physics. Does that then mean that no matter what we observe in the functioning of nature, however *prima facie* unexpected it might seem, we must (in some sense that lies at the centre of the debate) suppress any sense of surprise?

From the viewpoint of the ardent reductionist the answer is yes – there is never any *intrinsic* mystery to be found in higher-level processes such as biological functioning. Any sense of 'surprise', no matter how great, is taken by the reductionist to indicate not that biology is irreducible to fundamental physics but that we are simply ignorant of the all the underlying facts. Surprise tells the reductionist where research is still needed and fulfilled expectations where no more research is required. Since phenomena can always be consistently shelved

---

[21]   Quoted by J.C. Polkinghorne, *Science and Providence* (London: SPCK, 1989), 38.

[22]   This is 'a "throwing away of the prior", as Bayesians say', B.C. van Fraassen, *The Empirical Stance* (New Haven, CT: Yale University Press, 2002), 92.

[23]   Polkinghorne, *Science and Providence*, 38.

into one of these two categories (reduced and not-yet-reduced), it is clear that reductionism can never be disproven.

Reductionism is not only unfalsifiable, it is also transparently circular. It only 'explains' phenomena, ultimately, by positing entities equipped with just those properties that will reproduce the observed phenomena. The enterprise would therefore be rather suspect were it not for its tremendous success at *unifying*[24] so many seemingly disparate phenomena into so concise a conceptual scheme as given by modern science. As Polkinghorne remarks, 'the understanding gained thereby proves that this circularity is benign and not vicious'.[25] At the same time, Polkinghorne is careful to note the pragmatic nature of reductionism and that it therefore need not infringe on a broader view of the world:

> It is clearly worthwhile to pursue the program of reductionist explanation as far as it can legitimately be pursued, but that is a methodological strategy for investigation, not a metaphysical strategy determining the total nature of reality.[26]

In short, reductionism *gets results* and so we tend to overlook its question-begging shortfalls in virtue of other qualities such as 'elegance, economy and naturalness'.[27]

By the very nature of the program then, it is no surprise that with the progression of reductionist science there follows a general shift of mystery away from higher-level phenomena (of biology say) towards the lower-level phenomena of elementary particle physics.[28] The long hope of many scientists is that all the mystery and surprise in Nature would eventually disappear in some 'Theory of Everything' as envisioned by Steven Weinberg.

---

[24] The view of (scientific) explanation being highlighted here is that which emphasises the central (although difficult to expound) concept of unification. A summary statement might be '[s]cience advances our understanding of nature by showing us how to derive descriptions of many phenomena, using the same pattern of derivation again and again.' P. Kitcher, *Scientific Explanation*, edited by P. Kitcher and W. Salmon (Minnesota, MN: University of Minnesota Press, 1989), 423.

[25] J.C. Polkinghorne, *Belief in God in an Age of Science* (New Haven, CT: Yale University Press, 1998), 107.

[26] Polkinghorne, 'The Metaphysics of Divine Action', 150.

[27] Polkinghorne speaking on the problem of underdetermination; Polkinghorne, *Belief in God in an Age of Science*, 16.

[28] That is, the parts of Nature that are readily reducible get reduced and the rest gets stacked on the 'to-reduce' pile.

A fundamental theory [of everything] has to be simple – not necessarily a few short equations, but equations that are based on a simple physical principle … it has to give us the feeling that it could scarcely be different from what it is.[29]

Increasingly though, this metaphysical aspiration is being abandoned in virtue of the Anthropic Principle (as discussed) and, of particular significance, the recognition that the Universe appears to be 'fine-tuned' for life as we know it. It is simply too large a pill to swallow to believe that the only possible laws of physics, dimensionless constants and boundary conditions of a universe, in some metaphysical sense of necessary (for it is certainly logically possible that the Universe might not contain life), are those needed for carbon-based life. The serious alternatives then seem to be divine design or a Multiverse. Polkinghorne sees this as a welcome development,

This proposal of a prodigious multiverse is not a scientific suggestion but a metaphysical speculation, a way to accommodate anthropic fine-tuning within a recklessly enlarged naturalism. It seems to me that a much more economic understanding is offered by the belief that there is only one universe, which is the way it is because it is indeed not 'any old world' but a creation that has been endowed by its Creator with just those finely tuned laws that have enabled it to have a fruitful history.[30]

In either case, those who conclude that reductionism has, in important ways, compounded rather than dissolved the mysteriousness of the natural world (leading many to adopt a Many-Worlds or God hypothesis as their terminus of explanation rather than a 'simple physical principle' à la Weinberg) will be motivated to examine alternative strategies. However, suggestions of this sort can easily lead to anti-scientific positions, which we wish to avoid, and so it will be necessary to tread carefully in formulating a useful approach to this subject area.

Theological Arguments Discouraging Appeals to the Miraculous

Is the 'anthropic fine-tuning' then the final destination for any form of the argument from design – to place all the 'teleology' in the initial act of creation?[31] Many theologians believe so, as Polkinghorne reports,

---

[29]   S. Weinberg, 'Will We Have a Final Theory of Everything?', *Time Magazine*, April 2000, accessed 29 March 2010, http://www.time.com/time/magazine/article/0,9171,996607,00.html.

[30]   J.C. Polkinghorne, *Science and the Trinity* (London: SPCK, 2004), 71.

[31]   That is not to say of course that God must then be disconnected from the world – he is still involved in so far as he continually upholds it – only that the *design inference* is then off limits in some way.

Theology is a complement to science and not an alternative. Accordingly, contemporary natural theologians have turned from arguments about the outcomes of natural processes to the firmer ground that is provided by consideration of the laws of nature themselves. After all, those laws are science's given starting point, but it is conceivable that they are not so self-explanatory[32] that it is intellectually satisfying to regard them as brute fact. Cosmology and physics have now moved onto centre stage.[33]

Theology has thus withdrawn from the realm of biology and for sensible reasons. Firstly, appeals to irreducibility in biology and the need to invoke the supernatural will, probably, compound a sense of embarrassment that is perceived to have been wrought by positing a God of the Gaps in the past. Wishing to avoid any hindrance to progress, theologians have tried to steer clear of forebodings of the end of science and the need for divine intervention. In the eyes of many, the most famous blunder in this regard (besides Paley's perhaps) was Newton's 'solution' to the belief that the orbits are not gravitationally stable and thus require God's habitual intervention to set them right, a hypothesis Laplace famously declared superfluous in the court of Napoleon.

Secondly, though, is a deeper reason for this development in natural theology, one that stems from an analysis that positively concludes that God *prefers* to use natural processes, wherever possible, to bring about his unfolding purposes (I highlight 'wherever possible' for reasons I shall return to later). If correct, this would create theological (not just scientific–methodological) disinclination to appeal to miraculous contraventions of physical law in one's account of the natural world. How could this be? At first glance, it seems surprising that theism would disincline one to appeal to the miraculous. It is an counter-intuitive thesis to which Polkinghorne, who has spent a lifetime wrestling with paradoxical issues in the realm of quantum mechanics, has made valuable contributions.

His first line of thought comes about through contemplating the divine attributes in light of revelation. A principal quality of the Christian conception of God is his steadfast fidelity, a characteristic to be inferred from his creative expression.

---

[32]   (The early) Wittgenstein would have said that they are not explanatory *at all* (see propositions 6.371–2 of the *Tractatus*). Of course, Polkinghorne recognises this dilemma and cautiously leaves the question open. 'In all metaphysical discourse, there is always the question of how far one wishes to push the search for an intellectually satisfying explanatory basis. Is it enough to rest content with the brute fact of natural law or should one look further to an Agent whose steadfast will is taken to be the basis for the perceived regularities of nature and their fruitful consequences?' J.C. Polkinghorne, *Faith, Science and Understanding* (New Haven, CT: Yale University Press, 2000), 92.

[33]   Polkinghorne, *Faith, Science and Understanding*, 85.

Divine upholding of the cosmos, whose regular laws are understood as reflections of God's unchanging faithfulness, is part of the story of God's relationship with the unfolding history of creation.[34]

Not only is this an expression of the Creator's character, but it is a necessary aid to our comprehension of the world. Consistency in natural process is required to make rational sense of one's environment; it is a *sine qua non* of meaningful intentionality carried out by creatures to be able to predict the outcomes of their actions.[35]

The second line of thought as to why theists might want to think very deeply before invoking the miraculous is empirically motivated and concerns reconciling God's loving character with the fact of evil. The main problem seems to be an apparent capriciousness in so far as the Christian conception of God as Father, a being who is immanent in our lives and responsive to our

---

[34]   Polkinghorne, *Belief in God in an Age of Science*, 54.

[35]   A parallel line of argument that has been somewhat neglected in such discussions could also be pursued by scientific realists: the world needs to have been consistent in its development over cosmic time to help ground a faithful epistemology of the external world. As Polkinghorne notes, 'in terms of naked power, no doubt God could have created humankind fully fleshed, rather than allowing them to emerge after 15 billion years of cosmic history, but he did not do so. That is the patient way that love works', Polkinghorne, *Science and Providence*, 65–6. Not only is this expressive of the Creator's kenotic love – allowing Creation the freedom to be itself – it is also viewed as a source of confidence that we are not part of some contrived puppet show akin to Descartes's worst case scenario. By *not* creating the world *ex nihilo* in some ready-to-go state (with adult creatures finding themselves fully formed), God makes a world in which creatures can infer the past back to, in our case, a well-defined physical system as given in the Big Bang scenario. The fact that the same physical laws we observe in operation today, operating on the early state of the Universe, led to a Universe very much like the one we inhabit is a remarkable discovery of modern science. The correlation of prediction to observation and unification of initially disparate phenomena provide us with a startling sense of clarity, of the kind Descartes spoke of, that helps ground a realist epistemology of the world. Suppose, by contrast, cosmic history were a complete mystery to us, that looking out into the sky there was only darkness. In such a case there would be no possible way to ascertain much (if anything) of cosmic origins, whether the earth had existed forever or had been conjured up in the recent past at the whim of a powerful agent. Such a world would lend itself much more readily to metaphysical scepticism amongst its rational inhabitants, perhaps encouraging solipsism and discouraging concern for fellow agents. It is precisely because cosmic history is so coherent and intricately interwoven with other domains of human knowledge that the human psyche is impelled towards the dismissal of Boltzmann Brains and other sceptical scenarios, thus encouraging a realist (and empathetic) view of the world. As Polkinghorne puts it, 'so marvellously patterned is that experience that I, for one, cannot doubt that it is the discernment of an actual reality', J.C. Polkinghorne, *Science and Creation* (West Conshohocken, PA: Templeton Foundation Press, 2006), 85.

everyday petitions, can permit evils on a global scale. To this end, Polkinghorne lays out his free-process defence:

> I think the only possible solution lies in a variation of the free-will defence, applied to the whole created world ... In his great act of creation I believe that God allows the physical world to be itself, not in a Manichaean opposition to him, but in that independence which is Love's gift of freedom to the one beloved. The cosmos is given the opportunity to be itself.[36]

It is important to emphasise that, in Polkinghorne's view, God is not constrained by some external metaphysics, but it is his own steadfast desire to endow creation with the freedom to be itself that results in his *causal* passiveness . One must emphasise causal here since, at the same time, the Christian God is deeply present and affected in such circumstances, personally partaking in the suffering through the kenotic act of 'becoming vulnerable', as reflected in Christ's passion and passivity.

> He is not a spectator but a fellow-sufferer, who has himself absorbed the full force of evil ... The God revealed in the vulnerability of the incarnation and in the vulnerability of creation are one.[37]

For Polkinghorne then, divine inaction in a world of untold suffering is not an *ad hoc* supposition introduced to retain the coherence of theism, rather it stands at the very core of the Christian faith. 'The cross', says Polkinghorne, 'is the fundamental basis of Christian theodicy'.[38] It is thus Polkinghorne's deep reflection on the problem of evil that leads him to conclude how very much God must be constrained by his *own* nature.

> [T]his kenotic sharing of power has important implications for theodicy. No longer can God be held to be totally and directly responsible for all that happens ... this is a self-qualification, exercised within the divine nature and in accordance with that nature itself ... The classical theologians ... had not taken adequately into account the interior 'constraints' of the self-consistency of the divine nature.[39]

The classical theologians did have a genuine concern – this theodicy risks leaving no room for God to play an authentic role within the creative order. Is God so constrained by his nature so as to be *causally* indistinguishable from deism? This is a perplexing problem that Polkinghorne approaches from many different

---

[36] Polkinghorne, *Science and Providence*, 66.

[37] Polkinghorne, *Science and Providence*, 68.

[38] Polkinghorne, *Science and Providence*, 68.

[39] J.C. Polkinghorne, *The Work of Love* (Grand Rapids, MI: Eerdmans, 2001), 95–6.

perspectives, seeking to reconcile the steadfast character of natural law, free will and divine action; each perspective offering a complementary 'glimmer of how it might be that we execute our willed intentions and how God exercises providential interaction with Creation'.[40]

One such glimmer is Polkinghorne's notion of 'active information' motivated by, amongst other things, the pilot-wave theory of Bohmian mechanics.[41] Others come from insights afforded by chaos theory and quantum indeterminacy, which create an epistemological openness to the world that, he contends, implies an ontological openness in which God's 'active information' can effectuate without violating natural law.[42] At the same time, Polkinghorne recognises that, while the intriguing aspects of chaos, quantum mechanics and information theory allow a certain 'room to manoeuvre' with respect to free will and divine action, they cannot be stretched to accommodate all traditional claims of God's interaction with the world. In particular they cannot account for the doctrine of the resurrection, which Polkinghorne takes to have been physically prefigured in Christ.[43] He thus concurs that, 'in unprecedented circumstances, it is entirely conceivable that God will act in totally novel and unexpected ways',[44] while carefully avoiding the claim that God 'intervenes' in such cases. How one is to make sense of the miraculous without 'intervention' is the subject of the next section.

Recasting the Miraculous

So far, we have seen theological reason (distinct from, say, scientific reason) to think very deeply before appealing to divine intervention as God prefers, in some general sense, to achieve his purposes through natural process. This flows from his nature as a kenotic creator desiring to furnish creation with a genuine autonomy of its own. Yet, that same nature also allows for this *apparent* laissez-faire policy be overridden in 'unprecedented circumstances' where physical law, as it is usually conceived, is incapable of accomplishing some other, more important aspect of the Creator's will. For Polkinghorne, the resurrection is just such a case. His work implies that, although God desires the physical world to operate in a predictable (and therefore transparently consistent) manner for the sake of his creatures, the revelatory significance of the physical resurrection of Christ is more desirable still.

---

[40]   Polkinghorne, *Belief in God in an Age of Science*, 62–3.

[41]   A well-known deterministic interpretation of Quantum Mechanics.

[42]   That is, bringing about an intended state of affairs without, say, violating energy conservation.

[43]   'Also important, I believe, is the witness of the empty tomb, for the fact that the Lord's glorified body is the transmuted form of his dead body speaks to me that in Christ there is a destiny not for humanity only, but also for matter, and so for creation as a whole', Polkinghorne, *Science and the Trinity*, 86.

[44]   Polkinghorne, *Belief in God in an Age of Science*, 73.

The two are not compatible. If one asks, 'why didn't God use physical processes to bring about the resurrection?' the answer is simple: it is not *possible* given the usual laws of physics. In some sense of course God does not have to use 'physical' processes at all – he is free to act as his will calls for – but it is impossible for him to *both* adhere strictly to the laws of physics (as they are currently conceived) *and* to bring about the resurrection (or other 'extraordinary' events) at the same time.

Presumably then, if God could have used natural processes to bring about the resurrection, he would have,[45] but in such a case where his purposes require the execution of the physically impossible, the 'extraordinary' can be expected.

There therefore arises an implicit ordering of priorities within the divine will that is reflected in the world: for the sake of an autonomous and rationally intelligible creation, transparently consistent and open natural processes are the rule; for the sake of revelation in the case of 'unprecedented circumstances', miracles are the *apparent* exception.

I say apparent because, according to Polkinghorne, 'God must be utterly consistent in his relationship with the world, but consistency does not mean a dreary uniformity'.[46] In other words, although miracles are rare in his opinion, they still follow the same 'expanded' (constantly valid) principles that can span, not just the space of physical states, but the spiritual and moral as well. He explains,

> I am carefully trying to characterise the event as "unexpected" rather than using discontinuous language like "due to direct divine intervention" … My reason is simply that I believe that God's complete action in the world must be consistent throughout. In the end there is no sharp separation to be made between general providence and special providence and miracle.[47]

How then are we to understand the transition, or the 'switching', between the 'general' and the 'special'. To explain this, Polkinghorne uses the analogy of a phase change in physics (as in heated water turning to steam at boiling point), where the underlying law remains the same but a new regime is entered that acts with 'totally unprecedented, totally unexpected consequences'. George Ellis puts this idea into a more concrete example when he speculates,

---

[45]   That is unless, of course, it is entirely *because* of its physical impossibility that God brings about the resurrection. If the sole purpose is to demonstrate his power over nature in an indisputable manner, then God would have to contravene the normal course of nature, but as Polkinghorne says, 'God could not be whimsically capricious about deciding to do something unprecedented, as if engaging in an act of divine showing off', Polkinghorne, *The Work of Love*, 105.

[46]   J.C. Polkinghorne, 'God's Action in the World', *CTNS Bulletin*, 10(2), Spring 1990, accessed 29 March 2010, http://www.polkinghorne.net/action.html.

[47]   Polkinghorne, *Science and Providence*, 50.

[There is the possibility of the] existence of a new order, a new regime of behavior of matter (cf. a phase transition), where apparently different rules apply ... [W]hen the right "spiritual" conditions are fulfilled ... the extraordinary would be incorporated within the regular behavior of matter, and neither the violation of the rights of matter nor the overriding of the chosen laws of nature would occur. Thus the laws of physics are respected. The charge of capriciousness would then fall away ... This is related to collapsing the distinction between the natural and the supernatural, from God's point of view. An example could be Jesus' resurrection.[48]

If Polkinghorne is correct, this would essentially mean that the operation of matter is ultimately more *complicated* than how it is usually conceived in science, especially if the operation of matter were to depend on the mental or spiritual state of the environment (if indeed these can be distinguished from the physical state in some ontological manner). As noted earlier, the appearance of miracles can always be represented by an increase in the complexity of the world, which can itself be connected (via the analogy of the cosmic computer) to the implementation of an if-statement in the structure of reality: **if** certain conditions are met, **then** a new regime is entered.

Mathematically, this could make the physical representation of the Universe tremendously more complicated, perhaps with the inclusion of an infinite number of extra terms in the equations of motion, but as indicated earlier, a well-executed if-statement can do the work of an infinite number of mathematical operations. So while the apparent arbitrariness of (reported) occurrences of miracles arises because the mathematically equivalent representation of their enactment would be too complex to allow the discernment of any pattern, the underlying reason could depend on a comparatively simple explanation if one is willing to allow for a richer ontology than that which defines reductive materialism.

We then have a conceptual framework to help understand how top-down causality (the sort we wish to affirm for the first-person perspective of human agency) and the 'extraordinary' emerge from a world that would otherwise appear to be reducible to particles in motion. God relates to these processes in so far as he has established and continually upholds the Universe as well as authoring the 'cosmic code' that relates one temporal slice of the world to the next. This abstract code organises but does not (necessarily) determine the bounds of possibility. An analogous example would be a program that traces out a chaotic trajectory with inputs from a random number generator; although the exact output on the screen cannot be determined in detail, the algorithm constrains the results from being meaningless noise.

---

[48]   G.F.R. Ellis, 'Ordinary and Extraordinary Divine Action', in *Chaos and Complexity: Scientific Perspectives on Divine Action*, edited by R.J. Russell, N. Murphy and A.R. Peacocke (Berkeley, CA: Vatican Observatory Publications and Berkeley University Press, 2000), 386.

Moreover, when particular conditions are seen to have been met within the program (at either the macro- or microscopic scale), a phase transition can be implemented in the code via an if-statement. This can help make sense of the interplay between top-down and bottom-up causality that Polkinghorne has in mind when he writes,

> If one adopts the admirable stance of asserting that wholes are more than mere sums of their parts, and combines this with the concept of a relatively orderly world, one is implicitly suggesting that there are holistic as well as constituent laws of nature. The structured richness of reality then results from an interplay between these two kinds of laws, and there is the problem of how we should best think about their mutual interrelation.[49]

The example to follow is rather crude (pressing it for detail would require an essay in itself), but helps illustrate the basic idea of how such 'interrelations' might be implemented in the 'cosmic code' of the Universe via 'collapse of the wave-function':

if *macroscopic* agent[50] has intention X **and** certain physical conditions are met
then realise *microscopic* state such that X results

else realise *microscopic* state according to the Schrödinger equation (or some other causal procedure)

Three comments will be useful here. Firstly, scientists are so accustomed to thinking that nature only deals with expressions like the individual terms in Eq. 2 (i.e. smooth and differentiable functions) that it takes some getting used to before discontinuous functions, as given by an if-statement in Eq. 1, cease to feel 'unnatural'. This is probably because if-statements produce non-linear complexity[51] that one does not expect in fundamental laws given the way reductionistic science is presently conceived. Also, needless to say, it is well outside the paradigm of modern scientific methodology to suppose that top-down or holistic causality is part of the structure of reality (with some research programmes into quantum mechanics being the exception). This calls for a degree of open-mindedness in the manner advocated by Polkinghorne.

---

[49] J.C. Polkinghorne, 'The Laws of Nature and the Laws of Physics', in *Quantum Cosmology and the Laws of Nature*, edited by R.J. Russell, N. Murphy and C.J. Isham (Berkeley, CA: Vatican Observatory Publications and Berkeley University Press, 1996), 430.

[50] One might want to replace 'agent' here with 'configuration of matter corresponding to an agent' on Polkinghorne's dual-aspect monism.

[51] Or, equivalently, an infinite number of linear terms.

Physics is taking a holistic turn. The possibility of the existence of holistic laws of nature is one which should not be discounted. Certainly such laws would be more difficult to discover than the familiar laws governing the behaviour of parts, and their form would surely be different from that of the differential equations which are the staple of current localized mathematical physics. Yet it would be a Procrustean imposition on science to deny that it could have access to such laws.[52]

Secondly, it may appear at first from the code in the above example as though 'holistic' causes in some way trump the 'constituent' causes by taking precedence in the if-statement. This is until we remember that the microscopic gives rise to the macroscopic in the first place. There is therefore the potential for a rich feedback structure whereby constituent causes give rise to macroscopic structures that then 'switch on' new modes of causality that feed back into the microscopic. In this case, a totally consistent law, applicable throughout all space and time, would control the 'mutual interrelation' between the 'holistic' and 'constituent' causal modes of nature.

Thirdly, some might object that causality in this scheme seems too artificial and, therefore, too much like occasionalism – the idea that God straightforwardly determines the motion of matter in sync with, and on behalf of, the choices we make in some disconnected 'mind space'. In such a view the real 'us' is the dislocated mental substance and it becomes questionable whether one really needs a physical world at all. However, as stated earlier, the conceptual scheme at hand is metaphysically neutral. It is consistent with occasionalism in so far as such a puppet universe can be represented using the conceptual scheme laid out in the opening sections. Ultimately though, the cosmic-code representation merely describes the *form* of causal relationships in the real world without dictating their ontology.[53]

The scheme is therefore just as compatible with the open and temporal-becoming of Polkinghorne's critical realism. However, if one wishes to drape Polkinghorne's ontology explicitly over the proposed conceptual scheme, one will find that they link very naturally. In such a case, God continually upholds the world according to consistent laws (analogous to computer code) that describe the evolution of the Universe from one moment to the next in an open (i.e. involving a random number generator) but bounded manner. With each passing moment, the Universe is neither completely random nor determined, but is bounded by the state in the previous moment. God's grasp of the future comes from 'seeing' every detail on the cosmic screen and understanding the possibilities allowed by the code he has decreed. With this knowledge at hand, God is able to respond and act in the world in a similar way to a programmer at the keyboard, not by

---

[52]   Polkinghorne, 'The Metaphysics of Divine Action', 150.

[53]   Those who are rather Humean in their stance on causality (as is the author) will not be too bothered by this objection.

capriciously rewriting the code at any moment or magically altering the contents of the hard drive, but by feeding 'active-information' into the openness inherent in the program. Finally, the structure of the code is such as to interrelate the holistic and elementary through if-statements that switch between different regimes of behaviour. This mutual interrelation between the macro and the micro, the top-down and bottom-up, makes sensible the claim that 'there is no sense in which subatomic particles are to be graded as "more real" than, say, a bacterial cell or a human person'.[54] In such a world, there is proper freedom[55] and non-reducible emergence of the kind envisioned by Polkinghorne when he writes

> The everyday world is constructed of constituents from the quantum world but, as these entities combine together into systems of greater and greater complexity, new possibilities come into being, exhibiting properties (such as life and consciousness) that were unforeseeable in terms of the simpler constituents out of which they are made, while only realizable through the potentialities with which those same entities are endowed. Thus, the growth in organization produces genuine novelty, and each level (biological, human, social) enjoys its own autonomy in terms of concepts that are not simply reducible to those associated with lower levels.[56]

To summarise so far, Polkinghorne gives us strong theological reason to suppose that the Universe is implanted with a deeper structure than normally supposed by reductionist science, a structure that takes the form of completely new regimes of physics that are activated if non-physical (in the usual sense of the word) conditions are met. Although I do not claim to have definitively solved the puzzles as to how God acts in the world, the proposed conceptual scheme allows us to view the subject from the relatively untapped and, I believe, illuminating perspective of a programmer–computer relationship. Hopefully it can come to stand alongside and complement other ways that theologians have tried to express the nature of agency – both human and divine – in a world of unwavering natural law.

In the next section I shall return in more detail to the possibility that a related though more 'physical' type of if-statement[57] is implanted into physics and that anthropic reasoning, which has become mainstream in cosmology, offers reason to take this possibility seriously. Such if-statements might 'switch on' new phenomena at higher levels of biological process, perhaps in the regime of DNA structure, that would prove *immensely complicated* to represent in the usual reductionist scheme of biochemistry. Nonetheless, such processes would be entirely physical in so far as their operation would occur consistently throughout all space and time.

---

[54] Peacocke, quoted by Polkinghorne, *Science and Providence*, 29.

[55] Assuming of course that libertarian freedom is truly possible.

[56] Polkinghorne, *Science and Creation*, 46.

[57] That is, if-statements that do not depend on moral or spiritual conditions, but are strictly physical in the usual scientific sense.

Scientific Motivation for Cosmic If-statements

The Limits of Physical Intuition

In view of this discussion, what then are we to make of the sense of the 'unexpected' in the 'bias' of matter that Montefiore was trying to communicate? Does it merely reflect our ignorance of the intricacies of matter and physical law? Not necessarily. We are never totally ignorant about what matter, operating under (our current conceptions of) physical law, can and cannot do. Indeed, the very structure of physical law is designed to demarcate what is and is not possible.

In fact, it is very easy to cite extreme examples of counterfactual phenomena that would call physical reductionism into question. In particular, we all have some sense of what evolution can and cannot produce, although there is great dispute over the details of the divide owing to the complexity of such systems. As Dennett illustrates,

> One may ... be reasonably nervous about the size of the role of sheer, unfettered imagination in adaptationist thinking [in evolution]. What about butterflies with tiny machine guns for self-protection? This fantastic example is often cited as the sort of option that can be dismissed without detailed analysis ... It is just too distant a possibility in design space to be taken seriously. But as Richard Lewontin aptly notes, "My guess is that if fungus-gardening ants had never been seen, the suggestion that this was a reasonable possibility for ant evolution would have been regarded as silly".[58]

The point Dennett makes here is that, although we have *some* intuition about the capacities of matter in complex systems, it is extremely difficult to know in any detail how far these intuitions can carry us. If we then set aside any allegiance to reductionism as a methodology, and ask to what extent we actually *know* that biological processes are straightforwardly reducible to fundamental physics, we find that our intuitions tell us rather little (or, that intuitions on the matter vary radically from one individual to the next).

By straightforwardly reducible I mean, for example, that all energy levels in biochemical processes are in principle calculable by solving the Schrödinger equation using the established constituents of atoms (electrons, protons and neutrons). If an energy level were found that were not reducible in this way then the reductionist would have to add extra terms to the potential corresponding to new modes of energy propagation (i.e. we would have to posit new 'stuff' and/ or new properties that complicate the way particles couple with each other in the evolution of the system). Of course, it would be tremendously difficult to find such an energy level because of the problem of underdetermination – is the apparent discrepancy owing to an error in the experiment, inaccuracy in the *ab*

---

    58   D.C. Dennett, *Darwin's Dangerous Idea* (London: Penguin Books, 1996), 251.

initio calculation[59] or because our physics is genuinely incomplete and therefore requires expansion?

It is easy to understand from the practical point of view why it is that scientists would strongly resist adjusting fundamental theory in this way. This is usually a last resort since their goal is to represent the processes of nature in as simple a form as possible and adjusting the equations almost always complicates them. However, as argued earlier, the desire for ultimate simplicity is a pragmatic idealisation that must eventually run up against the minimal degree of complexity in our Universe required by the Anthropic Principle. The assumption that the world is ultimately simple at its core is not a promise that nature has made to us. Although humankind can rightly take pride in its collective discoveries given our many limitations, it is important to keep our capabilities in perspective. We are only able to write down those aspects of the Universe that are isolable and tractable and so it would be naive to suppose that we have already exhausted all the major surprises that nature has kept hidden. As William Stoeger explains,

> [The physical] phenomena, and therefore the theories and laws [that govern them], are not able to reveal all features of observed reality nor even its most fundamental features. Some of them are hidden from, or inaccessible to, our probing. This is simply because, in making our observations and measurements, we focus on those stable and characteristic features [of which] we are capable ... But there may be, and certainly are, many aspects of observed reality which are neglected or simply missed ... Certain parts of reality in which we are immersed are such that we can successfully model them in all their detail – they are algorithmically compressible. But that fortunate and mysterious trait of reality should not delude us into thinking that we have a direct access to reality as it is in itself – if indeed this term has meaning.[60]

The fact is, no one has an intimate enough knowledge of particle physics and the way it combines into chemistry and biochemistry to really know if the 'bias' in matter is something that is reducible to fundamental physics (as it is conceived today) without having to greatly complicate the equations such that, for example, effects come into play at larger (e.g. biological) scales that are negligible at lower (e.g. atomic) scales. Moreover, as Eugene Wigner pointed out, such 'hidden terms' are only likely to be found if one is already looking for them.

---

[59]   That is, solving the fundamental laws of physics bottom-up with little or no short-cuts or approximations.

[60]   W.R. Stoeger, 'Contemporary Physics/Laws of Nature', in *Quantum Cosmology and the Laws of Nature*, edited by R.J. Russell, N. Murphy and C.J. Isham (Berkeley, CA: Vatican Observatory Publications & Berkeley, 1996), 220–21.

The possibility that we overlook the influence of biotonic phenomena, as one immersed in the study of the laws of macroscopic mechanics could have overlooked the influence of light on his macroscopic bodies, is real.[61]

However undesirable it might be to complicate the equations of physics, it might ultimately prove necessary.[62] At the same time, it remains the case that we just do not know whether such bio-friendly regularities observed at the macroscopic are, in fact, straightforwardly reducible to fundamental physics (as it is presently conceived). In the face of such difficult questions, Polkinghorne is wise to discourage the equation of our ignorance of the facts with God's intervention. Montefiore went on to equate the 'bias' in matter with the 'work of the Holy Spirit'. Polkinghorne responds:

> The question of whether such effects are present [in biology] is a scientifically posable question and I see no reason why it should not be expected to receive a scientifically state-able answer. There may be more to evolution than has met the neo-Darwinian eye, but to call that missing ingredient in our understanding the Holy Spirit is to invoke the God of the Gaps.[63]

This is a common 'blunder' that Polkinghorne is sharp to denounce; the suggestion, that anything that at first seems physically intractable is indicative of divine intervention, leads, almost invariably, to a God of the Gaps that will one day prove superfluous (and even if it does not, it's not scientifically *useful*).[64] Polkinghorne urges that God's interaction is not one of *intervention* since God must act in a totally consistent manner. 'The true God is related to the whole of creation, not just the puzzling bits of it'.[65]

---

[61]   E. Wigner, quoted by P.C. Davies, *The Cosmic Blueprint* (West Conshohocken, PA: Templeton Foundation Press, 1988), 148.

[62]   A good example of this sort of problem is the debate over Dark Matter – does Newtonian physics enter a new regime of behaviour above a certain scale (requiring an adjustment to the equations), or do we need to posit a new and exotic form of invisible matter? That is, do we complicate the equations or add to the length of the state-vector (or both)?

[63]   Polkinghorne, *Science and Creation*, 70.

[64]   The relationship between scientific realism and human utility ('usefulness') is an important subject that deserves more attention than is possible here. It is worth noting in passing that Polkinghorne places a great deal of epistemic weight on the 'usefulness' of ideas – 'There is no logically inevitable way to proceed from epistemology to ontology … It can be resolved only by an act of metaphysical decision … by an appeal to the fruitful success of the strategy adopted', Polkinghorne, *Belief in God in an Age of Science*, 53.

[65]   Polkinghorne, 'The Laws of Nature and the Laws of Physics', 438.

A Practical Approach

The more scientifically useful and theologically informed question that Polkinghorne would wish to pose is not, therefore, whether God is 'intervening' in the course of biological processes, rather, Polkinghorne would prefer the more neutral question of whether 'biotonic laws' are to be found in nature. I wish to suggest that the most promising form of such a law would be that of an 'if-statement' (or their equivalent representation in the form of hidden terms whose effects become non-negligible, that is, 'switch on' under certain finely-tuned conditions) whose effect is to encode a degree of non-linear complexity that might be required for biology and evolution to take place.

It is a metaphysically neutral proposal because, if such if-statements are *anthropically* required, then they can be explained by the standard paradigms for the 'fine tuning of the Universe for intelligent life', namely, by divine design or a selection effect from a Multiverse realising a wide variety of logically possible and physically distinct domains.[66]

In the prior case, such if-statements would arise from the Creator's consistent, law-like intention to uphold the world in a manner habitable by (in our case) carbon-based life forms. Such if-statements, if they exist, implant matter with the bias to which Montefiore alludes, and hold true for all space and time in keeping with the Creator's consistent intention to make the Universe as open to inductive reasoning as possible. In that manner, they are distinct from the classical notion of a miracle as some sort of occasional and spatially localised contravention of physical law. These if-statements complicate the laws of physics, which is undesirable in and of itself, but are nonetheless necessary to achieve the functionality of biochemistry.

In the latter interpretation of biotonic if-statements, using the Multiverse, if it is the case that they are necessary for life as we know it to evolve and persist, then only universes that have them will have 'physical observers' to note their occurrence. In such a case all universes where physics *is* reducible to the Schrödinger equation as we presently envisage it (without any hidden terms or if-statements that 'switch on' in higher-level processes) would be sterile. That is, they would not be complex enough to furnish biochemistry. One would have to move to a different (presumably smaller)[67] subset of more complicated universes

---

[66]   See J. Leslie, *Universes*, first published in 1989, Routledge, London, for an excellent discussion of these interpretations of the Fine Tuning.

[67]   This brings up the 'measurement problem' with respect to Multiverses; how does one measure the relative frequency of one type of universe to another in the Multiverse and thus determine whether or not universes like ours are 'rare' in the Multiverse. It is the hope of Multiverse proponents that a physically motivated model of the Multiverse (as the 'String Landscape' is alleged to be) would turn out to predict that universes like ours are relatively common. This whole field is, however, fraught with difficulties of comparing infinities with infinities as well as putting substance into phrases like 'physically motivated'

to find life. However rare such universes might be though, in a sufficiently large and diverse Multiverse, they will be bound to occur.[68]

So far I have discussed the conceptual possibility of 'regime switching' in the laws of physics controlled by virtual if-statements and suggested theological and scientific motivation to take the notion seriously. The scheme fits well with Polkinghorne's theological reflections as to the steadfast character of the Christian God and his philosophical–scientific thoughts regarding emergence and openness in the physical world. He writes,

> I have considerable sympathy with the belief that the fruitfulness of cosmic and terrestrial history is such that it is reasonable to seek to supplement current received evolutionary ideas with the operation of possible teleological laws of nature ... Darwinian ideas provide partial insight into the developing history of a fruitful world but it is certainly not known that they tell the whole story.[69]

One might complain, though, that no *positive* argument has been given yet to think that physical if-statements are in fact needed for biology to function as it does. This relates to the difficult connection between epistemic possibility and actual possibility[70] and, given the complexity of the systems in question, must therefore come down to a judgement according to the individual's overall grasp of the physical situation in question. The purpose of the next section is to encourage contemplation of just how easily the constraints of 'fundamental law' could frustrate the bottom-up construction of biological functioning.

The Perils of 'Monkeying With Physics'

Consider a crude thought experiment. Suppose you are to design a Universe containing matter to be governed by natural law where, as a rule of thumb, you must make the laws as simple as possible whilst allowing for the emergence of intelligent life in the course of time. Suppose you begin with a simple system like a Hot Big Bang with Gaussian inhomogeneities that, under a simple law of attraction ($1/r^2$), will condense into structures. You find that, with only three other

---

and what it means to be an 'observer' (see D.W. Darg 'The Fine Tuning of Consciousness', in preparation, for 2012 publication).

[68]   This is especially true of the variety of Multiverse reflecting the philosophical position of modal realism where, crudely speaking, 'everything that can exist, exists'; cf. Max Tegmark, *The Mathematical Universe*, 2008, FoPH, 38, 101–50.

[69]   Polkinghorne, *Beyond Science*, 78–9.

[70]   Consider a deeply technical mathematical proposition that is, as yet, unproven. We would be able to say, in so far as we are ignorant of the truth value of the proposition, that it is possibly true (i.e. it is epistemically possible). Suppose then that someone comes up with a disproof that gains acceptance by the mathematical community. We would then no longer say that the proposition is possibly true but, rather, that it is necessarily false.

forces and some simple rules (quantum mechanics) exhibited by a modest number of fundamental particles, you are able to produce stars from these gravitational structures, which allows these particles to combine into heavy elements in their hot interiors. These stars explode in due course and scatter the elements into the interstellar medium available to re-condense into a proto-solar system. A chemically rich planet thus forms and oceans gather on its surface.

The water in these oceans proves to be a versatile solvent for atoms to begin to interact in accordance with their electron shells that are determined by the same laws of quantum mechanics that brought about their formation in the core of the stars. This leads to a crude form of chemical reproduction that progresses onto a self-replicating cell. Unfortunately, a problem then arises – a vital chemical reaction needed for larger self-replicating organisms does not quite work – an important energy level of catalyst X is a fraction of an electron volt (α eV) too small to bind and speed up an important protein folding. You try solving the problem by tweaking the fine-structure constant. That raises the energy level to the right amount but now another energy level in a different reaction is too large. You try to solve this by increasing the mass of the proton by a tiny fraction, but now nucleosynthesis in stars occurs at one tenth its previous rate, so stars need to burn longer to obtain enough elements. And so on. After exhaustive efforts you find that any attempt to fix a problem by changing the fundamental laws of physics ends up disrupting things elsewhere – the systems have become too complex and there are simply too many constraints welling up from the coincidences that you have already taken advantage of in basic physics. What you end up finding is that it is simply not *logically* possible for you to *both* use the physical laws so far established consistently across all space and time *and* bring it about that life will evolve by itself without further, specific acts of contravening the laws so-far decreed.[71] In this case, do you

(A) abandon the whole plan (or start all over from scratch);

(B) make the laws more complicated so that only *in this regime of physics* the necessary effect is actualised.

Although this thought experiment is highly simplistic, the fact that many of us would choose option B might make us sympathetic to the possibility of such 'regime changes' in the laws of nature. If a human programmer were tackling the above problem, the solution would be to simply implement an if-statement into the cosmic code: if configuration X obtains, then adjust the energy level by α eV.

Three comments are apt at this point. Firstly, those of a scientific orientation might be highly concerned that some deeply held principle of physics will not allow this (as though such principles are in some way inviolable). In this example, energy conservation would be broken. I do not believe this is a serious problem

---

[71] I assume of course that not even God can do the *logically* impossible.

at all. Maybe the Universe makes consistent exceptions – if Bohmian mechanics (a respected though seldom embraced interpretation of quantum mechanics) is true then particles do not travel inertially either. Moreover, it would be very easy to balance out the energy, for example, by increasing or decreasing the rest-mass of the molecule by the corresponding energy difference or absorbing/emitting a photon.

Secondly, the idea that God is constrained as to how the Universe operates (as portrayed in the above thought experiment) comes right out of theodicy. If God were to adjust physical law so that earthquakes never happen then this would produce massive ripple effects throughout the natural world that would almost certainly make life impossible for one reason or another. As Polkinghorne states, 'the existence of tectonic plates allows mineral resources to well up in the gaps between them, thereby replenishing the surface of the earth, but it also allows earthquakes and tsunamis to occur. You cannot have one without the other'.[72]

Thirdly, if one were to choose B in the above thought experiment, and if one were therefore willing to allow that God *might* use a single if-statement to solve a biochemical engineering problem vital to life, why stop there? Perhaps biology is so complicated at the cellular level that if-statements of this sort are required all over the place. It was, of course, the complexity of the cell that urged Elsasser, the father of systems biology, to posit the conceptual category of biotonic processes in the first place. It is difficult to observe the working of a cell and believe that all of this movement is essentially reducible to 'Lego blocks' in motion simply bouncing off each other seeking thermodynamic equilibrium.[73]

Where would one look for such if-statements then if they had the resources and motivation? The best choice would be biochemistry. This is the regime where complexity takes off like no other place in the Universe and is therefore the most likely regime where if-statements might be anthropically required. Also, chemistry provides a very 'neat' place to encode 'phase changes' since bonds and energy levels are quantised. The conditions that the if-statements would act on would then be questions of whether a configuration is in place and whether any adjustments need to be made. More detailed areas of investigation are suggested in the Appendix.

A Challenge to Intelligent Design

Politics and 'wedge strategies' aside, I wish to focus briefly on some of the philosophical questions that the intelligent design movement has prompted

---

[72]   J.C. Polkinghorne and N. Beale, *Questions of Truth* (Louisville, KY: Westminster John Knox Press, 2009), 65.

[73]   I highly recommend the reader watch the animation of the cell in the given link in order to fully appreciate the sense of non-reducibility, to which Montefiore alluded: http://www.astro.physics.ox.ac.uk/~ddarg/shtml/cell_animation.shtml.

within theological and scientific circles. In *Darwin's Black Box*, Michael Behe goes to great lengths to describe the intricacy of biochemical processes. The grandeur of such microscopic architecture sets the stage for his argument based upon 'irreducible complexity' – an argument so well-known now that it needs no repetition here. This leads to the proposition of 'intelligent design', which many have read as (ultimately) an appeal to direct divine action of the creationist variety.

How well does Behe's (implied) interventionism cohere with his affirmation of common decent? This is difficult to assess owing to the reticence of intelligent design proponents to posit a mechanism by which the Agent 'designs' the system. In any case, the proposal has a strong anti-uniformitarian flavour to it, suggesting that highly non-linear events took place in the past (the sort that we associate with actions carried out by intentional agents such as ourselves) that are no longer directly discernible since they are not embedded in the natural structure of the world. Such discontinuities are distressing to scientists (who, as discussed already, depend on Nature operating 'smoothly') and stand in contrast to what Polkinghorne describes as the 'gentle providential guidance exercised within the openness of natural process, of the kind "theistic evolutionists" tend to favour'.[74] In short then, there are two problems. Firstly, there is the theological problem that we have already discussed stemming from the problem of evil to Polkinghorne's thesis: God does not rewrite his code when (and as if) things fail to go to plan. Rather, he is consistent from start to finish, capable of foreseeing technical obstacles like 'irreducible complexity' and, therefore, capable of writing the laws of nature with sufficient complexity to overcome them. It is then the empirically motivated doctrine that God gives the world the freedom to 'create itself' that increases one's expectation that nature does have the requisite complexity built into its laws to accomplish this (so that these effects would still be accessible to science today). Polkinghorne summarises the thought as follows:

> God is never spoken of as a "designer" in the Bible: he is Creator and Father, and a Father does not "design" his children ... By endowing us with free will and giving us the capacity to love, God calls us to be in a limited but very important sense co-creators.[75]

The second problem is more practical. I am personally sympathetic (as is Polkinghorne – see quotations of his works above) to the claim that a degree of non-linear complexity might be required in biological processes that is not provided by the (relatively) simple physical laws that have been ascertained so far by reductionistic science. However, if these 'complexities' were instantiated exclusively in the past by some supernatural intervener, which are therefore inaccessible to science in the present, then it is difficult to see how any useful

---

74   Polkinghorne, *Faith, Science and Understanding*, 93.
75   Polkinghorne and Beale, *Questions of Truth*, 57.

research programme can result from this proposal.[76] This, many claim, disqualifies it from bearing the premium of 'science' as it does not comply with the (pragmatic) methodology of reductionism.

Moreover, it is very difficult to see how Darwin's challenge[77] could ever be falsified beyond doubt since one can *always* appeal to the future hope that new discoveries will lead to new and unexpected discoveries to solve problems that currently seem intractable.

A more useful and more ideologically neutral programme would result by taking the theological arguments of Polkinghorne seriously and re-orientating such research around the pursuit of biotonic laws – laws that emerge in higher level processes that are not reducible to physics as it is currently conceived. If one were able to find such 'if-statements' and thereby falsify current assumptions, biology and physics would be revolutionised. If none are found, then the sociological effect would no doubt serve to strengthen the *status quo* of reductionism à la Popper, but at least we would have learnt something new about nature and, from the theistic perspective, shown that God simply did not need to intervene over and above the laws he has set in place.

I do not wish to speak casually of the difficulties – conceptual and practical – that one would have to undertake in accepting such a challenge: scientific research demands tremendous resources and commitment. It also requires support from the human *community* that the intelligent design movement has made difficult for itself by being so forthright with its ideological agenda. This is a shame for those of us who, joined together as a philosophical community, wish to learn about those parts of the world that are most central to our origins and existence. Polkinghorne's work suggests both theological and scientific motivation to search for such biotonic phenomena in the structure of the world but, unfortunately, it is unlikely they will ever be sought so long as ideological struggles preclude such research programmes ever being taken seriously by the scientific community.

Summary

The conceptual scheme that compares the Universe with the operation of a computer operating according to a set of rules, that I have referred to as 'cosmic code', is a helpful analogy for God's relation to the world. In order to accommodate life, this code requires a minimal degree of complexity. A key concept in programming

---

[76] Again, the deep and perplexing question arises concerning the role of utility in science – a question that cannot be dealt with here except to point out that the two are intimately connected.

[77] 'If it could be demonstrated that any complex organ existed, which could not possibly have been formed by numerous, successive, slight modifications, my theory would absolutely break down', C.R. Darwin, *The Origin of Species* (New York: Oxford University Press, 1998), 154.

complexity into computer code is the use of an if-statement that switches between regimes of behaviour.

In this representation, miracles are the *complications* rather than the *contraventions* of natural law. Given that a minimal degree of complexity is required by the Anthropic Principle, one is confronted with the question whether this complexity is most efficiently represented with the occurrence of if-statements in nature. This proposal is compatible with both a theistic-design and a Multiverse-selection-effect scenario. Given the astounding complexity observed in biological processes, there is no (non-practical) reason to suppose *a priori* that such if-statements are not required and that all life processes are straightforwardly reducible to the Schrödinger equation in action.

This conceptual scheme lends powerfully to the important theological contributions that Polkinghorne has made. According to him, the Christian conception of God is that of a steadfast and consistent sustainer of the world who does not capriciously contravene the functioning of the Universe. The world is truly allowed to be itself within the bounds of natural law prescribed by the Creator. At the same time, Polkinghorne sees the structure of reality as being much richer than reductionist science would imply; nature is orchestrated such that top-down causality and 'the extraordinary' emerge in an irreducible manner from the bottom-up causes that constitute the world. The notion of if-statements in the cosmic code assists us in conceptualising how such transitions might take place within the consistent laws of nature that God has 'programmed'. Moreover, God can interact with creation as a programmer does during the operation of the computer, not by arbitrarily re-writing the code, but by feeding what Polkinghorne would call 'active-information' into the openness that was built in from the start.

Finally, I suggested some practical ideas about where one might look for such hidden structures. This is a more practical programme than those that have gone before it, namely, in search of 'irreducible complexity'. It would be a tremendous accomplishment if Polkinghorne's theological reflections lead to the discovery of scientifically describable structures that the theist would wish to interpret as the hallmarks of the Creator in a Universe given freedom to co-create itself.

Acknowledgements

I am grateful to Ard Louis, Bernard d'Espagnat and Kelly James Clark for useful feedback and discussion. I acknowledge the Templeton Foundation for financial support.

Appendix A: Water

Few appreciate just how difficult it is to solve the Schrödinger equation even for very simple systems. The hydrogen atom (one proton and one electron) is basically the one system that can be solved 'exactly'. Beyond that, one must employ approximations to greatly simplify the problem. By time one gets to proteins (with hundreds of protons, electrons and neutrons), the calculations are far removed from the *ab initio* ideal.

To illustrate the difficulties that beset this field, I shall say a word on water. Despite it being the most important liquid for life and thus the subject of much research, its structure and properties are still not fully understood. Water has several peculiar properties that make it vital for life such as its increased density in liquid state[78] and its high melting point.

Several of these properties arise owing to its bond angle (~104.5°) being close to that of a perfect tetrahedral (~109.5°). With a slight departure from this precise bond angle, the chemical properties of water change considerably. Heavy water, where the hydrogen atoms are replaced with deuterium (with nuclei of one proton and one neutron), is chemically similar to water, having only a slightly smaller bond angle. This small difference, though, disrupts the biochemistry substantially. 'D_2O in metazoans, both animals and plants, is completely inert and useless. In D_2O, seeds will not sprout and rats die of thirst given only D_2O to drink'.[79]

Is the bond angle of water a direct and determined result of the time-independent Schrödinger equation? Molecules of this size might be the best place to look; beyond this, it becomes too complicated.

Appendix B: DNA And Protein Structure

Protein structure is incredibly complex. Long polymers link up and fold into a shape that is representable by its 'solvent-accessible surface'. This is basically a constant-energy surface of the potential-energy distribution that results from all the charges within the molecule all 'added up'.[80] These shapes assume various roles: links for building larger structures, 'keys' for 'locks', platforms for other reactions, etc. The precision that these shapes are required to have in order to carry out their 'tasks' is remarkable.

Even for the polymers to fold into the required shape seems (metaphorically) paradoxical. The molecular biologist Cyrus Levinthal noted that, if an average folding protein were to explore every possible configuration before 'coming to rest', it would require timescales much greater than the age of the Universe. Yet, proteins fold into their required shape in a few milliseconds typically. This

---

[78]   This means that ice floats, which is important for the development of life; if ice were to sink, it would cause bodies of water to freeze solid and inhibit life. As it is, ice floats and insulates the water beneath, keeping it in a liquid state.

[79]   Barrow and Tipler, *The Anthropic Cosmological Principle*, 541.

[80]   Adding them up means solving the Schrödinger equation. This is practically impossible *ab initio*.

'paradox'[81] is resolved by the fact that the protein does not explore all possibilities, but follows a deterministic path down a funnel-like energy landscape. So not only does biochemistry have to have the right shapes, but it also has to get to those shapes *fast*.

This is the picture of how all bio-molecular processes are believed to occur – through deterministic paths where shapes and energy levels all conspire to keep organisms in constant flux. While it is possible[82] that this is all reducible to Schrödinger's equation, from the view point of ontologically rich scenarios such as theism and a Multiverse, the notion that there is 'emergent complexity' not discernible from the Schrödinger equation does not seem so implausible.

---

[81]   Whether there is a formal paradox here is questionable; the main point is that the problem of figuring out the folding structure of such proteins is short-handedly referred to by the phrase 'Levinthal's Paradox'.

[82]   That is, epistemically possible in so far as nobody knows; the point though is that it might not *actually* be possible.

Chapter 8

Bishop Berkeley's Castle:
John Polkinghorne on the Soul

Keith Ward

Professor Polkinghorne's writings on theology tend to be brief (although there are many of them), but they unerringly go to the heart of the topics he writes about, and provide insights that are important for any contemporary statement of Christian faith. In this short paper I intend to consider some of the things he says about the soul. I do not pretend to talk about Professor Polkinghorne's view of the soul in general. Instead I shall consider some of the specific things he has written about the soul, whether or not he now continues to hold those views as he stated them in the texts I shall consider. Therefore this paper is a consideration of some of his writings on the subject of the soul, rather than about his doubtlessly more complex and developing views.

The writings I will refer to are to be found in just three books: *One World* (SPCK, 1986 and 2007) [OW], *The God of Hope and the End of the World* (SPCK, 2002) [GH] and *Exploring Reality* (SPCK, 2005) [ER]. The title of this paper is suggested by a passing comment he makes in one of them: 'I am not about to retreat with Bishop Berkeley into the idealist castle' (OW, 109). I will put my cards on the table, and say that I think he should not be ashamed to enter into Berkeley's idealist castle. Indeed, at times he virtually does so, and I would like to suggest that this is not at all a bad place to be, and that he is not as far away from it as his comment suggests.

I need to say a word about Berkeley, although this paper is about Polkinghorne, not Berkeley, so I will be brief. It is a complete misunderstanding of Berkeley to suppose that he thought that physical objects do not exist, and that everything is in human minds, so that the world disappears when humans are not looking at it. He always claimed to be a common sense philosopher, and was quite sure that objects exist when humans do not perceive them. Berkeley's point was that physical objects cannot exist without some perceiving mind – so if there is a physical world independent of humans, it must exist in the mind of God. It does, although not exactly as it is perceived by humans. The form of the world's existence in God is veiled from our understanding, but it could not exist at all without the mind of God. Berkeley's castle is one in which minds have ontological priority. Matter exists as the content of mental acts, and could not exist on its own.

This is not very far, if it is any distance at all, from classical Christian theism. God, who is not material, can exist without a material universe, but matter cannot exist without God. If God is anything like a mind – and God is said to know, to act, to have purposes, and to be wise – then Christians must believe that mind can exist without matter. I doubt if Polkinghorne would have any problems with that, but it is already a sort of dualism or idealism. Mind is different from matter, and can exist on its own – that is dualism – and perhaps mind produces matter as its wholly dependent expression – that is idealism.

Polkinghorne would say, I think, that it may be very well for God, but it will not do as an account of human minds or souls. The universe may express the mind of God, but our human bodies do not express our minds. On the contrary, our minds seem to be largely dependent upon our bodies and brains, and to be the result of millions of years of material evolution. Some philosophers even argue that human minds are nothing but very complex material arrangements of molecules, and such minds could not exist if those arrangements, making up a human brain, ceased to exist.

The evidence for this claim is the observed dependence of human thought upon the functioning of the brain. If the brain is damaged, we may change our character or lose our memory or our sense of being a continuing agent. If we stimulate the brain, we can produce various conscious experiences in the mind, and consciousness itself seems to depend on the existence of a brain of a certain size and structure. This evidence does not show that the mind is nothing but the brain, but it does suggest that the human mind or soul (I shall use these words interchangeably for the purposes of this paper) depends upon the existence of the physical brain, and not vice versa.

It is not wholly surprising that, as a particle physicist, Polkinghorne takes this sort of evidence to show what he calls 'the psychosomatic integrity of human beings' (OW, 91). Souls are not stuck onto brains as a divine add-on. Souls and brains are welded indissolubly together, so as to form one thing, not two things miraculously working in complete agreement. This he calls an 'anti-dualist conclusion' (GH, 105).

From a Christian point of view, this seems not to be some sort of radical and threatening discovery, but a re-affirmation of what the Biblical view of human persons always has been. The Book of Genesis records that human are formed of dust, filled with *neshemah,* the breath of God – just as all animals are (Genesis 2, 7 and 7, 22). Humans are special in being made in the 'image and likeness of God' (Genesis 1, 26), but that does not consist of the addition of an immaterial soul. According to most Hebrew scholars, it is more likely to express the special role that humans have on this planet, as the stewards of the earth, those responsible for cultivating and caring for it and, when necessary, controlling it to make it fruitful and beautiful. In other words, human persons are material animals who have a sense of moral responsibility and the capacity for abstract intellectual thought.

The doctrine of the resurrection of the body may also be taken to stress the importance of the 'body', of the physical and material, to the continuance of human personhood. The Christian hope is not for the persistence of some immaterial soul, but for the possession of a fully embodied soul. That is true. However, what will the nature of that body be? And is this really an anti-dualist conclusion?

If we look carefully at what Descartes actually says, he affirms that 'I am not present in my body merely as a pilot is present in a ship. I am most tightly bound to it, and as it were mixed up with it, so that I and it form a unit'.[1] For Descartes, body and mind form a unity. This is a compound unity, just as water is a compound unity of hydrogen and oxygen. As hydrogen and oxygen are quite different from each other, but combine together to form water, so body and mind are quite different, but combine to form a human person. That is Descartes's form of dualism, although it is one of the most widely misunderstood doctrines in the history of philosophy.

For Descartes, as for Aquinas, there can be minds, things which think, feel, imagine and dream, without bodies, without being located and extended in physical space. However, human persons are essentially compounds of mind and body, integrated in the 'tightest' way. Cartesian dualism is in fact the doctrine that body and mind are different in kind, but are substantially integrated and united to form one entity, a human person. If so, Descartes would have been happy to affirm the psycho-somatic integrity of human beings. I wonder if Polkinghorne strongly disagrees with that form of dualism?

Why, though, call it dualism? Because, according to the New Testament, the resurrection body will not be the same as this physical body, which dies and decays. There will certainly be no spatio-temporal continuity between my body and my resurrection body, as my body will have ceased to exist long before the resurrection happens. Not only that. In 1 Corinthians 15, surely the crucial New Testament passage for any construal of what bodily resurrection is, the writer is clear that the laws of physics will be different in the resurrection world. There will be no decay, no entropy and, the writer says, the resurrection body will be as different from this physical body as corn is from the seed from which it sprang (1 Corinthians 15, 35–7). There is, this implies, a causal connection (and, in this case, a non-local causal connection) between the two, but no physical resemblance.

I personally will not care if, in the resurrection, I do not look like what I now am. On the contrary, I hope I will not do so. What age would my resurrected body be? Would babies still be babies when resurrected? These questions are faintly ridiculous, which helps to emphasise the point that such matters are not central to a hope for resurrection. What is central, however, is that I should remember what I have done and have been responsible for, that I should have some personal character that I have shaped throughout the course of my earthly life, and that I should have the same general desires, feelings and goals that I developed on earth. In other words, it is my mental characteristics that I care about, not my bodily characteristics.

---

[1]   'Meditations on First Philosophy' (1642), in *Descartes: Philosophical Writings*, trans. G.E.M. Anscombe and P. Geach (London: Nelson, 1954), Sixth Meditation, 117.

Those mental characteristics might be appropriately and naturally embodied in some way that allows me to express them and communicate with other persons, but I cannot envisage what precise way that would be, except that it would be very different from any stage of my earthly body. It follows that, whereas many of my mental properties depend upon my physical brain in this life, in a resurrection life whatever bodily properties I had would depend upon and express my mental properties, which would have been shaped in some quite different, pre-death, environment.

That is one reason why a dualistic view is important, because it allows my mental properties to be transferred to a different form of embodiment. The only relevant form of close similarity here is mental, not bodily. Embodiment may be essential to being fully human, but there are different forms of embodiment possible for the same person. It follows that my mind and my mental properties and capacities cannot be wholly dependent on the structure of this brain, since this brain will certainly cease to exist and will not simply be replicated in the world to come. Mind is essential to personal identity in a way that body is not.

You may not want to call this dualism, reserving that term for the view that minds exist more properly without bodies, as Plato held, although Descartes did not. Some philosophers, like John Searle, have called it 'dual-aspect monism', to stress that mind and body are distinct in kind, although together they form one unit. However, that view is ambiguous. For it is consistent with the belief that matter is the real causal basis of mind. Even if minds are different from brains, perhaps minds cannot exist without the brains that give rise to them, and minds cannot simply be decoupled and transferred to other forms of embodiment.

For this reason, I would prefer to speak of 'dual-aspect idealism', which postulates that minds can exist without brains, can be transferred to other form of embodiment, and indeed that matter exists primarily to enable certain sorts of mental properties to be expressed, so that in the end minds have causal and ontological priority over matter.

I have suggested that Christians should have no problems with this as a general statement, because God has causal and ontological priority over the material cosmos. However, are human minds not emergent from and dependent upon the material cosmos, so human minds are not causally prior to the environment in which they exist? However, Christians should not find this odd either. Christians have always believed that humans are creatures, wholly dependent for their existence upon God, so it is no surprise to know that they are dependent, and that they are not causally or ontologically prior to God. Therefore, why should they be causally prior to the environment that enables them to exist, and that God has created?

What matters is that matter has been created to enable minds to emerge and to exist, as natural parts of the cosmic process. Minds, once created, normally and naturally have the capacity to shape their own natures within limits, and to make significant moral decisions and relate to other persons in responsible ways. It is this responsible decision-making and self-shaping that will be judged by God at death, and will determine the future destiny of each human person. God will not judge people's bodies (except insofar as they have been responsibly shaped by conscious persons), but God will judge free actions. From that moment, what happens to minds will no longer depend on non-moral physical causes. It will depend upon what those minds have responsibly done during life. In that sense, life in the world to come will be shaped by mental, and not by physical, factors. Human minds may not be causally prior to human brains in this time, but in the world to come human minds, and what they have done and become, will be causally prior (with God's help) to their forms of embodiment in that resurrection age. We may be sophisticated 'dual-aspect' materialists in this world, but we will certainly be dual-aspect idealists in the next.

I believe Polkinghorne is committed to this view, and that this view is all that, and just what, Bishop Berkeley, wished to assert. So why does he not want to enter Bishop Berkeley's castle? A clue is given in his statement that 'The pattern (of atoms etc.) constitutes the physical expression of our continuing personality' (OW, 91). The hypothesis that a person is a specific pattern or structure of atoms or basic physical particles is quite important to Polkinghorne. Of course, when he says that such a pattern is the physical expression of our personality, this could mean that our personality might exist but not be physically expressed. There would then be more to a person than the physical pattern that expresses what they are. Is this the case?

This is not an easy question to answer. If we take a specific pattern of matter that constitutes the physical expression of a person and replicate that pattern, do we get the same person? In the TV series *Star Trek*, Captain Kirk has the physical configuration of his body dissolved and replicated in a different location, and then Captain Kirk is assumed to have been teleported. We can see it happen on television. In Vienna, sub-atomic particles can be teleported by transmitting their structure over a spatial interval. In the Vienna case, however, what actually happens is that, since all such particles are known to be exactly identical, if we replicate a specific structure of such particles and then destroy the original, we can be said to have teleported the structure. What has actually happened, however, is that we have replicated a physical structure and destroyed its original. What we have transported is information, not physical stuff. If that is what happens to Captain Kirk, will he be worried by the fact that he has been destroyed and an exact replica of him created from scratch?

The problem with the Kirk case is that we do not know that Kirk consists solely of a pattern of physical particles. Would a physical replica also be a mental replica, with all Kirk's memories, desires and character? Does the same physical basis entail the same mental content? For an outright materialist, the answer has to be 'yes' by definition. There is no separate mental content to consider. However, if there is an additional mental content (even as a distinct part of a 'psychophysical unity'), we cannot be sure. I think the honest answer is that this is a factual question that the moral prohibition on the killing of the innocent may forbid us to resolve. The connection between mental and physical phenomena seems to be a causal and contingent one, and such that the causal sequence does not just run in one direction, from physical to mental. Sometimes a mental act, like forming an intention, seems to cause physical effects. That means, logically, that the same cause could conceivably have different effects, or no effects at all, and that sometimes mental events (intentions, for example) cause brain events. If this is the case, a physical account of the brain would not be a complete account of the human person, since it would omit any mention of mental causes or of the mental effects that are contingently caused by physical states.

Of course, to say that causal sequences are contingent does not mean that they will actually be broken. The law of gravity is contingent. It could easily have been otherwise, but we do not expect it to cease to operate universally. Therefore, if we replicate a complete pattern of brain-states, the usual mental states associated with that brain may indeed be generated, if there is a contingent but general causal law to that effect. However, they may not be generated, and then we would have created a perfectly formed zombie, without any consciousness at all. Causal connections to mental states would simply be missing, and there would obviously be no conscious intentional actions. Otherwise, however, things may proceed very much as before, and we might be none the wiser. Zombies would perform on auto-pilot, and their behaviour might easily pass the Turing test for the existence of personhood. Yet there would in them be no conscious experiences or truly responsible actions. If this seems implausible, remember that some philosophers actually think consciousness is irrelevant to human personhood anyway.

My suggestion is that we should not perform a Captain Kirk experiment, which might well kill Kirk and beam up a zombie. I am not sure if Polkinghorne agrees with this or not. What he says is, 'We can accept a structural reductionism ... the units out of which all the entities of the physical world are constructed are just the elementary particles' (OW, 103). Under one interpretation, this is trivially correct. If and insofar as an entity is physical, it is constructed just out of elementary particles. Yet under another interpretation, it is radically false, at least for people who believe that human persons are entities in the physical world, but that they are not merely physical. They have irreducibly mental properties – a 'separate and additional spiritual component' – so they are not constructed just out of elementary particles. Structural reductionism is false.

Polkinghorne wants to deny 'conceptual reductionism', which says that we can give a complete description of a human person in purely physical terms. If you are a conceptual non-reductionist you say that there is nothing to humans but physical particles; that is the stuff, and the only stuff, out of which they are made. Yet when we come to describe humans, it is impossible to do so just by talking about the properties of the physical particles and the laws governing their interaction. I wonder if this really makes sense, however. It seems to me that speaking of intentions and experiences would then only be a sort of shorthand for the extremely long and unwieldy sentences mentioning all the movements of elementary particles that we do not have time for in real life. There is nothing going on but the physical; yet we find it necessary to have a different vocabulary that uses generalised descriptions involving human feelings and actions. I think this is only a matter of practical convenience. The physical is the only real. There is no additional mental stuff, and there are no additional mental causes.

That is, these days, a perfectly respectable philosophical position, but it does not differ significantly from reductive materialism. It is ontologically reductive materialism. All it adds is that we can talk about mental properties to save time and trouble. 'Psycho-physical dualism', on this reading, reduces ontologically to reductive materialism. It is not dualism, or dual-aspectism, at all. This impression is corroborated when Polkinghorne states (I do not claim that it represents his mature view, but he does say it): 'It is this information-bearing pattern that is the soul' (GH, 106). The soul is an information-bearing pattern, not a substantial entity.

There are well-known cases of information-bearing patterns. One is the chemical structure of DNA, which carries the information for constructing proteins that will build organic bodies. Another is the binary sequences on a CD disc, which carry the information for playing music when connected to appropriate translation devices. In such cases, there is a purely physical structure that carries information. Does Polkinghorne mean that the soul, as an information-bearing pattern, is a purely physical structure so organised as to carry information, that might in principle be transferred to a different physical structure? In this case, there would be no information without the physical pattern; the information lies in the pattern, and could not exist without it.

Or does he mean that the information is a mathematical sequence (like the string of 0s and 1s on a CD programme) that could be abstracted from any physical structure, and could exist in some sort of noetic world, waiting for possible material embodiments? Physicists sometimes talk of laws of nature in this way, as if they might exist without any physical universe, or even, in some unexplained way, give rise to physical universes.

Fully fledged materialists would have to select the former option, since whatever noetic mathematical sequences are, they are not material. And now Polkinghorne reveals his incipient Berkeleyan tendencies. For he says that there are 'noetic realms of rational skill, moral imperative and aesthetic delight ... forces are at work to draw out and enhance distinctive human potentialities' (ER, 56). These noetic realms are not material, and they are not parts of any existent human minds. The properties they have are those of rational intelligibility (truth), moral obligation (goodness) and aesthetic delight (beauty). Moreover, they are causally effective – they 'draw out' human possibilities. They are not passive abstract immaterial ideals to be contemplated, as they might be in Plato. They exert an attracting influence on human minds, leading such minds as respond positively to be shaped in a certain direction.

This is not really surprising, for Polkinghorne is a realist about God; he thinks God is supreme truth, intelligibility, goodness and beauty; that God exists and is not material; and that God draws human minds into greater knowledge of and unity with the divine being. The informational pattern that delineates the ideal form of fully actualised human personhood exists in the mind of God before it is embodied in any physical structure. Furthermore, if each human individual is unique, God may conceive of every unique human soul as an information-bearing pattern that may be more or less fully actualised in the physical universe. The soul would not be a purely physical structure, its genesis wholly dependent upon partly random physical processes. Each soul would be an eternal pattern in the mind of God, and that pattern would exert a causal influence on the way the physical universe develops to enable souls to be embodied and develop. The mind of God contains envisaged ideals and initiates a cosmos that progressively actualises many levels of consciousness, culminating so far in societies of partly self-developing sensitive and creative agents, whose potentialities it 'works to draw out'. These souls can be logically decoupled from this cosmos, for indeed as patterns they existed before the cosmos existed, and may well exist after it ends. This is quite a long way from materialism. The noetic realm has ontological and causal priority over the physical – Berkeley's castle begins to look more inviting.

Yet there is still a problem with this account of the soul as being identical with noetic patterns, for most Christians do not believe that each human soul pre-exists eternally (even though this thought gives sense to thinking of Jesus as eternally existent). Souls, Christians usually think, come into being with the genesis of a physical body. Moreover, 'eternal patterns' are rather static and impersonal, a bit like mathematical equations and not much like active and individual agents. Yet Polkinghorne says that the pattern that is the soul 'is modified with new experiences, insights and memories' (GH, 105). We can also speak of 'purifying and transforming the soul awaiting resurrection' (GH, 111). Can a *pattern* be modified, purified, transformed? Can it have new experiences and insights? Personal agents change and develop as they have new experiences and respond to them in uniquely creative ways, but information-bearing patterns are like blue-prints, wholly shaped by another, contents but not subjects of consciousness. The human soul is a subject and agent, not just a pattern.

Polkinghorne does think that 'basic personal experience of choice and responsibility' is a 'complementary aspect of the whole person' (OW, 114). This suggests that the soul is a subject of a unique history of experiences and agent of a unique sequence of responsible choices. It is inseparable from its mental content, its memory, character, intentions that have been formed as a result of its experiences. It needs an arena of knowledge and action, a material world from which it can receive experiences and in which it can act and interact with others. Therefore, an individual soul is not a separate substance, in the unrealistic and non-Cartesian sense that it could quite properly exist without any material or quasi-material environment, or even perhaps with quite different memories, character and intentions. It is a subject and agent that, with all its mental content, could be variously embodied if there was some means of transferring it to a different sort of body.

Polkinghorne believes in that possibility, and speaks of a 'reconstitution of the whole person in some other environment' (OW, 91), as the best way of thinking of the resurrection of the body. This is best conceived, I suggest, not as transferring a quasi-physical or mathematical pattern from one embodiment to another, but as transferring a living, acting subject with all its memories, feelings, thoughts and desires into another environment. The pattern constantly changes, and it changes partly by the conscious actions of a dynamic subject whose nature is expressed in the pattern, but who also changes the pattern by responsible action. The soul is not identical in a simple way to an information-bearing pattern. It is that which is expressed in the pattern, but which also changes the pattern, and which, in the Christian case, seeks to shape itself in its own uniquely appropriate way on the pattern of humanity that was definitively expressed in Jesus Christ.

Mention of the resurrection brings me to the gates of Berkeley's castle, from whence I hope to invite Professor Polkinghorne to cross over the drawbridge with me. I wonder whether replication is an adequate model for the resurrection of the body. If you take an information-bearing pattern and replicate it in another environment, what you are going to get is an exact copy (a perfect clone) of a person. St Paul does not seem to think that an exact copy will do the job, and it is not irrelevant to note that when he claimed to see the risen Lord what he saw was a blinding light, not a copy of Jesus' physical body. What Paul looks for is a transformation 'in the twinkling of an eye'. He is rather sceptical about whether we can imagine what such a transformed body would be like, but we can maybe go some way to sketching some possibilities.

If we are lucky, and we find ourselves living in the presence of God after death, what would be desirable is complete access to all our mortal experiences. We would certainly want painful experiences to be mitigated in some way, and even pleasant experiences to be placed in a richer context of the working out of God's purpose for creation. Yet if God is to judge us for what we have done, it would be desirable to be able to recall what we did, as well as to see what its consequences for others and for ourselves really were. We want a clearer vision of how we responded or failed to respond to the opportunities and challenges that we met during life, so that we know what we need to ask forgiveness for, and what the depth of God's forgiveness needs to be.

None of this can be given by the replication of any state of our earthly brains, for we have never, at any point in our lives, had such complete recall and extended knowledge of the context and consequences of our actions. It looks as though there is no conceivable brain-state that could give us such deepened awareness of and, we hope in many cases, deepened appreciation for, our earthly experiences. In other words, God will not be able to refer to any physical information-bearing pattern as the model for reconstituting us in the world to come. God will have to refer directly to those experiences in their distinctive ontological reality, and make them accessible to us, in ways that we are able to endure, in the light of God's wider knowledge of all experiences of other finite creatures that have ever been. Such accessibility to past experience will not depend upon the existence of any specific material state or brain state. It will be a form of direct access to our mental lives, independently of whatever physical basis those lives may have had on earth.

I also believe that part of Christian resurrection hope is that, as well as being forgiven for our sins and failures, we may have the possibility of realising many of the potentialities inherent in our characters that we failed to realise in this life. We hope to grow in the knowledge and love of God and of our fellow creatures, and in our understanding of the divine purpose for us and for creation. Such a possibility transcends any of the actual states of our brains during earthly life, for we have never at any time of our lives had the actual capacity to fulfil our potential to the full and without the frustrating elements of egoism, attachment and physical incapacity that are such a large part of our personalities. What we hope for in the world to come transcends by far any specific stage in the physical development (and degeneration) of our brains. In this respect also, God would not refer to any physical information-bearing pattern as a model for reconstituting us. God would not simply replicate some specific physical embodiment of our information-bearing pattern, for that would leave us with exactly the limitations and imperfections from which we hope to escape in resurrection. God needs to be able to transform our capacities in an environment that makes their realisation possible in a way that was never possible in our earthly bodies.

We will also live in an environment that is non-entropic, that will not decay and fade away. This is another respect in which the information that constitutes the physical structure of our bodies and brains will not be appropriate to an environment with a wholly different set of environmental laws and constraints. I am not pretending to be an expert on life in the world to come. Rather, building on the resurrection appearances of Jesus and on Christian beliefs about the resurrection of the body and eternal life, I have wished to suggest that these things point to our being able to exist in a very different world where our present physical structures will no longer be relevant. At this point, for Christians, materialism meets its nemesis, for it is we who will exist without physical bodies (bodies of 'flesh and blood') as we now possess them, and yet we will be the same persons, even if strangely renewed.

To enter Berkeley's castle is to see the distinctive importance of our spiritual lives as having immensely greater significance than the possession of physical bodies. Yet it is not at all to denigrate the physical. Berkeley's souls are not disembodied, as Plato's arguably were. They are properly and naturally expressed in a physical environment, within which they come to be and grow. They will never be wholly disembodied, but the form of their embodiment will be such that matter will be, as it is not yet, the unimpeded instrument and sacrament of spirit. Then we will know that matter cannot properly exist without mind, and that it is mind that gives to matter, in all its forms, its value and purpose.

In ending, I want to pay tribute to Professor Polkinghorne for his piercing insights into Christian beliefs, which arise from his scientific expertise. They are, I think, of fundamental importance for the future of Christian theology. I also want to affirm that I largely agree with Polkinghorne's general views of the nature and destiny of the human person. We are psycho-somatic unities, and we do hope to be resurrected in a new and more glorious environment. There is a noetic world – the mind of God – which is the pattern and ideal that exerts a causal influence on the genesis and development of this physical universe. Reductive physical accounts of the human person are grossly inadequate. The concept of 'information' in particular provides an additional resource to any purely physicalist account of the universe.

With all these things I agree, and am indebted to Professor Polkinghorne for their clear formulation by him. My comments in this paper are simply tweaks to his theological thinking, from a philosophical perspective – and a rather unfashionable one at present – of philosophical idealism. I hope it may persuade some that much modern science is wholly compatible with idealism, and that Polkinghorne's own view is much nearer to Berkeley's than he seems to think. Perhaps, after all, we do not have to retreat into the idealist castle, for that castle is the world in which we already exist: 'In God we live and move and have our being'.

Chapter 9

Theology and Scientific Cosmology

Fraser Watts

John Polkinghorne has made a towering contribution to the interface between theology and science, and I am greatly indebted to him. However, it would have been boring for me to focus on the many topics on which I agree with him. So, I have chosen to focus on a topic about which I have a different perspective from his: the interface between theology and cosmology. I do so with some trepidation, as this is very much his field of science rather than mine.

The interface between physics and scientific cosmology is a major theme in Polkinghorne's work. He has tackled a range of cosmological issues, including the origin of the universe, its fine-tuning, and its eventual end. He is particularly to be commended for tackling issues about the predicted demise of the universe, which raise difficult problems for the interface between science and theology, and which have been often been neglected.

However, I will suggest that Polkinghorne uses science rather differently in his treatment of the fine-tuned universe from his treatment of the end of the universe, building on science where it is theologically congenial, but using theology to sidestep the implications of science where they are inconvenient. I will advocate a more consistent use of a complementary perspectives methodology, similar to the one that Polkinghorne himself uses when handling the origin of the universe. According to this, I suggest that it makes no difference to the theological use of fine-tuning whether or not we have a scientific explanation of it.

I agree with Polkinghorne that there is no theological eschatology that can be recommended on scientific grounds. However, I will indicate a possible alternative approach to the end of the universe that has the merit of providing more continuity between the present and the eschatological future. Polkinghorne makes helpful use, in his treatment of eschatology, of the analogy to personal resurrection. I suggest that one of the most fruitful features of his approach is his interpretation of soul as an 'information-bearing pattern', and that it would be helpful for future work in theology and science to build on the use Polkinghorne makes of the concept of information.

Creation and Origins

Polkinghorne's work on the interface of cosmology and theology emphasises that the two disciplines are answering different questions, and I very much welcome that. He sees this particularly clearly when considering creation and origins. While cosmology is puzzling over the origin of the universe, the theology of creation is not primarily about its origin, but rather about how it arose from the purposes of God and has a continuing dependence on God. It is a good example, perhaps the best available example, of how theology and science are answering distinct but complementary questions. However, as I will indicate later, I am less sure that he stays with that same methodological approach when it comes to the anthropic principle and the end of the universe. I will suggest that, with the anthropic principle, science may become too determinative. In contrast, with the end of the universe, science may be too much side-lined.

I also very much welcome what Polkinghorne says about the way in which chance and necessity work together in creation.[1] He is, here, making at least two separate points. First, he is making a point about God. Using the terminology of Pannenberg (albeit using it to make a different point from the one Pannenberg makes), Polkinghorne is saying that God is both the 'ground of phenomenal order' and the 'free origin of contingent events'.[2] He is also making a point about how necessity and chance work fruitfully together in creation. Both orderliness and openness are needed for creation to be fruitful in the way it has been.

As far as terminology is concerned, I myself prefer 'order' and 'contingency' (terms that Polkinghorne also uses quite frequently) to 'necessity' and 'chance'. 'Necessity', taken at face value seems incompatible with chance, and 'chance' is a term that can too easily be used in misleading ways, such as the phrase 'due to chance', which seems to suggest that chance is some weird kind of non-causal causation.

However, the more significant point I want to make here is that all these terms, whether used in philosophy or in science, are terms that assume an inanimate or non-agency world. The discourse of theology is very different; it is a discourse that assumes agency, the agency of God.[3] There are other corresponding terms that belong to that kind of agency discourse; it is a discourse that speaks of purpose rather than necessity, and of freedom rather than chance. Agents have purposes, and agents allow (or achieve) freedom.

Purpose is, of course, an important concept in Polkinghorne's theology. Over the years he has also had an increasing amount to say about how God allows creation freedom.[4] On this latter point, incidentally, I think he has sometimes been misunderstood. I do not think that in his 'kenotic' theology he is implying that creation is in any sense independent of God; that would be incompatible with so much of what he has written. My main point here is that the transition from the

---

[1]   John Polkinghorne, *Science and Providence: God's Interaction with the World*, London, SPCK, 1989.

[2]   Ibid., 63.

[3]   Fraser N. Watts, ed., *Creation: Law and Probability*, Aldershot, Ashgate, 2008.

[4]   J.C. Polkinghorne, *The Work of Love: Creation as Kenosis*, Grand Rapids, MI, Eerdmans, 2001.

non-agency discourse of necessity and chance to the more distinctively theological and agency discourse of purpose and freedom is one that needs to be handled as explicitly and carefully as possible.[5]

Another recurrent theme in Polkinghorne's writing about creation concerns the intelligibility of the world, and he has become increasingly interested in the role of mathematics in that intelligibility. He has a strongly Platonic view of mathematics, which he sees as discovered rather than created.[6] Also, if I follow him, he sees mathematics as transcending creation, and eternal. If there is a dualism in Polkinghorne's thought (and I imply no disapproval in using the term 'dualism' here), it is perhaps a dualism of mathematics and matter; that is a point to which I will return.

Fine-tuning of the Universe

I turn now to the anthropic principle, and to how Polkinghorne handles that. It is a topic that I would want to handle somewhat differently, and I will explain why and how. I diverge from Polkinghorne in this area only with considerable hesitancy, because the scientific field involved is much more his than mine. I also have nothing to add to the admirable clarity with which he expounds the remarkable fine-tuning that has led to carbon-based life.

One terminological point is that I prefer to call this area the fine-tuned universe, rather than the anthropic principle. Polkinghorne would agree that 'fine-tuned' is more appropriate, although he often uses the better established 'anthropic principle'. There are three inter-related reasons for preferring 'fine-tuned': (i) It seems to me best to start as objectively and descriptively as possible. The 'anthropic principle' seems to me to be a theory to explain the facts of the fine-tuned universe, and not the only candidate in the ring; (ii) What is remarkable in cosmology is that the universe is fine-tuned for stable matter and for carbon. There is nothing in the cosmology that points to humans, or has anything to say about how we got from primitive carbon-based life to humans. That is a matter for evolution, not for cosmology; (iii) The phrase 'anthropic principle' can easily lead to a conflation of science and theology, although that is something to which Polkinghorne would in principle be opposed, as he has said very clearly in *Scientists as Theologians*.[7] Polkinghorne would not disagree with any of that.

---

[5]   See Watts, *Creation: Law and Probability*.

[6]   J.C. Polkinghorne, *Meaning in Mathematics*, Oxford, Oxford University Press, 2011; see also J.C. Polkinghorne, 'Mathematics and Natural Theology', in Russell Re Manning, J.H. Brooke and F. Watts, eds, *Oxford Handbook of Natural Theology*, Oxford, Oxford University Press, 2011.

[7]   J.C. Polkinghorne, *Scientists as Theologians: A Comparison of the Writings of Ian Barbour, Arthur Peacocke and John Polkinghorne*, London, SPCK, 1996.

Like most people, Polkinghorne implicitly assumes that a theological explanation of the fine-tuned universe is an alternative to multiverse theory. Although I am aware that I am in a minority here, I really want to question whether they are alternatives. In handling creation, Polkinghorne is very clear that theology and science are answering different questions, and so are not alternatives. It seems to me that he does not hold to that methodological principal quite so consistently in his treatment of the fine-tuned universe.

I suggest that it is perfectly possible to interpret the fine-tuning of the universe theologically, regardless of whether one assumes a single universe or multiple universes. In the former case, I would assume, as Polkinghorne does, that God chose a universe that would be uniquely fruitful. However, if you assume multiple universes, it is perfectly possible to assume that God used chance processes to ensure that at least one universe would arise that was remarkably fruitful.

In other contexts, as I have already indicated, Polkinghorne is very clear that chance can provide an opportunity for God's creativity. It is a point that has been made more frequently in the context of the evolution (especially by Arthur Peacocke[8]) than in cosmology. However, I see no reason why the same point does not apply in both cases. Therefore, I see no reason why multiverse theory cannot be interpreted theologically.

Even if that point is accepted, I suspect that most people would not see the theological interpretation of a single universe and of multiverses as being on the same footing. The difference is presumably that, if multiple universes are assumed, there is some kind of quasi-scientific explanation of why there should be one strikingly fruitful universe, but there is no such explanation if only one universe is assumed.

Actually, I do not think the resort to chance in multiverse theory is at all satisfying as a scientific theory. A good scientific theory includes insights about processes, and makes testable predictions. There is not much to be said in favour of multiverse theory as a scientific theory, on those grounds, except that it is not a theological explanation of why there is a fruitful universe.

However, I come back to the methodological point that theology and science are answering different and complementary questions; they are not offering competing answers to the same question. I suggest that if we really take that principle seriously it makes no difference to the credibility of a theological interpretation whether or not there is a scientific (or at least non-theological) explanation available. Although it is more hinted at than explicitly stated, I suspect that Polkinghorne makes too much of the fact that we have no scientific explanation for why a single universe might be fruitful. I suspect that he, like many others, assumes that a theological interpretation gains credibility from the lack of a scientific explanation.

You might like to engage in the thought experiment of imagining that we eventually get a scientific explanation of the fruitfulness of a single universe.

[8]   A.R. Peacocke, *Theology for a Scientific Age: Being and Becoming – Natural, Divine and Human*, 2nd edn, London, SCM, 1993.

Suppose, for example, that inflation theory develops over the decades to the point where it gives us a scientific understanding of why the balance between forces of expansion and contraction was exactly right to produce stable matter. Suppose also that nuclear resonances are not random, and that we eventually get some scientific explanation of why there is a resonance that facilitates the formation of carbon. You do not have to regard those as likely possibilities. My point is just that, if there were any such scientific developments, it ought to make no difference to the theological interpretation of a single, fruitful universe. If you accept that, it follows that it affords no advantage to such a theological interpretation that we currently have no scientific explanation.

I would make a converse point to atheists who are attracted to multiverse theory because of what they imagine to be its anti-religious implications. As I have already said, I see no problem in giving a theological interpretation of multiverses; they can be seen as God's way of ensuring that there is at least one remarkably fruitful universe. This is, admittedly, the additional question of the centrality of God's revelation of himself in Jesus Christ. However, I do not find it difficult to make the theological assumption that God will reveal himself in appropriate ways to any creatures in any universe who are capable of receiving that revelation, and will do so through the second person of the Trinity. Along those lines, Christian theologians can come to terms with multiverses.

The other reason why atheists are presumably attracted to multiverse theory is that they imagine that it deprives religious people of the opportunity to build any theological conclusions on a scientifically inexplicable single, fruitful universe. However, as I have also said, I do not assume that it is necessarily inexplicable from a scientific point of view. Even if it were, I would not want to take any theological advantage from it. Given the way I would approach a theological interpretation of the fine-tuned universe, it makes no difference to me whether fine-tuning is scientifically inexplicable or not. So, atheists do not need to try to deprive me of an advantage that I am not claiming in the first place.

Natural theology used to claim that there could be no explanation of why creatures were so well adapted to their habitats, other than that God made them so. With the wisdom of hindsight, it was a foolish claim. That kind of natural theology was hopelessly undermined by Darwin. I suggest that it is just as unwise to assume that the fine-tuned universe will never be explained by science. However, I can hear the objection to that, one that I think Polkinghorne himself would make, that the two cases are not comparable at all. The adaptiveness of species to habitats is the kind of thing that science can explain, whereas the fine-tuning of the universe is so fundamental that science could never explain it.

It is hard to be sure where the boundaries of science lie. I am sure that a careful historical study would show that there are many things that used to be thought to be outside science, but which science has eventually tackled successfully. What currently seems to defy scientific explanation is probably a poor guide as to where the boundaries of science actually lie. It is also hard to find compelling arguments of principle for why science can explain some things and not others.

It is an issue addressed in Michael Ruse's recent book on *Science and Spirituality*.[9] He rejects the old positivist assertion that all questions that cannot be answered by science are meaningless. He takes the view that there are some fundamental questions that are coherent and meaningful, which science cannot answer, but which religion may be able to answer. However, it is interesting that he has no very principled view about exactly which questions fall into that category. He gives examples (Why is there something rather than nothing? What is the foundation of morality? What is consciousness? What is the point of it all?[10]), but admits that others would give different examples. He is also explicit that his list of questions arises from the currently predominant version of science that is based on the machine metaphor, and that if science adopted a different fundamental metaphor it could lead to a different list of questions, and perhaps a more limited one.

It is beyond the scope of this paper to go deeply into all this, and I can do little more than state my instincts. I am suspicious of the idea that there are two clearly different sets of questions, one handled by science, and one handled by religion or in other non-scientific ways. I think an approach to these issues in terms of dimensionality and complementarity would be more helpful than a sharp distinction between two sets of questions. On this view, science and religion can each make a contribution to most questions, although in some questions the dominant contribution comes from science, and in others the main contribution comes from religion. I am not persuaded that every feature of the fine-tuned universe necessarily falls into the category of questions that science cannot explain.

Before leaving this topic, I must add that I very much welcome the fact that Polkinghorne does not believe in trying to build an argument for the existence of God on the basis of the puzzling facts of the fine-tuned universe. He repeatedly says that natural theology is a matter of 'insight', not of 'argument', and I completely agree that this is the character of the revived natural theology that he (and I) would wish to see. However, when he comes to the detail of the fine-tuned universe, he sometimes writes as though he were offering argument, and not just an insight (a point that Re Manning takes up in his chapter in this volume).

The End of the World

The third cosmological topic with which Polkinghorne deals is the end of the world,[11] and it is the one on which he has made the most original contribution. It is probably the most challenging topic in theology and science. If there is anything

      [9]   Michael Ruse, *Science and Spirituality: Making Room for Faith in an Age of Science*, Cambridge, Cambridge University Press, 2010.

      [10]   Ibid., 146.

      [11]   J.C. Polkinghorne and Michael Welker, eds, *The End of the World and the Ends of God: Science and Theology on Eschatology*, Harrisburg, PA, Trinity Press International,

in science that is inconsistent with a theological interpretation of the world, it is probably the predictions of cosmology concerning the future of the universe. This is not easy ground for anyone concerned with the integration of theology and science, and Polkinghorne has not shirked it, but has given it unrivalled care and attention. The only comparable collection of work on the end of the universe is that edited by George Ellis on *The Far-Future Universe*,[12] and the only individual who has made a contribution of comparable thoroughness to this difficult topic is Robert J. Russell.[13]

Of course, one can try to offer a theological interpretation of the predicted demise of the world, and some have attempted that. For those who want to offer a theological interpretation of the end of the world, of an apocalyptic kind, a big crunch is more richly suggestive than gradual dispersal and cooling, 'fry' is more in tune with Biblical apocalyptic than 'freeze'. However, it is 'freeze' that is now the standard prediction, and it lends itself less well to theological interpretation than 'fry'.

It is not easy for theologians to be methodologically consistent in how they handle the fine-tuned universe and the end of the universe. The facts of the fine-tuned universe are theologically congenial, so the natural response is to simply accept them, and to offer a theological interpretation. The facts of the predicted end of the universe are theologically inconvenient, so it is tempting to try to find ways of not accepting them, or at least not accepting their finality. Polkinghorne does not accept their finality, and neither do I. However, I remain uncomfortable about this methodological inconsistency, and I put that on record, although I see no good alternative.

If the bleak future for the universe that cosmology predicts is not the end of the story for the universe, how might it be transformed? The helpful methodological move that Polkinghorne makes is to draw an analogy between the death of the individual and the dispersal and cooling of the universe. In both cases, there is a problem about how to reconcile those bleak eventualities with a religiously based hope.

Polkinghorne thinks that the only pointer we have towards what a new or transformed creation might be like is the body of the risen Christ. He is surely right about that. Russell has made a similar point.[14] Polkinghorne would not want to dismiss reports of the risen Christ as mere wish fulfilment born of the strong faith of the early Christians, nor would he see resurrection discourse as just a way of talking about the presence of Christ in the social body of the early church.

2000; also J.C. Polkinghorne, *The God of Hope and the End of the World*, New Haven, CT, Yale University Press, 2002.

[12]   George F.R. Ellis, *The Far-Future Universe: Eschatology from a Cosmic Perspective*, Philadelphia, PA, Templeton Foundation Press, 2002.

[13]   Robert J. Russell, *Cosmology: From Alpha to Omega: The Creative Mutual Interaction of Theology and Science*, Minneapolis, MN, Fortress Press, 2008.

[14]   Ibid., chap. 10.

Polkinghorne and I would both assume that there *was* a risen body, and that it was a transformation of the pre-crucifixion body.

A key question here is whether the transformation that Jesus' body underwent is something about which science could ever at least speculate, or whether it is a question that is in principle totally outside science, and must remain so for all time. I see no reason why science should not eventually develop in such a way as to enable it to at least engage with this question, although I admit that I can see no arguments of principle one way or the other. If we do at least get some speculative understanding of how Jesus' body was transformed, that will help us to understand how the world may eventually be transformed in a way that will either change current cosmological predictions, or at least undermine their finality.

With both the end of the universe and the death of the individual, Polkinghorne, like most contemporary theological thinkers, is not attracted by a purely dualistic solution. He does not see the hope of the individual as lying in the survival of a disembodied soul. Similarly, he does not see hope for the universe as lying in some continuation of purely mental or spiritual life when the universe is no longer able to support physical life. However, if there is any kind of incipient dualism in Polkinghorne's thought, it is a dualism that contrasts matter with information. Polkinghorne also has a very strong view of the importance of information. Indeed I suggest that Polkinghorne's theology of information is one of the most significant aspects of his thought, and one that has become increasingly prominent.[15]

There are several inter-related strands in Polkinghorne's ideas about information:

1. He is sympathetic to an emerging ontology that sees information as the fundamental stuff of the universe (rather than matter or energy). It is a view most evocatively expressed by John Wheeler in his 'it from bit' soundbite, by which he meant that all things physical are information-theoretic in origin.[16]

2. Polkinghorne is also intrigued by the role that active information plays in self-organising systems, and how the whole can influence the parts in such systems; he has been influenced by the work of Stuart Kauffman in this area.[17]

3. He sees information as having a key role in the mediation of divine action, providing a non-energetic way in which God can influence events, and playing a role analogous to that of active information in self-organising systems.

[15]   See e.g. J.C. Polkinghorne, *Theology in the Context of Science*, New Haven, CT, Yale University Press, 2009.

[16]   John Wheeler, 'Information, Physics, Quantum: The Search for Links', in W. Zurek, ed., *Complexity, Entropy, and the Physics of Information*, Redwood City, CA, Addison-Wesley, 1990.

[17]   Stuart A. Kauffman, *At Home in the Universe: The Search for Laws of Self-Organization and Complexity*, New York, Oxford University Press, 1995.

4. He sees the human soul as an 'information-bearing pattern', and life after death as being the survival of that information-bearing pattern, pending its re-instantiation by God in a transformed body in the new creation.

Polkinghorne, like many contemporary thinkers in the Judeo-Christian tradition, favours a psychosomatic view of the human person in which the body continues in a transformed way. Similarly, he favours a new creation in which matter is also transformed. If an individual can survive as an information-bearing pattern, then perhaps there could be some future for the universe as information rather than as matter, making the inability of the material universe to continue to support carbon-based life of limited consequence.

Although Polkinghorne is no dualist, it would not be difficult for someone to take his emphasis on information, and to develop it in a more dualistic way than he does himself, although it would be a very integrative form of dualism (or a 'dual-aspect monism') as there is no sharp disjunction between information and matter. 'Matter' has increasingly been used in an expanded sense, as physics has developed. It no longer refers to irreducible hard stuff, but to whatever such hard stuff arises from, or even to what physics studies. So, information is distinct from, but not ultimately separable from hard matter. As Polkinghorne notes, this has continuity with the Thomistic tradition that sees soul as the 'form' of the body, not as some wholly separate substance.

Sudden or Gradual Transformation?

There are two basic approaches to the problem of how to reconcile the decay of the universe with the Christian hope. I think Polkinghorne settles too quickly for one of these rather than other, and I would like to see the choice debated in a more even-handed way. The basic question is whether to postulate a sudden or a gradual transition from the present condition to the hoped-for future. Polkinghorne envisages a sudden transition. He assumes that the universe will continue inexorably on its path towards being unable to support life but that, at some point, God will bring a new creation into being.

He is well aware of the problem of reconciling continuity with discontinuity here, and he tries to do that by saying that the new creation will not be *ex nihilo*, but *ex vetere*. The new creation will arise out of the decay of the old creation. It can therefore be said to redeem the old creation, and to justify hope arising within the old creation. Although this, in some sense, balances continuity with discontinuity, it seems to me to weight things on the side of discontinuity to a degree that I find theologically uncomfortable.

I am also uneasy, methodologically, about the nature of the interaction between science and theology in Polkinghorne's proposal for a new creation. There is little dialogue or collaboration between the two disciplines. Science poses the problem, and theology provides the solution.

Despite these problems, it would be a rash person who claimed to be able to do better. However, I suggest that a more gradualist view of the transformation of matter is at least worth considering as an alternative. Rather than assuming that there is a sudden transformation of matter at a point of new creation, one could propose a gradual transformation of matter within this creation. Teilhard de Chardin proposes a gradual spiritualisation of matter, and it is not difficult to find roots of that idea in the thinking of St Paul, especially in Romans Chapter 8.

It is hard to know how to develop such a proposal in terms that physics could understand, and it is not easy to see how to reconcile it with a thermodynamic drift to disorder. However, if a gradual spiritualisation of matter were to happen, it is doubtful whether the values of the basic forces would remain unchanged. The concept of spiritualisation of matter seems to imply a weakening of gravity, for example. If there began to be such radical changes to matter within the present universe, the basis of cosmological predictions would be undermined. It would be hard to know what to predict, but the present prediction of dispersal and cooling would not necessarily apply any more.

Robert J. Russell has made a similar argument for a transformation of the universe, brought about by the resurrection, and which changes the basis on which cosmological predictions are made.

> ... [I]f God is free to act in radically new ways (which of course God is!) not only in human history but in the ongoing history of the universe, then the future of the cosmos will not be what science predicts. Instead the cosmic far future will be based on a radically new kind of divine action which began with the resurrection of Jesus, and this new act of God cannot be reduced to, or explained by, the current laws of nature, that is, by God's actions in the past history of the universe. In short, we could say that the "freeze" or "fry" predictions for the cosmological future might have applied had God in Easter, and if God were not to continue to act to bring forth the ongoing cosmological transformation of the universe. Because of Easter and God's promise for its eschatological completion, however, the freeze or fry predictions will not come to pass.[18]

Theologically, I prefer a gradual transformation of the present creation to a sudden intervention by God to bring about a new creation. It also seems to me to provide a better balance between continuity and discontinuity, providing greater continuity with the present creation, and providing a better ground for hope in this creation, something that I have argued elsewhere is important in eschatology.[19] Such an approach allows more scope for us to participate in, and contribute to, the transformation of creation. It also, as Russell points out, gives more explicit credit to the role of the resurrection in the transformation of the universe.

---

[18]   Russell, *Cosmology*, 307.
[19]   Fraser N. Watts, *Theology and Psychology*, Aldershot, Ashgate, 2002.

So what is against this vision of a gradual transformation of the material creation? Science; there is absolutely no support for it in contemporary science. However, I am not too deterred by the fact that, a mere 2000 years after the resurrection, there is not yet any scientific evidence for a progressive transformation of matter. Let us wait and see (although we will have to wait far beyond any of our lifetimes). I do not want to rule it out, and I am not convinced that current cosmological predictions will last for ever.

It is interesting that the predominant stance on this issue has changed from one period to another. Peter Bowler has described how, in the interwar years, people were more interested in a religiously motivated program of building a less materialistic science.[20] Something similar was also evident in the approach to science and religion of the journal, *Theoria to Theory*, produced by the Epiphany Philosophers in Cambridge from 1966 to 1981, which was characterised by radical science, contemplative religion and rigorous philosophy. A vision of a theologically based transformation of science is currently out of fashion, but may not always remain so.

Metaphysics

Polkinghorne emphasises the importance of metaphysics in science, and in the dialogue between science and theology (and again I would agree with him). If theology is to challenge science, the main way in which it can do so is by challenging the metaphysical assumptions with which science is intertwined. I would want to emphasise the provisionality of contemporary science. One reason for that is the extent to which contemporary science is intertwined with particular metaphysical assumptions that are contingent, and quite likely to change. Another is that there are clearly major scientific questions that we so far have no idea how to tackle. That suggests to me that we are still at the foothills of building a complete science, and that much is likely to change as science advances through one paradigm shift after another.

Polkinghorne has often emphasised the role of metaphysics in cosmology, and I believe he is right to do so. The sciences differ in the extent to which they raise metaphysical issues, and I think it would be a correct generalisation to say that the more a particular area of science raises metaphysical issues, the more it also raises theological issues. Cosmology is certainly an area of science that engages very strongly with metaphysics. (So, in different ways, do evolutionary biology and artificial intelligence.) It is because of the metaphysics intertwined with cosmology that the interface between cosmology and theology is so rich and fruitful.

I think there are two rather different points to be made about metaphysics and cosmology, one from the perspective of science itself, the other from the

---

[20] Peter J. Bowler, *Reconciling Science and Religion: The Debate in Early-Twentieth-Century Britain*, Chicago, IL, University of Chicago Press, 2001.

perspective of popular interest in science. There has been increasing recognition by philosophers of science, especially since the 1960s, of the role of metaphysical assumptions in science. Rom Harré has been one of the key voices emphasising the metaphysical nature of science itself. I suggest that the notion of 'paradigm' is helpful in understanding the role of metaphysics in science, and that a fruitful way of understanding what changes when there is a paradigm shift is to say that the metaphysical assumptions of science change. The general trend in the development of science has been towards expanding the range of metaphysical assumptions, towards (i) recognising an increasingly rich ontology of the basic stuff of the universe, and (ii) recognising an increasingly rich diversity of processes in the universe. That is a metaphysical change that has been fruitful for the interface with theology.

However, I would also want to call attention to the popular fascination with cosmology, and suggest that such fascination largely stems from cosmology being an arena in which the public can do metaphysical thinking. Certain areas of science, cosmology especially, afford a contemporary secular language in which metaphysical assumptions can be explored. No doubt there was a time when metaphysics was done within the domain of theology. Now, people do metaphysics in a range of secular discourses, such as cosmology. Speaking as a psychologist, cosmology seems to provide a screen on which people can project their metaphysical assumptions.[21]

That raises the question of whether the contemporary cosmological metaphysics is anti-theological, in the sense that John Milbank would say that modern social theory is anti-theological,[22] or whether it is just a-theological, as Dixon, among others, suggests.[23] I suggest it is sometimes one and sometimes the other, and it is useful to notice which is going on. Cosmology can be developed in an anti-theological way, as multiverse theory currently is (even though I have argued that the anti-theological thrust of multiverse theory is unjustified), *or* it can be developed in a way that is incipiently but not necessarily theological.

Conclusion

John Polkinghorne has made an important contribution on the interface of theology and scientific cosmology, as he has across the whole sweep of topics on the interface of theology and science. However, I have raised issues about his treatment of both the fine-tuned universe and the end of the universe. On the fine-tuned universe, it seems to me very important to keep clearly in focus that science

---

[21]   Watts, *Theology and Psychology*.

[22]   John Milbank, *Theology and Social Theory: Beyond Secular Reason*, Oxford, Basil Blackwell, 1993.

[23]   Thomas Dixon, 'Theology, Anti-Theology and Atheology: From Christian Passions to Secular Emotions', *Modern Theology* 15 (1999): 297–330.

and theology are answering separate and distinct questions. A key corollary of that in this area is that it makes no difference to a theological interpretation of the fine-tuned universe that we currently have no scientific explanation of it. I would want to emphasise that there is no theological benefit in a lack of scientific explanation.

The end of the universe is one of the most difficult problems on the interface of theology and science, and one with which Polkinghorne has wrestled thoroughly and rigorously. The uncomfortable fact is that it is hard to make any proposal in this area that is acceptable theologically and for which any scientific support can be claimed.

There does not seem to be any satisfactory solution, or at least of not one that can yet be discerned. However, I have urged the gradual transformation of the universe as a possible alternative to the new creation theory that Polkinghorne favours. At least it is an alternative that merits careful discussion.

Chapter 10

Christian Hope in Dialogue with Natural Science: John Polkinghorne's Incorporation of Bottom-up Thinking into Eschatology

Junghyung Kim

This chapter aims to explore eminent scientist–theologian John Polkinghorne's original contribution to current dialogue between Christian eschatology and physical cosmology. I will first discuss how he brings scientific and meta-scientific insights into a fruitful dialogue with Christian hope for the redemptive transformation of our universe. Then, in order to highlight the significance of his contribution, I will put his eschatological discussion side by side with the cosmic eschatology of Jürgen Moltmann. Despite the fact that they represent different modes of thinking, I will show that they agree upon the cornerstones of Christian eschatology— divine faithfulness as the ultimate ground of hope, Christ's resurrection as the anticipation of cosmic destiny, continuities and discontinuities both required by *creatio ex vetere*, and *theosis* as the goal of God's creation. I will argue that these fundamental convictions should lay the foundation of subsequent eschatology– cosmology dialogues. The next discussion of Polkinghorne's threefold criticism of recent eschatological discussions will lead us into an interesting dialogue between the two theologians. In particular, I will discuss their different modes of thinking, different definitions of temporality of the eternal life, and different timescales. In the process, I hope, it will be revealed that the two theologians' eschatological ideas have greater affinities than they first appear to. Be that as it may, I will argue that Polkinghorne's emphasis on bottom-up thinking is to be taken as a legitimate challenge to Moltmann's top-down eschatology. In the final analysis, I will suggest that the attempt to overcome the current dissonance between biblical eschatology and physical cosmology needs to be continued.

Dissonance between Eschatology and Cosmology

Today Christian eschatology suffers from its "dissonance" with physical cosmology. It is a widespread consensus in today's scientific community that our universe will witness the inevitable death of all life on earth—probably in the near future, or definitely in the far future. There are three different cosmological scenarios of the ultimate fate of the universe: "open," "flat" and "closed." Unfortunately, all of them agree upon eventual cosmic futility. The first two scenarios describe an ever-expanding universe in which all the physical materials will come to a chilly equilibrium ("freeze"). According to the third scenario, the now expanding universe will some day cease to expand and begin to contract, eventually ending up with the hot Big Crunch ("fry"). Whether "freeze or fry," there seems no possibility that life can continue to survive in the far future universe.[1]

This bleak picture of the cosmic future led several leading scientists to believe that cosmic history is ultimately absurd. The prediction of eventual futility makes the present fruitfulness of life on earth look like a meaningless fluke. Steven Weinberg's aphorism is much-quoted: "It is very hard to realize that this [world of ours] is just a tiny part of an overwhelmingly hostile universe. It is even harder to realize that this present universe has evolved from an unspeakably unfamiliar early condition, and faces a future extinction of endless cold or intolerable heat. The more the universe seems comprehensible, the more it also seems pointless."[2] From this judgment it is a short step to argue that the ultimate absurdity of cosmic history would disprove that there is a creator who has good purpose for the creation and sufficient power to accomplish the purpose.

Owing to the dissonance between science's prediction of eventual cosmic futility and Christian hope for the final consummation of cosmic history, some theologians rejected the former in favor of the latter. For instance, John Macquarrie says, "if it were shown that the universe is indeed headed for an all-enveloping death, this might seem to constitute a state of affairs so negative that it might be held to falsify Christian faith and abolish Christian hope."[3] Likewise, Ted Peters argues that "if the future brings what scientific cosmologists predict, freeze or fry, then theological hope will be dashed."[4]

No one who takes seriously the bottom-up constraints of science upon theology[5] would dare deny that the current dissonance between cosmology and

[1]   Cf. William R. Stoeger, "Scientific Accounts of Ultimate Catastrophes in Our Life-Bearing Universe," in *The End of the World and The Ends of God: Science and Theology on Eschatology*, eds John Polkinghorne and Michael Welker (Harrisburg: Trinity, 2000), 30–31. As for the future of the universe, according to Stoeger, scientists predict many *contingent* possible catastrophic threats to the earth, on the one hand, and *definitely* expected events, such as the destruction of the habitable solar system and the death of the universe itself, on the other.

[2]   Steven Weinberg, *The First Three Minutes* (New York: Basic Books, 1977), 154.

[3]   John Macquarrie, *Principles of Christian Theology* (London: SCM Press, 1977), 256.

[4]   Ted Peters, introduction to *Resurrection: Theological and Scientific Assessments*, eds Ted Peters, Robert John Russell and Michael Welker (Grand Rapids, MI: Eerdmans, 2002), xiv.

[5]   For instance, Arthur Peacocke, speaking of "a hierarchy of disciplines" which reflects "hierarchies of complexity" among the phenomena, argues for what is often called "epistemic holism": cf. *Theology for A Scientific Age: Being and Becoming— Natural, Divine, and Human* (Minneapolis, MN: Fortress, 1993), 214–18. According to epistemic holism, disciplines of lower levels "constrain" those of upper levels, while the

eschatology poses a serious challenge to Christian hope. There are, however, only a few thinkers who have faced this challenge squarely. With this in mind, I believe it counts as one of the greatest achievements of eminent scientist–theologian John Polkinghorne that he insists on the implication of Christ's resurrection for the ultimate destiny of the universe.

This paper aims to explore Polkinghorne's original contribution to the current dialogue between Christian eschatology and physical cosmology. I will first discuss how he brings scientific and meta-scientific insights into a fruitful dialogue with Christian hope for the redemptive transformation of our universe. In order to highlight the significance of his contribution, I will then put his eschatological discussion side by side with the cosmic eschatology of Jürgen Moltmann. Despite the fact that they represent different modes of thinking (top-down vs bottom-up), I will show that they agree upon the major cornerstones of Christian eschatology— divine faithfulness as the ultimate ground of hope, the resurrection of Jesus Christ as the anticipation of cosmic destiny, continuities and discontinuities both required by *creatio ex vetere*, and *theosis* as the goal of God's creation. Also, I will argue that these theological convictions should lay the foundation of subsequent eschatology–cosmology dialogues.

The next discussion of Polkinghorne's threefold criticism of recent eschatological discussions will lead us into an interesting dialogue between two theologians. In particular, I will discuss their different modes of thinking, different definitions of temporality of the eternal life, and different timescales. In the process, I hope, it will be revealed that two theologians' eschatological ideas have greater affinities than first appears. Be that as it may, I will argue that Polkinghorne's emphasis on bottom-up thinking is to be taken as a legitimate challenge to Moltmann's top-down eschatology. In the final analysis, I will suggest that the attempt to overcome the current dissonance between biblical eschatology and physical cosmology needs to be continued.

Bottom-up Thinker Speaks of the Eschatological Future of the Universe

Polkinghorne is convinced that the ultimate destiny of the universe as God's creation will be fulfillment, not futility. However, the end of the universe cannot be conceived of in terms of evolutionary optimism, since such an optimistic expectation contradicts scientific prognostication of eventual cosmic futility. Nor

---

latter are not "reduced" to the former. Robert John Russell derives from this insight an invaluable conclusion for the eschatology–cosmology dialogue: "it makes abundantly clear that cosmology as a part of physics places constraints on all the supervening disciplines, including theology. Thus scholars who view the bodily resurrection of Jesus as a proleptic event of the transformation of the universe into the New Creation must face this challenge from scientific cosmology squarely and exhaustively." Robert John Russell, *Cosmology: From Alpha to Omega* (Minneapolis, MN: Fortress Press, 2008), 7.

is the universe supposed to come to an abrupt end followed by second creation out of nothing, for such an apocalyptic expectation weakens theological conviction of divine consistency. Instead, God will bring to fulfillment nothing but the present physical universe by transforming it through *creatio ex vetere* (creation out of the old).[6] Therefore, there will be both continuities and discontinuities between the old creation and the new creation.

Since *creatio ex vetere* presupposes both continuities and discontinuities in the redemptive fulfillment of the universe, Polkinghorne argues that science may contribute to Christian eschatology as regards the continuous aspects, even if the discontinuous aspects would belong to the province of theology.[7] Here lies Polkinghorne's original contribution: namely, meta-scientific or bottom-up exploration of continuities between the old creation and the new creation, the area thus far neglected. His discussion of "some questions and some insights from science" seeks to give "a modest degree of substance" to Christian hope, thus overcoming "implausible airy fantasies" widespread among eschatological discussions by systematic theologians.[8] In the following I will first explicate where Polkinghorne finds the ultimate ground of his cosmic hope, and then look at his discussion of continuities and discontinuities involved in *creatio ex vetere*.

Ultimate Ground of Hope

Despite his emphasis on science's contribution to eschatology, Polkinghorne does not think that Christian hope can be grounded solely upon bottom-up thinking, as if the potentiality of fulfillment were already built into present reality. The universal futility in the future, as science extrapolates from the past and present, effectively disproves any idea of cosmic fulfillment solely from within.[9] To our relief, however, "the ultimate future does not belong to scientific extrapolation but to divine faithfulness."[10]

This theological conviction leads Polkinghorne to distinguish eschatological hope from "Promethean presumption" or "utopian myth of progress." If scientific prediction of eventual futility is taken seriously, then the only possible source of a true hope is "the eternal faithfulness of the God who is the Creator and Redeemer

---

[6]   John Polkinghorne, "Eschatology: Some Questions and Some Insights from Science," in *The End of the World and The Ends of God: Science and Theology on Eschatology*, eds John Polkinghorne and Michael Welker (Harrisburg, PA: Trinity, 2000), 29–30.

[7]   Ibid., 30.

[8]   John Polkinghorne, *The God of Hope and the End of the World* (New Haven, CT: Yale University Press, 2002), 145.

[9]   Polkinghorne, "Eschatology," 29, 32–3; Polkinghorne, *God of Hope*, 11–12. For this reason, he rejects the "physical eschatology" of Freedman Dyson and Frank J. Tipler as well as the evolutionary optimism of Pierre Teilhard de Chardin.

[10]   Polkinghorne, *God of Hope*, 12.

of history."[11] "Only such a God," he rightly indicates, "could be the ground for [the] *hope against hope* that transcends the limits of any natural expectation."[12]

Only God's faithfulness to the present creation warrants a transcendent hope beyond its anticipated demise. Thus fails all the meta-scientific responses to cosmic futility from those scientists who "are unwilling to look to religion for the possibility of a wider prospect beyond the end of physical process."[13] In other words, "an unaided scientific account of the world alone cannot succeed in *making complete sense* of cosmic history."[14] Only something like the Christian resurrection hope can make complete sense of the universe.

Creatio ex Vetere *in Relation to* Creatio ex Nihilo

If divine faithfulness grounds the general possibility of Polkinghorne's transcendent hope beyond cosmic history, then the specific form of his cosmic hope—namely, *creatio ex vetere*—is decided by the resurrection of Jesus Christ; for Christ's resurrection is the anticipation of the new creation. The resurrection of Jesus Christ is "the beginning *within* history of a process whose fulfillment lies *beyond* history, in which the destiny of humanity and the destiny of the universe are together to find their fulfillment in liberation from decay and futility."[15] The ultimate destiny of the universe as anticipated in Christ's resurrection is epitomized in the phrase *creatio ex vetere* (creation out of the old).

The concept of *creatio ex vetere* deserves more explanation. If my reading of the works of Polkinghorne is right, the concept first appears when he addresses the problem of "fall" in the old creation in comparison with the "unfallenness" of the new creation; later, it becomes the overarching framework for his eschatological discussion which is in dialogue with science. Originally, his question was of a sort of theodicy: "if the laws of matter could be revised in such a way as to exclude physical evil, why did not the Creator ordain just those laws the first time round, rather than bothering with the old unsatisfactory variety? In short, if the world to come is to be physically 'unfallen,' why was that not true of this world also?"[16] Already, the idea of the redemptive transformation of matter

---

[11]   Ibid., 94.

[12]   Ibid., 95. My italics.

[13]   At first he mentions three metascientific responses to science's bleak picture of eventual futility: "heroic defiance" (Jacques Monod and Steven Weinberg), "physical eschatology," and multiverse of "endless fertility" (Christ Isham): Polkinghorne, "Eschatology," 30–34. Later, he adds another response, "a total view" of block universe (Isham): Polkinghorne, *God of Hope*, 21–7.

[14]   Polkinghorne, "Eschatology," 38.

[15]   Polkinghorne, *Science and Christian Belief: Theological Reflections of a Bottom-Up Thinker* (London: SPCK, 1994), 165. My italics.

[16]   Polkinghorne, *Reason and Reality: The Relationship between Science and Theology* (Philadelphia, PA: Trinity Press International, 1991), 102–103. Similar questions are found

and physical laws in the old creation is presupposed. The problem concerns primarily the *raison d'être* of the old creation, and secondarily, though not the least, the rationale of the new creation.

The answer is given by distinguishing the good of the old creation as *creatio ex nihilo* from the good of the new creation as *creatio ex vetere*: the former lies in the universe's self-realization of its fruitful potentiality, and the latter in the new relationship between God and the world. The point is that the *new* creation will not be "replacement," but "redemption," of the old creation.[17] In this regard Polkinghorne appeals to Gabriel Daly, who says, "The word 'new' could mislead here. It does not imply an abolition of the old but rather its transformation. It is a 'new creation' but, unlike the first creation, it is not *ex nihilo*. The new creation is what the Spirit of God does *to* the first creation."[18]

In short, the whole history of God's creative activity is divided into two distinct, albeit not completely separate, phases:[19] *creatio ex nihilo* of "raw material"[20] and *creatio ex vetere* as the former's redemption. Polkinghorne's recent eschatological discussion assumes these two phases in God's history of creation and explores continuities and discontinuities between them, with particular help from scientific and meta-scientific insights.

Continuities and Discontinuities in Creatio ex Vetere

In Christian hope, the ultimate future of our universe, *creatio ex vetere*, requires both a certain degree of discontinuity and a certain degree of continuity with the old creation in order to make sure of both the latter's redemption and identity at the same time.[21] The question of "coherence" of such a hope for *creatio ex vetere* now comes to the fore in Polkinghorne's eschatological discussion. His answer to the question begins with an insight in complexity theory: the *complementary dichotomy* of energy and pattern.[22] Simply put, the transmutation of matter will bring about the necessary discontinuity, while the carryover of information pattern will guarantee the necessary continuity.

To be more specific, as for discontinuity Polkinghorne highlights the significance of the empty tomb, for it implies that the risen Lord's body was transmuted and glorified. Likewise, the "matter" of the new creation will be given

---

in his later works as well: see *Science and Christian Belief,* 167; *Serious Talk: Science and Religion in Dialogue* (Valley Forge, PA: Trinity Press International, 1995), 106.

[17] Polkinghorne, *Reason and Reality,* 102; cf. *Science and Christian Belief,* 167.

[18] Gabriel Daly, *Creation and Redemption* (Wilmington, DE: Glazier, 1989), 100. My italics.

[19] Polkinghorne, *God of Hope,* 116.

[20] Polkinghorne, *Science and Christian Belief,* 168. Here *creatio ex nihilo* is to be understood as including *creatio continua.*

[21] Polkinghorne, "Eschatology," 38–9.

[22] Ibid., 39.

a totally different character from that of this creation, in order to make sure that the new creation is free from death and suffering. Of course, the transmutation of matter is expected to involve a corresponding change in the physical laws as well. On the other hand, as regards continuity through re-embodiment of patterns, Polkinghorne rehabilitates the Aristotelian–Thomistic notion of the soul as the form of the body, while overcoming the individualistic reduction of the traditional discussion by employing twentieth-century scientific insight into the relational character of physical reality. The pattern of a person includes her relationships with other persons and, especially, with God. This whole complex information pattern will be retained in divine memory and then re-embodied in the transmuted "matter" in the new creation.[23]

The assumption that information patterns of the old creation will be retained in its eschatological transformation is supplemented by two other assumptions about continuities between the old creation and the new creation.[24] Of them the first assumption is that the intrinsically dual-aspect (energy-pattern) character of creaturely nature will continue to exist even in the world to come; the second, derived from general relativity theory, is that the nexus of relationship between space, time and matter—which is characteristic of the created order in general—will also continue to be valid even in the new created order. Given them, the continuities between the old and new creation include not only the identity of information patterns, but also the fundamental structure of creatures as psychosomatic unity and spatiotemporal being. I would say, then, that Polkinghorne has accomplished to a considerable extent what he has intended: namely, "clarifying what will be the necessary degree of continuity required"[25] for the hope for *creatio ex vetere*.

Owing to its implications for our later discussion, the second assumption needs a little more discussion. The insight of general relativity theory into the nexus of inextricable relationship between space, time and matter encourages Polkinghorne to emphasize the existence of dynamic change "in time" even in the new creation. He says,

---

[23]   It seems, however, that this idea of the re-embodiment of information-patterns ("soul") in transmuted matter ("body") does not adequately describe the Christian hope for the resurrection of the *body*. Ted Peters wonders why Polkinghorne "limits continuity to the divinely remembered soul." Appealing to the biblical phrase *soma pneumatikon* ("spiritual body"), Peters argues that our identity will be carried forward "physically," not simply by a divinely remembered information pattern: Peters, *Anticipating Omega: Science, Faith, and Our Ultimate Future* (Göttingen: Vandenhoeck & Ruprecht, 2006), 39. I suspect that the empty tomb, so central to Polkinghorne's eschatological vision, entails not only a transmutation of matter, but also a physical continuity in that transmutation. Also, from the perspective of the gospel of salvation from sin, it is in fact information patterns that need judgment or redemption all the more than matter–energy; in that sense, I think, we need to affirm "transfiguration of pattern" as well as "transmutation of matter."

[24]   Polkinghorne, "Eschatology," 39.

[25]   Polkinghorne, *God of Hope*, 13.

> [R]esurrected beings will not only be embodied in the 'matter' of the new
> creation, they will also be located in its 'space' and immersed in its 'time.'
> Understood in this way, the continuity of human nature would imply for
> humanity an everlasting destiny, rather than some timeless experience of
> eternity. The modern recognition of the role of becoming in the unfolding
> history of the present creation encourages a dynamic concept of being and of
> being's perfection. Change does not imply imperfection ... The beatific vision,
> then, will not be an atemporal experience of illumination but the unceasing
> exploration of the riches of the divine nature.[26]

The point is clear that the dynamic nature of temporal experience in the old
creation will continue to exist even in the new creation. The eternal life will not
be a timeless or atemporal experience, but an "everlastingly" unfolding process.[27]
Anthropologically speaking, as much as embodiment, "temporality is constitutive
of being truly human,"[28] whether in the old creation or in the new creation.
Theologically speaking, God is "the patient God" in both worlds: "In my view,
part of the continuity that we may expect to hold between the two halves of God's
great creative/redemptive acts is that the patient God who acts through temporally
unfolding process in the old creation, will continue to act in a similar fashion in the
unfolding fulfillment of the new creation."[29]

As far as the relation between time of the old creation and "time" of the new
creation goes, Polkinghorne seems not so much concerned about discontinuity as
continuity. Yet, it seems evident that in the passage quoted above Polkinghorne
also assumes a transformation of space and time (or, space–time) in the old
creation into "space" and "time" (or, "space–time") of a different character in the
new creation, in an analogous way to the transformation of perishable matter into
imperishable "matter." This might be what he means by "continuing, if *redeemed*,
temporal process" as part of the new creation.[30] To my disappointment, however,
he does not explicate further what constitutes the discontinuity in that redemptive
transformation of time into "time." Be that as it may, I suspect that by "time"
Polkinghorne does not mean simply an infinite extension of linear, irreversible
time which is subject to transience and mortality, suppose that "matter" is free from
transience and mortality and that "space," "time," and "matter" are inextricably
connected.[31]

For Polkinghorne, in the final analysis, the discontinuities between the old
creation and the new creation do not consist only of the transformation of matter–
energy (and therefore of physical laws and space–time). The decisive discontinuity

26   Polkinghorne, "Eschatology," 40.
27   Cf. Polkinghorne, *God of Hope*, 117.
28   Cf. ibid., 100.
29   Ibid., 120.
30   Ibid., xxi (my italics).
31   Cf. ibid., xxi.

lies rather in the different modes of God's presence among the creation.[32] The new creation will be, he says, "totally infused with the presence of the Creator." In this sense, *panentheism* is accepted as an eschatological reality, if it does not describe the present reality. If in the old creation God's presence is most transparently perceived in particular covenanted occasions called sacraments, the new creation will be *wholly sacramental*, for then God will be "all in all" (1 Corinthians 15:28). In addition to all these ideas, he embraces the Eastern Orthodox view of the eschatological fulfillment as an attainment of *theosis*, or creatures' full sharing in the divine life and energy.

Theological Foundations for the Eschatology-cosmology Dialogues

Polkinghorne's eschatological vision, as I have discussed thus far, shows remarkable affinity with that of Jürgen Moltmann, one of the most influential eschatological theologians today. These agreements demand much more attention than the disagreements between them, which I will discuss later, because those points of their convergence lay the foundation for subsequent dialogues between Christian eschatology and physical cosmology. Of many, I focus on four major points: the ultimate ground, the specific source, the eschatological model, and the final vision of Christian hope.

First, both theologians find the ultimate ground of their hope in the faithfulness of God, who "gives life to the dead and calls into existence the things that do not exist" (Romans 4:17).[33] Faith in divine faithfulness to the promise underlies their hope for the final consummation of creation *despite* the scientific prediction of eventual cosmic death (Polkinghorne) or all the realistic possibilities of End-time exterminism (Moltmann). Hence, they follow the biblical example of Abraham who held "hope against hope" (Romans 4:18), and of the legendary Luther, who declared that, even if he knew that tomorrow the world would end, he would plant an apple tree today.

As Moltmann succinctly expresses, the eschaton is not something that develops out of the potentialities built into the present world (*futurum*), but something new that comes from the future of God (*adventus*).[34] In this sense, Christian hope is distinguished from naïve optimism, which is found in the ancient notion of *entelechy* and modern belief in in-built progress. As a consequence, the method of Christian eschatology is to be different from that of science, which relies solely upon the extrapolation of the present into the future.[35] Christian eschatology

32   Polkinghorne, "Eschatology," 40; cf. Polkinghorne, *God of Hope*, 115.
33   Polkinghorne, *God of Hope*, 102; Moltmann, *The Coming of God: Christian Eschatology* (Minneapolis, MN: Fortress, 1996), 235.
34   Moltmann, *Coming of God*, 25.
35   Moltmann, *The Future of Creation* (Philadelphia, PA: Fortress, 1979), 20–23.

begins with divine promise of the ultimate consummation and is sustained by faith in divine faithfulness to the promise.

Second, both theologians derive their specific vision of the cosmic future from the event of the resurrection of the crucified Christ,[36] which they believe is the revelation and confirmation of God's promise of the new creation as *creatio ex vetere*. In this regard, their emphasis on the cosmic significance of the Christ event is to be highly regarded.

For Moltmann, just like for Polkinghorne, the eschatological perspectives on the future of the universe do not derive from the general observation of nature or history, but from a particular experience of God, the sort of experience that he calls "root experience."[37] For Israel it is the Exodus, whereas for Christianity it is the cross and resurrection of Christ. These root experiences are special and historical in origin, yet embrace the general horizons of experience in the form of universal expectations of the future; for they are experiences in time of the eternal God. The God of Exodus is the Creator of *all* things; the God of resurrection is the one who brings *all* things to completion. Therefore, cosmic eschatology is integral to Christian eschatology and provides it with the most comprehensive horizon.[38]

Since Christian eschatology takes its bearings from nothing but the Christ event of cross and resurrection, Moltmann argues, it combines two different ideas of the "end of the world" as *finis* (end) and *telos* (goal).[39] In Christian eschatology there are both an end and a beginning, both a catastrophe and a new start, and both apocalyptic and millenarian; for Christ's end on the cross was not the last thing, but became his true beginning in the resurrection into the eternal life of the future. Thus, in the end is the beginning.[40] Moltmann believes that this "dialectical mystery of Christian eschatology" is also true of the destiny of the universe. Expecting a

---

[36] Polkinghorne, *Science and Christian Belief*, 165; Moltmann, *Coming of God*, 233–4.

[37] Moltmann, "Creation and Theosis," in *The Far-Future Universe: Eschatology from a Cosmic Perspective*, ed. George Ellis (Philadelphia, PA: Templeton Foundation Press, 2002), 250. Here Moltmann defines root experience as an experience of events in which God reveals himself and thus from which a human community acquires her identity.

[38] Cf. Moltmann, "Creation and Theosis," 252.

[39] Moltmann, "Creation and Theosis," 255.

[40] Moltmann's interpretation of cross and resurrection in terms of the combination of apocalyptic and millenarian looks formally akin to Polkinghorne's idea of the new creation beyond the anticipated cosmic demise. However,, as I will discuss later, a closer look reveals that their contents are quite different from each other. For Moltmann, apocalyptic and millenarian are so intrinsically connected that it is the advent of the new creation that brings the old creation to the end; for Polkinghorne, however, there seems to be no intrinsic connection between the anticipated death and transformation of the present creation: cf. Polkinghorne, *God of Hope*, 120–21.

definite yes, he asks, "Could the 'death and [resurrection] of the universe' be the prelude to an unexpected new creation of all things?"[41]

Third, suppose that the unexpected new creation of all things is already anticipated in the resurrection of the crucified Jesus, Moltmann believes, the ultimate destiny of the universe will not be its extermination (*annhilatio mundi*), but rather its transformation (*transformatio mundi*): "the universe will be transformed from the state in which we see it now into a condition that is qualitatively new."[42] The old world of sin, death, and transience will be transfigured into the new world of righteousness, eternal life, and imperishability. "Behold, I make all things new" (Revelations 21:5)—from this passage Moltmann infers that what is promised is not second *creatio ex nihilo*, but "the new creation of everything that has already been created " or "the fundamental alteration of the existing one."[43] Thus, the eschatological transformation of the universe "embraces both the identity of creation and its newness, that is to say both continuity and discontinuity."[44] Therefore, Moltmann also affirms the idea of *creatio ex vetere*[45] as the eschatological model of cosmic fulfillment.[46]

Thus, both Moltmann and Polkinghorne agree that God's creation consists of two distinct, although not completely separate, phases. As we have seen, Polkinghorne understands God's total creative intent as "intrinsically a two-step process":[47] first *creatio ex nihilo* and then *creatio ex vetere*. Likewise, Moltmann suggests that the history of the universe as God's creation is divided into "two qualitatively differentiated eons": that is, "the time of this [transitory] world— 'this world-time'—and the time of the [eternal] world to come—'the future world-time.'"[48] As for the specific relation between two distinct worlds or times,

---

41 Moltmann, "Creation and Theosis," 255.

42 Ibid., 257.

43 Moltmann, *Science and Wisdom* (London: SCM, 2003), 52.

44 Moltmann, "Creation and Theosis," 257.

45 Moltmann, *Coming of God*, 27.

46 In light of this theological perspective of the transformation of the present universe, Moltmann does not agree to Weinberg's pessimistic interpretation of the place of humanity in the universe as an island of meaning in an ocean of meaninglessness, because he believes the ultimate destiny of the universe will not be the eventual return to nothing (*reductio ad nihilum*), but its participation in the eternal life of God: "Creation and Theosis," 252. Nor does he find desirable the utopian vision of "an endless future for life and the universe as we know," as suggested in physical eschatology or multiverse models. Instead, he argues, a radical transformation of the physical structure of the universe is required to overcome "death and the transitoriness of time"; for a "world without end" in its genuine sense would not be possible without the "end of the world" in its present form: "Creation and Thesis," 253–4. This is comparable, albeit not identical, with Polkinghorne's rejection of heroic defiance (Weinberg) and "physical eschatology" (Dyson/Tipler).

47 Polkinghorne, *God of Hope*, 116.

48 Moltmann, "Cosmos and Theosis," 259.

I will discuss it in a while. For now, it is important to note that both theologians expect the future time to be of a different sort than simply an extension of the present time.

Finally, both theologians understand the genuine novelty of the new creation with regard to the old creation in terms of the radical change in God's relation with creatures; that is, the discontinuity between two worlds does not consist simply in the transformation of the physical structure of creation. In this regard, they both appeal to the biblical promise that in the new creation God will "be all in all" (1 Corinthians 15:28) and interpret this vision in terms of eschatological panentheism, divine *Shekinah*, the sacramental world, and *theosis* or *deificatio mundi*.[49] All of these ideas describe the new creation redeemed by a radically new mode of God's presence among creatures and the consequent participation of creatures in God's eternal life.

In short, Polkinghorne and Moltmann converge upon the fundamentals of Christian cosmic eschatology: that is, God's promise and faithfulness as the only ground for ultimate hope, Christ's resurrection as the prefiguration[50] of cosmic transformation, *creatio ex vetere* as the proper eschatological model, and *theosis* as the final goal of God's creation. These theological foundations will serve as the cornerstones for the following dialogue between two theologians and also, I believe, for the subsequent dialogues between Christian eschatology and physical cosmology.

Bottom-up Thinking Challenges Top-down Eschatology

It is on the top of this theological agreement that Polkinghorne brings scientific and meta-scientific insights to give "a modest degree of substance" to Christian eschatological hope. Drawing from complexity theory and general relativity theory, as I have discussed earlier, he suggests that the continuities between the old creation and the new creation will include not only the information patterns, but also the fundamental structures of creaturely beings. This is Polkinghorne's original contribution, which could not be expected from systematic theologians like Moltmann.

In addition, Polkinghorne challenges systematic theologians to reflect upon their own assumptions and motivations in their eschatological discussions. This is, I think, another great contribution of Polkinghorne to contemporary Christian eschatology. Assuming that scientist–theologians like himself have different concerns and different concepts than systematic theologians like Moltmann

---

[49]   Cf. Polkinghorne, *God of Hope*, 114–15; Polkinghorne, "Eschatology," 40; Moltmann, *Coming of God*, 295; Moltmann, "Creation and Theosis," 258–9; Moltmann, *Science and Wisdom*, 45.

[50]   For the concept of prefiguration or prolepsis, see Peters, *Anticipating Omega*, 28–36.

do, Polkinghorne accuses "mainstream systematic theologians" of the three shortcomings: neglect of the bottom-up approach, devaluation of temporality, and anthropocentric timescales.[51] In the subsequent discussion I will make each of these critiques the starting point for the continuing dialogues, reconstructed in my own way, between Polkinghorne and Moltmann.

Bottom-up Thinking Within Top-down Eschatology

One of the fundamental differences between scientist–theologians and systematic theologians, Polkinghorne believes, relates to "the method by which one seeks to explore the fundamental eschatological theme of continuity/discontinuity."[52] His specific critique concerns the latter group's neglect of a bottom-up approach in an exclusive preference for a more top-down matter of eschatological assertions. Although Moltmann is not explicitly mentioned in this criticism, I suspect it may apply to him as well, at least to some extent.

In the first place, the approaches of two theologians show a striking contrast: while scientist–theologian Polkinghorne insists on science's possible contribution to eschatology, systematic theologian Moltmann asks about the eschatological perspectives on the cosmic future: "What can a theology of hope tell us about the far-future cosmos that has relevance from a human perspective?"[53] Although both theologians embrace the eschatological vision of *creatio ex vetere*, one gives more heed to its continuous part (*ex vetere*) in which science may have something to contribute, while the other puts more emphasis on the novelty that its discontinuous part (*creatio*) brings to the present universe.[54] In this sense, yet in this sense only, I would say, Polkinghorne's discussion moves from science to theology, while Moltmann's moves from theology to science.

It is also important to note, however, that neither of two theologians' discussions follows simply a unidirectional approach. Recall that Polkinghorne's bottom-up approach to the theme of continuity/discontinuity already presupposes his top-down commitment to the theological vision of *creatio ex vetere*, which is grounded upon a specific interpretation of Christ's resurrection. In spite of his emphasis on the eschatological perspective, on the other hand, Moltmann too is aware of the need to set Christian eschatology "critically and self-critically" in the context of modern astrophysics.[55] Their difference seems to consist more in emphasis than in substance, so that their different approaches do not lead to a mutually incompatible contradiction. In principle, they may complement each other; that is, in order to make fully intelligible the eschatological vision of *creatio*

---

51 Polkinghorne, *God of Hope*, 140–5.
52 Polkinghorne, *God of Hope*, 144.
53 Moltmann, "Cosmos and Theosis," 255.
54 Moltmann, *Coming of God*, 27. Here Moltmann discussion of *creatio ex vetere* aims to explicate the category *novum*.
55 Moltmann, "Cosmos and Theosis," 249.

ex vetere, we need to discuss both its continuous and discontinuous aspects and to make them into a coherent whole. Then, Polkinghorne's contribution may be subtly redefined as incorporation into the dominantly top-down discussions of the so far neglected bottom-up thinking.

Temporality of the Eternal Life

Next, Polkinghorne claims that systematic theologians devalue temporality. In this regard, his criticism concerns specifically Moltmann, who conceives the eschatological consummation of creation primarily in terms of a redemptive transformation of time into eternity. As a result, he says, Moltmann negates "the role of continuing process within the eschaton" and resists "the concept of creative change."[56] Instead, Polkinghorne believes, dynamic becoming is the form of perfection appropriate to creatures. Hence, it is both congenial and necessary to conceive that the eternal life in the new creation is everlastingly exploratory in character: "The new creation will not be a timeless world of 'eternity,' but a temporal world whose character is everlasting."[57]

I agree that Moltmann affirms the idea of "the end of time" in the advent of divine eternity. For him, however, the "end" does not mean simply "cessation," but primarily "fulfillment."[58] The end of time means the end of linear, irreversible, transient time of this creation, on the one hand, and the beginning of cyclical, reversible, eternal time of the new creation.[59] Drawing the Orthodox terminology "aeon," which refers to creatures' relative eternity distinct from God's absolute eternity, Moltmann calls the time of the new creation "aeonic time."[60] The "aeonic" time is not "a deathlike silence"; rather, it is "the time of eternal life," "the time of eternal livingness," "the fulfilled time," "the time filled with eternity," and "eternity filled with time."[61] In this sense, Moltmann compares the cyclical movements of eternal life to dance and music. All things considered, I would disagree with Polkinghorne that Moltmann's concept of aeonic time is "static" or

---

[56]   Polkinghorne, *God of Hope*, 143.

[57]   Ibid., 117.

[58]   Moltmann, *Coming of God*, 279–95. Polkinghorne's critique of Wolfhart Pannenberg's idea of the end of time is more severe than his critique of Moltmann's. However, for Pannenberg too the end of time means primarily its fulfillment, although I admit that his definition of eternity as the whole of time gives less room for the dynamic nature of the eternal life than Moltmann's appeal to the notion of aeon: cf. Pannenberg, *Systematic Theology* vol. 3 (Grand Rapids, MI: Eerdmans, 1997), 580–607.

[59]   Moltmann, "Creation and Theosis," 261–2.

[60]   Moltmann, *Science and Wisdom*, 109.

[61]   Moltmann, *Coming of God*, 295. Elsewhere, he describes the eternal life as "cyclical and full of repetition" and as "life in depth," meaning "the intensity of the lived life, not its endless extension": see Moltmann, *The Way of Jesus Christ* (Minneapolis, MN: Fortress, 1993), 331.

"dull."[62] Rather, in my opinion, the *spiral* image[63] Moltmann employs to describe aeonic time is one of the best images to express both its fullness and dynamism at the same time.

It seems to me, then, that the real question at stake is not whether the eternal life is temporal or not, but what is the specific nature of temporality in the eternal life. The latter question is closely related to another "theological" question of the nature of temporality of the eternal God, for the eternal life is nothing but participation in the life of the eternal God. At this point, Moltmann seems to have a different understanding of divine eternity from Polkinghorne.[64] In the eschatological moment which "ends time in time" and "gathers all times into eternity,"[65] Moltmann believes, "the time of the Creator's long-suffering and patience with his creation ends too."[66] On the contrary, Polkinghorne believes that "the patient God who acts through temporally unfolding process in the old creation will continue to act in a similar fashion in the unfolding fulfillment of the new creation."[67] This difference in their ideas of God's relation to creation may explain, at least in part, the fact that Polkinghorne discusses temporality primarily in terms of continuity between old creation and the new creation, and Moltmann primarily in terms of discontinuity.

One way to bring forward the dialogue between two theologians would be to ask how Polkinghorne understands discontinuity in the transformation of time to "time," on the one hand, and how Moltmann understands continuity in the transformation of transient time to eternal time, on the other.

In his discussion of the relation between time and "time," Polkinghorne argues that they do not stand "in a strictly sequential relationship," as if the new "time" begins only "after" the old time ends. Instead, the "time" of the new creation lies "beyond" the time of the old creation.[68] The basic insight derives from Christ's resurrection, which, albeit an event *within* history, anticipates an event *beyond* history; that is, Christ's resurrection is "an event within, as well as beyond, present history."[69] Hence, Polkinghorne suggests a more nuanced model of the relation between the present time and the future "time," than a simply sequential model, appealing to the mathematical idea of two distinct, albeit somehow connected,

---

[62]   Cf. Polkinghorne, *God of Hope*, 117–19.

[63]   Cf. Moltmann, *Science and Wisdom*, 109.

[64]   Polkinghorne's view of divine eternity/temporality seems close to the process theism: *Science and Theology: An Introduction* (Minneapolis, MN: Fortress, 1998), 90–92. On the other hand, Moltmann's view of divine eternity/temporality embraces Boethius' famous definition of eternity as a total, perfect and simultaneous possession of unlimited life: Moltmann, *Science and Wisdom*, 96.

[65]   Moltmann, *Way of Jesus Christ*, 318.

[66]   Moltmann, *Science and Wisdom*, 106.

[67]   Polkinghorne, *God of Hope*, 120.

[68]   Polkinghorne, "Eschatology," 40.

[69]   Polkinghorne, *God of Hope*, 120.

space–times: "Mathematicians can readily think of the spacetime of the old creation and the 'spacetime' of the new creation as being in different dimensions of the totality of divinely sustained reality, with resurrection involving an information-bearing mapping between the two, and the redemption of matter as involving a projection from the old onto the new."[70] "If time and 'time' are related in this way," he believes, Karl Rahner's view of the intermediate state—namely, the idea that, although we all die at different times in this world, we may all arrive "simultaneously" on the day of resurrection in the world to come—would be "a coherent possibility, with mappings from different times all leading to the same 'time' in the world to come."[71] To my surprise, Polkinghorne here comes close to Moltmann's concept of "the eschatological moment."[72]

Moreover, like Moltmann, Polkinghorne suggests music as the best image for the dynamic character of the everlasting life in the new creation: "Each one of Bach's thirty Goldberg variations is perfect in itself and we do not need to opt for just one of them. They present us with an image of *change without either repetition or loss*. It is the exploration of the endless variations of divine perfection that will constitute the harmony of the heavenly realm."[73] I find it particularly significant that of many musical forms Polkinghorne appeals to variations, in which, even in an improvised one, a basic musical theme is repeated with modifications in rhythm, tune, harmony or key.[74] A certain degree of repetition of the basic theme seems indispensable to give all the variations unity or identity.[75] Also, I wonder what he means by the idea of change without *loss*; does he refer to something other than what Moltmann means by "aeonic time" or relatively eternal time?

If I turn to Moltmann's idea of the continuous aspects between "transitory time" of the old creation and "eternal time" of the new creation, it also shows a striking affinity with Polkinghorne's idea. This is most evident in Moltmann's discussion of creation as an open system. The point is that creation will continue to be "open" even in the world to come. Since creation is to be completed in the indwelling of the unlimited fullness of God's potentialities, he argues, new creation means "the openness *par excellence* of all systems of life." It is "participation in the unbounded liberty of God." He continues to say, "in the kingdom of glory too there will be time and history, future and possibility." There will be "change without

---

[70]   Ibid., 120–21.

[71]   Ibid., 122.

[72]   Like Polkinghorne, Moltmann also interprets Paul's phrase "in the twinkling of an eye" (1 Corinthians 15:52–3) as meaning that all the different times in this world will arrive "simultaneously" at what he calls "the eschatological moment." Cf. Moltmann, *Science and Wisdom*, 102.

[73]   Polkinghorne, *God of Hope*, 120, my italics.

[74]   Cf. "Variation 4." *Merriam–Webster's Collegiate Dictionary*, 11th edn, 2005.

[75]   In this sense, "a certain degree of repeated dullness" is indispensable even in his own concept of the everlasting life: cf. Polkinghorne, *God of Hope*, 119.

transience, time without the past, and life without death."[76] It seems difficult to fail to see the convergence between this statement and Polkinghorne's emphasis on the "everlastingly exploratory" character of the life to come in the new creation.

In sum, as far as the nature of temporality in the eternal life is concerned, the difference between two theologians seems slighter than Polkinghorne assumes. Be that as it may, it does not undermine Polkinghorne's unique contribution. By drawing from the scientific insight of general relativity theory into the nexus of relationship between space, time and matter, he reminds us of the intrinsic value of temporality for creaturely life.

Cosmic Eschatology Covering a Genuinely Cosmic Scale

Finally, Polkinghorne criticizes the narrow timescales with which many systematic theologians foresee the future of creation. Systematic theologians, he says, seldom "reflect the expectations that cosmic history will continue for many billions of years." The criticism goes directly against Moltmann:[77] "It is too anthropocentric to write, as Jürgen Moltmann did, that we are living in a 'nuclear and ecological end time' and to 'deduce from this that before the final end of history there will be a concentration of humanity's both constructive and destructive opportunities." That is, there is no serious consideration of the scientific prediction that the whole earth will continue to exist until the explosion of the Sun into its red giant phase. Polkinghorne suspects that this human scale of thinking encourages Moltmann to expect at the last stage of history the advent of Christ's kingdom on the earth, which will serve as a "relatively smooth transition" from the old creation to the new creation. According to him, this millenarian expectation "sounds a little cosily terrestrial," and reflects "a residual reluctance ... to give up some ultimate form of political hope within the course of present history." Also, such an expectation does not give due attention to the radical distinction between the old and the new creation; on the contrary, Polkinghorne believes, "the new creation must be endowed with a totally different 'physical fabric' from that of the old creation and, of course, this must be on a universe-wide scale."

This criticism may count as one of the most serious challenges ever raised against Moltmann's eschatological theology. For an efficient discussion here I distinguish three, otherwise closely connected, elements: the anthropocentric–terrestrial scale of eschatological imagination; adherence to the idea of the completion of history as the goal and the final condition of history; and neglect of the radical discontinuity involved in the transformation of present physical conditions.

(1) I wonder whether Moltmann's eschatology has a "cosmic" scope in a genuine sense. It seems that it still remains "ecological" at most. In his cosmic eschatology

---

76 Moltmann, *Science and Wisdom*, 46.
77 Polkinghorne, *God of Hope*, 142–3.

he emphasizes "the ecological unity of human being and the earth,"[78] yet is not much concerned with the interdependence of the earth and the universe. Even the ecological crisis is often reduced to an anthropological problem. Moreover, the fate of the earth (and of the universe) is understood as contingent upon the destiny of humanity, not vice versa.[79]

Agreeing with Polkinghorne's criticism, I believe we need to distinguish cosmic eschatology from historical–political–ecological eschatology even more sharply than Moltmann does. The transformation of the physical fabric of creation needs a separate discussion, which cannot be simply reduced to other aspects of Christian eschatology. The scientific insight needs be taken into eschatological discussion that neither the catastrophic end nor the fulfillment (whatever that may be) of human history on the earth may have no intrinsic relation to the end or fulfillment of the cosmic history.

(2) As Polkinghorne rightly notes, the anthropocentric scale of thinking underlies Moltmann's idea of the fulfillment of the earthly history in the form of Christ's millenarian kingdom. However, the "optimistic" expectation for the final stage of history before the ultimate end of history poses a different set of problems from the anthropocentric scale of thinking. If, as Moltmann insists, Christians hope for the "consummation of history" within the old creation, which is distinguished from, and precedes, the "consummation of creation" in the new creation,[80] then it is unavoidable that Christian eschatology contradicts the scientific theories of the fate of the universe, in a quite different way than Polkinghorne assumes.

For Polkinghorne, the new creation lies "beyond" the old creation, while there are substantial continuities between them. To use his expression, the "space–time" of the new creation is distinct from the space–time of the old creation.[81] In principle, therefore, this "transcendent" hope for the new creation is compatible with the scientific prediction of the ultimate futility of the old creation.[82] There is

---

[78]   Moltmann, *Coming of God*, 277.

[79]   Behind this anthropocentricism and consequent neglect of cosmological considerations, lies Moltmann's commitment to "strong anthropological principle" of biblical traditions: "Creation and Theosis," 252. Among systematic theologians, Moltmann is not unique at this point: as for Karl Rahner's anthropocentricism in relation to Christian eschatology, see Denis Edwards, *Jesus and the Cosmos* (New York: Paulist Press, 1991), 93–7. Interestingly enough, Teilhard de Chardin's cosmic vision of the Point Omega also proves to be terrestrial: cf. Russell, *Cosmology*, 279–80.

[80]   Moltmann, *Coming of God*, 294, 193, 195, 197.

[81]   Polkinghorne, *God of Hope*, 120–21.

[82]   It is understandable, then, that Polkinghorne disagrees with Macquarrie that the eventual cosmic death would amount to the falsification of Christian hope. Polkinghorne says, "I do not think that the eventual futility of the universe, over a timescale of tens of billions of years, is very different in the theological problems that it poses, from the eventual futility of ourselves, over a timescale of tens of years. Cosmic death and human

neither theological necessity, nor scientific probability, to posit "the last moment" as a critical moment of fulfillment that leads to the new creation. Also, he believes it is "unwise" to suppose that God will intervene to end the cosmic history "before science expects," although he does not rule out that possibility.[83] In short, the last moment does not claim any privilege over the previous moments; every time in the old creation is equidistant from the "time" of the new creation.[84]

Meanwhile, Moltmann believes that God will bring to consummation the present cosmic history along with the human history within it before its final end. Hence, as time passes, the history comes closer to its goal, something similar to the Point Omega in Teilhard de Chardin's cosmic vision. Unlike Polkinghorne's transcendent hope, it seems evident that this immanentist hope for fulfillment within the present universe stands in striking contrast to the scientific picture of eventual demise.

Does Christian hope need to adhere to such an immanentist aspect in addition to its transcendent one? Polkinghorne would agree with Richard Bauckham, who argues against Moltmann that "for Christian eschatology which does envisage such a new creation, I do not see why history should not have its goal beyond itself, in God's fulfillment and transfiguration of history in eternity."[85] From a theological perspective alone, however, I think there are several convincing reasons why we should put our hope not exclusively upon the transcendent realm beyond history, but also upon the real future of our cosmic history:

- last century biblical scholarship discovered that Jesus and the early Church expected the coming of God's kingdom in the real, futurist sense;[86]
- the resurrection of Jesus Christ is not simply the anticipation of the consummation lying beyond history, but also the initiation within history of the new creation; thus, we may expect that the present creation is in the process of transfiguration into the new creation by the power of God, not by the immanent force of creatures;
- God has always brought "to" the world something new, like Exodus or Christ's resurrection; thus, we may expect that God will bring the eschatological *novum* "to" this universe, not beyond its history;
- God's creation is not yet complete or finished, it is still ongoing; thus, it is expected to consummate in the final end of the ongoing creation;

---

death pose equivalent questions of what is God's intention for his creation." Polkinghorne, *Science and Christian Belief*, 163.

83   Polkinghorne, *God of Hope*, 140–41; also, see 121.

84   Cf. Polkinghorne, "Eschatology," 40.

85   Richard Bauckham, "Millennium," in *God Will be All in All: The Eschatology of Jürgen Moltmann*, ed. Richard Bauckham (Edinburgh: T&T Clark, 1999), 140.

86   Cf. Johannes Weiss, *Jesus' Proclamation of the Kingdom of God* (London: SCM, 1971).

• the idea of the completion of history leading to its final end preserves the unity of God's creative activity from creation to consummation, more than the idea of the consummation beyond history.

If what Christians expect in the last moment of history is not only its end, but also its fulfillment, the mere projection of the new creation "beyond" the old creation can neither properly express Christian hope, nor address the current dissonance between Christian hope and physical cosmology. The current dissonance between eschatology and cosmology is not simply apparent, but in fact amounts to a contradiction. There are only two possible options: first, adjusting the Christian hope to science, and second, adjusting science to the Christian expectation. Moltmann follows the second option. Starting from the controversial concept of the whole cosmos as an open system, he suggests that the universe as a whole is open to a qualitative leap into a radically new whole.[87] It is evident that he is expecting a consummating event in the real future of the present cosmic history, rather than beyond it. This is a praiseworthy attempt to find a scientifically tenable cosmological model that might be consonant with the Christian eschatology he is espousing. However, the problem is that the primary assumption is scientifically untenable: that is, the universe as a whole is not an open system.[88]

(3) According to Polkinghorne, Moltmann's expectation that in the end, not in the beyond, God will consummate history blurs the radical discontinuity between the old creation and the new creation. This point leads to another interesting dialogue between two theologians. It is right that, unlike Polkinghorne, Moltmann emphasizes the inseparable connection between the end of the old creation and the beginning of the new creation: in the end is the beginning. The eschatological moment, in which temporal creation ends and is transformed into eternal creation, is at the same time an exit out of the old creation and an entrance to the new creation.[89] Also, between the present history and the eschatological moment lies

---

[87]   Moltmann, "Creation and Theosis," 263–4.

[88]   For a critique of Moltmann's concept of open system, see Ted Peters, *God as Trinity: Relationality and Temporality in the Divine Life* (Louisville, KY: Westminster/John Knox Press, 1993), 160: "we cannot work with the notion that the universe as a whole is an open system receiving energy input from outside. If there were such an energy source, our notion of the universe would expand to include it, and then we would be right back where we started. The result is that the second law of thermodynamics applies to the cosmos as a whole." Also, note his alternative concept of "temporal holism": Peters, *God as Trinity*, 168–70. Polkinghorne also speaks of "an open universe," yet in a different sense than Moltmann does: cf. Polkinghorne, *Science and Theology*, 89–90. His discussion confines itself to quantum theory and chaos theory. He does not give us any hint that our universe as a whole is open to a radical transformation in its very physical fabric.

[89]   For Moltmann's concept of the eschatological moment, see *Science and Wisdom*, 98–100.

Christ's millenarian kingdom, which begins with the parousia of Christ and the special resurrection of believers. In this way, Moltmann's discussion gives us an impression that there is a stepwise progress from the present history to the eschatological new creation.

In my view, Moltmann's premillenarian interpretation of two resurrections is highly suspicious. Moltmann distinguishes the first special resurrection of believers *from* the dead during millennium from the second general resurrection *of* the dead at the eschatological moment.[90] Note that the first resurrection occurs within the physical structure of the old creation, that is, before its radical transformation in the new creation.[91] If the resurrection of the body is not something radically new in the new creation, the transition from the old creation to the new creation may look "relatively smooth," as Polkinghorne says.

This does not imply that Moltmann has no idea of the radical transformation of the physical structure of the old creation. In this vein, it is interesting to see how differently two theologians understand what will be different in the physical fabric of the new creation. For Polkinghorne, it is primarily the transmutation of matter and the corresponding transfiguration of physical laws that bring about discontinuity between the old creation and the new creation; for Moltmann, on the other hand, it is primarily the transformation of spatiotemporal structure of the old creation into "simultaneity" and "omnipresence."[92] This difference between them does not need to imply that their views are mutually exclusive. Given the inextricable relationship between matter, time and space in general relativity theory, it seems better to conceive the transformation of the physical universe in all those respects: matter, physical laws, time and space. Yet we are still far from attaining any clear and coherent vision of the new creation.

Unsolved Problems:
Toward a Consonance between Eschatology and Cosmology

As regards the relation between science and theology, Polkinghorne prefers a "consonance" approach to an "assimilation" approach. The "consonance" approach "lays particular stress on theology's *conceptual autonomy*, but it recognizes that there must be a *consistent fit* with science where there is some degree of overlapping concern." Then, in the case of Christology, Polkinghorne emphasizes "theology's conceptual autonomy," while in the doctrine of creation he insists on theology's "consistent fit with science." Eschatology is located between two extreme cases; thus, he says, "Theology's expression of its hope must be *consistent* with science's prediction of physical futility, but theology is entitled to *look beyond* that and to

---

[90]   Moltmann, *Coming of God*, 195.
[91]   For a critical comment on this point, see Bauckham, "Millennium," 141.
[92]   Moltmann, *Science and Wisdom*, 105–107.

make use of insights derived from its own conviction of the faithfulness of God."[93] To put it otherwise, Christian eschatology is constrained, albeit not exhausted, by current physical cosmology. This is the way Polkinghorne arrives at the "consonance" between eschatology and cosmology.

For Moltmann, however, this might amount to a distortion of the authentic Christian hope for the consummation of history at its final stage. Instead of adopting a relatively easy way of compromise, as I have discussed, he would confront the dissonance as it is. He may feel more sympathetic with Pannenberg than with Polkinghorne. Noting that science's prediction of eventual futility contradicts biblical eschatology, Pannenberg suggests accepting the current conflict between scientific cosmology and biblical eschatology as a challenge to the human mind.[94] Both Moltmann and Pannenberg would argue against Polkinghorne that, as far as eschatology is concerned, "theology's conceptual autonomy" must be taken more seriously than its "consistent fit with science."

With Moltmann, I believe that hope for the coming Kingdom of God at the end of history belongs to a non-negotiable core of biblical faith. If nothing but divine faithfulness is the ultimate ground of our hope, if scientific extrapolation cannot restrict God's freedom in the future, and if our universe is genuinely "open" to an unexpected new divine action that will affect and transform the physical fabric of the whole universe, then it does not seem unreasonable to hold onto the biblical hope for the future consummation.

With Polkinghorne, however, I believe that theology's consistent fit with science is mandatory if we want to make our Christian hope intelligible to the contemporary world. We may have been called to "hope against hope" (Romans 4:18) However, we are also admonished to be always ready to make a defense to everyone who asks us to give an account for our hope (1 Peter 3:15). Therefore, even if we find ourselves still far from a consensus on the concrete form of consonance between eschatology and cosmology, I am convinced that the attempt to attain a "consonance" needs to be continued.[95]

---

[93]   Polkinghorne, *Science and Theology*, 118.

[94]   Pannenberg, *Toward a Theology of Nature* (Louisville, KY: Westminster/JKP, 1997), 26–7.

[95]   Robert Russell proposes us an interesting thesis that I hope may finally bring about the consonance between eschatology and cosmology: that is, biblical eschatology (Theological Research Project, TRP) may indirectly influence the formation of an alternative scientific cosmology (Scientific Research Project, SRP). For the details, see his *Cosmology*, 298–327.

Chapter 11

Subtle and Supple: John Polkinghorne's Engagement with Reality

Pat Bennett

I love you, gentlest of Ways,
who ripened us as we wrestled with you …
You are the deep innerness of all things.

Rilke[1]

All my life, I have been trying to explore reality.

John Polkinghorne

'Subtle' and 'supple' are terms in which John Polkinghorne has often described the reality he has encountered and attempted to unravel in his long career as both physicist and priest. They are also quintessential characteristics of his own exploration and articulation of such reality as a pre-eminent first generation scientist-theologian. This essay in honour of his 80th birthday examines and evaluates elements of the epistemological strategy he has employed for engaging that reality and which, despite some inherent tensions, has been fruitfully brought to bear in the evolving science–theology field. It also suggests that he stands in the vanguard of those pointing towards the possibility of a more *trans*disciplinary engagement between the two disciplines, and that this is an important part of the legacy and challenge he bequeaths to those following him into the field of science–theology engagement.

The paper presents a critique of the two key planks at the heart of Polkinghorne's approach to that field, viz. his appropriation of a critical realist stance, and his efforts to establish an equality of relationship and areas of consonance between the two disciplines. Both of these bring their own particular difficulties that he has also had to address and accommodate, sometimes explicitly and sometimes more obliquely. In the case of the former, there are inherent tensions for his theological thinking and commitments located at both poles of the critical realist label; in that of the latter, there are questions to be answered regarding the asymmetry of the dialogical and constraining relationship between the two disciplines. In each case I will delineate the key features of the strategy, discussing their associated challenges and examining how Polkinghorne responds to these, and the degree

---

[1]   The Book of Hours: I, 25; II, 22.

or not to which he is successful in meeting them. In the light of this critique I will suggest that Polkinghorne's talent for subtle and supple thinking, and the way in which he himself has engaged in the arena of science–theology debate, have many similarities with both the flexible transversal rationality developed by J. Wentzel van Huyssteen and his associated model of transversal space dialogue.[2] When seen from this perspective I believe that Polkinghorne's contribution points to possibilities for a new way forward for the science–theology field, and that it is in this respect, the value of his many and varied other contributions to it over the last 40 years notwithstanding, that he presents the strongest and most exciting challenge to new scholars entering the arena of engagement.

Of central importance to Polkinghorne's attempt to build a constructive dialogue between science and theology is his espousal of the philosophical stance of critical realism and his claim that this characterises the approach of both disciplines. It is beyond the scope of this piece to give a comprehensive account of the position and thus I will merely deal with certain key aspects as they relate to his work here. In terms of its usage in the context of the modern engagement between science and theology, the label precedes Polkinghorne, having been first introduced by Barbour in the inaugural edition of *Zygon*.[3] Barbour's initial offering connected it with scientific attempts to describe reality through the use of symbolic and abstract language and with models that were necessarily partial, limited and without exact correspondence to that reality. Subsequently he linked it more explicitly to an acknowledgement of both the indirectness of reference and the realistic intent of the language used by the scientific community.[4] In the decades following this introduction, critical realism has been the predominant philosophical mode of engagement in the science–theology debate and has been taken as a clear way to bridge the gap between them and thus to facilitate engagement and dialogue.

In itself, then, there is nothing particularly unique about Polkinghorne's adoption of the strategy. Moreover, along with Barbour, he confidently asserts that it is actually the assumed stance of almost all scientists, even if they are neither explicitly aware of it nor acknowledge this to be the case.[5] Whether or

---

[2]   J. Wentzel van Huyssteen, 'Postfoundationalism in Theology and Science: Beyond Conflict and Consonance', in *Rethinking Theology and Science: Six Models for the Current Dialogue*, ed. Niels Henrik Gregersen and J. Wentzel Van Huyssteen (Grand Rapids, MI: Eerdmans, 1998), 13–50; *The Shaping of Rationality: Towards Interdisciplinarity in Theology and Science* (Grand Rapids, MI/Cambridge: Eerdmans, 1999).

[3]   Ian G. Barbour, 'Commentary on Theological Resources from the Physical Sciences', *Zygon* 1, no. 1 (1966): 29.

[4]   Ian G. Barbour, *Issues in Science and Religion* (Englewood Cliffs, NJ: Prentice-Hall, 1966), 172.

[5]   J. Polkinghorne, *Exploring Reality. The Intertwining of Science and Religion* (New Haven, CT: Yale University Press, 2005), 4.

not this is so, what is beyond dispute is that, from his earliest[6] through to his most recent work in the field, Polkinghorne himself *has* explicitly claimed it as central to his own vision of the epistemological task.[7] The term is not without a certain ambiguity of its own, a somewhat chequered history in association with a variety of epistemological strategies[8] having led to a number of reinventions.[9] Howbeit, its recent usage by the scientist–theologians essentially delineates an acceptance of Kantian empirical realism coupled with a rejection of Kant's transcendental idealism. This is certainly the sense in which Polkinghorne appropriates the term: for him the world is supremely knowable, albeit with the essential need to engage one's critical faculties when moving from experience to understanding, and of retaining a certain degree of fallibilism.[10] Thus his stance carries with it a clear commitment not only to referentiality, but also to a theory of truth involving correspondence, coherence and pragmatism – as evidenced by what is probably Polkinghorne's favourite aphorism, viz. that 'Epistemology models Ontology'.[11]

Polkinghorne situates his choice of critical realism as the most appropriate epistemic stance for engaging with reality, firmly in the context of on-going debates about the nature of that reality and the human ability to access objective knowledge. Here it functions as a necessary and effective bulwark against both constructionism and postmodern fragmentation with its intimations that all intellectual life is 'strictly à la carte'.[12] Additionally it provides him with a way of negotiating a path between this latter and continued modernist claims to the possession of, and search for, clear and certain ideas as the basis of all knowledge[13] – an Enlightenment project that he deems to have definitively failed.[14] In its actual shape and out-workings, as with that of both Barbour and Peacocke, Polkinghorne's critical realism is indebted to the vision of scientific realism expounded by Ernan

---

[6]   J. Polkinghorne, *One World: The Interaction of Science and Theology*, rev edn (West Conshohocken, PA: Templeton Foundation Press, 1986, 2007).

[7]   J. Polkinghorne, *Theology in the Context of Science* (London: SPCK, 2008), 17.

[8]   Kees van Kooten Niekerk, 'A Critical Realist Perspective on the Dialogue between Science and Theology', in *Rethinking Theology and Science. Six Models for the Current Dialogue*, ed. Niels Henrik Gregersen and J. Wentzel Van Huyssteen (Grand Rapids, MI/ Cambridge: Eerdmans, 1998), 51–2.

[9]   Andreas Losch, 'On the Origins of Critical Realism', *Theology and Science* 7, no. 1 (2009): 98.

[10]   J. Polkinghorne, *Reason and Reality* (London: SPCK, 1991), 7.

[11]   J. Polkinghorne, , *Science and the Trinity: The Christian Encounter with Reality* (London: SPCK, 2004), 79.

[12]   J. Polkinghorne, *Exploring Reality. The Intertwining of Science and Religion*, 2.

[13]   J. Polkinghorne, *Science and the Trinity: The Christian Encounter with Reality*, 51–2.

[14]   J. Polkinghorne, *Scientists as Theologians: A Comparison of the Writings of Ian Barbour, Arthur Peacocke and John Polkinghorne* (London: SPCK, 1996), 16.

McMullin.[15] In this, constructions based around scientific models and theories
were seen as the best way to gain reliable and increasing knowledge of the world;
and any theories gaining long-term success were deemed as giving good grounds
for believing that 'something like the entities and structure postulated by the
theory actually exists'.[16] Such a belief clearly informs Polkinghorne's view of
the mechanisms and successful progress associated with the scientific project,[17]
in which the ultimate hallmark of the real is not that it is *observable* but that it is
intelligible.[18]

Important tools in Polkinghorne's critical realist approach are the use of
metaphor, models and theories, and he employs these in both his scientific and
his theological explorations but in different proportions in each discipline. Thus
theology, because it deals with the uncapturable infinity of the divine, needs
the indefinite open-endedness which metaphors provide – in a way that science
simply does not.[19] With respect to models and theories Polkinghorne, in contrast
to Barbour,[20] places a much greater emphasis on the latter. Essentially regarding
models as useful tools but of 'recognised inadequacy',[21] his preference is always
to work towards a theory as the locus of any claimed verisimilitude. Since models
do not aspire to ontological accuracy, they need not be treated with ontological
seriousness and so may legitimately neglect or completely omit certain details.[22]
It is thus possible to simultaneously work with completely incompatible models
in the attempt to understand the behaviour of phenomena.[23] In contrast to this,
theories offer an account that affords consistent explanation of phenomena over a
wide and clearly demarcated range of well-winnowed physical experience. Unlike
models, they have 'serious ontological pretensions within the acknowledged limits
of critical realism'[24] and thus it is not usually possible to work with more than one at

[15]   Ian G. Barbour, *Religion and Science. Historical and Contemporary Issues*
(London: SCM, 1998), 118. Arthur Peacocke, *Intimations of Reality* (Notre Dame, IN:
University of Notre Dame Press, 1984), 24. Polkinghorne, *Reason and Reality*, 6.

[16]   Ernan McMullin, 'A Case for Scientific Realism', in Scientific Realism, ed. Jarrett
Leplin (Berkley, CA: University of California Press, 1984), 26.

[17]   Polkinghorne, *Reason and Reality*, 49.

[18]   Polkinghorne, *Scientists as Theologians: A Comparison of the Writings of Ian
Barbour, Arthur Peacocke and John Polkinghorne*, 14.

[19]   J. Polkinghorne, *Scientists as Theologians* (London: SPCK, 1996), 20.

[20]   Ian G. Barbour, *Myths, Models, and Paradigms: A Comparative Study of Science
and Religion* (New York: Harper and Row, 1974).

[21]   Polkinghorne, *Reason and Reality*, 23.

[22]   Polkinghorne, *Scientists as Theologians: A Comparison of the Writings of Ian
Barbour, Arthur Peacocke and John Polkinghorne*, 19.

[23]   Ibid., 21. J. Polkinghorne, *Quantum Physics and Theology. An Unexpected Kinship*
(London: SPCK, 2007), 74.

[24]   Polkinghorne, *Scientists as Theologians: A Comparison of the Writings of Ian
Barbour, Arthur Peacocke and John Polkinghorne*, 21.

a time. Polkinghorne understands the basic nature of this scientific quest to engage reality not as being the attainment of exact truth – which he deems impossible – but of working towards increasing verisimilitude,[25] a term that originated with Popper. Polkinghorne employs it throughout his writing as a way of describing the best obtainable approximation to reality, although in Popper's original usage the term designated a formal metalogical concept of 'truth-likeness'.[26] However, Polkinghorne's use would seem to be in keeping with Popper's later assertions that its chief value was not formal but as intuitive and heuristic.[27]

These then are the key features of Polkinghorne's critical realist stance; and while his uncompromising statement that

> any metaphysical world view that did not seek to take reality on reality's terms
> in the way that I have briefly sketched it, would be unacceptable[28]

may read as a little arrogant, in fact it simply reflects the strength of his commitment to the strategy. However, and particularly in the light of his explicitly acknowledged debt to Polanyi,[29] there are some inevitable tensions associated with this claim. These condense mainly around the theological pole of Polkinghorne's contribution and the extent to which, in this context, he can legitimately appropriate the adjectival element of the critical realist label.

One obvious difference between science and theology is in the nature of the evidence to which they are deemed to appeal. Whilst the evidential element of scientific exploration inheres in its experimental data, that on which the theologian draws and expands is a mixture of historical and contemporary experiential data that is understood to be in some sense revelatory. By its very nature as singular, often private and not amenable to repetition and testing under controlled conditions, the latter not only stands in stark contrast to the former, but appeal to it also represents the very antithesis of scientific method.[30] In addition, theology also draws on a corpus of foundational texts that, by their nature, form and history, have no direct counterpart within the scientific canon. There is thus a clear potential threat here to any claim that theology can legitimately hold a critical stance. In response to this Polkinghorne, like Barbour,[31] is very clear – unambiguously stating that he

---

[25]   Ibid., 3.

[26]   Karl Popper, *Conjectures and Refutations* (London: Routledge and Kegan Paul, 1969), 228–34, 391.

[27]   Karl Popper, *Objective Knowledge. An Evolutionary Approach* (Oxford: Clarendon Press, 1979), 59.

[28]   Polkinghorne, *Exploring Reality. The Intertwining of Science and Religion*, 6.

[29]   Polkinghorne, *Reason and Reality*, 53. Polkinghorne, *Quantum Physics and Theology. An Unexpected Kinship*, 6.

[30]   Ibid., 9.

[31]   Ian G. Barbour, *Religion in an Age of Science*. Gifford Lectures 1989–91, Vol. 1 (London: SCM, 1990), 64–5.

understands the Christian concept of revelation in terms of human encounter with divine grace, not as the uncritical acceptance of some 'unquestionable propositional knowledge made known by an infallible decree'.[32] He is similarly firm in his assertions that religious insight is not derived from 'unhesitating acceptance of fideistic assertion', although at same time he also maintains that it cannot simply be based on arguments controlled by the conventions of secular thought.[33]

A second line of defence comes from holding that the Christian interpretation of experience is properly located within, and accountable to, the life of a worshipping community.[34] Whilst arguably this insistence on active Christian practice might thereby exclude the thinking of a significant portion of the theological community, it is possible to draw at least some parallels with scientific process here: what Polkinghorne seems to be describing is a species of epistemic accountability that, in theory at least, winnows out the more eccentric ideas and interpretations of individuals. In many respects this could be seen as similar in kind to the process of critical evaluation and scrutiny of ideas that happens in any academic community, or at least in the early and informal stages of such. However whether many worshipping communities really encourage or achieve any level of critical reflection of this kind is perhaps somewhat more debatable. Similarly there would also seem to be a parallel of sorts between the 'universe-assisted logic'[35] that Polkinghorne's sees as having informed the scientific quest for understanding and the 'liturgy-assisted logic' that he sees as flowing from the worshipping life of the religious thinker – although this is not an entirely convincing comparison.

A potentially more serious difficulty, however, arises elsewhere: something that Polkinghorne leans on heavily in his understanding and application of critical realism is the understanding of knowledge advanced by Polanyi. Central to this is the fact that

> into every act of knowing, there enters a tacit and passionate contribution of the person knowing what is being known, and that this coefficient is no mere imperfection, but a necessary component of all knowledge.[36]

This is something on which Polkinghorne draws explicitly, particularly in his arguments that, in both science and theology, there are inevitable metaphysical components introduced into things such as data selection and theory choice.[37]

---

[32] Polkinghorne, *Scientists as Theologians: A Comparison of the Writings of Ian Barbour, Arthur Peacocke and John Polkinghorne*, 13.

[33] Polkinghorne, *Quantum Physics and Theology. An Unexpected Kinship*, 9.

[34] Polkinghorne, *Reason and Reality*, 59.

[35] Ibid., 1.

[36] Michael Polanyi, *Personal Knowledge: Towards a Post-critical Philosophy*, corrected edn (London: Routledge & Kegan Paul, 1962), 312.

[37] Polkinghorne, *Reason and Reality*, 6. Polkinghorne, *Science and the Trinity: The Christian Encounter with Reality*, 37, 39.

However within this personal contribution to knowledge, Polanyi also discerns a spectrum of commitment[38] in which movement from 'knowing' in the context of the sciences to that of the humanities/arts is also a movement from more 'external' to 'internal' sources of evidence, and from *verification* to *validation*.[39] Although the structure of the commitment is unchanged, and although both types of knowledge lay claim to the presence of a reality external to the knower, Polanyi argues that with this progression 'the emotional coefficient of the assertion is intensified'.[40] Thus it could also be argued, as indeed Losch has done, that the concept of 'critical reality' is only applicable within the domain of the natural sciences, since with other types of knowledge there is a corresponding and inevitable decline in criticality.[41]

Polkinghorne himself acknowledges this tension, at least implicitly, since he makes it quite clear that he has a portfolio of non-negotiable theological commitments – as exemplified for example by his comment that 'I am unwilling to relinquish the grand scheme of Trinitarian theology, anchored in the narratives of the canonical tradition'.[42] However, whilst this seems fairly uncompromising, it belies the flexibility of Polkinghorne's approach both in how he uses theological models and in how he understands the concept of being 'anchored in the narrative of the canonical tradition'. In this regard, the manifesto given in the introduction to his Gifford lectures is illuminating:

> [I am seeking] a basis for Christian belief that is certainly revised in the light of 20th century insights but which is recognisably contained within an envelope of understanding in continuity with the developing doctrine of the church throughout the centuries.[43]

He has also frankly acknowledged that the historical defence of critical realism in theology is a much more difficult undertaking than with science, since the former clearly cannot make similar claims for the substantial, cumulative and, most importantly, communally agreed, advances that the latter has achieved. However he argues that, for example in the tradition of western Christianity within which he himself is situated, it is possible to discern 'a continuing exploration and

---

[38]   Polanyi, *Personal Knowledge: Towards a Post-critical Philosophy*, 202.

[39]   Ibid., 321.

[40]   Ibid., 202.

[41]   Andreas Losch, 'Our World is More Than Physics: A Constructive-critical Comment on the Current Science and Theology Debate', *Theology and Science* 3, no. 3 (2005): 280.

[42]   Polkinghorne, *Science and the Trinity: The Christian Encounter with Reality*, 10.

[43]   J. Polkinghorne, *Science and Christian Belief: Theological Reflections of a Bottom-up Thinker* (London: SPCK, 1994), 8.

appropriation of the foundational riches of the New Testament'.[44] It is clear that he sees himself as not only standing in, but faithfully continuing that tradition. Thus what is apparent is that for Polkinghorne, whilst his view of theological thinking involves commitment to a map of a particular landscape containing certain key landmark features, precisely how these are to be delineated is in no way definitively prescribed; and moreover that this activity is, and always has been, an evolving process:[45] the historic councils of Constantinople, Ephesus, Nicaea and Chalcedon, each in response to a particular contemporary philosophical challenge, produced an understanding of the nature and role of Christ which was both increasingly sophisticated and yet retained a clear connection with the original belief-motivating experience; similarly the understanding of other key features of the Christian landscape can continue to evolve in the light of contemporary understandings, both philosophical and scientific.

In Polkinghorne's case, this willingness to address and re-think key elements of understanding, even if this goes against the grain of a dominant mode of Christian thought, is clearly demonstrated in his firmly stated belief that

> the distant God of classical theism, existing in isolated transcendence is a concept in need of correction by a recovered recognition of the immanent presence of the Creator to creation.[46]

This quest has seen him increasingly embrace and use the ideas and insights of kenotic theology to articulate an understanding of God's relationship with the created order.[47] This, while strikingly different to that of classical theism, still retains both a strong connection with an important early text in the biblical cannon (Philippians 2: 1–11) and also stands in continuity with a historically identifiable and evolving strand of thought within mainstream Christianity.[48] In conjunction with contemporary scientific insights, this has allowed Polkinghorne to explore a range of themes encompassing the issues of freedom for the created order and thus to articulate possible answers to perennial and vexing problems of theodicy in respect to both 'moral' and 'natural' evil.[49]

---

[44]   Polkinghorne, *Scientists as Theologians: A Comparison of the Writings of Ian Barbour, Arthur Peacocke and John Polkinghorne*, 17.

[45]   Polkinghorne, *Science and the Trinity: The Christian Encounter with Reality*, 29.

[46]   Ibid., 98.

[47]   See for example: J. Polkinghorne, 'Kenotic Creation and Divine Action', in *The Work of Love. Creation as Kenosis*, ed. J. Polkinghorne (Grand Rapids, MI/London: Eerdmans/SPCK, 2001), 90–106.

[48]   Jürgen Moltmann, 'God's Kenosis in the Creation and Consummation of the World', in *The Work of Love: Creation as Kenosis*, ed. John Polkinghorne (Grand Rapids, MI/London: Eerdmans/SPCK, 2001), 138–42.

[49]   Polkinghorne, *Exploring Reality. The Intertwining of Science and Religion*, 143–4.

Such an understanding of God as self-limiting in terms of the divine triad of omnipresence, omniscience and omnipotence is radically different from the traditional view rooted in classical theism (itself of course a product of philosophical ideas prevalent in the early centuries of Christian development). As such it is fiercely opposed by those who see it as compromising God's essential character in various ways,[50] but it nevertheless retains continuity with canonical texts, with foundational experiences of the early church, and with strands of theological exploration throughout the development of Christian thought. Thus it remains clearly 'within [the] envelope' and yet is critical of certain elements of Christian understandings of God, seeking to revisit, revise and rearticulate these in ways which are illuminated by the light of contemporary understandings of the nature of reality. In this respect, Polkinghorne's approach exemplifies the 'developmental' category of his revision[51] of the two positive stations of Barbour's classic taxonomy.[52] In maintaining a recognisable connection with tradition, Polkinghorne also manages to avoid Westhelle's criticism[53] that re-workings of Christian motifs in the light of contemporary knowledge, in which they are stripped down to 'newly conceived essentials',[54] reduce theology to an 'anaemic myth', and one that is debased as both specific and universal coinage.

However, this in itself does not decisively settle the issue of criticality since a charge could still be levelled that, given the sense across his writings that there are some irreducible elements of the portfolio of Christian belief and theological concept that admit no reworking,[55] there will still inevitably be a point at which it fails. Even with regard to these seemingly fixed landscape features though, Polkinghorne maintains an approach that demonstrates both suppleness and subtlety. An archetypal example would be his apparently non-negotiable belief in the 'sacramental principle' that Christian salvific symbols are always anchored in actual occurrence,[56] with all the difficulties this seems to raise in connection with events such as the virgin birth, or the resurrection of Jesus. However with respect to the former, although he is 'prepared to believe [it] actually took

---

[50]   Thomas R. Thompson and Cornelius Plantinga Jr, 'Trinity and Kenosis', in *Exploring Kenotic Christology: The Self-emptying of God*, ed. Stephen C. Evans (Oxford: Oxford University Press, 2006), 165–6.

[51]   Polkinghorne, *Science and the Trinity: The Christian Encounter with Reality*, 10–29.

[52]   Ian G. Barbour, *When Science Meets Religion* (London: SPCK, 2000), 2–4.

[53]   Vitor Westhelle, 'Theological Shamelessness? A Response to Arthur Peacocke and David A. Pailin', *Zygon: Journal of Religion and Science* 35, no. 1 (2000): 171–2.

[54]   Arthur Peacocke, 'Science and the Future of Theology: Critical Issues', *Zygon: Journal of Religion and Science* 35, no. 1 (2000): 136.

[55]   Polkinghorne, *Scientists as Theologians: A Comparison of the Writings of Ian Barbour, Arthur Peacocke and John Polkinghorne*, 80, for example.

[56]   Polkinghorne, *Science and the Trinity: The Christian Encounter with Reality*, 31.

place',[57] there is a feeling that, unlike with Peacocke,[58] it is not a critical matter for Polkinghorne as to precisely how Jesus obtained his human genome, since the proof of his total humanity does not depend on this so much as on his complete sharing in the experience of human death.[59] By contrast, his approach to the matter of the resurrection of Jesus carries a much more inescapable sense that, because of Polkinghorne's eschatological commitments, the witness of scripture is unambiguously that this must constitute an actual physical event.[60] He is, however, prepared to imagine and explore a range of ways as to how this might be understood, using these to show that such a belief does not violate either the possibilities inherent in current models being explored in theoretical physics,[61] nor his own understandings of God's interaction with the created order.

In tandem with this, whilst continuing to affirm the traditional Christian belief in the resurrected afterlife, Polkinghorne is able once again to think in an evolving and more supple way about possible shapes for this. These are clearly located outside of both a strict (and currently rather popular) biblical literalism and of the mainstream evangelical positions on judgement and hell, envisioning instead a continuous unfolding of salvation and union with the divine.[62] Similarly, whilst retaining a commitment to the Christian idea of an eternal soul, he is in no way constrained by the traditional dualistic conception of this, once again demonstrating that he is able and willing to rethink this doctrine in an alternative and creative fashion. In this instance he draws on a concept of 'information' (i.e. the specification of dynamical patterns of behaviour in complex systems) to produce an alternative 'information bearing pattern' conception of soul.[63] This takes account of growing scientific understanding of chaotic and complex systems, and simultaneously maintains a recognisable connection with traditional ideas of the soul as the distinct locus of identity and individuality.

Inevitably, considerations about the evaluation of biblical (or other) evidence, and of whether or not a certain corpus of such is sufficiently convincing to sustain a particular belief, raise the perennial matter of the 'hermeneutic circle' and the extent to which this is, or is not, escapable. This is a point that Polkinghorne has himself repeatedly discussed in his evaluation of the status of science and theology as critical realist disciplines; indeed it has been one of his ways of establishing the legitimacy of parity between them in this respect. His argument, following

[57] Ibid.

[58] Arthur Peacocke, *Theology for a Scientific Age*, enlarged edn (Minneapolis, MN: Fortress, 1993), 275–9.

[59] Polkinghorne, *Science and the Trinity: The Christian Encounter with Reality*, 30.

[60] Ibid., 23, 30–31, 167–9. Polkinghorne, *Exploring Reality. The Intertwining of Science and Religion*, 82–7.

[61] Ibid., 171–3.

[62] Polkinghorne, *Science and the Trinity: The Christian Encounter with Reality*, 159–60.

[63] Ibid., 161.

Ricoeur, is that any act of knowing is inevitably tied into a circle in which the encounter with reality is inescapably linked to an interpretative viewpoint in 'a relationship of mutual illumination and correction':[64] as Ricoeur has it 'We must understand in order to believe, but we must believe in order to understand'.[65] Polkinghorne argues that this is just as much the case for science as for religion; indeed science's own commitment to the idea of an accessible, ordered and explainable world can be seen as already assuming a prior metaphysical belief about how the world essentially *is*.[66] Thus all knowing inevitably involves an element of metaphysical choice. The paradigmatic example of Bohr and Bohm, and their different interpretations of the inherent unpredictability of the quantum world laid bare by Heisenberg, clearly illustrates that empirical adequacy alone may be an insufficient ground for theory choice. We could legitimately argue then that since no-one, not even the scientist, comes to the noetic situation as merely a passive receptor of value-neutral data, and since all data interpretation requires an element of choice that will be conditioned by prior metaphysical commitment, then the nature of the choices Polkinghorne makes as a theologian are, as regards the issue of criticality, essentially no different in kind from those that he makes as a particle physicist.

Thus by Polkinghorne's own definition of the term, it is possible to argue from a variety of perspectives that he does maintain a suitably critical stance with respect to his theological commitments – proving himself willing to rethink the shape these might take whilst still maintaining a recognisable connection with the general topography of the Christian thought-map. Hence the potential issue of whether, in regard to Polkinghorne's theological thinking, the intensification of Polanyi's 'emotional coefficient of the assertion' inevitably entails a potential and fatal loss of criticality proves, because of his willingness and ability to bring both suppleness and subtlety to his thinking, to be much less of a problem than might have initially appeared to be the case. There is however another potential, although more subtle, source of tension in Polkinghorne's assumption of a critical realist stance, which I would also like to explore, albeit somewhat more briefly. In this instance the incipient difficulties, whilst again connected with Polkinghorne's theological commitments rather than his scientific ones, are associated with the 'realist' element of the description, and in particular the extent to which he believes it is possible for God to be known and spoken of.

Polkinghorne's writings consistently and clearly indicate that his assumption of a realist stance is located in his belief that knowledge, rooted in interpreted experience, can be taken as a reliable guide to the nature of reality;[67] and that,

---

[64]   Polkinghorne, *Quantum Physics and Theology. An Unexpected Kinship*, 8–9.

[65]   Paul Ricoeur, *The Symbolism of Evil*, trans. Emerson Buchanan, ET edn (Boston, MA: Beacon Press, 1967), 351.

[66]   Polkinghorne, *Reason and Reality*, 49.

[67]   Polkinghorne, *Scientists as Theologians: A Comparison of the Writings of Ian Barbour, Arthur Peacocke and John Polkinghorne*, 14.

cultural constraints notwithstanding, it is thus possible to attain best explanations of experience that correspond to a *verisimilitudinous* account of the nature of reality.[68] However, when it comes to articulation of the extent to which experience of *God* gives access to any understanding of his nature, Polkinghorne's response is variable. There would seem to be a number of possible elements to this, the most obvious of which is that it reflects the ancient and perennial question as to the degree of equivalence possible between human language and the divine attributes. On the one hand, God is mysteriously ineffable and cannot be captured or exhaustively contained in the finite categories of human thought. On the other, he has 'acted to make the divine nature known in humanly accessible ways', most particularly in the life death and resurrection of Christ.[69]

Polkinghorne is obviously aware of this tension and urges his fellow theologians to strike the correct balance between apophatic and cataphatic utterance about God. In as much as this call seems to be more in the way of a challenge to them to be sufficiently bold than a plea for them to be more retiring in their God-talk,[70] one might take it as in keeping with commitment to maintain a realist stance within theology, the difficulties of that notwithstanding. Further evidence of this commitment could be adduced from Polkinghorne's personal willingness to commit himself extensively to both kenotic[71] and perichoretic[72] theologies as a means of trying to articulate in theological terms a verisimilitude with what he believes modern scientific insights (particularly those from physics) are revealing about the nature of reality. Against this, he freely admits that theology knows that 'all its models of God, if pressed too far, will eventually become inadequate idols'.[73]

However, the realist commitment notwithstanding, and despite his adamant view that 'the mystery card should be the last one played in the theological discussion',[74] there are also times when Polkinghorne clearly feels that it is impossible to access certain elements of reality in connection with God or with spiritual matters, and thus we must simply 'wait and see'.[75] In part this seems to stem from further issues relating to his understanding of *how* we come to know things. Along with the hermeneutic circularity already referred to, Polkinghorne also discerns the existence of an epistemic circularity as an equally inescapable part of the process of knowing: for both theology *and* science, the way in which

[68] Ibid., 4.
[69] Polkinghorne, *Exploring Reality. The Intertwining of Science and Religion*, 95–6.
[70] Polkinghorne, *Science and the Trinity: The Christian Encounter with Reality*, 90.
[71] Polkinghorne, 'Kenotic Creation and Divine Action', 90–106.
[72] Polkinghorne, *Science and the Trinity: The Christian Encounter with Reality*, 88–117.
[73] Polkinghorne, *Scientists as Theologians*, 23.
[74] Polkinghorne, *Exploring Reality. The Intertwining of Science and Religion*, 96.
[75] J. Polkinghorne, *The God of Hope and the End of the World* (New Haven, CT: Yale University Press, 2002), 138.

we gain knowledge of the nature of an object is itself determined by that nature.[76] Thus we can only know objects in their own terms.[77] In respect to the argument that it is difficult to maintain a realist position in light of some aspects of modern scientific knowledge and theory, particularly those relating to quantum theory, this is in fact a pleasingly supple way of resisting the charge. However it seems somewhat more problematic with regard to knowing God, since in this instance the nature of the revelation is arguably under the active control of the object (God) in a somewhat different way from that operating with the particles of subatomic physics. When Polkinghorne speaks of a 'necessary veiling' and a process whereby 'God can progressively begin to be revealed with greater clarity',[78] he seems to acknowledge that at any given time, our knowledge of God will not necessarily correspond in any very exact respect to the reality of how God is.

A further difficulty for the realist project would also seem to be raised by the question of how exactly the theological investigation of God relates to the religious experience of encounter. Once again there is a hint as to the nature of the issue in Polanyi's thinking about knowledge, to which, as was earlier noted, Polkinghorne is explicitly indebted. However this time the issue is more complex than merely that of personal commitment to the object of enquiry diminishing criticality. Thus it is correspondingly more elusive to pin down in regard to Polkinghorne's work. Essentially, Polanyi holds that, as the objects of knowledge move to higher levels of existence (for example from physical processes to organisms), so there is a corresponding and 'an ever more ample ... sharing of existence between the knower and the known'. This finally reaches the point with another person that 'our knowledge of him has definitely lost the character of an *observation* and has become an *encounter* instead'.[79] This is very reminiscent of the distinction that Marcel draws between first and second reflection and of the inevitable clash between them. In the former, the reality encountered is subjected to a process of abstraction and categorisation, being objectified and problematised in an attempt to discover its true nature.[80] However, those very manoeuvres preclude the possibility of a true encounter and thus of gaining any real knowledge of it. The question might therefore be asked as to whether the realist project of attempting to move from experience through interpretation to attempting a verisimilitudinous account of reality could, at least in respect to certain aspects of God, actually have the opposite effect.

At first sight, this might appear to be a variation of the apophatic theme discussed above but it is, I think, somewhat different. The issue would seem instead to be whether, in the case of certain types of encounter with reality, the approach

---

[76] Polkinghorne, *Scientists as Theologians*, 15.

[77] Polkinghorne, *Science and the Trinity: The Christian Encounter with Reality*, 77.

[78] Polkinghorne, *Exploring Reality. The Intertwining of Science and Religion*, 142–3.

[79] Michael Polanyi, *The Study of Man* (Chicago, IL: University of Chicago Press, 1959), 94–5, my emphases.

[80] Gabriel Marcel, *Being and Having* (Glasgow: Robert MacLehose, 1949), 116–7.

of interrogating and interpreting experiential data might cause that knowledge that we seek to understand and articulate to slip through our fingers. The sense of this is clearly expressed in the line from Marcel's play *L'Iconoclaste* that 'Knowledge exiles to infinity whatever it claims to clasp'.[81] On this point, and given the strong sense throughout his corpus that, just as for Rilke, observation of the world is often synonymous with encountering its creator,[82] one could also raise the admittedly much more speculative question as to whether there might be an implicit issue here for Polkinghorne's *scientific* work and thinking as well. However there is nothing in his writing to suggest that his scientific explorations of the world place God at a greater distance, quite the contrary in fact; and there is certainly no sense of Marcel's 'hypostasis of absence'.[83] Nevertheless it is interesting to note that, ultimately, Polkinghorne seems more willing to think and talk of a grand unified theory in terms of the inherent mysteries of Trinitarian theology,[84] rather than in the explicitly delineated mathematical shape of a string theory, no matter how elegant the latter might be.

For Polkinghorne then, there are certain inherent tensions associated with the first of the major planks of his epistemological approach to the science–theology dialogue but which, by employing a flexible and subtle approach, he manages to negotiate reasonably successfully. However if we turn to the second of his key strategies, the difficulty is less easily resolved. This is in part because it is less under Polkinghorne's direct control, and in part because it seems built in to the very structure of the interaction between theology and science.

Polkinghorne is deeply committed to a view that the essential character of human experience is inescapably many-layered, with the same event capable of bearing interpretation from a variety of perspectives. Hand-in-hand with this is the conviction that crass physical reductionism will only ever render a very impoverished account of such experience, and thus that to give the fullest account of it will inevitably and always require different epistemes. However he has no truck with the notion that, as per Gould's NOMA,[85] these different modes of discourse can have nothing to say to each other. On the contrary, his theological commitments demand that, as one who 'endeavours to speak of God as ground of all', he has a responsibility to seek a way in which to 'incorporate all forms of

---

[81]   Gabriel Marcel and Katharine Rose Hanley, *Ghostly Mysteries*, trans. Katharine Rose Hanley, ET edn (Milwaukee, WI: Marquette University Press, 2004), 99.

[82]   For example, J. Polkinghorne, *Belief in God in an Age of Science* (New Haven, CT: Yale University Press, 1998), 1–2, 19.

[83]   Louis Pamplume and Beth Brombert, 'Gabriel Marcel: Existence, Being, and Faith', *Yale French Studies* no. 12 (1953): 92.

[84]   Polkinghorne, *Science and the Trinity: The Christian Encounter with Reality*, 61. Polkinghorne, *Quantum Physics and Theology. An Unexpected Kinship*, 110.

[85]   Stephen Gould, *Rocks of Ages: Science and Religion in the Fullness of Life* (New York: Ballantine Books, 1999).

specific knowledge into a single reconciled account'.[86] In this respect he embodies the essence of McMullin's assertion that:

> The Christian cannot separate his science from his theology as though they were incapable of interrelation ... He may, indeed *must* strive to make his theology and his cosmology consonant in the contribution they make to this world view.[87]

Thus the second part of his strategy is to underline that theology and science *both* operate in a critical realist mode, and in tandem with this, to demonstrate and substantiate a claim that there is also a close and 'cousinly kinship' between them, making dialogue both possible and permissible. However, there is no question of theology being relegated to a peripheral role as merely a possible source of insight only for specific limit-type questions.[88] On the contrary he believes that distinct areas of consonance can be found that will prove to be mutually illuminating.

In order to establish this close relationship, Polkinghorne argues that there are a number of areas in which the disciplines display essential similarities, even if within this, aspects of precise detail are sometimes quite widely different. He has recently presented a detailed analysis of this with respect to quantum physics and theology, believing that the argument is better made through worked examples than through an appeal to general principle.[89] However, it is taken as a given that the patterns thus discerned can be understood to apply across the spectrum of science/ theology kinship. It should perhaps be emphasised here that, in making such claims, Polkinghorne is not following Murphy in trying to establish that theology is *itself* a scientific discipline.[90] Rather he is building a case for relatedness that then allows him to search for and explore areas of consonance between the two disciplines. Foundational to this argument is his understanding that both science and theology employ an essentially similar heuristic in their approach to expanding knowledge.[91] Thus he claims that both work through a dialectical engagement between experience and interpretation; and that, while the fundamental elements of this, namely the data drawn on and the type of elaborations made from it, clearly take a different shape, each discipline approaches the task in the same way, and

---

[86]   Polkinghorne, *Scientists as Theologians: A Comparison of the Writings of Ian Barbour, Arthur Peacocke and John Polkinghorne*, 12.

[87]   Ernan McMullin, 'How Should Cosmology Relate to Theology?', in *The Sciences and Theology in the Twentieth Century*, ed. A.R. Peacocke (Notre Dame, IN: University of Notre Dame Press, 1981), 52.

[88]   Willem B. Drees, *Religion and Science in Context: A Guide to the Debates* (London: Routledge, 2010), 96–8, 106.

[89]   Polkinghorne, *Quantum Physics and Theology. An Unexpected Kinship*, 15.

[90]   Nancey Murphy, *Theology in the Age of Scientific Reasoning* (Ithaca, NY: Cornell University Press, 1990).

[91]   Polkinghorne, *Quantum Physics and Theology. An Unexpected Kinship*, 25.

each makes a conscious selection of appropriate tools (for example a specific type of maths or philosophy) from within an available range.[92]

Within this basic dialectical heuristic, Polkinghorne sees both science and theology as displaying a similar pattern of conceptual development – one that has elements typical of the critical realist *modus operandi*. The key features here are firstly that thinking is 'bottom-up' – in other words that the quest for motivated belief essentially involves a movement from experience to understanding, rather than from *a priori* concepts downwards to interpretation of experience; and secondly that in this upward development, understanding progresses, via the use of models, metaphors and theories, through different levels of conceptualisation of increasing complexity and depth. Each level maintains a contact with the original motivating evidence but, through the generation of novel concepts, also attains increasing explanatory power. Thus each stage also encompasses an appropriate level of both generality and the depth to yield fruitful insight.[93] The net result is an overall movement beyond the simple matching with experiential particulars through to the formulation of ideas with both wider generality and more profound significance.[94]

Whilst initial attempts at explanation of experience are typically fairly conservative, the usual pattern is that, under the stimulus of a succession of challenges – which may be experimental/theoretical in the case of science, and experiential/conceptual in the case of theology – they gradually develop into a much richer account that does justice to the actual complexity of the underlying reality and thus displays an increasing level of verisimilitude. As a typical example of this from the world of particle physics, Polkinghorne cites the progression of ideas that accompanied the evolving understanding of nuclear properties: here the notion of equivalent potential gave way to a quantum field theory sufficient for understanding directly observable experimental particles; this in turn was then supplanted by the concepts of quantum chromodynamics essential for understanding quarks.[95] A theological equivalent offered is the progressive elucidation of the nature of Christ which flowed from the statements issued by the historic church councils at Nicaea, Constantinople, Ephesus and Chalcedon in response to a series of philosophical challenges.[96] The final formulation, whilst retaining its connection with the initial experiential data, is far more sophisticated and potentially fruitful than the earlier ones; yet at the same time, each successive development does justice to the level of understanding from which it arose and provides the foundations for the next stage of the process.

In their pursuit of understanding, often in the face of encounter and struggle marked by the surprising and the frankly counter-intuitive, Polkinghorne discerns

[92]   Ibid., 25–9.
[93]   Ibid., 76.
[94]   Ibid., 73.
[95]   Ibid., 75–6.
[96]   Ibid., 85–90.

another similarity in the trajectories of the disciplines. Their shared journey through the stages of enforced radical revision, unresolved confusion, new synthesis and understanding, continued wrestling with unresolved problems and the eventual realisation of deeper implications allows him once again to claim a cousinly relationship as existing between them.[97] It is on such bases as these that Polkinghorne builds his case for a close connection between the disciplines. This then allows him to search out and explore areas of consonance between them as they pursue their search for truth via the careful evaluation of well-motivated belief.[98] Once again, Polkinghorne's capacity for supple and imaginative thinking is revealed in his suggestions of areas in which there might be consonances worth further excavation and exploration. A typical example is his comparison between the discovery of superconductivity and the nature of miracles: Here he examines how Onnes' work (with its seeming disproof of the universal applicability of Ohm's law) led eventually to the understanding of how apparent inconsistencies at a certain level could still be connected to the same deep underlying and unchanging law; he then draws out parallels with theological attempts to understand and give an account of miracles as connected to divine consistency.[99]

Nevertheless, and despite Polkinghorne's championing of epistemological kinship, and his identification of multiple areas of consonances, there remains across all arenas of science–theology engagement, an apparent and seemingly inescapable asymmetry between the two disciplines. There are a number of strands to this, some of which inhere in the nature of the reality that each discipline studies and attempts to articulate, and some of which are linked to a persistent tension between their different domains and associated efforts to claim cognitive parity between these. In part at least, this would seem to be related to the fact that, as van Huyssteen has noted, theology as a discipline is caught in something of a double-bind: on the one hand, it is firmly enveloped in and must grapple with the issues presented by the radical pluralism of postmodern discourse; on the other, somewhat paradoxically, it is still trapped in a modernist dilemma in which an allegedly superior scientific rationality continues to oppose religious faith and designate any experience or thinking associated with it as being inescapably private and subjective, and thus barred from contributing anything meaningful to shared or public discourse.[100] Current scientific polemic directed against religious and theological discourse would seem to offer support for this reading. However, interestingly and perhaps tellingly, Polkinghorne prefers to understand any inescapable asymmetry as directly relating to the nature of *theology* and its specific task, rather than to any presumed rational superiority of science. Moreover he holds that this is because theology, dealing as it does in discourse about God,

---

[97]   Ibid., 15–22.

[98]   Ibid., x.

[99]   Ibid., 33–5.

[100]   J. Wentzel van Huyssteen, *Duet or Duel? Theology and Science in a Postmodern World* (London: SCM Press, 1998), xii–xiii.

is necessarily concerned with 'the totality of what is real'.[101] This same sense
of theology's wider remit and loftier project is also implicit in Polkinghorne's
observation that the success of science is ultimately due to the modesty of its
ambitions.[102]

Nevertheless there would still seem to be a serious tension between
Polkinghorne's account of theology's aspirations to the regal position of 'The
Queen of Sciences'[103] and his assertion that science, in telling us about the nature
of the physical world, 'imposes conditions of consonance which the broader
considerations of theology must respect'.[104] Whilst this might be relatively
unproblematic (at least for some) in terms of the example which Polkinghorne
uses of the geological age of the earth and the doctrine of creation, it is unclear
exactly where the lines might eventually be drawn in this respect. A similar
opacity surrounds *how* this demarcation is to be determined, especially when
considered in tandem with Polkinghorne's related comment that such constraint
is a useful brake on theology's occasional propensity for indulging in ungrounded
speculation. Given that Polkinghorne is himself, in some respects, a very creative
speculative thinker, this would seem to lead us back to earlier discussions of the
tensions involved in critical realism, the prior metaphysical commitments implicit
in the hermeneutic circle, and Polkinghorne's own clear statements about elements
of religious understanding on which he is not prepared to concede ground.

Moreover, it could also be argued that Polkinghorne's concession of the
right of science to constrain theology in some respects, coupled with his candid
statement that science, operating within its own domain, needs no assistance from
theology,[105] constitutes a tacit assent to Gregersen's observation that, while science
is self-validating, theology falls short of its agenda if it does not engage with
science.[106] In effect this would seem to be tantamount to accepting that science
plays a role in the justification of theology as a rational discipline – a position that
does not sit entirely easily with some of Polkinghorne's other statements on the
relationship between the two. It is not clear quite how this tension is to be resolved,
since Polkinghorne's main concern here lies not necessarily in a specific defence
of the rationality of theology in the face of scientific hostility, but in establishing,
through similar patterns of operation and developmental history, enough of a
cousinly relationship to admit of a search for consonance.

---

    [101]   Polkinghorne, *Reason and Reality*, 75.

    [102]   Ibid.

    [103]   J. Polkinghorne, *Science and Creation* (London: SPCK, 1988), 1.

    [104]   Polkinghorne, *Reason and Reality*, 75.

    [105]   J. Polkinghorne, 'Where Is Natural Theology Today?', *Science and Christian
Belief* 18, no. 2 (2006): 171.

    [106]   Niels Henrik Gregersen, 'A Contextual Coherence Theory for the Science–
Theology Dialogue', in *Rethinking Theology and Science: Six Models for the Current
Dialogue*, ed. Niels Henrik Gregersen and J. Wentzel Van Huyssteen (Grand Rapids, MI:
Eerdmans, 1998), 185.

What is clear is that, over the years, Polkinghorne has shown a great talent for identifying and exploring these areas of consonance, particularly those between perichoretic and kenotic theologies and aspects of modern physics. Nevertheless, despite the subtle and supple ways in which he has used these to explore complex issues such as the balance between freedom and order within creation, the nature of time and of God's connection with the temporal world and the possibility of divine action in the world,[107] it is hard to escape the feeling that the only beneficiary of this dialogue is the believing community. Thus its primary result, despite Polkinghorne's denial of such an aim,[108] might in fact be viewed, not as a contribution to a more widely accepted expansion of human understanding of the nature of reality, but as the development of a more sophisticated form of Christian apologetics, one that enables those involved or interested in scientific discourse to successfully defend themselves against charges of committing 'intellectual suicide' by attempting to hold onto religious belief. This is not of course tantamount to saying that such constitutes an unimportant result; and indeed Polkinghorne has clearly stated that theology cannot excuse itself from its duty of enabling believers to be able to make a coherent defence of their faith as necessity arises.[109] Thus one can appreciate and applaud, for example, Polkinghorne's attempt to articulate a scientifically coherent view of the resurrection in response to his belief that part of the Christian community has lost its nerve about affirming 'the hope of destiny beyond death', partly because of 'an inability to make some sort of sense of what that prospect might actually mean'.[110]

Polkinghorne does of course offer some thoughts about what he sees as the possible contribution that theology makes to science – for example in his comment that it can provide science with answers to the meta-questions that it raises but cannot itself answer.[111] However it is difficult to find much evidence in his corpus of any sense of what theological thinking has *actually* contributed to the scientific enterprise or understanding of the world, except perhaps for those working in the science–theology field, who might be supposed to have some prior commitment to finding it useful. Indeed it is not always clear in which direction the flow goes for Polkinghorne himself: for instance, with respect to kenosis, there is some opacity around whether kenotic theology has provided him with a fruitful resource for thinking about scientific data, or whether it was the latter that made fertile ground for his development of kenotic understandings of different aspects of God's relationship with the created order. Comments in the introduction to *The Work of*

---

107   J. Polkinghorne, 'Kenotic Creation and Divine Action', in *The Work of Love: Creation as Kenosis*, ed. J. Polkinghorne (Grand Rapids, MI/London: Eerdmans/SPCK, 2001), 97–100.

108   Polkinghorne, *Belief in God in an Age of Science*, 85.

109   Polkinghorne, *Exploring Reality. The Intertwining of Science and Religion*, 95.

110   Ibid., 170.

111   Polkinghorne, *Reason and Reality*, 75.

Love[112] seem to hint at the former, whereas those in a *Zygon* article are strongly suggestive of the latter.[113] This is not in itself a particular problem, and indeed one could easily and aptly think of the two disciplines as interacting in a perichoretic way in Polkinghorne's thinking. However, the underlying questions as to what precisely flows from theology to science, and what its fruitfulness has been in a wider sense, must be considered in any attempt to claim a mutually meaningful and illuminating interaction between the disciplines. This in turn leads inevitably to a consideration of ways in which the science–theology field might be developed in the future and whether this inequality should and can be addressed. Thus I want finally, in the light of the account of Polkinghorne offered in this essay, to venture a suggestion as to one of the chief challenges I see him offering to new theologians such as myself, who are currently entering this field.

In this essay I have endeavoured to demonstrate that, in both his deployment of a particular epistemological strategy and the way in which he has negotiated some of its inherent tensions, Polkinghorne has shown a subtlety and suppleness in his thinking to reflect that which he has encountered in his own explorations of reality. In these respects, he stands as an exemplar of how to undertake interdisciplinary dialogue from a critical realist perspective. However I believe that his example also points the way forward towards the possibility of a bolder venture, something that would of course be completely in keeping with his own calls for a willingness to take intellectual risks in the pursuit of a greater understanding of the rich reality that we inhabit and encounter.[114]

Polkinghorne has always specifically defined himself as a critical realist; however, I would contend that, just as with his own suggestion that such a stance could be, and often has been, adopted and employed unknowingly, so too his own mode of engagement down the years, and over the range of his contributions to assorted discussions at the science–theology interface, actually embodies and displays precisely the kind of flexible transversal rationality which J. Wentzel van Huyssteen has delineated, developed and employed in his own Gifford lectures.[115] Like Polkinghorne, van Huyssteen has attempted to chart a course between the twin perils of modernistic foundationalism and post-modern relativism, both of which he too rejects as untenable.[116] However, rather than employing critical realism as a tool, his approach has been to creatively refigure the concept of rationality itself. The key features of this reconfigured *post-foundational* rationality, viz. the recognition of the epistemic quest as being to make progress

---

[112]   J. Polkinghorne, ed., *The Work of Love. Creation as Kenosis* (Grand Rapids, MI/ London: Eerdmans/SPCK, 2001), x–xiv.

[113]   Polkinghorne, 'The Continuing Interaction of Science and Religion', *Zygon* 40, no. 1 (2005): 44–5.

[114]   Polkinghorne, *Belief in God in an Age of Science*, 83, for example.

[115]   J. Wentzel van Huyssteen, *Alone in the World? Human Uniqueness in Science and Theology* (Grand Rapids, MI: Eerdmans, 2006).

[116]   Ibid., 12.

towards intelligibility and optimal understanding, the exercise of the epistemic skill of responsible judgement and the notion of experiential accountability,[117] all find, as I have illustrated in this essay, a ready and strong echo in the understanding and approach of Polkinghorne.

In van Huyssteen's model, acceptance of these basic tenets opens the way for the development of a different sort of interdisciplinary dialogue predicated on the understanding that, whilst participants remain rooted and connected to their base communities or disciplines, they are not constrained by them. Again I would argue that just such transcendence-in-rootedness is a key characteristic of Polkinghorne's approach. In van Huyssteen's proposed model, although we may come into dialogue with strong beliefs, commitments and even prejudices, a commitment to a post-foundational understanding of rationality, by enabling the identification of shared resources of rationality between different modes of knowledge, allows us to reach beyond disciplinary boundaries.[118] Moving forward requires a complex and multileveled approach that is not located within the confines of the disciplines involved but in 'transversal spaces between them'.[119]

Drawing on Schrag's mathematically informed picture of multiple intersecting lines,[120] van Huyssteen develops this idea of interdisciplinary dialogue as an enterprise in which the participating disciplines move on convergent trajectories (for example shared research foci) towards a 'transversal space'. Here the different voices do not see themselves as in contradiction or needing to be assimilative; instead they can be dynamically interactive, exchanging information, ideas and insights. This opening up of transversal spaces is key to the enterprise, allowing as it does the connection of different domains of rationality in a non-competitive way. The resultant interdisciplinary networks enable the possibility that

> different disciplines in dialogue, though never fully integrated, can learn from one another and actually benefit from taking over insights presented in that dialogue.[121]

I would argue that Polkinghorne, particularly in his creative attempts to identify and explore areas of consonance between physics and theology, has already been opening up just these sorts of transversal spaces. Moreover, his own subtle and supple ways of thinking and engaging, whilst remaining both rooted in, and

[117]   van Huyssteen, *The Shaping of Rationality: Towards Interdisciplinarity in Theology and Science*, 179–234.

[118]   J. Wentzel van Huyssteen, 'Fallen Angels or Rising Beasts? Theological Perspectives on Human Uniqueness', *Theology and Science* 1, no. 2 (2003): 162.

[119]   van Huyssteen, *Alone in the World? Human Uniqueness in Science and Theology*, 9.

[120]   van Huyssteen, *The Shaping of Rationality: Towards Interdisciplinarity in Theology and Science*, 246.

[121]   van Huyssteen, *Alone in the World? Human Uniqueness in Science and Theology*, 20.

accountable to, a religious epistemic community, exemplify just the sort of flexible transversal rationality that van Huyssteen has described.

However I also want to suggest that the challenge this presents to young scholars entering the field behind Polkinghorne goes further and relates to the final tension identified in his work, and to a way in which this imbalance might be taken on and addressed. It seems to me that there are strong points of intersection not only between Polkinghorne's mode of engagement and these ideas of transversal space dialogue, but also with the developing fields of transdisciplinarity: for example, van Huyssteen's designation of transversality as 'a vibrant and constructive postmodernist move to integrate all our ways of knowing without again totalising them in any modernist sense'[122] is very close in many ways to the idea and structure of the 'complex thinking' developed and deployed by Edgar Morin.[123] This works towards the reintegration of knowledge deriving from different disciplines and sub-disciplines into an expanded complex whole. Polkinghorne has not only shown that it is unnecessary to be reticent about the contribution that theology can make to developing a richer understanding, but has also demonstrated *how* this contribution can be taken into creative dialogue with other disciplinary voices. Thus I want finally to suggest that the next stage in this process is for theologians to draw on his example, heed his call for intellectual daring and, in light of theology's anthropological interests and insights, look for ways to move forward into a true *trans*disciplinary engagement with the biological sciences, particularly the neurosciences, in which it can stand as an equal contributing partner. I believe that such a move would be a fitting tribute to John Polkinghorne's rich, subtle and supple contributions to the science–theology field.

---

[122]   Ibid., 19.

[123]   Edgar Morin, *On Complexity*, trans. R. Postel and S.M. Kelly, ET edn (Cresskill, NJ: Hampton Press, 2008).

Chapter 12

On Revising Natural Theology:
John Polkinghorne and the False Modesty
of Liberal Theology

Russell Re Manning

Introduction

John Polkinghorne is rightly acknowledged as a 'living icon' of the renewal of
the dialogue between science and religion.[1] Throughout his prolific career as a
scientist–theologian he has been at the forefront of much creative work that has
challenged the (sadly still widespread) assumption of a basic conflict between
Christian faith and the scientific worldview. Polkinghorne, however, goes further
than simply affirming the mutual compatibility of religious belief and a commitment
to scientific truth. For him, 'belief in God in an age of science' is not just presented
as a valid option amongst others but he equally defends Christian theology as
'a true Theory of Everything' that is 'much grander and more comprehensive
and intellectually satisfying than any Grand Unified Theory of particle physics
could ever be'.[2] This essay will consider Polkinghorne's theological project in the
context of the tradition of theological liberalism and its central rhetorical posture
of modesty.

Liberal theology is in a situation of crisis. Assailed by scientistic naturalisms
on the one hand and various theological dogmatisms on the other, the previously
secure *via media* of the mediation of religious faith and its cultural setting has
become increasingly unsettled. Just as the reductionism that currently dominates
in the natural sciences denies the autonomy of the religious, so the regnant
dogmatism of much confessional theology exposes what it designates as the empty
nihilism of contemporary secular culture.[3] The result is that a liberal theology that

---

[1]   Edward M. Hogan, 'John Polkinghorne and Bernard Lonergan on the Scientific
Status of Theology', *Zygon: Journal of Religion and Science* 44(3) (2009): 559.

[2]   John Polkinghorne, *Quantum Physics and Theology. An Unexpected Kinship*
(London: SPCK, 2007), 110; John Polkinghorne, *Faith, Science and Understanding* (New
Haven, CT: Yale University Press, 2000), 25.

[3]   See Steven Weinberg, *The First Three Minutes: A Modern View of the Origin of the
Universe* (New York: Basic Books, 1977), Daniel Dennett, *Breaking the Spell: Religion as
a Natural Phenomenon* (London: Allen Lane, 2006), Pascal Boyer, *Religion Explained. The*

aims to adopt Schleiermacher's reciprocal 'perpetual alliance' between Christian faith and modern knowledge without threatening the autonomy of either party is increasingly being squeezed and risks collapsing into either simply a theological baptism of scientific naturalism or a *de facto* theological positivism.[4] The other alternative, more frequently adopted than explicitly defended, is a retreat from normative metaphysical judgements in favour of a lazy agnostic pluralism.

Of course, none of this is new and the modern form of the dilemma is as old as modern, that is, post-Kantian, philosophy; what is pressing, however, is the urgency of the need for a robust defence of the possibility of a liberal mediating theology given the clamour of scientistic new atheism outside the academy and the rising prominence of aggressive forms of theological dogmatism within. It is here that the renewal in recent years of the dialogue between theology and the natural sciences is particularly important: is a constructive mediation between Christian theology and the natural sciences possible that both recognises the autonomy of both disciplines and defends the truth of the Christian conviction that it – and not naturalism – is 'the "best explanation" of the many-levelled character of human encounter with reality'?[5]

This essay will consider John Polkinghorne's complex and subtle account of a 'scientific theology' as an attempt to give an affirmative answer to this contemporary formulation of Schleiermacher's dilemma.[6] My thesis is that Polkinghorne's work as a scientist–theologian is partially successful in this aim and a clear example of the characteristic strengths and weaknesses of this strand of theological apologetics. Central to my analysis is the determinative role played by the defining rhetorical posture of liberal apologetic theology, namely that of *modesty*. Polkinghorne's work is a rich synthesis of insights from the natural

---

Human Instinct that Fashions Gods, Spirits and Ancestors (London: Vintage, 2001) and Richard Dawkins, *The God Delusion* (London: Bantam Press, 2006) for a representative sample of scientistic naturalism and John Milbank, Catherine Pickstock and Graham Ward, eds, *Radical Orthodoxy. A New Theology* (London: Routledge, 1999) for an indication of the developing neo-dogmatism of the turn to 'radical orthodoxy' in recent Christian theology. For a fuller discussion of the liberal tradition, see John Powell Clayton, *The Concept of Correlation. Paul Tillich and the Possibility of a Mediating Theology* (Berlin: Walter De Gruyter, 1980), Michael Langford, *A Liberal Theology for the Twenty-first Century. A Passion for Reason* (Aldershot: Ashgate, 2001) and Russell Re Manning, *Theology at the End of Culture. Paul Tillich's Theology of Culture and Art* (Lueven: Peeters, 2005).

[4]   Clayton, *Correlation*, 39.

[5]   John Polkinghorne, *Science and Creation. The Search for Understanding* (London: SPCK, 1988), xii.

[6]   A note about terminology here: I characterise Polkinghorne as a 'scientist–theologian' and hence his project as that of a 'scientific theology'; what is meant by this is simply that Polkinghorne's overall aim is to write Christian theology 'in an age of science', that is to say as a thinker whose habit of mind is that of a trained empirical scientist and whose audience accepts the autonomous authority of the natural sciences as capable of describing what the natural world is like (as we encounter it).

sciences, philosophy, the theological tradition and the Christian Scriptures; his writing is a model of clarity and successfully presents complex ideas in an accessible and conversational prose; whilst striving to give a fair hearing to alternative interpretations, he is not afraid to state his own view, and in spite of his prolific output, his position has remained remarkably consistent. His writings are also characterised by a golden thread of humility, self-effacement and modesty (in spite of his acknowledged eminence, there is little of the condescension and bombast that one might expect). It is this rhetorical style, as much as the content of his writings, that positions Polkinghorne's scientific theology firmly within the tradition of liberal apologetics and provides the key to unlocking the successes and failures of his project.

By developing his own account of the two roles of theology, I will identify two critical moments of Polkinghorne's characteristic modesty, the first of which I will endorse, the second of which I will challenge. The first concerns Polkinghorne's (characteristically liberal) prioritising of religious experience in the first role of theology, namely a systematic defence of the validity of Christian belief. Unlike Richard Swinburne, whose rationalist apologetics builds a cumulative case argument for theism *before* turning to the evidences of religious experiences as the crucial final step, Polkinghorne instead begins with personal religious experience.[7] This starting point enables Polkinghorne to develop a theological methodology that is a 'critical rationalism' analogous to that of the natural sciences. Modestly, Polkinghorne does not – at this stage at least – affirm the superiority of theology over or against the natural sciences, but argues instead for their complementarity as rational discourses. As a systematic account of the experience of what he calls the 'religious dimension' of our encounter with reality, theology should for Polkinghorne take its place in the contemporary university alongside the other specialist sciences.[8] Further, he is insistent that theology should never close itself off from dialogue with the other scientific disciplines, which should be given priority within their particular domains. Clearly, for Polkinghorne, the quantum physicist, *qua* quantum physicist cannot prove or disprove the existence of divine action, for example, but s/he can be expected to give an account of how such intervention could occur, were that to be believed to take place. Polkinghorne's account of this position is a significant and helpful defence of this important characteristic of the liberal mediationist programme.

The second instance of Polkinghorne's theological modesty by contrast however is, I will argue, a step too far. This concerns Polkinghorne's reformulation of the basis of theology's claim to truth. Just as in his account of theological method Polkinghorne develops a 'critical rationalism', his treatment of theological truth is developed by means of a defence of a 'critical realism'. In effect he argues that the reality that theological utterances refer to (that is to say, the religious dimension of

---

[7]   In particular, see Richard Swinburne, *The Coherence of Theism* (Oxford: Clarendon Press, 1977) and *The Existence of God* (Oxford: Clarendon Press, 1979).

[8]   Polkinghorne, *Faith, Science and Understanding*, ch. 1.

our experience that is the original basis for theology) can indeed be shown to be real on the basis of the way in which it enables the intelligibility and fruitfulness of our experience of the world. In the absence of such theological reality we are left without any sufficiently satisfying explanation of the characteristics of our experience of the way the world is. This line of argument Polkinghorne correctly recognises as a form of natural theology. However, with undue humility, he immediately qualifies this position as a 'revised natural theology', according to which theology's status as the meta-science that alone can integrate the findings of the various particular sciences (including theology in its first function) is denied. Instead of the bold claim that theology provides '*the* best explanation' of the character of our experience of reality, Polkinghorne's revised natural theology effectively amounts to the claim that theology can provide an 'intellectually satisfying' explanation. This theological modesty is, however, problematic on at least three accounts. Firstly, and perhaps most trivially, Polkinghorne's account of the 'old-style' natural theology that he proposes to revise is partial, superficial and inaccurate. Secondly, such modesty is not true to the ambitions of the liberal tradition to which he belongs because it fails to make full use of the available cultural resources to develop a more robust rebuttal of the inadequacy of scientific naturalism to account for the intelligibility and fruitfulness of the world, the very assumptions upon which empirical science itself is predicated. Thirdly, Polkinghorne's caution fails to do justice to the apologetic ambition of his theology: he cannot simultaneously categorise theology as a metaphysical discourse and deny the legitimacy of metaphysical arguments without lapsing into precisely the perspectivism that he wishes to avoid.

Polkinghorne's Systematic Theology:
Theology as First-order Science of Interpreted Experience

Like Paul Tillich before him, Polkinghorne identifies two roles for theology: firstly a systematic presentation of the contents of religious experience and secondly a philosophical reflection on 'the whole of human knowledge'.[9] Again, along with Tillich, Polkinghorne insists that the first task of theology is to be understood as the application of 'the conceptual tools of its period' in the service of an expression of the Christian *kerygma*, this latter based upon a participation in the communal religious experience of the Christian church.[10] As Polkinghorne puts it, theology in this first sense is 'the specialist investigation of particular types of experience and insight which we label religious'.[11]

---

    [9]   Ibid., 20.

    [10]   Paul Tillich, *Systematic Theology*, Vol. 1 (Chicago, IL: University of Chicago Press, 1951), 7.

    [11]   John Polkinghorne, *Science and Christian Belief. Theological Reflections of a Bottom-up Thinker* (London: SPCK, 1994), 46.

What is immediately striking about Polkinghorne's account of the nature of systematic theology is the primacy given to religious experience. Perhaps surprisingly for someone well known for his work in natural theology, Polkinghorne unequivocally bases his theological project on what he calls 'the religious dimension of personal experience'.[12] The theologian, in keeping with Anselm's 'splendid phrase' *fides quaerens intellectum*, is a systematiser or organiser of that which strikes as an unavoidably religious 'domain of human experience'.[13] As he puts it,

> theology is reflection upon religious experience, the attempt to bring our rational and ordering faculties to bear upon a particular part of our interaction with the way things are.[14]

As such, theology, in its primary sense for Polkinghorne is not natural theology, but *revealed* theology; faith for Polkinghorne is not assent to certain religious propositions or acceptance of certain creedal statements but an awareness of what Tillich calls '*der Erfahrung des Unbedingten*' ('the experience of the unconditioned').[15] No theological thinking is possible without a 'deeply personal experience that is the foundation for a religious faith' within the community of the 'holy common people of God'.[16] Writing with Michael Welker, Polkinghorne designates two conditions for theological utterances, the first of which is that any such 'must show a minimum of conviction and a minimal degree of having been existentially influenced'.[17] Interestingly, though, Polkinghorne is remarkably reserved in his writings about the *personal* character of such an existential influence, preferring a more detached definition, according to which 'the data for Christian theology are to be found in scripture and the tradition of the Church (including, of course, the contribution of our own experience), and in such general insights about order and purpose that may be brought to light by the play of reason on the process of the world'.[18]

Of course, the priority of experience is consistent with Polkinghorne's self-designation of his approach as that of a 'bottom-up thinker', moving from

---

[12]   Polkinghorne, *Faith, Science and Understanding*, 19.

[13]   Ibid., 27.

[14]   John Polkinghorne, *One World. The Interaction of Science and Theology* (London: SPCK, 1986), 28.

[15]   Victor Nuovo, *Visionary Science. A Translation of Paul Tillich's 'On the Idea of a Theology of Culture' with an Interpretive Essay* (Detroit, MI: Wayne State University Press, 1987), 24.

[16]   John Polkinghorne and Michael Welker, *Faith in the Living God. A Dialogue* (London: SPCK, 2001), 139.

[17]   Ibid., 140, italics in original.

[18]   Polkinghorne, *Science and Christian Belief*, 35.

experience to understanding.[19] This stance, which Polkinghorne describes as 'instinctive' for a scientist, underlines the primacy of experience – data – for theology's self-understanding of its first task. However, it is crucial to emphasise that Polkinghorne's bottom-up approach is far from a naïvely exclusive reliance upon 'raw data'. As Polkinghorne clarifies, the move from experience to understanding is 'by no means ... a Baconian accumulation of particular instances, assembled in the hope of making an inductive leap'.[20] By rejecting the empiricist ideal of a 'confus'd heap' of facts, Polkinghorne qualifies his strictly bottom-up approach with a recognition of the virtuousness of the hermeneutical circle of data and theory. Indeed, Polkinghorne presents such a qualified bottom-up approach as precisely that which the basic scientific commitment to empiricism demands. In writing of the 'epistemological pragmatism' of bottom-up thinkers like himself, he claims that they are 'not disposed to believe in the existence of a universal method but instead they seek to tailor their approach according to the nature of the particular reality as it is apprehended'.[21] It is this 'improvisatory approach' that provides the best characterisation of what we might call Polkinghorne's 'critical rationalist' theological methodology; the same particularist perspective that best describes the practise of the sciences as data-driven interpretations of the experience of specific features of reality.

> Experience and interpretation will always intertwine in hermeneutic circularity, but one should try to make the circles as tight and as small as possible. Bottom-up thinking is an instinctive stance for a scientist to adopt. Study of the physical world has shown us many surprises (quantum theory is, perhaps, the outstanding example). In consequence, scientists are loath to give much credence to *a priori* or transcendental notions of what is reasonable. Experience often breaks the mould of our prior expectation, and so we have to be open and humble enough to submit to the way things actually are.[22]

This scientific criterion of the experiential 'checking' of run-away speculative theories by unanticipated data is equally applied to theology, in keeping with Polkinghorne's commitment to using the best available cultural resources for its development, 'least it should succumb to the temptation to turn its current idea of God into an unrevisable icon'.[23] At the same time, Polkinghorne recognises the theory-laden nature of scientific 'facts' as 'interpretations which are themselves

---

[19]   Ibid., *passim*; Polkinghorne and Welker, *Faith in the Living God*, 134.

[20]   Polkinghorne and Welker, *Faith in the Living God*, 134–5. It is worth noting that even Bacon himself was far from a naïve bottom-up thinker, see Dorothea Krook, 'Two Baconians: Robert Boyle and Joseph Granville', *The Huntingdon Library Quarterly* 18(3) (1955).

[21]   Polkinghorne and Welker, *Faith in the Living God*, 135.

[22]   Ibid., 135.

[23]   Ibid., 135.

embedded deep in current theoretical understanding' and further stresses that it
would not be appropriate for a scientist to 'throw in the towel at the first encounter
with problematic data.[24] A certain degree of courageous persistence, open to the
possibility of correction but not prone to the hasty dismantling of theories well-
winnowed by experience, has been the way in which further understanding has
frequently been achieved'.[25]

Just as the sciences progress, so ought theology, as the on-going enterprise of
the refining of theoretical understanding of our experience of the nature of God and
of our relation to Him.[26] Recently, Edward M. Hogan has criticised Polkinghorne
for his affirmation of the 'cousinly relationship' or analogical similarity of
theology and the natural sciences given his methodological particularism, or
what I have called here his critical rationalism.[27] For Hogan, Polkinghorne cannot
simultaneously embrace both the 'accommodation' of theological method to the
'idiosyncratic nature of God' as transcendent and the methodological similarity of
theology and the natural sciences, the objects of which, no matter how peculiar
and unexpected they may be, are by definition not transcendent.

This accusation, however, fails to do justice to the second condition that
Polkinghorne and Welker place upon an utterance for it to be recognised
as theological, namely, that it 'must be formulated in words and must be
comprehensible. It must be such that others can follow its logic and it must be
capable of material development'.[28] Of course, this is not to say that an affirmation

---

[24]   Polkinghorne, *Science and Christian Belief*, 34.

[25]   John Polkinghorne, *Reason and Reality. The Relationship between Science and
Theology* (London: SPCK, 1991), 50.

[26]   It is important to note that Polkinghorne also acknowledges the dissimilarity
between theology and the natural sciences in at least two respects. Firstly, he argues that
the data of theological science are such that it 'does not enjoy the luxury that equipment
grants to [natural] science, of being able to deal with essentially controllable and repeatable
experience. It has to look to the given and unrepeatable revelatory events in which God has
chosen to make the divine nature known'. John Polkinghorne, *Belief in God in an Age of
Science* (New Haven, CT: Yale University Press, 1998), 47. Secondly, as a consequence
of the character of his foundational experience, 'the task of theology is so difficult that
it is unreasonable to expect the fully successful accomplishment of theory construction'.
Polkinghorne, *Science and Christian Belief*, 36. Given that 'theology has no words adequate
to encompass the mystery of the divine nature' it must instead 'make use of the open and
living language of symbol [such that] its discourse will never be able fully to encompass
God within the limits of finite human understanding'. Polkinghorne, *Belief in God*, 37–8.
For a fuller discussion of the differences between theology and science, see Polkinghorne,
Quantum Physics, 9–22.

[27]   Ibid., *passim*; Hogan 'Polkinghorne and Lonergan'.

[28]   Polkinghorne and Welker, *Faith in the Living God*, 140, italics in original. It is
interesting to note how precisely these two conditions map onto George Lindbeck's
characterisation of liberal theology as 'experiential–expressivist'. See George Lindbeck,
The Nature of Doctrine. Religion and Theology in a Postliberal Age (London: SPCK, 1984).

of divine transcendence is not comprehensible and thus not theological; rather the point is that the theologian, in seeking to systematise – and hence understand – religious experience, does not take as her 'object' a God of an unbreachable transcendence. Such a God can surely only be the product of an extreme apophatic speculative imagination and not the God whose presence is believed to generate the experiential basis of religious faith. In other words, if Polkinghorne were aiming to construct his defence of the scientific critical rationality of theology on the basis of a speculative or rationalist conception of the nature of God, then the apparent inconsistency that Hogan objects to would be problematic; however, if we acknowledge the foundation of Polkinghorne's understanding of theological methodology in revelation then the objection loses its force.

Systematic theology, in Polkinghorne's scheme, is able to develop a comprehensible validity, methodologically similar to the natural sciences precisely because it, as they, takes as its starting point an interpreted – and hence interpretable – experience of what is taken to be real. Whether the theologian is in fact justified in her assumption that the religious experience *is* of reality is another question, which I shall consider in the next section of this essay. What is important here is that Polkinghorne's strategy of accommodation – the classic stance of post-Kantian liberal protestantism – is that of an accommodation of theological method to the ways in which God is experienced within the contemporary situation.[29] In all this, Polkinghorne's writings encapsulate the liberal ideal of a dialogic modesty: the theologian takes her place alongside the other scientific practitioners in an attitude of humble responsiveness to her interpretable data and an inter-disciplinary openness to the insights of her colleagues. That such an approach is a fruitful one is confirmed by Polkinghorne's creative development of central theological questions, in particular his contributions to discussions of divine action, eschatology, and the Fall.[30]

---

[29]   As such, Polkinghorne is very close to Tillich's 'method of correlation' even if he does not use this language.

[30]   For a sample of Polkinghorne's work on divine action and its critical reception, see Polkinghorne, *Reason and Reality*, ch. 3, Polkinghorne, *Science and Christian Belief*, ch. 4, Polkinghorne, *Belief in God*, ch. 3, Christoper C. Knight, 'Theistic Naturalism and "Special" Divine Providence', *Zygon: Journal of Religion and Science* 44(3) (2009): 533–42, Robert Larmer, 'Divine Action and the Principle of the Conservation of Energy', *Zygon: Journal of Religion and Science* 44(3) (2009): 543–57, Robert John Russell, 'Quantum Physics and the Theology of Non-Interventionist Objective Divine Action', in *The Oxford Handbook of Religion and Science*, ed. Philip Clayton with Zachary Simpson (Oxford: Oxford University Press, 2006), 579–95. For Polkinghorne's discussion of eschatology, see Polkinghorne, *Science and Christian Belief*, ch. 9, John Polkinghorne and Michael Welker, eds, *The End of the World and the Ends of God. Science and Theology on Eschatology* (Harrisburg, PA: Trinity Press International, 2000) and John Polkinghorne, 'Christianity and Science', in *The Oxford Handbook of Religion and Science*, ed. Philip Clayton with Zachary Simpson (Oxford: Oxford University Press, 2006), 68–70. For the Fall, see *Reason and Reality*, ch. 8.

Polkinghorne's Natural Theology:
Theology as Second-order Integrating Meta-science

Having reconstructed Polkinghorne's understanding of the first role of theology as a critical rationalist systematic theology characterised by a methodological analogy to the natural sciences and a representation of doctrinal commitments in language and concepts appropriate to an age of science, it is now possible to turn to the second role assigned to theology by Polkinghorne. Here the discussion shifts from questions of systematic validity to those of truth; otherwise put, for Polkinghorne, theology is not concerned simply to articulate its own internal comprehensibility but should also defend the truth of its assertions to those who do not share its particular experiential basis. It is at this point that we move from systematic theology to natural theology. Of course, to say this is not to imply that any defence of the truth of Christian belief must inevitably take the form of natural theology; fideist, expressivist and coherentist accounts of religious truth will be content to assign this task to systematic theology itself.[31] However, Polkinghorne, in keeping with the tradition of a liberal theology of mediation, rejects any account that exempts theology from what he calls the 'generality of account' according to which the *Anknupfungpunkt* between revealed and natural knowledge of God is unavoidable.[32] As we have seen, Polkinghorne's recognition of the analogical similarity of theological method to that of the natural sciences does not entail the reduction of theology to a natural science; theology retains its own autonomous domain of experience. Similarly, the liberal insistence upon the defence of theological truth-claims in terms accessible to the non-believer does not amount to the reduction of theology to the scientific study of religion. In this respect, the liberal tradition is characterised by a commitment to a two-pronged defence of the legitimacy of natural theology via the claims of critical realism and of the unity of knowledge. As is to be expected, Polkinghorne embraces both these positions. Before turning to these – more assertive – aspects of Polkinghorne's scientific theology, it is important to clarify place of natural theology in Polkinghorne's overall project by considering his account of the second function of theology, namely as a 'second-order reflection upon the whole of human knowledge'.[33]

As its second role, Polkinghorne gives to theology the task of integrating the findings of all the particular sciences into an overarching (or fundamental) unity. This synthetic task he describes as the second-order discipline of metaphysical

---

[31]   See *inter alia*, Don Cupitt, *Taking Leave of God* (London: SCM Press, 1980), D.Z. Phillips, *Religion Without Explanation* (Oxford: Blackwells, 1976) and Lindbeck, *Nature of Doctrine*.

[32]   Polkinghorne, *Science and Christian Belief*, 42. Of course, the canonical statement of this position is Emil Brunner, 'Natur und Gnade: Zum Gespräch mit Karl Barth', in *Ein offense Wort. Vorträge und Aufsätze 1917–1934*, ed. Rudolf Wehrli (Zürich: Theologischer Verlag., 1934). See also Tillich, *Systematic Theology*, 6–11.

[33]   Polkinghorne, *Faith, Science and Understanding*, 20.

theology that seeks 'the integration of the partial perspectives, afforded by the first-order disciplines, into a single consistent and coherent account of reality … to provide a more profound and comprehensive understanding than could be acquired through any single primary mode on its own'.[34] This, I contend, is equivalent to the role of natural theology, explicated in terms of its two central themes of intelligibility and fruitfulness or purpose (expressed, for Polkinghorne in terms of the Anthropic Principle), such that Polkinghorne ought to acknowledge that his arguments for critical realism and the unity of knowledge themselves form part of his natural theology. In fact, however, Polkinghorne equivocates. At times he presents natural theology as an alternative first-order discipline; at others he describes it as 'the arena for [the] interaction' of science and theology, whilst all along what he actually does under the rubric of natural theology is in fact what he identifies as the second role of theology.[35] The equivocation seems to rest on a curious acceptance of a rather restrictive definition of natural theology and an undue modesty as to its scope and ambition, in spite of his actual development of a more broadly conceived understanding.

When introducing a defence of the legitimacy of natural theology in his Gifford lectures, Polkinghorne defines natural theology as 'the search for God through reason and general experience'; similarly in a chapter arguing for the 'continuing role' of natural theology 'within the Judaeo-Christian tradition', he gives the definition as 'the search for the knowledge of God by the exercise of reason and the inspection of the world'.[36] This way of defining natural theology is widespread and has a certain intuitive appeal in as much as it clearly differentiates natural theology from revealed theology and as such is frequently advanced by those who wish to affirm that only one of these two types of theology is legitimate.[37] It is,

---

[34]   Ibid., 20.

[35]   Polkinghorne, *Science and Creation*, 2.

[36]   Polkinghorne, *Science and Christian Belief*, 42; Polkinghorne, *Science and Creation*, 2.

[37]   Perhaps the clearest expression of these opposing views come from Karl Barth on the one hand and John Toland on the other. See for example, Barth's claim (cited by Polkinghorne) that God 'cannot be known by the powers of human knowledge, but is apprehensible and apprehended solely because of His own freedom, decision and action. What man can know by his own power according to the measure of his natural powers, his understanding, his feeling, will be at most something like a supreme being, an absolute nature, the idea of an utterly free power, of a being towering over everything. This absolute and supreme being, the ultimate and most profound, this "thing in itself", has nothing to do with God'. Karl Barth, *Dogmatics in Outline* (London: SCM Press, 1949), 23. By contrast see Toland's confidence that 'The New Testament (if it be indeed Divine) must consequently agree with Natural Reason, and our own ordinary Ideas. The Apostles commend themselves to every Man's conscience, that is, the appeal to every Man's Reason, in the Sight of God. Peter exhorts Christians to be ready always to give an Answer to everyone that asks them a Reason of their Hope. Now to what purpose serv'd all these Appeal, if no Regard was to be had to Men's Understandings? If the Doctrines of Christ were incomprehensible,

however, a profoundly misleading conception of the nature of natural theology in its demarcation of two radically distinct forms of religious experience – the revealed and the natural – with corresponding distinct data for any subsequent theological consideration. On at least one occasion, Polkinghorne falls into this trap in the passage already quoted from his Gifford lectures concerning the data of theology in which he distinguishes that 'found in scripture and the tradition of the Church' from 'such general insights about order and purpose that may be brought to light by the play of reason on the process of the world'.[38] If this is to be taken as Polkinghorne's conception of natural theology, then the consequence is that natural theology is concerned with certain specific interpreted experiences of order and purpose in the processes of the natural world (be those physical or biological) and as such it must be considered alongside revealed theology as a further particular sub-discipline of the first role of theology, rather than as the second-order discourse that aims to integrate the particular sciences. If this were to be the case, it then would be difficult to substantiate Polkinghorne's claims for the meta-scientific (or metaphysical) status of theology and hence to defend the truth of theological utterances.

Interestingly, a parallel equivocation occurs with his presentation of 'systematic theology', which whilst 'officially' characterised, as above, as the first-order rational ordering of the religious domain of experience, is sometimes described as synonymous with theology's apologetic function, such as his gracious acceptance of the description of his Gifford lectures as a 'mini-systematic theology'.[39] Such a description, however, is mistaken on Polkinghorne's own grounds; as he himself acknowledges, his Gifford lectures are concerned with the truth of the Nicene Creed and as such are properly speaking an exercise in natural theology 'which falls within the provisions of Lord Gifford's will'.[40] It is the Creed and not Polkinghorne's lectures that should be recognised as the 'mini-systematic theology'! Crucially my point here is not so much to quibble with Polkinghorne's terminological inconsistency, as to draw attention to the way in which he tends to conflate the two roles for theology that he so carefully (and helpfully) distinguishes: there is a difference between attempting to 'articulate Christian belief in ways that seem natural and congenial to the scientific mind' (bottom-up systematic theology) and defending the claim that his religious beliefs are 'founded on the truth'.[41]

Fortunately, however, in spite of some misleading tendencies arising from his uncritical acceptance of an admittedly 'well-winnowed' but nonetheless unsatisfactory definition of natural theology, what Polkinghorne actually does with his work in natural theology is far more constructive than simply identifying

---

contradictory; or were we oblig'd to believe in reveal'd Nonsense?' John Toland, *Christianity Not Mysterious* (1696) (New York: Garland, 1978), Preface.

[38]   Polkinghorne, *Science and Christian Belief*, 35.

[39]   Ibid., 84.

[40]   Ibid., 2.

[41]   Polkinghorne, *Belief in God*, 84; Polkinghorne, *Science and Christian Belief*, 30.

certain naturally mediated religious experiences – up to a point. To see this it is necessary to outline the constructive work of Polkinghorne's revival of natural theology, namely his defence of a synthetic critical theological realism via the arguments of intelligibility and fruitfulness, before turning to his unnecessarily modest revision of natural theology from 'demonstration' to 'insight'.[42]

In his 1996 Terry Lectures, published as *Belief in God in an Age of Science*, Polkinghorne devotes the first lecture to what he describes as 'natural theology'.[43] Strikingly, he does not therefore simply outline a series of observations of the apparently religious character of the interpreted order and purpose of the world. Instead, he sets out to make the case for 'the fundamental content of belief in God', namely 'that there is a Mind and a Purpose behind the history of the universe and that the One whose veiled presence is intimated in this way is worthy of worship and the ground of hope'.[44] He presents this belief, which he goes on to abbreviate to 'theism', as providing 'a way of making sense of the broadest possible band of human experience, of uniting in a single account the rich and many-layer encounter with the way things are'.[45] In short, 'theism is concerned with making *total* sense of the world' and 'the force of its claims depends upon the degree to which belief in God affords the best explanation of the varieties, not just of religious experience, but of all human experience'.[46] This is unambiguously a statement of the second role of theology, that of integrating the insights of all the particular sciences into a synthetic meta-science; this is unquestionable natural theology as theological metaphysics. Here we see a bold and sophisticated apologetic theology, centred around the twin themes of the tradition of natural theology – intelligibility and purpose – in a defence of the truth of Christian belief via the affirmation of the reality of God. This is 'doing natural theology [as] part and parcel of doing theology'.[47]

At this point it should be clear that Polkinghorne's defence of a critical theological realism on the basis of the recognition of intelligibility and purpose is the substance of his natural theology. Although he has a tendency to separate out his discussions of critical realism and natural theology, they are in actual fact coincident: both aim, in effect, to show that the foundational insight of the systematic theologian of a God who creates and sustains the world according to His loving will is, as Polkinghorne characteristically puts it, 'a coherent and intellectually satisfying understanding'.[48]

It is not necessary here to rehearse in full Polkinghorne's well-known argument in favour of a critical theological realism on the basis of the intelligibility and

42 Polkinghorne, *Reason and Reality*, 51.
43 Polkinghorne, *Belief in God*, xi.
44 Ibid., 1.
45 Ibid., 24.
46 Ibid., 24.
47 Polkinghorne, *Science and Christian Belief*, 3.
48 Polkinghorne, *Belief in God*, 5.

fruitfulness of our interpreted experience of the world as multi-layered.[49] What is crucial, however, is to recognise the extent to which this argument, a theological variant of an important strand of the philosophy of science, is doing the work in Polkinghorne's natural theology. A second recognition is also called for: namely its metaphysical boldness. In spite of Polkinghorne's apparent commitment to a sceptical view of the potential of metaphysics (a view consistent with the state of philosophical reflection of the Cambridge of Polkinghorne's formative years), it is disingenuous of him to claim of an argument for the reality of the divine mind behind the rational beauty of the cosmos that its conclusion is not a 'logical demonstration' because 'we are in the realm of metaphysical discourse where such certainty is not available' when in the same book he develops at length an argument for critical realism in science (and hence scientific theology), concluding by endorsing 'a realist trust in the rational reliability of our understanding of experience'.[50] Clearly, Polkinghorne is correct in recognising that *critical* realism does not entail deductive certainty as is the case with *naïve* realism; however, it is surely mistaken to conclude that the qualification 'critical' refers to a lessening of the degree of certainty involved. An argument for a critical realist position can – and ought to – be just as logically demonstrative as a competing argument for naïve realism, or idealism for that matter. The crucial difference lies not in the strength of their conviction but in what it is that they are arguing for.[51] Polkinghorne's confusion here, I propose, stems from a combination of a residue of his scientific training (the habits of empiricist naïve realism are hard to shake, even for a quantum physicist!) and, crucially, from his liberal theological modesty that restrains him from developing his apologetic insights to their full.

An indication of how this theological humility is manifest can be seen in Polkinghorne's repeated claim that he is concerned 'not only with a revived natural theology but also with a *revised* natural theology', which he describes as 'more modest in its tone than its predecessors of earlier centuries. It [revised natural theology] speaks of insight rather than demonstration. Its aim is not the classic goal of proving the existence of God. Rather, it seeks to exhibit theism as providing a coherent and deeply intellectually satisfying understanding of the total

---

[49]   See Polkinghorne, *One World*, chs 1–3; Polkinghorne, *Reason and Reality*, chs 1–3; Polkinghorne, *Belief in God*, ch. 5; Polkinghorne, *Faith, Science and Understanding*, 78–84 and Polkinghorne, *Quantum Physics*, ch. 1.

[50]   Polkinghorne, *Belief in God*, 4–5; ibid., 124.

[51]   Interestingly, when discussing critical realism *per se*, Polkinghorne seems to acknowledge this, the slippage occurs when he applies the critical realist position in his reflections upon the nature of natural theology. For example, he writes of critical realism that 'the adjective acknowledging the need to recognise that something is involved that is more subtle than the encounter with unproblematic objectivity, while the noun signifies the nature of the understanding that it actually proves possible to attain'. Polkinghorne, *Quantum Physics*, 6.

way things are'.[52] The limited ambition that Polkinghorne places on his revised natural theology is surprising given the way in which he sets out the integrative task of his apologetic scientific theology and problematic on at least three accounts.

To begin with it is unclear whether Polkinghorne's account of the history of natural theology does justice to the differentiated and complex character of this genre of theological thought. To some extent this is unexpected, given the available literature on the historical and conceptual varieties of natural theology.[53] At the same time, it should be apparent, even to a non-historian, that a facile identification of 'the old-style natural theology of Paley and the *Bridgewater Treatises*' with 'the God of the Gaps' will simply not do.[54] Admittedly, Polkinghorne does recognise

---

[52]   Polkinghorne, *Belief in God*, 15, italics in original; Polkinghorne, *Reason and Reality*, 51. Polkinghorne is by no means alone in his desire to revise natural theology. For a comparable project, see Alister McGrath, *The Open Secret. A New Vision for Natural Theology* (Oxford: Blackwell, 2008).

[53]   There is, as yet, no comprehensive account of the historical and conceptual varieties of natural theology, although the forthcoming Russell Re Manning, ed., *Oxford Handbook of Natural Theology* (Oxford: Oxford University Press, 2013) aims to make a significant initial contribution to filling this lacuna. One important element of *this* revisionary account will be the shift in focus from an almost obsessive preoccupation with a minimal cast of 'the usual suspects' – Anselm, Aquinas, Paley the *Bridgewater Treatises* – towards a more synoptic view of the tradition. For a seminal discussion of the complexities of the relations between science and theology (including natural theology) in the modern period, see John Hedley Brooke, *Science and Religion. Some Historical Perspectives* (Cambridge: Cambridge University Press, 1991). Interestingly, those wishing for any revival of natural theology to be simultaneously a revision of 'old-style' approaches, tend to accept (as Polkinghorne does) the account of natural theology's implication in the rise of modern atheism given by Michael Buckley, *At the Origins of Modern Atheism* (New Haven, CT: Yale University Press, 1987). Recent work by Stephen Gaukroger, however, has questioned Buckley's interpretation, see Stephen Gaukroger, *The Emergence of a Scientific Culture. Science and the Shaping of Modernity, 1210–1685* (Oxford: Oxford University Press, 2007). It is important to distinguish this broad-based understanding of natural theology from that of its other revival, namely in the area of Christian apologetic analytical philosophy of religion. For this latter, see the definition of natural theology as 'that branch of theology that seeks to provide warrant for belief in God's existence apart from the resources of authoritative, propositional revelation'. William Lane Craig and J.P. Moreland, eds, *The Blackwell Companion to Natural Theology* (Oxford: Blackwell, 2009), ix.

[54]   Polkinghorne, *Science and Creation*, 13. For a sample of the revisionary literature on Paley and the *Bridgewater Treatises* see John T. Baldwin, 'William Paley's Argument from Perfection Tradition: A Continuing Influence', *The Harvard Theological Review* 85(1) (1992): 109–120; Aileen Fyfe, 'The Reception of William Paley's *Natural Theology* in the University of Cambridge', *British Journal of the History of Science* 30 (1997): 321–35; William Paley, *Natural Theology, or Evidence of the Existence and Attributes of the Deity, Collected from the Appearances of Nature* (1802), ed. Matthew D. Eddy and David Knight (Oxford: Oxford University Press, 2006), ix–xxix; Niall O'Flaherty, 'The Rhetorical Strategy of William Paley's *Natural Theology* (1802): Part 1, William Paley's

the possibility of interpreting the character of the arguments of Aquinas' 'Five Ways' as 'more subtle' than 'that of knock-down demonstration', and yet the repeated insistence is that the new natural theology differs from the old 'by refraining from talking about "proofs" of God's existence and by being content with the more modest role of offering theistic belief as an insightful account of what is going on'.[55] That Anselm and Aquinas are concerned to 'prove' the existence of God is a highly contested claim and whilst it is indeed possible to find 'Enlightenment' natural theologians, such as Paley, who do explicitly argue for the existence of God, even then it is important to recognise that their arguments are far from deductive 'knock-down' proofs. (Paley, for instance, writes directly in reply to Hume's inductive arguments against Christian theism by proposing a 'best explanation' argument analogous to Polkinghorne's own!)

Polkinghorne, however, presents his revised natural theology not only as different in terms of the type of argument it uses (insight not demonstration), but also in terms of the data that its arguments employ. He writes that 'it differs from the old-style natural theology of William Paley and others by basing its arguments not upon particular occurrences (the coming-to-be of the eye or of life itself), but on the character of the physical fabric of the world, which is the necessary ground for the possibility of any occurrence (it appeals to cosmic rationality and the anthropic form of the laws of nature)'.[56] In this shift of focus, however, Polkinghorne is in good company: ever since its inception in Plato's late dialogue, *The Laws*, through to William Whewell's contribution to the *Bridgewater Treatises* (*Astronomy and General Physics Considered with reference to Natural Theology* (1833)) natural theologians have argued from the general intelligibility and providential order of the world.[57] Much more could be said here, in particular concerning the origins of natural theology in Greek philosophical thought and the perhaps surprising persistence of post-Darwinian natural theology; however, one final observation will suffice. As is typical of many contemporary commentators on the history of natural theology, Polkinghorne repeats the commonplace accusations that 'old-style' natural theology is guilty simultaneously of naïve anthropomorphism and impersonal deism.[58] Surely, however, the incompatibility of these accusations

---

Natural Theology in Context', *Studies in the History and Philosophy of Science* 41 (2010): 19–25 and J.R. Topham, 'Beyond the "Common Context": the production and reading of the Bridgewater Treatises', *Isis* 89(2) (1998): 233–62.

[55] Polkinghorne, *Science and Creation*, 11; Polkinghorne, *Belief in God*, 10.

[56] Ibid., 10.

[57] On Plato, see Gerard Naddaf, 'Plato. The Creator of Natural Theology', *International Studies in Philosophy* 36(1) (2004): 129–50. On Whewell, see David Knight, 'Religion and the "New Philosophy"', *Culture, Theory, and Critique* 26(1) (1982): 147–66 and John Hedley Brooke and Geoffrey Cantor, *Reconstructing Nature. The Engagement of Science and Religion* (Edinburgh: T & T Clark, 1998).

[58] For the first point, see Polkinghorne's claim that 'this shift from design through making to design built into the rational potentiality of the universe ... answers a criticism

must lead one to question whether natural theologians were really so confused as to be promoting a bizarre and incoherent 'deistic–anthropomorphic' theology and to wonder whether the real history might be somewhat more differentiated and complex (and interesting) than is routinely assumed.[59]

The second respect in which Polkinghorne's revisionary modesty is inappropriate relates to his unnecessary separation of his philosophical defence of critical realism in science and theology from his account of natural theology. As already stressed above, Polkinghorne's robust metaphysical engagement in favour of critical realism in science and theology ought to present him with a powerful natural theology true to the liberal commitment to the application of contemporary cultural resources to the articulation and defence of the Christian faith. Whilst Polkinghorne is surely correct to draw attention to the 'serious problems' challenging the argument for a theological critical realism, this concession should not diminish the power of the philosophical case he advances for a 'realist trust' in theology as much as in the natural sciences.[60] As he himself says, the idea of critical realism for science and theology 'is deep enough to encompass the character of both these forms of the human search for truthful understanding'.[61] Polkinghorne's liberal modesty should not prevent him from recognising and unapologetically employing the arguments for critical realism in the philosophy of science in the service of the cousinly discipline of theology.[62]

---

of the old-style natural theology so trenchantly made by David Hume. He had asserted the unsatisfactoriness of treating God's creative activity as the unseen analogue of visible human craft. The new natural theology is invulnerable to this charge of naïve anthropomorphism, for the endowment of matter with anthropic potentiality has no human analogy. It is a creative act of a specially divine character'. Polkinghorne, *Belief in God*, 11. For the second, Polkinghorne quotes with approval from Thomas F. Torrance that 'if we reject a deistic disjunction between God and the world, which we are bound to do, natural theology cannot be pursued in its traditional abstractive form'. Polkinghorne, *Science and Creation*, 14, citing Thomas F. Torrance, *Reality and Scientific Theology* (Edinburgh: Scottish Academic Press, 1985, 40).

[59]   It should be noted, on the other hand, that, unlike many recent accounts of natural theology, Polkinghorne does recognise the aesthetic aspects of the tradition and the points of intersection between what is normally thought of as scientific natural theology and theologies of culture and the arts. See Polkinghorne, *Science and Christian Belief*, 44–6 and Polkinghorne, *Belief in God*, 18–19. For an alternative appreciation of the role of the Platonic transcendentals in natural theology, see McGrath, *Open Secret*, pt 3.

[60]   Polkinghorne, *Belief in God*, 113.

[61]   Polkinghorne, *Quantum Physics*, 15.

[62]   For a sample of (now classic) important defences forms of critical realism in the philosophy of science, see Roy Bhaskar, *A Realist Theory of Science* (London: Verso, 1975); Hilary Putnam, *Reason, Truth and History* (Cambridge: Cambridge University Press, 1981); Ian Hacking, *Representing and Intervening. Introductory Topics in the Philosophy of Natural Science* (Cambridge: Cambridge University Press, 1983) and Nancy Cartwright, *How the Laws of Science Lie* (Oxford: Clarendon Press, 1983).

More than even this, however, Polkinghorne is obliged, given the emphasis on the unity of knowledge in his characterisation of the second role of theology, to give an account of that which can act as the basis of such a unity. Unless his perception of the unity of knowledge, initially provoked for Polkinghorne by the quest for Grand Unifying Theories in theoretical physics, is to be dismissed as an arbitrary imposition upon his experience of reality, it is incumbent upon him to draw on critical realist arguments against the self-sufficiency of the scientific enterprise to make sense of itself, a position famously dubbed the 'no miracle argument' by Hilary Putnam. Here Polkinghorne's engagement with Bas van Fraassen's arguments for the 'empirical adequacy' of science are important, as are his rebuttals of the expressivist school; there is scope, however, for a more robust philosophical defence of theological critical realism and Polkinghorne's liberal modesty should not prevent him (or others) from developing this position. As Polkinghorne himself recognises, whilst philosophers are likely to be suspicious of theologians adopting philosophical arguments to support the motivations for their beliefs, that suspicion should not be allowed to bar theologians from appropriating such arguments. After all, they might just be true.

It is with the fundamental question of truth that the most significant problem with Polkinghorne's liberal theological modesty is to be found.[63] Without wanting to deny the importance of belief for Polkinghorne's theological apologetics (indeed his recognition of the role of belief in science is itself a significant contribution to the science–theology debates), I do wish to question Polkinghorne's reluctance to advocate any apologetic conclusions stronger than what he calls 'motivated belief', given the resources he deploys in his writings in defence of theology's second role as the meta-scientific discipline. To argue, as Polkinghorne does, that only theology (in this second sense) can provide an explanation of the possibility and unity of knowledge is to make a claim that goes beyond Torrance's restriction of natural theology to 'the necessary *infra-structure* of theological science' and instead presents natural theology (whatever Polkinghorne may *say* it is) as 'the fullest possible understanding of the world'.[64] Torrance's inclusion of natural theology 'within the body of positive theology' is indeed an advance on Barth's total rejection and yet it entails at most a postliberal (postmodern) '*ad hoc* apologetics' that conflicts with Polkinghorne's advocacy of a robust critical realism for theology.[65] Here, once again, the separation of his arguments for critical realism and his defence the legitimacy of natural theology in Polkinghorne's work

---

[63] For trenchant accounts of the 'false modesty' of such liberal theological approach (albeit in very different contexts), see John Milbank, 'Only Theology Save Metaphysics. On the Modalities of Terror', in *Belief and Metaphysics*, eds Peter M. Chandler and Conor Cunningham (London: SCM Press, 2007), 452–500 and Quentin Meillassoux, *After Finitude. An Essay on the Necessity of Contingency* (London: Continuum, 2008).

[64] Torrance, *Reality*, 40; Polkinghorne, *Science and Creation*, 16.

[65] Torrance, *Reality*, 40. See also William Werpehowski, 'Ad Hoc Apologetics', *Journal of Religion* 66(3) (1986): 282–301.

is crucial; a robust theological critical realism, such as that which Polkinghorne consistently defends, is at odds with a *revised* natural theology that restricts the ambition of the natural theologian from demonstrating the truth of her beliefs in the intelligible unity of reality to merely presenting her 'motivated insights' into such a metaphysical view. Instead, a robust theological critical realism requires a robust apologetic natural theology. At this point the otherwise commendable liberal posture of modesty must give way to an assertive confidence to avoid the danger of lapsing into the parochialism and metaphysical agnosticism of a perspectivist position. If Polkinghorne is indeed to make the case for 'theological understanding as providing he kind of motivated belief that can alone expect to command respect in a scientific age', he ought, I propose, to gain that respect as much by the strength of his arguments as by the courage and coherence of his convictions.[66] Here, in conclusion, it is interesting to note his characteristic ambivalence – and posture typical of the liberal tradition to which he clearly belongs – when he turns from his primary focus of the defence of Christian belief in an age of science to engaging that other pressing aspect of our contemporary situation, namely the context of religious pluralism. Just as Polkinghorne is convinced of the error of scientism and yet unable to bring himself to follow through on his 'knock-down' argument against, for example Dawkins and Weinberg (in whose categorical affirmation of the pointlessness of the universe Polkinghorne acknowledges an 'austere nobility'), so he restrains himself from making a robust defence of Christian truth even as he realises the dangers of the vacuous pieties of postmodern religious pluralism. As he writes in the final chapter of his Gifford lectures concerned with non-Christian alternative 'theological metaphysics':

> Integrity requires us to speak for the truth as we see it, and we need to remember Farrer's warning that 'the acknowledgement of a vital truth is always divisive until it becomes universal.' I sometimes fear that Christianity is a little too eager for dialogue, a little lacking in nerve to hold fast to what it has learned of God in Christ.[67]

That said, however, his concluding words return him to a characteristic modesty:

> I do believe, however, that those questions of physical reality, and the related questions of natural theology which arise in an unforced way from them, constitute a modest but promising area of interaction for the world faiths … In this way we humble bottom-up thinkers might make our modest contribution even to the ecumenical encounter of the world's great religious traditions.[68]

---

[66]   Polkinghorne, *Faith, Science and Understanding*, 49.

[67]   Polkinghorne, *Science and Christian Belief*, 191, citing Farrer from Brian Hebblethwaite, *The Incarnation. Collected Essays in Christology* (Cambridge: Cambridge University Press, 1987), 123.

[68]   Polkinghorne, *Science and Christian Belief*, 192.

Conclusion

Polkinghorne's careful and humble exploration of the extent to which it is possible to 'use the search for motivated understanding, so congenial to the scientific mind, as a route to being able to make the substance of Christian orthodoxy our own' deserves praise and respect.[69] In his many wide-ranging books and articles, he has done much to advance the application of the insights of the natural scenes, in particular, of course, those of quantum physics, to issues in Christian systematic theology. His contributions to the on-going task of the revitalisation of the Christian theological imagination, in particular through his proposals for an understanding of divine action in terms of God's 'nonenergetically influencing chaotic systems' have been rightly celebrated.[70] This essay has taken a slightly different track by considering Polkinghorne's characterisation of the task of theology itself, in particular his distinction between the two roles of theology as a first-order discipline of the systematisation of a specific 'data set' of interpreted experience and as a second-order meta-scientific integration of the results of first-order sciences into a comprehensive 'Theory of Everything'. This, I have argued, corresponds to the characteristic move of liberal theologies of mediation, such as that of Paul Tillich, to consider theology as an apologetic enterprise that makes 'use of the conceptual tools of its period' both to establish the systematic coherence of its message and to argue for its truth.[71] These two steps I have characterised as the distinctive roles of systematic and natural theology.

In addition, I have noted the tendency of such liberal theologies to a rhetorical posture of modesty that sits ill at ease with their apologetic ambition and I have argued that Polkinghorne's work in systematic and natural theology shares this ambivalence and that, whilst this liberal modesty is commendable in theology's systematic role, it is problematic when manifest in theology's second task, in particular, when as with Polkinghorne's arguments in favour of theological critical realism, resources are available that would commend a more robust apologetic stance. Of course, it is the defining characteristic of a creative thinker that their work inspires further reflection and it is for this reason that – if his modesty permits – I conclude by placing Polkinghorne's work both within the tradition of the 'pragmatically minded English [who] have made their own characteristic contribution to a dialogue between science and theology that has been continuing for centuries' and amongst those who ensure that 'exciting times lie ahead for the international exploration of the relationship between the truths of science and the truth of God'.[72]

---

[69]   Ibid., 1.

[70]   Larmer, 'Divine Action', 548.

[71]   Tillich, *Systematic Theology*, 7.

[72]   Polkinghorne, *Faith, Science and Understanding*, 206.

Chapter 13

John Polkinghorne's Kenotic Theology of Creation and its Implications for a Theory of Human Creativity

James M. Watkins

Introduction

This paper brings the work of John Polkinghorne and W.H. Vanstone into dialogue for the purpose of exploring the implications of Polkinghorne's theology of creation for a theory of human creativity. The influence of Vanstone upon Polkinghorne is well known, and it is attested to by Polkinghorne's numerous references to Vanstone's book *Love's Endeavour, Love's Expense*.[1] While Polkinghorne clearly draws upon Vanstone's phenomenology of love, connections between Polkinghorne's theology of creation and Vanstone's observations of human creativity have not been explored. This paper will argue that Vanstone's description of human creativity can serve as a metaphorical background for Polkinghorne's theology of creation. Furthermore, Polkinghorne has not worked out the implications of his theology for a theory of human creativity, and connecting Vanstone and Polkinghorne in this way puts one in a position to do so.

It might be objected that this project presupposes a connection between divine and human creativity that need not be there. Why should human creativity have anything in common with God's creation of the universe? This is an important objection, and there is not enough time to develop a full response to it in this paper. However, two reasons can be offered for why it is reasonable to link human and divine creativity in this way. First, several philosophical and historical studies on the concept of the artist in Western society suggest a strong correlation between how the artist is envisaged and how divine creation is described.[2] Even

---

[1] For example, John Polkinghorne, *Science and Creation* (London: SPCK. 1988), xiii, 62–4; *Science and Providence*, 2nd edn (London: Templeton Foundation Press, 2005), 25, 78, 110–11; *Belief in God in an Age of Science* (New Haven, CT: Yale University Press, 1998), 74; *The Work of Love*, ed. John Polkinghorne (Grand Rapids, MI: Eerdmans, 2001), x, 93. Significantly, *The Work of Love* is also dedicated "to the memory of the late Canon W. H. Vanstone."

[2] Milton Nahm, "The Theological Background of the Theory of the Artist as Creator," *Journal of the History of Ideas*, 8 (1947): 363–72; Nahm, *Genius and Creativity* (New

postmodern criticism of originality and authorial intention is sometimes aware of the theological connections between Creator and artist: "We know now that a text is not a line of words releasing a single 'theological' meaning (the 'message' of the Author—God) but a multi-dimensional space in which a variety of writings, none of them original, blend and clash."[3] Second, Christian practice commonly looks to models of God as parent or lover for helpful insight into how one might live more fully and ethically as a parent or lover. Why should it be any different for human creativity? Certainly there will be places of disanalogy (such as God's transcendent *creatio ex nihilo*), but the same could be said of analogies of God as father or king. There is even some biblical precedent for such an analogy in the popular Old Testament image of the potter and the pot. Analogies of this sort have the potential to deepen one's understanding of what it means to be human, and their usefulness and applicability may ultimately be rooted in the Christian doctrine of the *imago dei*. Nevertheless, one must tread carefully when making comparisons between God and humanity.

This paper is organized according to a three-step movement from a model of divine creation to a theology of creation and to a theory of human creativity. First, I isolate Vanstone's observations of human creativity and suggest four important connections that they have with Polkinghorne's theology of creation. Second, I look closely at how Polkinghorne develops those four elements of his theology of creation. In order to draw out the distinctive character of Polkinghorne's theology of creation I differentiate him from some contemporary panentheists and from classical theism. Third, in light of Vanstone's analogy and the following development of Polkinghorne's theology of creation, I advance two implications for a theory of human creativity. Ultimately, I hope to show that Polkinghorne's theology of creation provides a meaningful background for a theory of human creativity that values artistry as open to *relationship* and *risk*.

W.H. Vanstone's Artistic Analogy

It is clear that Polkinghorne's theology of creation has been greatly influenced by Vanstone's thought. Vanstone develops a phenomenology of love in order to describe the Creator–creature relationship. Polkinghorne, who uses Vanstone's insights about love, argues that divine love (like logic) places restrictions on what God can and cannot do.[4] However, Vanstone also develops the Creator–creature relationship through an analogy with artistic creativity that cannot be altogether separated from his phenomenology of love. In fact, in Vanstone's

York: Harper and Row Publishers, 1956); Erwin Panofsky, *Idea: A Concept in Art History*, trans. Joseph J.S. Peake (Columbia, SC: University of South Carolina Press, 1968).

   [3]   Roland Barthes, "The Death of the Author," in *Image–Music–Text*, by Roland Barthes, ed. and trans. Stephen Heath (New York: Hill and Wang, 1977), 142–8.

   [4]   Polkinghorne, *Creation*, 51–2.

writing, the human activities of love and creativity are so closely connected that he often uses "lover" and "artist" interchangeably.[5] Although references to artistic creativity are uncommon in Polkinghorne's writing, it seems reasonable to suggest that Vanstone's artistic analogy (as well as his phenomenology of love) shapes Polkinghorne's kenotic theology of creation. In what follows, I isolate the most pertinent aspects of Vanstone's observations about creativity that may serve as a metaphorical background for Polkinghorne's theology of creation.

In *Love's Endeavour, Love's Expense*, Vanstone recounts a story about two boys who were looking for something to do on their holiday break from school. The boys came to Vanstone searching for ideas. Vanstone suggested that they build a model of "an area around a waterfall in the West of Ireland" that both he and the boys had recently visited. He told them where they could find materials, offered them a room for their project, and gave them some instruction on how to begin.

Although the project began without much excitement, it quickly became an obsession: they would work long hours and miss meal times. He notes how

> the placing of each stone and twig was a matter for careful discussion. Each was, as it were, surveyed and its possibilities assessed. One would be split or cut so that it would fit a certain place. It would be placed: and then came the moment of *waiting* to see if it was "right."[6]

Vanstone goes on to say that

> As the model grew and became of greater value, each step in its creation became of greater moment and was taken with greater intensity of care. Each item that was placed seemed to possess greater power to make or to mar. [...] The once contemptible sticks and stones now had a certain power over those who were using them—a power to effect or negate the completion of that which was being made, and so to satisfy or frustrate those who were making it. The two boys became vulnerable in and through that which, out of virtually nothing, they had brought into being.[7]

Vanstone draws out two important aspects of his story. First, the boys had to wait and "see if that which emerged was 'right.'"[8] And, second, the boys become

---

5   For example, "The awareness of need generates a sharper sensitivity or a wider receptivity which is not wholly unlike the sensitivity or receptivity of *the lover or the artist*" (W.H. Vanstone, *The Stature of Waiting*, London: Darton, Longman, and Todd, 1982, 107; emphasis mine).

6   W.H. Vanstone, *Love's Endeavor, Love's Expense* (London: Darton, Longman, and Todd, 1977), 31.

7   Ibid.

8   Ibid., 33.

vulnerable to their workmanship, giving it a "certain power"[9] over themselves. Everything that Vanstone says about creativity must be understood in the context of the activity of love. He calls creation the "work of love,"[10] and it is only love that solves the mystery of why creation is so important to the creator, or why "contemptible sticks and stones" can become the holiday obsession of two boys.

Vanstone's observations about human creativity can serve as a metaphorical background for Polkinghorne's theology of creation. It is possible to develop at least four points of connection between Vanstone and Polkinghorne. The first two points of connection between Vanstone and Polkinghorne illustrate ways in which they are both drawing upon traditional Christian theology. First, both Polkinghorne and Vanstone maintain the ontological distinction between Creator and creature. Furthermore, Polkinghorne's use of kenosis, like Vanstone's, ascribes otherness and independence to creation that is constitutive of its relation to the Creator. In terms of Vanstone's artistic analogy, this is affirmed by the obvious fact that the boys are separate from their work. I argue below that this feature of Vanstone's analogy is significant in contrast to metaphors used by some contemporary panentheists to describe the Creator–creature relationship. Second, Vanstone offers a *mimetic* model of artistic creation, which connects his analogy to the long tradition of seeing God as a craftsman and to the classical concept of formal causation. Thomas Aquinas, drawing from Aristotle's work on causation, describes formal causation as the arrangement of matter in accordance with a form or model. He applies this notion of causation to divine creation to describe how God creates the world according to the ideas in His mind. Vanstone's observations of human creativity bear similarities to formal causation (the form is "an area around a waterfall in the West of Ireland"), and Polkinghorne's theology of divine action also has significant ties to the concept of formal causation.

The next two points of connection between Polkinghorne and Vanstone suggest how they depart from classical theism. In particular, the classical notion of formal causation is problematic for Vanstone and Polkinghorne because it threatens to undermine the otherness of creation. Third, in Aquinas' theology of creation, formal causation has the effect of eliminating risk, but Polkinghorne argues that the world is metaphysically unpredictable, and that God freely limits his epistemic relation to creation such that he knows the world in its unpredictability. Polkinhorne's emphasis upon *intrinsic* unpredictability could be seen as a theological interpretation of Vanstone's observation that the boys must wait and see if each additional piece is "right." Polkinghorne's theology of creation, therefore, incorporates an analogous sense in which divine creativity is discovery. Fourth, unlike Aquinas' timeless description of formal causation, Vanstone's model takes very seriously the element of time. Through the process of creation, the boys become vulnerable to the success of their project. This suggests, as does Polkinghorne's theory of divine dipolarity (the idea that God has temporal

---

9   Ibid.

10   Ibid., 34.

and eternal poles), that God acts in and through the temporality of his creation, and is, in some sense, vulnerable to its success.

In these four significant ways, Vanstone's artistic analogy can be seen as a metaphor lying behind Polkinghorne's theology of creation. In what follows, I develop Polkinghorne's theology of creation in light of these four points of connection with Vanstone. Then, I am in a position to draw out implications from Polkinghorne's theology of creation for a theory of human creativity.

Polkinghorne's Kenotic Theology of Creation

Kenosis and the Creator–Creature Relationship

Both Polkinghorne and Vanstone maintain the ontological distinction between Creator and creature, and they both emphasize the independence and otherness of creation. Polkinghorne often situates his description of the Creator–creature relationship in contrast to panentheism: the affirmation that "the Being of God includes and penetrates the whole universe, so that every part of it exists in Him, but His Being is more than, and not exhausted by, the universe."[11] He sees the value in panentheism, but he is hesitant to endorse it:

> The word 'penetrates' need imply no more than the immanent divine presence to the created universe, but the word 'includes,' placed in parallel with it, seems to point to some closer form of ontological relationship.[12]

Polkinghorne suggests that it is the idea of divine kenotic creation—God's gift of love "that creatures should be allowed to be themselves and to make themselves in the veiled presence of God"[13]—that separates him from panentheism. Although panentheism may simply be an affirmation of God's presence in creation, there are panentheists who emphasize, to a greater degree than Polkinghorne, the immanence of God and the dependence of creation. For example, Michael Brierly writes: "The cosmos is not 'independent' of God in any way; indeed, it is radically dependent on God at every moment and at every level."[14] Complicating matters, however, is

---

[11] F.L. Cross and E.A. Livingstone (eds), *The Oxford Dictionary of the Christian Church*, 3rd edn (Oxford: Oxford University Press, 1997), 1213. Quoted in John Polkinghorne, *Science and the Trinity* (London: SPCK, 2004), 95.

[12] Polkinghorne, *Trinity*, 95.

[13] Ibid., 164–5.

[14] Michael Brierly, "The Potential of Panentheism for Dialogue between Science and Religion," in *The Oxford Handbook of Science and Religion*, ed. Phillip Clayton and Zachary Simpson (Oxford: Oxford University Press, 2006), 640.

the fact that many panentheists also describe divine creation as kenotic.[15] Because of the similarities between Polkinghorne and panentheists, some scholars see little or no difference between them.[16] How can one distinguish between the different ways that Polkinghorne and some panentheists use kenosis?

This distinction ultimately rests upon two different ways of conceiving the God–world relation.[17] Polkinghorne emphasizes the otherness of God and world, while contemporary panentheists emphasize the unity of God and world.[18] Otherness and unity are not necessarily mutually exclusive, but they are clearly different focuses or emphases. It is helpful to consider these different emphases in light of their extremes. Pantheism emphasizes the unity of God and world by dissolving the ontological gap between. Deism emphasizes the otherness of God and world by removing God's special and personal action from creation. These

---

[15]   The following examples are not meant to be a comprehensive description of how panentheists use kenotic creation, but simply some examples that gesture at the variety that is possible. Niels Henrik Gregersen connects kenotic creation to an "expressivist" or Hegelian account of panentheism in "Three Varieties of Panentheism," in *In Whom we Live and Move and Have Our Being*, ed. Phillip Clayton and Arthur Peacocke (Grand Rapids, MI: Eerdmans, 2004), 30. Arthur Peacocke also draws on Vanstone's theology to develop an account of kenotic creation that seems to emphasize divine vulnerability more than Polkinghorne's use of kenosis (*Theology for a Scientific Age* (Oxford: Basil Blackwell, 1990), 124). Celia Deane-Drummond speaks of kenosis as self-emptying, but rejects versions, such as Polkinghorne's, that describe God as 'giving up' properties or in terms of spatial self-limitation (*Christ and Evolution* (Minneapolis, MN: Fortress Press, 2009), 54). Denis Edwards employs the concept of kenosis but it is couched within Rahner's notion of creation as divine self-bestowal so that God waits actively upon creation. "A Relational and Evolving Universe Unfolding within the Dynamism of the Divine Communion," *In Whom*, 199–210 (*How God Acts* (Minneapolis, MN: Fortress Press, 2010), 25–56). Philip Clayton develops kenosis as creation in a way that is very close to Polkinghorne's understanding, but, as we will see, differs owing to Clayton's picture of the Creator–creature relation (Phillip Clayton, "Kenotic Trinitarian Panentheism" *Dialog* 44, No. 3 (Fall 2005): 250–55).

[16]   For example, Kevin Vanhoozer argues that Polkinghorne's "position with regard to the God–world relationship is virtually indistinguishable from that of other contemporary panentheists" (*Remythologizing Theology* (Cambridge: Cambridge University Press, 2010), 131, n. 242).

[17]   Keith Ward, *Rational Theology and the Creativity of God* (Oxford: Blackwell, 1982), 1–3. Ward distinguishes between two traditional views of God: inclusive and exclusive infinity. Polkinghorne and contemporary panentheists respectively stand in line with these two different traditions. Christianity, Ward argues, significantly modifies both of these traditions with the notion of a "self-giving God."

[18]   Celia Deane-Drummond seems to occupy a position similar to Polkinghorne's in relation to panentheism. She prefers the label "modified classical theism" to "panentheism." She finds value in the classical tradition because it asserts that "creation is mysteriously *other* than God, and furthermore, that only in declaring creation as other can we begin to think in terms of relation" ("The Logos as Wisdom: A Starting Point for a Sophianic Theology of Creation," *In Whom We Live*, 235).

two extremes serve as boundaries for a Christian doctrine of creation, and it is reasonable to suggest that Polkinghorne is closer to the extreme of deism while contemporary panentheists are closer to the extreme of pantheism.

The emphases of otherness and unity found in Polkinghorne and some contemporary panentheists, respectively, are seen even more clearly in the metaphors that each employs for the God–world relation. Owen Thomas argues that contemporary interest in panentheism may be related to what he calls the "new Romantic movement."[19] He argues that the metaphors panentheists use support his thesis, for "Romantic movements always favour organic metaphors over interpersonal ones, and therefore 'internal presence' over personal presence."[20] Behind panentheistic metaphors is the claim that "to know something is to be directly related to it."[21] Philip Clayton writes, "I am internally related to my body, immediately aware of stimuli and feelings in a way vastly different from my knowledge of the physical world. But God's relation to the world is no less intimate than my relation to my own body."[22] By way of contrast, Polkinghorne typically employs interpersonal metaphors that envisage the external relatedness of two distinct entities. In light of their differences of metaphor, one could say that some panentheists view relation as more fundamental than otherness, while Polkinghorne understands otherness as constitutive of the Creator–creature relation.

The dominating metaphor of all panentheisms is that the world is "in" God, but God is more than the world. Owen Thomas draws attention to a wide variety of interpretations of panentheism.[23] Phillip Clayton argues that the "in" metaphor has an irreducibly two-fold structure that corresponds to the "interdependence of God and world."[24] In contrast, Polkinghorne's emphasis upon the otherness of creation could be interpreted as the view that the world is "outside" of God. Polkinghorne qualifies the idea that God creates *ad extra* by appropriating Jürgen Moltmann's

---

[19]   Owen C. Thomas, "On Doing Theology during a Romantic Movement," in *The Subjective Eye: Essays in Culture, Religion, and Gender in Honor of Margaret R. Miles*, ed. Richard Valantasis (Eugene, OR: Pickwick Publications, 2006): 136–56.

[20]   Owen C. Thomas, "Problems in Panentheism", in *The Oxford Handbook of Religion and Science* ed. Phillip Clayton (Oxford: Oxford University Press, 2006), 652–64.

[21]   Phillip Clayton, "God and World", in *Cambridge Companion to Postmodern Theology*, ed. Kevin J. Vanhoozer (Cambridge: Cambridge University Press, 2003), 212.

[22]   Ibid.

[23]   Thomas, "Problems in Panentheism," 653. This results, he suggests, not from the theological richness of the position itself, but from the ambiguity of their primary metaphor that the world is "in" God.

[24]   Philip Clayton, *Adventures in the Spirit*, ed. Zachary Simpson (Minneapolis, MN: Fortress Press, 2008), 128. He writes, "The world depends on God because God is its necessary and eternal source; without God's creative act it would neither have come into existence nor exist as this moment. And God depends on the world because the nature of God's actual experience depends on interactions with finite creatures like ourselves."

use of *zimsum* to describe *creatio ex nihilo*.[25] Moltmann argues that the only way one can really conceive of an *extra Deum* is to assume a "self-limitation by God Himself preceding his creation which can be reconciled with God's divinity without contradiction. In order to create a world 'outside' Himself, the infinite God must have made room beforehand for a finitude in Himself."[26] Moltmann does emphasize the immanence of God in creation, but he envisages this as God entering the "God-forsaken space"[27] that He first makes for creation. Creation is "in" God by virtue of being contained by God. Some panentheists distance themselves from *zimsum* because they "wish to establish a closer relationship than that implied by God as a mere 'container.'"[28] However, it must be said, both Polkinghorne and Moltmann advocate a *kind* of panentheism. Polkinghorne argues that he is an *eschatological* panentheist[29] (the world will eventually be "in" God), which suggests that, even within Polkinghorne's theology, there is a way to conceive of creation as "in" God.

Polkinghorne worries that the "in" metaphor may blur distinctions between God and the world that render creaturely encounter with God less than personal.[30] In spite of Polkinghorne's worries, contemporary panentheists have argued that God encounters and acts in the world as a personal agent.[31] The logic of panentheism proceeds, in contrast to what Peacocke calls the notion of "God as necessary 'substance,'"[32] from the understanding that an infinite God includes everything within Himself. There is, then, nothing "outside" God. Philip Clayton, for example, rejects the notion that the world is "ontologically outside God" as this inevitably leads to a view of divine action as "interventions from outside into the world's order."[33] Clayton defends the view that God is radically immanent such that His identification with the world is "ontological as well as soteriological."[34] It is significant that, in his discussion of creation as kenosis, Clayton emphasizes the *difference* between Creator and creature, in contrast to Joseph Bracken's process

---

[25]   Polkinghorne, *Creation*, 61–2.

[26]   Jürgen Moltmann, *God in Creation*, trans. Margaret Kohl (London: SCM Press, 1985), 86.

[27]   Ibid.

[28]   Brierly, "The Potential of Panentheism," 637.

[29]   John Polkinghorne, *The God of Hope and the End of the World* (London: SPCK, 2002), 115.

[30]   Polkinghorne, *Providence*, 20.

[31]   Arthur Peacocke, *All That is*, ed. Philip Clayton (Minneapolis, MN: Fortress Press, 2007), 24; Philip Clayton, *Adventures in the Spirit*, ed. Zachary Simpson (Minneapolis, MN: Fortress Press, 2008), 121–2. Both Peacocke and Clayton argue that God is not an impersonal "system," but that he also transcends, and cannot be defined by, personhood.

[32]   Peacocke, *All That Is*, 21.

[33]   Ibid., 147.

[34]   Ibid., 251.

approach to creation.[35] Clayton also invokes the idea of divine aseity, the language of "ad extra" and that which is "beyond the inner-divine relations" to distance creation as kenosis from process theism.[36] Kenosis and the language of otherness introduce a tension into Clayton's panentheism by suggesting that God might relate to something "outside" himself.[37] For Polkinghorne, the tension takes the opposite form as he uses kenosis to address the problem of God acting "within" that which was already "outside" Himself.[38]

Because the "in" metaphor is the controlling metaphor of panentheism, most other metaphors that panentheists employ tend to develop the implications of the "in" metaphor further. This does not mean, however, that other panentheistic metaphors contribute nothing valuable to the panentheists understanding of the God–world relation. The world as God's body metaphor has come to be recognized as quintessentially panentheistic. Clayton finds a non-dualistic understanding of the mind–body relationship to be illuminating:

The analogy with God is intriguing: the mental subject of the universe has access to all occurrences in the world as input (although, of course, not by means of physical structures in the world, such as a sort of cosmic optic nerve or nervous system), and God's causal input into the world is best understood as analogous to that level of mental experience which, monitoring and responding to the various inputs from the world, makes decisions and carries out actions at a mental level that stands above, without being fully separate from, the level of physical functioning.[39]

This metaphor clearly suggests the interiority of God's relationship to creation. According to Peacocke, the world as God's body metaphor draws upon a way of relating human intention and action where "the action of the body just is the intended action of the person."[40] Thus, Peacocke strongly affirms the immanence of God in creation as "the processes [of the created order] are not themselves God but are the action of God-as-Creator—rather in the way that the processes and

---

[35]   Ibid., 182.

[36]   Ibid.

[37]   Ibid., 212. Clayton seems to recognize this tension as it relates to his participatory theory of agency. He notes that "*Paradoxically*, in recognizing [one's absolute dependence upon God], one also recognizes that she is an individual who must act, and who is capable of acting, either consonant with the whole or in opposition to it. (Is not the emphasis on kenosis or self-emptying in part III above an expression of this same principle?)" Clayton freely embraces this paradox, as indeed it seems he should, but it raises questions about whether the metaphor of the world "outside" God is not also an important metaphor for articulating the proper autonomy and integrity of creation.

[38]   Polkinghorne, "Kenotic Creation," 90–106. He applies the concept of kenosis to the topic of divine action and argues that God adapts Himself to work in and through the created order.

[39]   Clayton, "God and World," 210.

[40]   Peacocke, *All That Is*, 23.

actions or our bodies as psychosomatic persons express ourselves."[41] Peacocke
has also proposed the similar metaphor of the fetus in the womb to articulate the
close relationship of Creator and creature.[42] However the analogy is articulated,
at its root is the insistence that "the infinite God is ontologically as close to finite
things as can possibly be thought without dissolving the distinction of Creator and
created altogether."[43]

Polkinghorne is critical of divine embodiment. He writes, "It seems that
divine embodiment will force God to destroy the liberty of creation if he seeks
to safeguard his own independence. God and the world are so closely linked
by embodiment that one must gain the mastery over the other."[44] Although his
critique is aimed at Grace Jantzen's theology, which clearly has connections with
process theism, it seems that he intends it to apply to all panentheists who develop
divine embodiment.[45] Polkinghorne is suggesting that, if the world is essential
to God, then it will lose its distinct otherness and creatureliness.[46] Furthermore,
Polkinghorne argues that identifying God's actions too closely with creaturely
processes raises the classical problem of primary and secondary causality all over
again.[47]

In addition to embodiment metaphors, Peacocke develops an analogy with
musical composition that is particularly pertinent to the topic of this essay. He
imagines God as the composer of a grand and complex fugue. He writes:

> With the luxuriant and profuse growth that emanates from the original simple
> structure, whole new worlds of emotional experience which are the result of the
> interplay between an expectation based on past experience (law) and an openness
> to the new (chance in the sense that the listener cannot predict or control it).
> Thus might the Creator be imagined to enable to be unfolded the potentialities
> of the universe which he himself has given it, nurturing by his redemptive and
> providential actions those that are to come to fruition in the community of free
> beings—an Improvisr of unsurpassed ingenuity.[48]

---

[41]   Ibid., 19.

[42]   Arthur Peacocke, *Creation and the World of Science* (Oxford: Clarendon Press, 1979), 142.

[43]   Phillip Clayton, "The Panentheistic Turn in Christian Theology," *Dialog*, 37 (1999): 290.

[44]   Polkinghorne, *Providence*, 27.

[45]   Ibid. See his comments regarding Peacocke's metaphor.

[46]   Owen Thomas recognizes the same problem, in general, for panentheism (Thomas, "Problems in Panentheism," 657).

[47]   Polkinghorne, *Trinity*, 95. Clayton recognizes that panentheism is close to the classical affirmation of divine *concursus* (*Adventures*, 147).

[48]   Peacocke, *Theology for a Scientific Age*, 175. See also *All That Is*, 19–20.

Although Peacocke points out that the composer is transcendent in relation to the music, it is immanence that he chooses to stress. The immanence of God is emphasized by construing the musical piece as "thinking Beethoven's musical thoughts with him."[49] For Peacocke, the work of art (in this case the performed music) is a vehicle for communication. However, Peacocke is not content to speak about the communication of an idea, and suggests that, through music, the composer communicates his or her personality. He writes, "The music would in some sense be Beethoven's inner musical thought kindled in us and we would genuinely be encountering Beethoven-qua-composer. The whole experience is one of profound communication from composer to listener."[50]

Polkinghorne does make some positive use of Peacocke's model, but he mentions only the improvisatory nature of God's interaction with the world, and says nothing of divine communication.[51] However, the difference between Peacocke and Polkinghorne becomes clearer if we assume that Polkinghorne is drawing upon Vanstone's artistic analogy. In contrast to Peacocke's analogy, Vanstone does not include artistic communication in his analogy. While Peacocke's model shows how the composer is present in the musical composition, Vanstone's analogy describes the relationship between the boys and something that is other to them. The difference between Vanstone and Peacocke may have something to do with the respective artistic mediums they choose for their analogies.[52] An inherent drawback in the musical analogy, because so much of the creative activity seems to be mental, is that it is a difficulty to establish what, exactly, is independent of the composer. Peacocke could have emphasized creaturely independence within his model, however, had he considered the relationship between the musical performance and the composed sheet music.

In contrast to these panentheist analogies, Polkinghorne relies upon interpersonal metaphors for the God–world relation, such as Vanstone's artistic analogy. By "interpersonal metaphors," I do not mean to suggest that Polkinghorne's conception of God is personal whereas the contemporary panentheists' conception of God is impersonal. Rather, interpersonal metaphors logically imply an external relation, even if they envisage a degree of internal relation, such as the empathy of one person for another. Vanstone's phenomenology of love, which Polkinghorne explicitly uses, is based upon interpersonal relationships. Polkinghorne also makes use of Vanstone's suggestion that the vulnerability of the Creator can be understood in terms of a family that chooses to adopt a child. Polkinghorne writes,

---

[49]   Ibid., 176.

[50]   Ibid.

[51]   John Polkinghorne, *Theology in the Context of Science* (London: SPCK, 2008), 74; "Jürgen Moltmann's Engagement with the Natural Sciences," in *God's Life in Trinity*, ed. Miroslav Volf and Michael Welker (Minneapolis, MN: Fortress Press, 2006), 64.

[52]   In *All That Is*, p. 20, however, Peacocke does suggest that his metaphor could be extended to include painting.

> Though God was under no compulsion to undertake the risk of creation, by that
> free act the world has become necessary to him and he is intimately involved
> with its fate. Vanstone compares this to the way in which the act of adoption
> makes a child necessary to a family, and his welfare the active object of their
> concern, whilst before that deed of adoption the family was complete in itself.[53]

Polkinghorne emphasizes the importance of seeing the kenotic creative act as
bringing the other into the midst of relationship. In contrast, panentheist metaphors
tend to give priority to unity and relationship before establishing otherness
between God and world. An interpersonal model suggests how the object of love
can remain other while at the same time being in relationship to the lover.

Although Polkinghorne and some contemporary panentheists use kenosis to
describe the divine creative act as a self-limitation that establishes otherness,
Polkinghorne places greater emphasis upon the otherness of God and world, while
panentheists tend to place greater emphasis upon the unity of God and world. Of
course, both would want to affirm that God and the world relate to each other
as a unity-in-difference, perhaps modeled upon Trinitarian relationality, but the
difference between Polkinghorne and some contemporary panentheists appears to
be lodged in the metaphors that they use. The "in" metaphor, the world as God's
body metaphor and Peacocke's musical analogy clearly favor an understanding
of relation that preferences interiority. For some contemporary panentheists, it
would appear that relationality is more fundamental and primary than otherness.
Polkinghorne, on the other hand, remains content to work with a qualified notion
that the world is "outside" God, as well as to rely on interpersonal metaphors that
emphasize bringing the other into the midst of relationship. Although Polkinghorne
does write about the vulnerability and immanence of God, his use of kenosis should
be interpreted, in contrast to some panentheists, as the granting of otherness to
creation that establishes the possibility of and opportunity for relationship with
the Creator. For Polkinghorne, "God shares the unfolding course of creation with
creatures, who have their divinely allowed, but not divinely dictated, roles to play
in its fruitful becoming."[54]

Divine Action and Formal Causation: The Interaction of Creator and Creature

Vanstone's artistic analogy has strong connections to classical models that
describe divine creation in terms of craftsmanship. Formal causation, a concept
that Aquinas borrowed from Aristotle and placed at the heart of his doctrine of
creation, relies upon an analogy with an artisan who intellectually conceives a
design and executes it in material:

---

[53]   Polkinghorne, *Creation*, 63.

[54]   Polkinghorne, "Kenotic Creation," in *The Work of Love*, 94.

In other agents, namely those which act through intellect, the form of a thing to be produced already exists in its intelligible condition: thus the form of the house already exists in the mind of the architect. This can be called the idea of the house: because the architect intends to make the house to the pattern of the form which he has conceived in his mind.[55]

Formal causation assumes that the agent has conceived the end of his activities in the beginning. Furthermore, the form is a vision or concept of the whole, and so formal causality operates in a holistic manner. For Aquinas, God shapes the world according to an intellectual image, idea or form. Some contemporary theories of divine action, especially those called "top-down causality," have conceptual ties to formal causation. Clayton, for example, argues that top-down causality is a kind of formal causation, and he explicitly formulates his theory of divine action in Thomistic terms:

God could guide the process of emergence through the introduction of new information (formal causality) and by holding out an ideal or image that could influence development without altering the mechanisms and structures that constrain evolution from the bottom up (final causality).[56]

Similarly, Polkinghorne's version of "top-down causality" is the activity of God upon the whole of creation through active information input.

Polkinghorne's theory of divine action must be seen against the backdrop of the successful scientific explanation of the natural world. The scientific method appears capable of describing the universe as a closed causal chain, which suggests "that God can act in the world only by breaking in upon it and disrupting its internal structures."[57] Polkinghorne refuses to accept a God of the gaps or an interventionist God. He also distances himself from "the picture of the divine clockmaker."[58] Polkinhorne is committed to the idea that God acts in particular times and places, and so he must find room for divine causality without destroying the integrity and autonomy of creation. Furthermore, he must find this room within his commitment to scientific methodology, and within a theological commitment to incompatibilism.[59] Formal causation suggests the possibility of God acting in such a way that is non-energetic (non-interventionist), but that can affect particular events.

---

[55]   Thomas Aquinas, *Summa Theologiae*, ed. Thomas Gilby and Thomas C. O'Brien (London: Eyer and Spottiswoode, 1964–1976), Ia.15.1.

[56]   Phillip Clayton, "Divine Action and Natural Law," *Zygon* 39, no. 3 (2004): 633.

[57]   Thomas Tracy, "Theologies of Divine Action" in *The Oxford Handbook of Religion and Science*, 601.

[58]   Polkinghorne, *Providence*, 9.

[59]   John Polkinghorne, *Exploring Reality* (New Haven, CT: Yale University Press, 2005), 10.

Polkinghorne's theory of divine action is similar to Aquinas' notion of formal causation because it can be understood in terms of information input on the *whole* of creation.[60] Polkinghorne suggests an analogy with our experience of being embodied and willing agents. He writes "As embodied beings, humans may be expected to act both energetically and informationally. As pure spirit, God might be expected to act solely through information input."[61] Polkinghorne's theories of top-down causality and active information input assume "the metaphysical possibility that there are further causal principles at work in bringing about that future beyond those that are described by science's bottom-up notion of the exchange of energy between constituents."[62] Somewhat controversially, Polkinghorne locates the possibility of low energy active information input within the indeterminism he believes is intrinsic to chaotic systems.[63] Arthur Peacocke criticizes Polkinghorne's emphasis on the indeterminism of chaotic systems as simply another gap into which God places an "intervening finger."[64] In response, Polkinghorne writes:

> I do not suppose that either we or God interact with the world by the carefully calculated adjustment of the infinitesimal details of initial conditions so as to bring about a desired result. The whole thrust of the proposal is expressed in terms of the complete holistic situation, not in terms of clever manipulation of bits and pieces.[65]

In spite of potential problems, Polkinghorne intends his theory of active information to apply to the whole of creation and also to the individual part, and chaotic systems provide a way of imagining *how* this might happen.[66] Thus, he suggests that "we

---

[60]   As John Polkinghorne graciously pointed out to me in a personal correspondence, active information input may also be used to understand special divine action. However, it would seem that special divine action is always related to divine action upon the whole of creation. He writes, "One might call such causality 'active information' and denote its holistic character by the phrase 'top-down causality,' meaning by that an influence of the whole on its parts." ("Kenotic Creation and Divine Action," in *The Work of Love*, 100.)

[61]   Polkinghorne, *Belief*, 63.

[62]   Polkinghorne, *Theology in the Context of Science*, 57.

[63]   John Polkinghorne, "Natural Science, Temporality, and Divine Action," *Theology Today* 55 (1998): 340; For critique see Nancey Murphy, "Divine Action in the Natural Order: Buridan's Ass and Schrodinger's Cat," in *Chaos and Complexity: Scientific Perspectives on Divine Action*, ed. Robert John Russell et al. (Vatican City State: Vatican Observatory Publications, 1995), 327–8; Nicholas Saunders, *Divine Action and Modern Science* (Cambridge: Cambridge University Press, 2002), 186–96.

[64]   Peacocke, *Theology for a Scientific Age*, 154.

[65]   John Polkinghorne, "The Metaphysics of Divine Action," in *Chaos and Complexity*, 154.

[66]   Polkinghorne, *Theology in the Context of Science*, 78. Polkinghorne insists that no attempts to articulate "instrinsic unpredictability ... should be taken with undue detailed

think of information, in the widest sense, as being the dynamical principle that underlies the patterns of developing form and unfolding behaviour."[67]

The majority of connections between Polkinghorne and Aquinas (or classical theology in general) are negative. For example, Polkinghorne explicitly rejects Aquinas' thought on divine simplicity,[68] God as *actus purus*,[69] and the distinction between primary and secondary causality.[70] Yet Polkinghorne does draw upon Aquinas' notion of formal causation in his description of the human person as a soul, or "information-bearing pattern," that is embodied.[71] Aquinas' description of the human soul as "constituted on the boundary line between corporeal and separate substances"[72] is quite consonant with Polkinghorne's idea that human beings are "mental/material amphibians."[73] Furthermore, if we accept that Vanstone's analogy is influencing Polkinghorne's theology of divine action, then the connection with Aquinas and formal causation becomes stronger.

However, formal causation, as we find it in Aquinas, is problematic for Polkinghorne's theory of divine action. Divine formal causation, associated as it is in Aquinas with the Platonic forms, can rob the created order of its otherness and independence. Michael Foster, for example, points out that the independence of creation depends upon an understanding of divine creation not wholly governed by reason. The Platonic demiurge, he argues, produces a technology that has a design and meaning theoretically separable from its material, but "the voluntary activity of the Creator terminates on the contingent being of the creature (i.e. on that element of its being which eludes determination by form, namely its matter and the characteristics which it possesses qua material). If such activity is essential to God, it follows that the element of contingency is essential to what he creates."[74] For Foster, formal causation is problematic because it operates primarily because it is an operation of divine intellect rather than, or more than, divine will.[75] Also

---

seriousness. They are what a physicist would call 'thought experiments', attempts to explore and try out ideas in a simplified way, rather than purporting to be complete solutions to the problem of divine action."

[67]   John Polkinghorne, "Evolution and Information: The Context," *Currents in Theology and Mission* 28, Nos 3–4 (June/August 2001): 249.

[68]   Polkinghorne, *Trinity*, 110.

[69]   Polkinghorne, *Providence*, 95.

[70]   Polkinghorne, "Kenotic Creation," 97.

[71]   Polkinghorne, *The God of Hope*, 106; "Evolution and Information," 253.

[72]   Thomas Aquinas, *Questions on the Soul*, trans. James H. Robb (Milwaukee, WI: Marquette University Press, 1984), 48.

[73]   Polkinghorne, *Providence*, 33.

[74]   Michael Foster, "The Christian Doctrine of Creation and the Rise of Modern Natural Science," *Mind* 43 (1934): 464.

[75]   Ibid. Foster argues that Christianity distinguishes itself from Greek cosmology with the doctrine of creation: "In the creative act the will must exceed any regulations which reason can prescribe. That is to say, the 'insubordination' of will to reason, which

recognizing the problem of formal causation in Aquinas, Colin Gunton writes, "It is not that Aquinas does nothing to ensure the reality of the creature; it is rather that the contingence of the creature on God (its dependence) is given more adequate weighting than its contingency: its freedom to be itself."[76] Thus, adopting Aquinas' theory of formal causation into Polkinghorne's theory of divine action produces problems for his theology of creation: it threatens the very independence that God's kenotic choice grants to creation.

Polkinghorne's theory of divine action significantly modifies Aquinas' theory of formal causation in two important ways. First, Aquinas uses formal causation to eliminate risk in God's creative activities, but Polkinghorne argues that creation is *metaphysically* unpredictable. Because metaphysical unpredictability implies that God's epistemic relationship to creation is, to some degree, incomplete, this can be seen as a theological articulation of Vanstone's observation that the boys must wait and see if each addition to their project is "right." By affirming the metaphysical unpredictability of the universe, Polkinghorne preserves the otherness and independence of creation. Second, Aquinas' craftsmanship analogy leaves out an element of time, but Polkinghorne chooses to use formal causation within the temporal process of creation's becoming. Vanstone's analogy also includes time as an important aspect of the creative process. Polkinghorne's understanding of divine dipolarity allows him to argue that God knows creation in its temporal succession, while maintaining the idea (essential to formal causation) that God has an eternal purpose for creation. For Polkinghorne, both metaphysical unpredictability and divine dipolarity flow naturally from God's act of *kenotic* creation.

Metaphysical Unpredictability

In Aquinas' theology of creation, formal causation has the effect of eliminating risk. In his own words, Aquinas assumes that "for a thing to be produced an exemplar is required so that it may achieve a determinate form."[77] Formal causation determines what creation will be and, to the extent that the form of a creature is identical to its essence, all properties of that creature are *logically* necessitated by its form. In a world fully determined by the divine intellect there is little room for contingency, and certainly no room for chance: "Now since the world is not made by chance, but is made by God acting as an intellectual agent ... there must be in the divine mind a form."[78] Polkinghorne's metaphysical picture of the world, however, does include chance, and so, in relation to Aquinas, one might say that God is not the only agent of formal causation in the world, but, to some extent, the world makes

could be only a defect in God so long as God is conceived as Demiurge, becomes essential to his activity so soon as he is thought of as Creator. It is what constitutes him, not a bad Demiurge, but something altogether more than a Demiurge."

76   Colin Gunton, *The Triune Creator* (Grand Rapids, MI: Eerdmans, 1998), 101.
77   Aquinas, *Summa*, Ia.44.3.
78   Ibid., Ia.15.1.

itself. In terms of Vanstone's analogy, the creative activity of God also includes the ability to wait and see what the creature is becoming.

Polkinghorne argues that the world contains an element of "flexibility": a complex interplay between chance and necessity.[79] He argues that this flexibility arises not from "quantum phenomena," but from "the subtlety of behaviour enjoyed by complex dynamical systems."[80] Polkinghorne wrestles to put his finger upon precisely what this term—flexibility—means. He writes, "It is important to realize that chance is being used in this 'tame' sense, meaning the shuffling operations by which what is potential is made actual. It is not a synonym for chaotic randomness, nor does it signify just a lucky fluke."[81] Polkinghorne reminds us that Newtonian mechanics is not a deterministic account of the universe, but, rather, an "approximation to a more supple reality."[82]

To illustrate what is meant by flexibility, both Polkinghorne and Peacocke refer to the work of Jacques Monod on evolution. Monod "contrasts the 'chance' processes which bring about mutations in the genetic material of an organism and the 'necessity' of their consequences in the well-ordered, replicative, interlocking mechanisms which constitute that organism's continuity as a living form."[83] In this way, the remarkably ordered human organism has emerged after a long process involving the interplay of chance and necessity. Another way that Polkinghorne illustrates flexibility is through the behavior of chaotic systems. He observes that "Chaotic systems are not totally random in their behaviour but are confined to a certain set of possibilities called a strange attractor."[84] Although the strange attractor is a limiting factor, the behavior of chaotic systems is, ultimately, a matter of chance and unpredictability.

Polkinghorne argues that the unpredictability observed in evolutionary process and chaotic systems is not merely a result of human ignorance, but it is actually a clue to the metaphysical unpredictability of the universe. His view that the world *intrinsically* contains chance follows from his realist position that epistemology models ontology.[85] Polkinghorne recognizes that there is simply no way to prove that unpredictability is an intrinsic quality of the universe. Claiming the world to be flexible is a "metaphysical choice and not a logically forced move."[86] How, then, does the flexibility of the universe affect his theology of divine action?

First, flexibility is the grounds or opportunity for divine action in the universe. This can be observed in his analogy between divine action and the willed agency

---

[79]   Polkinghorne, *Providence*, ch. 2.

[80]   Ibid., 34.

[81]   Ibid., 46.

[82]   Ibid., 36.

[83]   Peacocke, *Creation and the World of Science*, 92.

[84]   Polkinghorne, "Natural Science," 340.

[85]   Polkinghorne, *Creation*, 43. For a critique of Polkinghorne's movement from epistemology to ontology see Murphy, "Divine Action in the Natural Order," 327.

[86]   Ibid.

of psychosomatic unities. He argues that the "mental pole emerges from a material pole ... by the indirect analogy of an *indefinitely flexible* degree of organization of the matter."[87] Just as human willed interaction arises from what Polkinghorne calls the "flexibility" of the universe, so "God's action would then relate to the presumably much greater flexibility present within the total flux of cosmic process. That flexibility would be the ground necessary for God's particular action, but not for his being."[88] According to Polkinghorne's description of divine action, God interacts with the world as a whole, and the flexibility of the universe makes this possible.

Second, flexibility also preserves the otherness of creation by requiring that God take on a particular epistemological relationship in regards to creation. As Vanstone's model illustrates, the Creator must wait and see if His creation has come "right." Humanity's imperfect ability to predict the outcomes of events is ascribed to God. Here one might question the consistency with which Polkinghorne employs his theology of kenotic creation. If kenotic creation involves God's voluntary self-limitation upon his omniscience,[89] then how does one make sense of this voluntary self-limitation when it would seem that the created universe requires it? Ian Barbour, from the position of process theology, critiques kenotic theology for this very reason: "It would make no sense to say that God might have had knowledge of the future but set aside such a capacity."[90] From a more traditional Christian perspective, Denis Edwards argues that there is an "unwarranted logical leap" between "the assertion that natural processes are unpredictable" and that "God cannot foresee their outcome."[91] God may choose to limit His foreknowledge, but suggesting that the observation of unpredictability in natural processes entails this limitation does not do justice, argues Edwards, to "the mystery and incomprehensibility of God" or to the relationship between eternity and time.[92] In light of these arguments, it is difficult to see how Polkinghorne can maintain both of his positions on divine kenosis and metaphysical unpredictability, but it is clear that he describes an epistemic gap between Creator and creature.

Divine Dipolarity

In contrast to Aquinas' static description of formal causation, Polkinghorne argues that creation is a universe of true becoming. He writes, "It is impossible today to think about created reality without acknowledging its evolutionary character and its

87   Polkinghorne, *Providence*, 32. Emphasis mine.

88   Ibid., 33.

89   Polkinghorne, "Kenotic Creation," 104.

90   Ian G. Barbour, "God's Power: A Process View," in *The Work of Love*, 13.

91   Denis Edwards, "The Discovery of Chaos and the Retrieval of the Trinity," in *Chaos and Complexity*, 157–75.

92   Edwards, "The Discovery of Chaos," 171.

radical temporality."[93] Polkinghorne develops a theory of divine action that affirms the temporality of creation, and he argues that "God knows all that can be known, and so possesses a current omniscience, but the divine engagement with the reality of time implies that God does not yet know all that will eventually be knowable, and so does not possess an absolute omniscience."[94] Polkinghorne reconciles the notion of a God who has a transcendent and eternal purpose for creation with the notion of a God who knows all events "in their succession"[95] through the concept of divine dipolarity. Thus, for Polkinghorne, God is vulnerable towards creation, but He cannot be manipulated by it.

Divine dipolarity provides Polkinghorne with a way of conceptually holding together God's eternal purpose for creation and the independence of creation from God. Polkinghorne writes that the concept "suggests that there is in the divine being both an atemporal eternal pole (which it calls the divine primordial nature) and a temporal pole (the divine consequent nature)."[96] He borrows the language of dipolarity from A.N. Whitehead and Charles Hartshorne, but he refuses to accept the metaphysical system of process theism.[97] His reasons for taking a dipolar view of God are his reading of scripture as "God's engagement with temporal process,"[98] as well as his concern to maintain certain classical notions of God. He writes, "There has to be an eternal and unchanging dimension to the divine reality, in order for there to be a basis for the steadfast love that is God's nature, and for the certain hope for creation that is God's promise."[99] This view of God is, perhaps, an attempt to bring some coherence to "Vanstone's description of the Christian God as *Deus non passibilis sed passus*—the God who is impassible but vulnerable."[100]

Ascribing a temporal pole to the eternal God suggests that He is vulnerable to changes in His creation. This is not to say that God can be manipulated by creation, but rather that his relationship to it cannot be static. Polkinghorne writes,

> While there must be in the divine essence that which is wholly free from the possibility of variation, so that God's loving mercy is eternally unchangeable, there must also surely be that which corresponds to the changing but perfectly appropriate relationship to the varying circumstances of a temporal creation.[101]

One can see a parallel here with Vanstone's suggestion that the boys' creative activity, as their model nears completion, takes on a new level of poignancy and

---

93   Polkinghorne, *Trinity*, 104.
94   Ibid.
95   Ibid.
96   Ibid.
97   Ibid., 105.
98   Ibid.
99   Polkinghorne, *Trinity*, 106.
100   Polkinghorne, *Providence*, 25.
101   Polkinghorne, "Kenotic Creation," 101.

intensity. Indeed, the work exerts a kind of power over the boys, but it obviously cannot coerce or manipulate them. By ascribing vulnerability to God, the otherness of creation is not only preserved, but it is also emphasized by suggesting that God accommodates himself to it. Divine dipolarity is the assertion that changes in creation matter to God, and that His relationship to creation must take these into account.

Implications for a Theory of Human Creativity

Polkinghorne's theology of creation grounds the value of relationship and risk for human creative practice within the divine kenosis. Vanstone observes that otherness and vulnerability are important elements in human creative activity, and, in Polkinghorne's theology, it is possible to see how these aspects of human creativity are grounded in God's *kenotic* creative activities. Polkinghorne's emphasis upon the otherness of creation easily lends itself to a theory of human creativity that is described in relational, rather than individualistic, terms. In contrast to Aquinas' notion of formal causation, Polkinghorne's theology of creation is more consonant with a theory of human creativity that values risk and unpredictability. Polkinghorne's kenotic theology of creation is suggestive of a theory of human creativity that is distinctive in its emphasis upon relationship and risk.

Creativity and Relationship

Polkinghorne emphasizes the Creator's ability to respect the otherness of creation and to incorporate its creativity within His own. In contrast to Polkinghorne's relational description of divine creativity, it is possible to develop a theory of human creativity that is individualistic. The Romantic theory of artistic genius, for example, emphasizes the autonomy of the artist. The theory of artistic genius describes human creativity in the isolation of creation *ex nihilo*: as original without respect for conventions, self-expressive without respect for an "other," and individualistic without respect for community. This theory of creativity is fundamentally monological. Nancy Fraser writes:

> The monologic view [of art] is the Romantic individualist view in which ... a solitary voice [is] crying out into the night against an utterly undifferentiated background. The only conceivable response to this voice is uncomprehending or identificatory imitation. There is no room for a reply that could qualify as a different voice.[102]

---

[102]   Nancy Fraser, *Unruly Practices* (Cambridge: Polity Press, 1989), 103.

The popular metaphor "expression" is very important to such a theory, for it suggests that creativity is fundamentally a unidirectional movement from an inner reality to an outer one. Peacocke's focus on the communication of the artist's personality seems liable to an individualistic interpretation, in spite of his emphasis upon divine vulnerability and evolution as creaturely self-making. The difficulty arises for Peacocke's metaphor because he overemphasizes the capacity of a material medium (in this case sound) to communicate authorial intent to the neglect of the proper autonomy of materials.[103] The musical metaphor, as well as the world as God's body metaphor, runs the risk of not doing justice to the full contingency of creation[104] and, thus, to the full contingency of the artist's materials. Polkinghorne's theology of creation, because it emphasizes the otherness of creation, offers an analogy with human creativity that likewise emphasizes the otherness and independence of artistic materials.

Consonant with Polkinghorne's theology are those who describe creativity in dialogical terms. Something like a dialogue is suggested by Vanstone's observation that the boys had to wait and see if each piece would come right. Nicholas Wolterstorff writes that "the work of art emerges from a dialogue between artist and material."[105] He goes on to say that

> If one is genuinely willing to hold conversation with one's material and not determined, come what may, to wrest it into shape, then to set about creating a work of art is to be willing, with apprehensive anticipation, to be led along in conversation to destinations unknown.[106]

Wolterstorff uses, somewhat unfortunately, the word "mastering" to describe the creative relationship between the artist and his materials. While the word seems less than able to fully grasp Wolterstorff's dynamic and dialogic description of the creative process, what is meant by it is clear: the artist who masters his material

---

[103]   This is not to say that panentheism necessarily leads to an individualistic notion of human creativity. With its "systems" approach to reality, contemporary panentheism profoundly expresses the interrelatedness of all things, and it could be quite fruitful to explore panentheism as a theological framework for human creativity as an open and collaborative process. However, if this musical analogy for the God–world relation is taken as an analogy between divine and human creativity, it is difficult to see how it could break free of Romantic assumptions about human creativity without a great deal more emphasis upon the autonomy of the material medium.

[104]   I am using "contingency" in the same way that T.F. Torrance does. He argues that "in virtue of its contingence the universe has an orientation at once toward God and away from him." The musical metaphor risks reducing the universe's relation to God as simply "toward God." See T.F. Torrance, in "Divine and Contingent Order," *The Sciences and Theology in the Twentieth Century*, ed. A.R. Peacocke (London: Oriel Press, 1981), 86.

[105]   Nicholas Wolterstorff, *Art in Action* (Grand Rapids, MI: Eerdmans, 1980), 94.

[106]   Ibid., 95.

excels in the knowledge of and the use of his material. Similar to Wolterstorff's notion of a "conversation to destinations unknown," Monroe Beardsley describes the creative process in the following way:

> as the poet moves from stage to stage, it is not that he is looking to see whether he is saying what he already meant, but that he is looking to see whether he wants to mean what he is saying.[107]

For Beardsley, the creative process boils down to two alternating postures, *invention* and *selection*, that generate the dialogic structure of artistic creativity. The artist is always switching between forming new ideas and looking to see what the work of art is "saying."

Framing artistic creativity in terms of a dialogue suggests that it is, in some sense, a journey of discovery. Polkinghorne's theology of creation certainly includes an element of discovery in his commitments to divine dipolarity and the metaphysical openness of the future. Polkinghorne emphasizes that this is a kenotic choice on the part of the Creator, but, for the artist, discovery is a necessary aspect of the creative process. The personal journals and creative work of contemporary Scottish environmental artist Andy Goldsworthy are a profound reflection upon the creative process, and, in many respects, they emphasize the importance of discovery in human creativity. For example, he writes:

> I have an art that teaches me very important things about nature, my nature, the land and my relationship to it. I don't mean that I learn in an academic sense; like getting a book and learning the names of plants, but something through which I try to understand the processes of growth and decay, of life in nature. Although it is often a practical and physical art, it is also an intensely spiritual affair that I have with nature: a relationship.[108]

There is a strong epistemic aspect to Goldsworthy's work as an artist, but he is careful to point out that he is not trying to "learn in an academic sense." Instead, Goldsworthy's exploration of the landscape takes place within the intimacy of a committed relationship to the landscape. He chooses to fully immerse himself in the physical terrain, and thereby gather a kind of "working" knowledge of the world as a whole.

While the relationship between the artist and materials is important, this does not exhaust all of the artist's relationships. The artist can choose to be open toward a tradition of art making, and develop the potential he or she discovers there. As many psychologists and anthropologists have pointed out, human creativity cannot be divorced from culture and society. Mihalyi Csikszentmihalyi, for

---

[107]   Monroe Beardsley, "On the Creation of Art," *Journal of Aesthetics and Art Criticism*, 23 (1965): 291–304.

[108]   Andy Goldsworthy, *Hand to Earth* (London: Thames and Hudson, 1990), 164.

example, argues that "creativity is a process that can be observed only at the intersection where individuals, domains, and fields interact."[109] Similarly, art theorist and curator Nicholas Bourriaud argues that "artistic activity is a game, whose forms, patterns and functions develop and evolve according to periods and social contexts; it is not an immutable essence."[110] Also, some recent philosophers of art emphasize the important role that the audience or viewer plays in completing a work of art, and in shaping the creativity of the artist through the expectation of the work's presentation.[111] However, the connection between the artist and her wider society is not a completely necessary one: the artist must choose to be open to influences beyond her own creative impulses. Polkinghorne's kenotic theology of creation provides a model that values openness to relationships as a part of the creative process. Moving beyond human relationships, Polkinghorne's theology also suggests that human creativity is fundamentally grounded in and related to divine creativity.

Creativity and Risk

The notion of formal causation can be used, as it seems to have been by Aquinas, to rid divine creativity of risk. The careful craftsman is able to execute his plan exactly as it was conceived. However, as we have seen, Polkinghorne is able to use the concept of formal causation and speak of God taking a risk in creation. He argues that creation is offered a share in making itself, and so God is not the only formal cause of creation. Furthermore, Polkinghorne's use of divine dipolarity suggests that the Creator's teleological purposes remain transcendent, even though God accomplishes them through the temporality of creation. Polkinghorne's theology, therefore, implies a theory of human creativity that is both risk-laden and teleological.

Some philosophers of art assume that ideal human creativity involves a small amount of risk and proceeds in a more programmatic way. There are two common ways to introduce "controls" into a theory of creativity. Monroe Beardsley calls these the propulsive and the finalistic theories of creativity.[112] The propulsive theory assumes that there is something prior to the creative act that exerts a controlling pressure. Beardsley takes R.G. Collingwood's theory of art as expression as his primary example of the propulsive theory. Collingwood argues that the process

[109]   Mihalyi Csikszentmihalyi, "Implications of a Systems Perspective for the Study of Creativity" in *Handbook of Creativity*, ed. Robert Sternberg (Cambridge: Cambridge University Press, 1999), 315.

[110]   Nicholas Bourriaud, *Relational Aesthetics*, trans. Simon Pleasance et al. (Paris: les pressus du reel, 2002), 11.

[111]   See Hans-Georg Gadamer, *Truth and Method* (London: Continuum Press, 2006), esp. 102–130; Kendall Walton, *Mimesis as Make-believe* (Cambridge, MA: Harvard University Press, 1990).

[112]   Beardsley, "On the Creation of Art," 293–7.

of creating a work of art begins with an "artistic emotion" that exerts a pressure on the artist to express it. The creative process is the unfolding and growing awareness of this emotion and so, in this way, the artistic emotion guides artistic creativity. The finalistic theory, on the other hand, controls the creative process by assuming that the artist has a goal or final product in mind. Beardsley associates this theory with "problem-solving" theories of creativity. The artist has a problem or goal in mind and takes the appropriate steps to achieve the end he has in sight. By attempting to "manage" risk, however, both the propulsive and the finalistic theories can potentially explain away creativity. In its most extreme idealistic form, the propulsive theory can reduce creativity to a mental activity. Collingwood, for example, argues that the physical making of a work of art is merely incidental to the mental work that goes before.[113] On the other hand, the finalistic theory can reduce the creative process to a superficial "playing out" of a required routine. In contrast, Polkinghorne's kenotic theology of creation suggests that risk may be a valuable element in God's creative activity. God's kenotic choice to grant otherness and independence to creation also establishes the creature's free response that, although it may further evil in the world, also has the potential to bring glory to God's creative purposes.

For Polkinghorne, divine kenotic creativity *freely* embraces risk as an important element in its activities, but a theory of human creativity must reflect the *necessity* and value of risk. Berys Gaut, in his essay "Creativity and Skill," argues that risk is an important and inherent element in human creativity. He argues that traditional "product-oriented" theories of creativity are problematic because they are "compatible with any story about that process."[114] For example, a product may be novel or valuable, but one would hesitate to call it "creative" if the process by which it was made is exposed as "completely accidental" or "mechanical."[115] Gaut suggests, in contrast to a product-oriented definition, that the creative process must involve an element that he calls "flair."[116] To put it succinctly, flair is the use of one's skills without following a set routine. Creativity, therefore, involves the freedom to stand back from a routine and make evaluative judgments. Skills, of course, are a means to an end, and so Gaut's account of creativity is teleological. However, in his description of the freedom of the artist, Gaut is careful to leave a great deal of room for risk, serendipity and chance as valuable elements of the creative process. Indeed, he argues that human creativity is "inherently risky. That is why an essential virtue of the creative person is *courage* exhibited in the realm of his creative activity."[117]

---

[113]   R.G. Collingwood, *The Principles of Art* (London: Oxford University Press, 1938), 37.

[114]   Berys Gaut, "Creativity and Skill," in *The Idea of Creativity*, ed. Michael Krausz, Denis Dutton and Karen Bardsley (Leiden: Koninklijke Brill, 2009), 85.

[115]   Ibid.

[116]   Ibid., 86.

[117]   Gaut, "Creativity and Skill," 102.

Although there is risk present in the divine creative action, this should not destroy the hope that Christians have in the New Heavens and New Earth. Polkinghorne writes that "hope is based neither on certainty, as if it were simple extrapolation of the present, nor on fantasy, as if its object bore only a tenuous relation to the present ... For the Christian, hope arises out of endurance in the face of adversity in the love of God."[118] The reality of hope is not eliminated by risk, but actually made all the more palpable and important. On the topic of Christian hope, Polkinghorne quotes Vanstone: "If creation is the work of love, its 'security' lies not in its conformity to some predetermined plan but in the unsparing love which will not abandon a single fragment of it."[119] The Christian's confidence in the triumph of God's work does not lie in His ability to orchestrate an air-tight plan of redemption. Rather, the Christian has confidence in the strength of God's persuasive love. She knows that the weakness of God is stronger than human strength.

Conclusion

Vanstone's artistic analogy provides an excellent metaphorical background for Polkinghorne's theology of creation. In contrast to panentheist metaphors that emphasize interior relationships, Vanstone's model provides a context in which one can understand Polkinghorne's kenotic theology of creation as establishing creaturely otherness that constitutes the Creator–creature relationship. Vanstone's model, again, provides a helpful metaphorical background because formal causation often relies, as it did for Aquinas, upon an analogy with craftsmanship. However, formal causation is problematic for Polkinghorne's theology of creation because it threatens to destroy the otherness and independence of the creature. Polkinghorne's theories of metaphysical unpredictability and divine dipolarity can be seen as solutions to these problems. Furthermore, these aspects of his theology of creation are connected to specific elements in Vanstone's model.

In light of Vanstone's artistic analogy, it is possible to suggest some implications from Polkinghorne's theology of creation for a theory of human creativity. Panentheist metaphors and the classical notion of formal causation provide descriptions of divine creativity that, by way of contrast, emphasize the distinctive character of these implications. In contrast to Peacocke's musical metaphor, Polkinghorne's theology of creation emphasizes the otherness of the creature, and so lends itself more easily to a theory of human creativity that respects the autonomy of the artist's materials as well as the various relationships in which the artist is embedded. In contrast to divine formal causation, Polkinghorne's theology of creation makes room for risk in divine creativity, and so is consonant with a theory of human creativity that incorporates unforeseen possibilities within

---

[118] Polkinghorne, *The God of Hope*, 29–30.

[119] Vanstone, *Love's Endeavour*, 66, quoted in Polkinghorne, *Providence*, 110.

a teleological and purposeful process. While these two implications clearly do not amount to a complete theory of human creativity, it is reasonable to suggest that Polkinghorne's theology of creation can provide a meaningful and fruitful theological background for human creative practice.

Chapter 14
Science-and-Theology from the Standpoint of Divine Kenosis

Philip Clayton

It pleases me immensely to be able to submit this chapter in honor of John Polkinghorne. Over many years of Vatican/ Center for Theology and the Natural Sciences consultations, throughout the seven years of "Science and the Spiritual Quest," during an extended stay at the University of Cambridge, and in countless international conferences and meetings, I had the privilege of watching John in action—his lectures, his prowess in debate, and his organizational leadership. Without his mentorship, I would never have been the scholar that I became. It is a testimony to John's influence that many, many of the leading science-and-religion scholars of our age can repeat the same testimony.

Undeniably, science–religion debates during the last few years have taken on a hostile, war-like tone that is very unlike the calm, affirming prose of John Polkinghorne's publications. "The culture wars are a big tent," writes Louis Ruprecht in the influential progressive online magazine *ReligionDispatches.org*. "The gap separating traditionally religious people from everyone else is wide, and growing wider by the day ... no one seems to dispute the fact that this dispute will be, and probably must be, increasingly strident and increasingly shrill."[1]

Can John Polkinghorne's approach still be effective in this increasingly bitter climate? Indeed, can the civil dialogue and cooperation between science and religion that the International Society for Science and Religion stands for still play a major cultural role in this age? Or, like medieval monks, must we now do our work behind monastery walls, faced with the disinterest (if not outright hostility) of the surrounding society?

In this essay I will single out one central thesis of Polkinghorne's work, which I believe offers a key guide and test case in this age of animosity: the concept of divine kenosis. It is well known that Polkinghorne has extended the theme of self-emptying from Philippians 2 to become the orienting point for his Christology, doctrine of God, doctrine of creation, theory of divine action, and view of the God–world relation. In addition to its theological strengths, I suggest, kenosis effectively conveys the tone that Christian voices need to take in religion–science

---

[1] Lou Ruprecht, "Einstein's Religion, Darwin's Agnosticism," *ReligionDispatches. org* (April 18, 2010). Dr Ruprecht clearly sides with Darwin in this debate.

debates today. In the end, though, I will urge Polkinghorne toward an even more radically kenotic approach to the field.

What Science/Religion Failed to Accomplish

In discussions going back to the early 1990s, Polkinghorne and I disagreed on what science–religion discussions could be expected to accomplish. At that time I believed that our field could become a distinct discipline within the Academy. Inspired by Ian Barbour's early work, Nancey Murphy and I had independently developed frameworks for the science–religion discussion based on Imre Lakatos's "research program" methodology.[2] Here is a five-step formulation of that program, adapted from the volume on quantum mechanics that we coedited with Bob Russell:[3]

1. The discussion partners agree on the state of the science—on what is textbook science, what are the emerging frontiers, and where are the unsolved problems.
2. We list the major interpretive options of the science. That is, in this case, we list the major options for interpreting the collapse of the wave function. We thus do philosophy of quantum mechanics—the kind that is closely tied to the physics and that attempts to interpret the physical theories and data successfully.
3. We evaluate these interpretations; we select the best one and argue for it, which means that we argue that one interpretation is superior to the others.
4. From here we move, directly or gradually, into philosophy proper. We look for ways in which philosophical positions are constrained by the best interpretation of quantum mechanics, and we defend some philosophical positions over others. Done well, this move requires one to develop sophisticated arguments about the theory of knowledge, the nature of physics, indeterminacy, emergent properties, the nature of mind or consciousness and how it is related to the physical world, and other topics.
5. This philosophy of mind or philosophy of nature then constrains the kind of theology that one can develop. The theology can use other sources, of course; it can draw on scriptures, creeds, the history of Christian thought, systematic theology proper, and so forth. Nonetheless, important guidelines for whatever theology one finally develops are derived from these five steps.

---

[2]   Philip Clayton, *Explanation from Physics to Theology: An Essay in Rationality and Religion* (New Haven, CT: Yale University Press, 1989); Nancey Murphy, *Theology in the Age of Scientific Reasoning* (Ithaca, NY: Cornell University Press, 1990).

[3]   Robert J. Russell, Philip Clayton, John Polkinghorne and Kirk Wegter-McNelly, eds, *Quantum Mechanics: Scientific Perspectives on Divine Action* (Vatican City State: Vatican Observatory/Berkeley, CA: Center for Theology and the Natural Sciences, 2001).

Something like this five-step movement represents the core of the approach that I brought to the dialogue for a number of years. When I first read Polkinghorne saying that he was a "bottom-up thinker," I assumed this is what he meant. After all, what could be more "bottom-up" than this five-step movement from the science, through its careful interpretation and philosophical analysis, on to theology proper? I still think this would be the quintessentially bottom-up approach.

However, Polkinghorne did not actually construe the method of our field in this way. He was happy to enter into dialogue with me and those in my school, criticizing concrete assertions and arguments that we made, but he claimed that he did not need to follow these five steps in order to do work in theology and science.

Take, for example, step 2: interpretations of the quantum mechanical formalism. When we were working on the quantum mechanics book, we and the others meeting at Castel Gondolfo agreed on the textbook quantum mechanics. However, John insisted, when it comes to interpreting the quantum mechanical phenomena, all of us are at the level of "a zeroeth-level approximation"—not an encouraging analysis by any stretch of the imagination! Not surprisingly, then, when it came to the philosophical arguments that were supposed to be built upon the step 2 interpretations, John expressed even greater levels of skepticism.

I must say that religion–science (or theology–science) scholarship would have been in many ways a more interesting endeavor if scholars had followed the five-step model. It would have built from the foundational science upward, step by step, according to a pre-defined order of succession. It would have been open to evaluation by a broader range of scholars; and because it would have had pre-stated criteria, it would have allowed for more robust ways of reaching consensus (or at least *trying* to get there). It would have been intellectually more demanding. It would also have exhibited a more technical kind of rationality, because participants in the debates would have possessed some criteria for deciding between competing philosophical and theological claims.

However, as it turned out, history went with Polkinghorne's *de facto* rejection of a truly bottom-up program. Apart from a few exceptions, the rigorous five-step movement from foundational science through interpretive issues and philosophical analysis and on to theology did not come to represent the science–religion field. Let us pause for a moment to explore the reasons – indeed, the central reason— that suggests why Polkinghorne was right in the end *not* to be a bottom-up thinker of this sort.

What happened instead in the history of the field over the last 10–15 years is that the discussions came to be driven by the religious (or anti-religious) interests and convictions of each individual author or group of authors. Each major participant began with her own starting position—her assumptions, convictions, values and beliefs. Each would then come to the science and try to make some sort of case that the science somehow supports her beliefs, or is at least compatible with them. It is not that the science could have *no* critical push-back under this approach; I return to this topic below. However, in the approach that came to dominate, the interests that one brings to the debate are really the driving forces that seem to determine where one looks and what conclusions one reaches.

Let us consider some examples, starting with two instances of interest-based reasoning that many people who write about science and religion would endorse. First, Intelligent Design (ID) arguments support conservative evangelical views on the status of scripture. The theological conviction about the status of scripture comes first, the science second. When a given candidate for "irreducible complexity" is debunked (say, the evolution of hemoglobin), the ID theorist goes looking for other science-based examples to use.

Second, the New Atheism has started with the methodological naturalism that is basic to the practice of science and turned it into a highly effective weapon against all things religious. As Christopher Hitchens says in his famous subtitle, "religion poisons everything." The interest of the New Atheist authors is to find *anything* in science or philosophy that might debunk "supernatural" or theological claims and to wield it against religion *tout court*. If this is true of books and articles, it is true with a vengeance in the blogosphere. I recall a gentle post in the *Huffington Post*, in which the online magazine's religion author merely announced a new forum for science and religion and invited constructive dialogue on the topic. When I checked the site again four days later to see what kinds of responses he had received, I found no less than *1000 responses* to his proposal for a dialogue forum. The majority were overwhelmingly negative, using hostile and devastatingly harsh rhetoric. Little actual science was cited; in fact, the only scientific fact I saw wielded was the claim that 30 percent of our DNA changes every year, which is blatantly false.

The dominance of the authors' own religious or anti-religious interests is patently clear across every area of our field today: the interest in demonstrating the factual accuracy of the Qur'an or in encouraging more symbolic readings (and likewise for other sacred scriptures); the interest in finding the sources of modern science in the Vedas or authenticating Ayurveda (traditional Indian medicine) through science; or the interest in neuroscience as substantiating the spiritual achievements of monks and yogis. Within Christianity alone the range is immense. The "Divine Action Project," led by CTNS and the Vatican Observatory, sought to preserve the possibility of non-interventionist, objective divine action, but it did not share the interest of many evangelicals in substantiating direct miracles and the bodily resurrection of Jesus. Amos Yong's brilliant work[4] is written out of the interests of the Pentecostal–charismatic community, whereas John Cobb's important recent book, *Back to Darwin*, works toward the interests of the community of process theologians;[5] and the "evolutionaries" at *EnlightenNext* serve yet another community. Completely different interests are served by those

---

[4]   See Amos Yong, *The Spirit of Creation: Modern Science and Divine Action in the Pentecostal–Charismatic Imagination* (Grand Rapids, MI: Eerdmans, 2011).

[5]   John Cobb, Jr, *Back to Darwin* (Grand Rapids, MI: Eerdmans, 2010).

who write to support the environmental movement, to foster ethical uses of technology, or to deepen human spiritual experience of nature.

Of course, there are some ironies here. One's own interests tend to be less visible to oneself and more visible to others. Like the water in which the fish swims, one's core interests can be so determining that they become invisible. Also, in the Academy, if your project is to show that naturalism undercuts theism (and therefore all religion), it is not considered an "interest" at all; you are free to pursue your project at most universities worldwide without anyone accusing you of lacking objectivity. Evolutionary explanations and the cognitive science of religion are thus seen as purely objective—even when they are explicitly motivated by an interest in undercutting religion. If your religious interests are Buddhist, they are generally more acceptable than most other religions, since they are not seen as conflicting with science. Social scientific studies of religion ("religious studies") and histories of religion–science relations are also taken to be interest-free.

Now let us return to the five-step research program discussed above. Although it is an inspiring ideal, it would work only if religion–science were a discipline, i.e. only if participants acknowledged common ground and were together committed to finding the best positions and arguments—*wherever* they might lead the discipline. It turned out, however, that religion/science over the last 20 years did *not* evolve into a discipline in this sense. Instead, it became a series of interpretations of science offered from the standpoints of a variety of non-scientific interests— interests that sometimes overlap and sometimes widely diverge from one another, as in the competing interests of Intelligent Design and the New Atheism. Those in the field *do* sometimes manage high levels of scholarship that are motivated by our divergent interests, but also rise above them. In the conclusion I will come back to when, and how, we are at our best.

What does all this mean? If we accept as a given that no higher-level criteria can adjudicate between the competing interests of authors in religion/science, then we should speak even more boldly from our particular perspective. I will thus accept John Polkinghorne's invitation and speak unapologetically as a Christian theologian. I will begin unapologetically with the Christian interest in Jesus, known as "the Christ." However, perhaps things are not as staid and predictable as they might seem when one begins in this way. For when we circle back to apply the central Christian notion of kenosis to the field of religion/science itself, we will find that it brings with it some surprising consequences.

Kenosis in Polkinghorne

Many scholars believe that the famous text on divine self-emptying in Philippians 2 is the oldest Christian hymn recorded in the New Testament:

Your attitude should be the same as that of Christ Jesus:
Who, being in very nature [form: μορφή] God,
    did not consider equality with God something to be grasped,
but made himself nothing [emptied himself: εκενωσεν; cf. κενωσις],
    taking the very nature [from μορφην] of a servant,
    being made in human likeness.
And being found in appearance as a man,
    he humbled himself
    and became obedient to death—
        even death on a cross. (Philippians 2:5–8, NIV)

Like other "kenotic theologians," Polkinghorne has extended this ancient hymn of divine self-emptying to become the orienting point for a variety of other doctrines.

1. Not surprisingly, Christology is the first. Kenotic theologians read Philippians 2 not just as a story but as the heart of Christology. The primary action of self-revelation of the Trinitarian God is *ekenōsen*, self-limitation. And the response of the Father is love. "Death on a cross" led to Christ's exaltation, so that "every knee shall bow, in heaven and on earth and beneath the earth" (Philippians 2:9–11).

2. The next step is the doctrine of God: what if kenosis expresses the eternal nature of God? C. Stephen Evans explains this move in his article in *Exploring Kenotic Christology: The Self-Emptying of God*: "If the Incarnation is indeed our best window into the nature of God, then it makes sense that a kenotic Christology should lead to a kenotic theism, in which the self-giving love shown in Christ is seen as central to God's very nature."[6] Elsewhere I have sought to describe a systematic theology that would work outwards from this central insight.[7]

3. Kenotic theologians move from here to develop a kenotic understanding of creation and divine action. As Polkinghorne writes in *Science and the Trinity*:

> The God of love has not brought into being a world that is simply a divine puppet theatre, but rather the Creator has given creatures some due degree of creaturely independence. Trinitarian theology does not need to see the history of the world as the performance of a fixed score, written by God

---

[6] C. Stephen Evans, ed., *Exploring Kenotic Christology: The Self-Emptying of God* (New York: Oxford University Press, 2006), 9. See also Ivor J. Davidson's interesting review of *Exploring Kenotic Christology* in *Ars Disputandi*, vol. 7 (2007), at http://www. ArsDisputandi.org, accessed July 10, 2010.

[7] Philip Clayton, *Adventures in the Spirit: God, World, Divine Action* (Minneapolis, MN: Fortress, 2009).

from all eternity, but may properly understand it as the unfolding of a grand improvisation in which the Creator and creatures both participate.[8]

The importance of rejecting the divine puppet theater recurs frequently in Polkinghorne's writings; clearly this is a central motif for him. The *locus classicus* is perhaps the famous passage from *Faith, Science, and Understanding*:

> The central Christian kenotic paradox of the incarnation centres on ... an act of divine self-limitation, so that God's nature is manifested ... through the Word's assumption of humanity and consequent participation in human life and human death in Jesus Christ. As the Fathers liked to say, the Ancient of Days lay as a baby in a manger ... If we believe that Jesus is God incarnate then, there in first-century Palestine, God submitted in the most drastic way to being a cause among causes ... The incarnation does, however, suggest what character that governance might at all times be expected to take. It seems that God is willing to share with creatures, to be vulnerable to creatures, to an extent not anticipated by classical theology's picture of the God who, through primary causality, is always in total control.[9]

In fact, Polkinghorne locates no fewer than *four* different spheres of divine kenosis:[10]

1. *The kenosis of omnipotence* implies that God allows creatures to develop through their own agency. God makes space, as it were, for real finite agents to exist. Those who know the Western philosophical traditions (e.g. al Ghazzali and Malebranche) will know how far from obvious this conclusion has been.
2. *The kenosis of simple eternity* implies that time is a reality that pertains also to God in God's eternity. God in his eternity still knows events *as they happen*, rather than knowing them only timelessly.
3. *The kenosis of omniscience* means that God's knowledge is limited to what is currently knowable. God's is a "current omniscience, temporally indexed."[11] Open theists have supplied strong arguments for accepting this temporalized understanding of divine omniscience.

---

[8]   John Polkinghorne, *Science and the Trinity: The Christian Encounter with Reality* (New Haven, CT: Yale University Press, 2004), 67.

[9]   John Polkinghorne, *Faith, Science and Understanding* (New Haven, CT: Yale University Press, 2000), 125f.

[10]   See, e.g., John Polkinghorne, ed., *The Work of Love: Creation as Kenosis* (Grand Rapids, MI: Eerdmans, 2001), 103–105. See also the helpful review of *Science and the Trinity* by Amos Yong at http://www.metanexus.net/magazine/tabid/68/id/9285/Default. aspx, accessed July 24, 2011.

[11]   Polkinghorne, *Science and the Trinity*, 108.

4. *The kenosis of causal status* means that God allows himself to be a cause among other causes. In this way, God allows creatures to be co-creators. However, it is not the kenosis of *zimzum*, of complete divine withdrawal. God limits himself in order to be present.

Affirming these four forms of divine kenosis makes Polkinghorne and me both like and unlike most process theologians. Unlike, because we do not think that God created the world out of necessity, or that the limitation of God's agency vis-à-vis other agents is a necessary limitation on God. However, like process theologians we affirm that God, having created the world, ceases to be omnipotent in relation to that world, on pain of contradicting the divine creative intent. Polkinghorne quotes Whitehead with approval, "God is a 'fellow sufferer who understands'." As theologian Thomas R. Thompson (who is not uncritical of kenotic theologies) writes,

> The virtually new axiom of divine passion—that God indeed suffers, not out of deficiency of being but connaturally out of love—both exhibits and parallels the reassessment of immutability, cut as they are from the same metaphysical cloth: God can and indeed does change in significant respects, but never in contradiction to God's character, understood along the lines of God's faithfulness to the good, the true, and the beautiful that God essentially is. The linchpin of a fixed and plenary set of essential divine attributes therefore has been loosened, particularly when thinking about the Incarnate Son. ... The classic kenotic question remains: To what extent could God change without becoming untrue to God's essential self?[12]

Of course, kenotic theologians are not without our critics. Some complain that we disregard historical precedents, using kenosis in ways that (say) Patristic theologians did not. Others have charged that kenotic theologians stretch the notion of divine self-emptying beyond where it should go. When kenosis becomes everything, they say, it becomes nothing—the kenotic night in which all cows are black.

The broader theological applications, Thomas Thompson complains, "shade in meaning into any divine or human moment of love, humility, self-giving, letting-be, enabling-to-be, and the like, in reference to the inner-Trinitarian life, creation and providence, God's revelation or grace-laden initiatives, the Christic pattern of life, basic human freedom or relations, and such"; in short, "Kenosis has now become a highly fruitful but diffuse motif of manifold application." Thompson goes so far as to represent Polkinghorne's *The Work of Love: Creation as Kenosis* as a "prolific promiscuity of the kenotic," whose "kenotic focus runneth over into all areas in, around, and under Creator and creature."[13]

---

[12]   Thomas R. Thompson, in Evans, ed., *Exploring Kenotic Christology*, 105.
[13]   Thompson, 103. Sarah Coakley has similarly criticized kenotic theologies.

This criticism is superficial, however. A rich systematic theology can be written by taking kenosis in Philippians 2 as one's guiding principle. The results are extremely useful in the theology–science dialogue; this theology has strengths in pneumatology, ecclesiology, eschatology, and other areas; and it is as christocentric as one could wish.

A More Radical Kenosis

My reservation about Polkinghorne's use of kenosis is a different one. I suggest that the implications of the kenosis concept are rather more radical than his writing suggests or admits. In the review cited earlier, Amos Yong asks

> whether or not this reformulation of the classical doctrine of divine omniscience is so radical that Polkinghorne becomes a revisionary rather than developmental theologian, to use Polkinghorne's own terms. If the former, then the lines between Polkinghorne and Peacocke (who is labeled a revisionist by Polkinghorne), for example, become blurred. In this case, for all of Polkinghorne's desire to remain faithful to historical Christian teachings, has his own "bottom-up" thinking led him to cross the line of orthodoxy?[14]

The answer to Yong's rhetorical questions, I suggest, is: yes, but in ways that may be truer in the long run to the Spirit of Christian theology. In order to get clear on this urgent question, let us look in turn at each of Polkinghorne's four kenoses. It will turn out that Yong is right; they do in fact lead us further from High Orthodoxy than one would have expected at first glance:

1. *The kenosis of omnipotence* becomes a God who binds himself to the natural world, to genuine relationship with finite beings—a God who becomes, in Pannenberg's famous phrase, "der Gott der Geschichte" (the God of history). Pannenberg writes, "The divinity of God is at stake in history. Without the actualization of his always-becoming faithfulness to himself, Jahweh would not be God, i.e. neither the ultimate truth nor the ground of all that exists outside of him."[15]

2. *The kenosis of simple eternity* becomes a God whose experience of the world is much more similar to ours than orthodox theism accepts. Polkinghorne writes, "if God's creation is intrinsically temporal, surely the Creator must

---

14   Yong; see note 10 above.

15   Pannenberg, "Der Gott der Geschichte," in *Grundfragen systematischer Theologie: Gesammelte Aufsätze*, vol. 2 (Göttingen: Vandenhoeck und Ruprecht, 1980), 112–28, quote p. 118: "Denn Gottes Gottheit selber steht in der Geschichte auf dem Spiel. Ohne den Vollzug seiner immerwährenden Treue zu sich selber wäre Jahwe nicht Gott, nämlich nicht Wahrheit schlechthin, noch Grund alles außer ihm Bestehenden."

know it in its temporality. In other words, God will not simply know that events are successive but God will know them according to their nature, that is to say, in their succession."[16] God experiences our experience as we experience it—a radical notion indeed.

3. *The kenosis of omniscience* means God's choice to limit Godself, so that God knows finite decisions as they are made. Elsewhere, Polkinghorne puts this bluntly: "God does not yet know the unformed future, simply because it is not yet there to be known."[17] To affirm this is to affirm that God is radically temporalized, caught up in the drama of history in ways that Augustine and other Patristic theologians would never have imagined or affirmed.

4. *The kenosis of causal status* means freely allowing other agents to exist alongside God, becoming full causal agents in their own right. As a result, God becomes a person-like agent, one whose actions are responses to others' decisions. A full explanation of divine action thus includes both the divine nature and the free decisions of other agents. This makes God much more similar to us as finite personal agents than the orthodox traditions would have been willing to grant. As Moltmann notes, one must now "ask about God's presence in the history of nature and in the chance events that herald a future which cannot be extrapolated from the past or present."[18]

This is not theological business as usual. For example, a radically kenotic theology could not affirm an incarnation of the Son that leaves the Father untouched. The position would have to draw closer to the more radical sections of Moltmann's *Crucified God*. It is not just that the Son suffers while the Father turns his back, so to speak; the Father suffers as well in this event (*patripassionism*). The interaction with the vagaries of human history is not limited to the incarnate Son; God as a whole enters into the flow of history. As Pannenberg (quoted above) sees, the very divinity of God is at stake in history.

This is a God who in some ways really does not know the outcome of your free decisions. *If* God is God, as we believe and hope, then "All shall be well, and all shall be well and all manner of thing shall be well" (Julian of Norwich), and "there will be no more death or mourning or crying or pain" (Revelations 21:4). We affirm these things by faith, however, and not by knowledge. In some sense, God lives through the process as fully as we do—and perhaps more so.

The implications permeate through the major questions of systematic theology and far outward into how the Christian life is lived. George Ellis describes "the virtues of kenosis as a unifying theme in the understanding of both human life and cosmology." Because God expresses kenosis, we ought to "be tuned to the welfare of others and of the world," which entails self-sacrifice for the good of others.

---

16   Polkinghorne, *Science and the Trinity*, 104.

17   Ibid., 54.

18   Moltmann in Polkinghorne, ed., *The Work of Love*, 138.

Divine kenosis is a voluntary choice whereby God exercises "total restraint in the use of God's power," suggests Ellis, "for otherwise a free response to God's actions is not possible."[19] A little reflection shows that Ellis's insights imply a vastly different understanding of God's ability to be present to evil rather than needing to draw away from it.[20]

Of the many lines of implication we could follow, allow me to mention just one: the question of panentheism. If I am right, Polkinghorne's main argument for limiting the double "in" of panentheism—God is *in* the world, and the world is *in* God—only to the eschaton is undercut. In that case the need for the adjective "eschatological" in "eschatological panentheism" is eliminated, and the kenotic Trinitarian theologian can also be a panentheist.

Conclusion

In these few pages we have looked at the diverse interests that define the field of religion/science, at Polkinghorne's kenotic doctrine of creation and divine action, and at the more systematic extension of kenotic theology that I believe is unavoidable once one has affirmed the "four kenoses" that lie at the heart of Polkinghorne's theology. What happens when we tie together the various parts of my argument?

I began by admitting that Polkinghorne turned out to be right about religion–science discourse, in opposition to my early "research programs" proposal. The differences between Jew and Hindu, between liberal theologian and evangelical theologian, are just too great for us to use the five-step program to do genuinely bottom-up work in our field. Because, historically, Polkinghorne turned out to be right about the development of our field (at least to date), we can be at best *quasi*-bottom-up thinkers. Scholars in our field—whether pro-religious or anti-religious—generally do not do the kind of disinterested reflection that I defended in my earlier publications. The commitments that people writing about religion and science have to their individual (and vastly diverging) interests is just too strong. Generally, and in contrast to much natural science, the diverging interests are more salient to the participants than the dialogue as such; *these interests*, and not a common pursuit of knowledge across religious differences, determine where common ground exists and who one is prepared to talk productively with.

However, now let us bring our conclusions about kenosis to bear. What would a kenotic approach to the science–religion dialogue look like? Well, think about what defines a discipline. Disciplines manifest mutual respect and an advocacy

---

[19]   Ellis in Polkinghorne, ed., *The Work of Love*, 107, 114.

[20]   See Craig Boyd's excellent article in *Theology and Science* 7/4 (2009), 391ff. See also the third-place winner of the Polkinghorne prize for 2010, James Watkins, whose prize-winning essay was entitled, "John Polkinghorne's Kenotic Theology of Creation and its Implications for a Theory of Human Creativity."

of the work of others, even when it lies outside one's own areas of interest. For example, in a physics faculty you have the specialty that has earned you a place among the faculty. You have not specialized in solid-state physics or biophysics, but you support the work of your colleagues in those fields and value it—in part because you know that the success of your faculty and university as a whole depends on its quality in *all* of the different fields of physics. The same is equally true, by the way, in most history or philosophy departments, certain visible exceptions notwithstanding.

The strength of our interests in religion–science—the strength of our religious convictions—makes it difficult (and many would now say, impossible) to act in a similar manner in our field. We tend to shun or even ostracize those with different positions. We are often harshest with our co-religionists, whom we view as too liberal or too conservative, and sometimes as deeply and culpably wrong. Conservative Christians may actively undercut the work of liberal Christians (and vice versa), just as Orthodox Jews tend to dislike the work of Reform Jews (and vice versa).

Still, "a house divided against itself cannot stand." When our activities in religion–science or theology–science are determined by our religious interests, we play right into the hands of New Atheist critics such as Richard Dawkins, who emphasize how unlike science our theological debates are. When our individual religious interests determine the bulk of our activities in the field, rather than letting outcomes reflect the commonalities of a shared discipline, do we not provide a *de facto* admission that our critics are right?

What then would it mean to take a kenotic approach to the field? I know that I begin as a Christian thinker; the pretense to neutrality is nothing more than that: a pretense. Yet I also know that the One whom I follow "emptied himself," taking on the form of a servant, being born in the likeness of man (Philippians 2:5–8). I can even describe my theological location (my "interest") with some precision: a Trinitarian open theist with a fairly high Christology; a kenotic panentheist deeply influenced by process thought but resisting a number of Whitehead's basic assumptions; and so forth. I know the areas of science in which I have the greatest expertise, the philosophies I find most helpful, and the answers I have defended in various books and papers. However, a *kenotic* approach to our field means that my professional activities are not carried out with the primary purpose of defending this list of causes and interests come what may. I will also act to support the work of those who bring different religious interests to our field: my Jewish and Muslim colleagues, Hindu and Buddhist scholars, naturalists like Willem Drees and "ground of being theists" like Wesley Wildman.

The hardest challenge for our field is to exercise this sort of kenotic charity toward members of one's own religious community whose views differ from one's own on the theological issues we hold most dear. In Christianity, the most vicious battle ground is Christology: is yours too low, or too high? In American evangelicalism, it is the doctrine of scripture. In Judaism it is about observance, and about the question of Israel. In Islam it is about the authority of the sacred

Qur'an, the status of God's Prophet, Mohammed, and the interpretation of *shuria*. And the list goes on.

Most of us by this point genuinely encourage engagement with science on the part of the other religions, although the level of support by individual scholars and by organizations such as the International Society for Science and Religion is not at the level that it should be when it comes to supporting and engaging with Jewish, Muslim, Buddhist and Hindu scholars. Far more serious, however, is the current trend within large organizations led primarily by members of a single religious tradition. The founder of the John Templeton Foundation, for example, sought to build cooperation between science and "the beneficial ancient scriptures of all religions," as he wrote in the Foundation's Charter. Yet in recent years, when the Foundation has funded theological work, it has tended to be mostly Christians who have been funded—and indeed, Christians toward the conservative end of the spectrum.

Overall, however, scholars in our field are supportive of blossoming religion–science dialogue across the religious traditions. It is those just outside our own theological clan, our theological neighborhood as it were, of whom we are the most suspicious. A kenotic approach to religion–science or theology–science means genuinely encouraging the work of those with whom one most disagrees.

Let me close with a vision for our field, inspired by John Polkinghorne's work and by the kenotic theology that I first learned from him. We are at our worst when we become a series of special-interest groups, each engaging science and constructing interdisciplinary dialogues to advance its own interests. We are at our best when our interests do not block but actually encourage a shared search for truth. (Think of it as *fides quaerens intellectum* in the broadest sense of the word.) At these times we welcome and even seek out those with divergent points of view, for we know that they are our best critics. Like science at its best, we formulate claims that can be rationally assessed, and then we look for the kind of critical feedback that can expose flaws in our own reasoning.[21] When criticism comes, we revise and improve our theories or, if necessary, throw them out and find better ones. In short, kenotic religion–science is not a wimpy, weak-willed, "walk all over me" approach. It is about courageous hypotheses, sharp critical feedback, and vigorous defense of one's own claims.

When we strive for this vision, when we are at our best—and leaders in our field like John Polkinghorne often are—we begin to make the transition from a loose collection of partially overlapping interests to a genuinely new discipline, ready to take our place proudly alongside the other interdisciplinary fields in the Academy. This is a noble and moving vocation. It is inspiring, in the way that Sir John Templeton's vision of a partnership between science and the world's religions in a common quest for truth was inspiring. It is intellectually exciting. It

---

[21]   We have tried to model this approach in dealing with the six chief grounds for doubting Christian claims in Philip Clayton and Steven Knapp, *The Predicament of Belief: Science, Philosophy, and Faith* (Oxford: Oxford University Press, 2011).

is demanding. It does not undercut religion, as the New Atheists think, but actually strengthens it.

Finally, this partnership between the religions with their vastly different theologies, in dialogue with the whole range of sciences, is indispensable. It is indispensable not only for the integration of fact and value, of knowledge and understanding, of science and wisdom, of heart and heart. It may also be indispensable for the survival of our species and our planet.

Chapter 15

Processes of Discovery in Science and Theology: Bottom-up Approach, Critical Realism and Interdisciplinary Inspiration

Michael Welker

In his illuminating books on quantum theory, John Polkinghorne reconstructs the complex process of discoveries that led to this scientific revolution in modern physics. Brilliant scientists from various countries had paved the way for the new theory. The sequence of discoveries is marked by physicists such as James Clerk Maxwell, Max Planck, Albert Einstein, Ernest Rutherford, Niels Bohr, Arthur Compton, Werner Heisenberg, Louis de Broglie, Erwin Schrödinger, Max Born, Paul Dirac and Richard Feynman – to name only the most glorious dozen![1]

In his book *Quantum Physics and Theology: An Unexpected Kinship*,[2] John Polkinghorne proposes that we see structural similarities between this scientific revolution and the great doctrinal achievements in the early church, particularly with respect to Trinitarian theology and Christology. It will be a future task for scholars in church history and patristics to reconstruct a similar process and to come up with a glorious dozen too. In both the sciences and theology, John Polkinghorne sees the search for truth progress through similar phases. Each goes through 'moments of enforced radical revision', 'a period of unresolved confusion', 'new synthesis and understanding' and a 'continued wrestling with unsolved problems', before finally attaining an awareness of 'deeper implications' – implications that challenge scientists and theologians alike to reformulate their theoretical frameworks in order to reach a new plateau of discovery.[3]

In his writings, John Polkinghorne not only describes and compares research processes in the search for truthful understanding. He has also been personally engaged in this search in several topical areas. According to the title of his 1993–94 Gifford Lectures, he regards himself as a 'Bottom-up Thinker'.[4] In other contexts

---

[1]   John Polkinghorne, *Quantum Theory: A Very Short Introduction*, Oxford University Press: Oxford, 2002.

[2]   Yale University Press and SPCK: New Haven, CT and London, 2007.

[3]   Cf. *Quantum Physics and Theology*, 15, 17, 18, 19 and 21; see also John Polkinghorne, *Theology in the Context of Science*, SPCK: London, 2008.

[4]   John Polkinghorne, *The Faith of a Physicist: Reflections of a Bottom-Up Thinker*, Princeton University Press: Princeton, NJ, 1994.

he describes himself as a 'critical and self-critical realist', who does not avoid 'top-down speculation', but who looks for experiential, empirical and even historical validation of truth claims. This is why he has always welcomed a strictly topical concentration in the science-and-theology discourse and has remained sceptical of merely methodological and meta-theoretical approaches.

This attitude, together with his insistence on 'cousinly relations' between science and theology, reminds me of an observation made by Alfred North Whitehead in his book *Science and the Modern World*. Whitehead saw the Reformation and the modern scientific movement as:

> two aspects of the historical revolt which was the dominant intellectual movement of the later Renaissance. The appeal to the origins of Christianity, and Francis Bacon's appeal to efficient causes over against final causes, were two sides of one movement of thought [...] It is a great mistake to conceive this historical revolt as an appeal to reason. On the contrary, it was through and through an anti-intellectualist movement. It was the return to the contemplation of brute fact; and it was based on a recoil from the inflexible rationality of medieval thought.[5]

This statement fits very well with Luther's repeated insistence that we cannot reach God through metaphysical speculation, but rather only by focussing on the incarnation and the kenosis of Jesus Christ. It fits with the attempts of the Reformers to concentrate their theology on historical and philological studies in order to take seriously God's revelation in human history.

It is characteristic of John Polkinghorne's work that he connects his passion for the science-and-theology discourse with a deep interest in the topics of Christology, pneumatology and eschatology. He shows, in this way, that we do not have to limit the dialogue between science and theology merely to the doctrine of creation or anthropology. Nor must we shy away from historical and biblical studies. In this interdisciplinary discourse, Polkinghorne, as a critical realist, seeks to strengthen common sense and its appeal to experience. Yet he also wants to heighten and sensitise common sense, to sharpen it in its confrontation with scientific and theological facts and discoveries.

It was this style of research and interdisciplinary cooperation that convinced me to invest time and energy in the dialogue at a point in my life when I had more or less given up on the science-and-theology discourse. During the 1980s, I had taken part in several consultations on science and theology, mostly within church-related academies in Germany. Yet in my experience, it was almost impossible to introduce the rich complexity of theological topics and forms of thought into this discourse. Science came in with all its glory; theology contributed only some poor metaphysical, transcendental or moral ideas. Most of the seminars and

---

[5]   Alfred North Whitehead, *Science and the Modern World*, The Free Press: New York, 1925, 1997, 8.

consultations focussed merely on historical questions of the relation between science and theology, or concentrated on general methodical reflections and general ethical concerns. In some cases it tried to test philosophy as a potential interface for the dialogue, yet as a rule it remained at the level of religiously or rather metaphysically interested and sometimes morally engaged common sense.

The more interesting German science-and-theology discourses, which began before my time, became mired in discussions about open and closed systems, or got lost in experiments with multiple modalised time systems. In the 1970s, the physicist A.M. Klaus Müller stimulated a theology-and-science discourse on time with his book *Die präparierte Zeit [Dissected Time]*.[6] However, brilliant historians such as Reinhard Koselleck, with his book *Futures Past: On the Semantics of Historical Time*,[7] and interdisciplinary geniuses such as the sociologist Niklas Luhmann would soon take over, and the topical discourse moved out of the domain of science and theology. Yet neither was the discourse able to provide leadership on issues of systems theory. After its engagement with biology and neuroscience, the academically sophisticated and creative discourse on systems theory moved into sociology. The names of Niklas Luhmann, Humberto Maturana and Francisco Varela mark this phase of the discourse.[8] We related to it in research and publications, but only in connection with legal studies and sociology and not in the framework of a theology-and-science discourse.[9]

Over against such unsatisfying developments, the new style favoured by Polkinghorne and others proved to be fruitful for academic cooperation – so much so in fact that by now I and many colleagues across the globe have gratefully participated in more than 10 international and interdisciplinary projects together with John Polkinghorne, most of them multiyear consultations, the results of which have been or will be published in several books. In the following I will attempt to offer an impression of John Polkinghorne's many seminal contributions to structuring international and interdisciplinary cooperation and some of his specific contributions to topic-oriented searches for insight and truth as I have experienced them over the years. Of course, this only covers a segment of his thought and publications over the last two decades. It will be limited to questions

---

[6]   A.M. Klaus Müller, *Die präparierte Zeit*, Stuttgart, Radius Verlag, 1972; Jürgen Moltmann, *Gott in der Schöpfung. Ökologische Schöpfungslehre*, Kaiser: München, 1985, 135ff.

[7]   Reinhard Koselleck, *Vergangene Zukunft: Zur Semantik geschichtlicher Zeiten*, Frankfurt, Suhrkamp Verlag, 1979 (*Futures Past: On the Semantics of Historical Time*, MIT Press: Cambridge, MA, 1985 [NY 2004]).

[8]   N. Luhmann, *Soziale Systeme. Grundriss einer allgemeinen Theorie*, Suhrkamp: Frankfurt, 1984; H. Maturana and F. Varela, *Autopoiesis and Cognition: The Realization of the Living*, Springer: Heidelberg, 1991.

[9]   Werner Krawietz and Michael Welker (eds), *Kritik der Theorie sozialer Systeme. Auseinandersetzungen mit Luhmanns Hauptwerk, stw 996*, Suhrkamp: Frankfurt, 1992, 2nd edn 1998.

regarding the way in which the theology-and-science discourse is organised, and how we might gain crucial topical insights in some areas of theology.

I first met John Polkinghorne in 1993 in a consultation organised by Dan Hardy at the Center of Theological Inquiry (CTI) in Princeton. The theologians were a minority among colleagues from the fields of cosmology, physics, chemistry, biology, environmental studies and philosophy – such as Owen Gingerich, William Stoeger, Robert Russell, Holmes Rolston and Ernan McMullin.

For about half a day the scientists talked about the spatio-temporal dimensions of the universe. Did we really need 13.7 billion years in order to bring forth the stellar constellations that then needed to turn to dust in order to provide the carbon material for our physical life? One of them concluded with the remark: 'Our life on earth should be compared with the survival of a person condemned to death. Twelve well-trained sharp-shooters shoot at him and he survives. He might say: This was just good luck. But he also might want to find out what really went on.' The scientists then addressed us theologians with burning questions that challenged us to deal with biblical notions about creation and salvation. Several of them said: 'You should take your traditions and texts as seriously as we take our materials.' 'We do not just want reductionistic ideas like the "unmoved mover" and the "ultimate point of reference".' Given my previous experiences, I was astonished to find scientists interested in systematic theological and even biblical thought. Although curiosity and excitement were building up on both sides, we saw that our areas of knowledge and modes of thought were too far apart to generate serious cooperation.

So we asked each other for very short papers on a specific topic that would allow us to relate our thoughts and insights from different disciplinary perspectives. For the second year we selected the notion of 'divine agency' and then found, after another lively discussion one year later, that this was still too broad. In the third year we discussed 'the temporality of God's acting in the world', and in the fourth year 'eternity and temporality in God's acting'. I found this process of narrowing down the focus in order to increase consistency and coherence in the interdisciplinary discourse extremely helpful. Sadly, when Dan Hardy was replaced at the CTI, the project came to a sudden end.[10]

The new director of the CTI, Wallace Alston, agreed to organise another multiyear international discourse on science and theology. John Polkinghorne and I proposed the topic of eschatology and were asked to develop a research programme. We started with sobering scientific insights into the finitude not only of individual but also of cosmic life. In this round, we also involved biblical scholars who confronted us with complex eschatological symbol systems. We thus experimented with a delicate balance of a topic-centred reduction of complexity on the one hand with complexity-enhancing symbolic potential on the other.

---

[10]   Some of the contributions were published in *Theology Today* 55 (1998), No. 3; cf. Patrick D. Miller, 'Theology and Science in Conversation', ibid., 301–304.

It was John Polkinghorne who offered the most helpful duality of 'continuity and discontinuity' in order to deal with complex eschatological thought and reality. This duality of continuity and discontinuity proved to offer much better orientation than the 'dialectic of unity and difference' proposed by most classical philosophical and theological modes of thought. The biblical emphasis on *new* creation, *new* heaven and *new* earth stressed discontinuity, whereas talk about *creation, heaven and earth* stressed continuity. On the one hand, 'Flesh and blood will *not* inherit the reign of God!' – yet on the other, 'We believe in the resurrection of the body!' We also saw that the classical opposition of 'future eschatology' and 'present eschatology' was of no help in understanding the emergent reality of the reign of God. We tried to explain the texture of emergent realities with the help of scientifically trained modes of thought. The many fruitful results of this project were published in the book entitled *The End of the World and the Ends of God: Science and Theology on Eschatology*,[11] which found strong resonance, and has since been translated into Korean and Chinese.

This work in the area of eschatology stimulated our interest in the topic of the resurrection. If resurrection is not some form of resuscitation, then what kind of reality is it? Together with Ted Peters, Robert Russell and several New Testament scholars, we explored the continuity and discontinuity between the bodily and the spiritual presence of the resurrected and exalted Jesus Christ. We also began discussing the correlation between present and future eschatology in the emerging reign of God in connection with the strange inner logics of so-called 'end-time eschatology'. End-time eschatology is an area that is heavily polluted by all sorts of speculation, and still requires a great deal of interdisciplinary work to achieve further clarification.[12] Some of our insights from our project on 'Divine Agency, Temporality and Eternity' helped us to avoid often-made eschatological mistakes, such as the abstract opposition of time and eternity or the confusion of end-time eschatology with an abstract synthesis of all times. John Polkinghorne contributed reflections on 'Eschatological Credibility: Emergent and Teleological Processes', attempting to discern eschatological speculations and expressions of 'evolutionary optimism' from an eschatological discourse that 'is reasonable and [with] its hopes well motivated'.[13] This was an example of how, even when dealing with the most complicated topics of the faith – ones which really challenge common-sense thought – the 'bottom-up approach' and 'critical realism' must not be given up in favour of lofty speculation.

[11]   John Polkinghorne and Michael Welker (eds), *The End of the World and the Ends of God: Science and Theology on Eschatology*, Trinity: Harrisburg, PA, 2000, Korean 2002, Chinese 2010; see also John Polkinghorne, *The God of Hope and the End of the World*, Yale University Press: New Haven, CT, 2002.
[12]   Ted Peters, Robert Russell and Michael Welker (eds), *Resurrection: Theological and Scientific Assessments*, Eerdmans: Grand Rapids, MI, 2002.
[13]   Ibid., 43–55, 55.

John Polkinghorne and I then moved on to examine the methodological insights that resulted from this work on eschatology. Some years before, we had already engaged with colleagues from around the world in a consultation at the *Internationales Wissenschaftsforum* in Heidelberg on more or less successful 'Models of Dialogue in Science and Theology'. We had also worked with students and doctoral students on theory issues such as symbolism in Cassirer, Whitehead, Susanne Langer and others. Now we reflected on methodological issues based on specific experiences from our interdisciplinary cooperation on topics in eschatology. Furthermore, we had also been active in the 'Pastor–Theologian Project' launched by Wallace Alston, in which 60 American pastors dealt with our contributions on eschatology over the course of one year – and confronted us with many helpful questions and comments. We published our findings in two contributions: *Opening Windows onto Reality* and *Springing Cultural Traps*. They highlighted the great potential of the science-and-theology discourse, but also a set of systemic distortions that block fruitful insights and discoveries. *Opening Windows onto Reality* and *Springing Cultural Traps* first appeared in the journal *Theology Today*[14] and then in a book jointly written by John Polkinghorne and myself: *Faith in the Living God.*[15]

Over the years John Polkinghorne had argued that the academy and the church should be seen, and should regard themselves, as 'truth-seeking communities'. We had a wonderful chance to reflect on this idea and the methodological procedures connected with it when John Polkinghorne visited Heidelberg for longer periods after he had been awarded the prestigious Von Humboldt Prize. We saw that correspondence-, coherence- and consensus-theories of truth must be combined in order to gain an adequate picture of truth-seeking communities. Truth-seeking communities are communities that do not claim to possess the truth, but rather raise truth-claims and develop agreed modes to test these claims. On the one hand, truth-seeking communities seek to enhance certainties, convictions and consensus, which must not be confused with truth. On the other hand, they also seek to enhance topical insight and the coherence of knowledge. This dual interest challenges the search for correspondence and serves to question and test those certainties, convictions and consensus that have already been reached, and to transcend the levels of topical insight in the search for truth.

We also used the Heidelberg times for discussions on issues of Trinitarian theology. John Polkinghorne's work on the topic resulted in his book *Science and the Trinity: The Christian Encounter with Reality.*[16] We both sought to explore the reality of the resurrected and exalted Christ and the work of the triune God by referring to the experiential basis of the sacraments, in particular Holy Communion. John Polkinghorne spoke of a 'liturgy-assisted logic', which can

---

[14]   *Theology Today* 58 (2001), 145–54 and 165–76.
[15]   John Polkinghorne and Michael Welker, *Faith in the Living God. A Dialogue*, SPCK: London, 2001; German 2005, Chinese 2006.
[16]   SPCK: London, 2004.

help in making modest steps in areas that many regard as totally inaccessible.[17] We were also increasingly drawn to issues in pneumatology, the doctrine of the Holy Spirit. The resurrected Christ is present in the power of the Spirit. In a context that thinks primarily naturalistically, this is hard to grasp. It raises the suspicion that this 'reality' of the Spirit is simply wishful thinking or an illusion, and it invites fundamentalism and agnosticism into agonising debates on the pros and cons of the idea of resuscitation, which completely misses both the central theological points and the substantial weight of the topic. Yet the mind–body dualism that dominates modern thought also needed to be overcome in order to be able to approach the reality of the resurrection.

In another attempt to explore so-called bridges between natural and spiritual realities, John Polkinghorne focussed on the topic of love. In 1998, with the assistance of Mary Ann Meyers from the Templeton Foundation, John initiated an interdisciplinary research project on the topic: 'The Work of Love: Creation as Kenosis'.[18] Several contributions were concerned with the question of how we understand the work of love beyond the boundaries of intimate I–Thou relations. How can we comprehend God's creative power as love? Can we see kenotic love already at work in the act of God's creation? Can these perspectives open up further insights into the reality of the exalted Christ and the working of the Holy Spirit?[19]

Again with the help of Mary Ann Meyers and the Templeton Foundation, we organised a consultation with the first generation of academically interested theologians from Pentecostal and charismatic backgrounds.[20] John Polkinghorne's insistence on understanding the work of the Spirit also with respect to creation has been extremely helpful in bringing critical realism into the pneumatological discourse and in overcoming a merely mentalist understanding of the Spirit. John Polkinghorne also helped me to answer a question that had plagued me for years. In my work on pneumatology I had come to realise that the self-referential spirit of Aristotle and Hegel must not be confused with the Holy Spirit of the biblical traditions.[21] The Holy Spirit is not self-referential and does not witness to itself.

---

[17]   Polkinghorne, *Science and the Trinity*, 118–42; Michael Welker, *What Happens in Holy Communion?*, translated by John Hoffmeyer, Eerdmans and SPCK: Grand Rapids, MI and London, 2000; second printing 2004.

[18]   John Polkinghorne (ed.), *The Work of Love: Creation as Kenosis*, Eerdmans and SPCK: Grand Rapids, MI and London, 2001.

[19]   Cf. John Polkinghorne, 'The Corporate Christ', in Andreas Schuele and Günter Thomas (eds), *Who is Jesus Christ for us Today? Pathways to Contemporary Christology*, Westminster John Knox: Louisville, KY, 2009, 103–111.

[20]   Michael Welker (ed.), *The Work of the Spirit: Pneumatology and Pentecostalism*, Eerdmans: Grand Rapids, MI, 2006.

[21]   Michael Welker, *God the Spirit*, translated by John Hoffmeyer, Fortress: Philadelphia, PA, 1994, esp. 279–302; see also 'The Holy Spirit', in J. Webster, K. Tanner and I. Torrance (eds), *The Oxford Handbook of Systematic Theology*, Oxford University Press: Oxford, 2007, 236–48.

Yet how then are we to understand the personhood of the Holy Spirit when it lacks basic self-referentiality? His helpful answer to this question came by suggesting that the personhood of the Holy Spirit is grounded in its context-sensitivity.[22] This insight opens up new perspectives on the power and subtlety of the emergent working of the Spirit in creation in general, but also in the human mind and body in particular.

These insights are also sorely needed in the areas of anthropological research. John Polkinghorne and I participated in two multiyear theology-and-science discourses on anthropology. Our shared interest was to overcome reductionistic and dualistic anthropological frameworks. Would it be possible to develop a theoretical and theological framework that allows us to develop a multidimensional anthropology that can host interdisciplinary approaches from the sciences and from the humanities?[23] The anthropology of Paul – with his ingenious differentiation of flesh, body, heart, soul, reason, conscience and spirit – proved to be extremely helpful for a multidisciplinary discourse. John Polkinghorne and I also became interested in the theories and practices of shared memory – communal, collective, cultural and canonical memories – which could offer further topics in future interdisciplinary cooperations.[24]

In recent years we have tried to connect this work on specific topics with our attempts to extend the science-and-theology discourse into those regions of the world where it is not yet maturely established. Together with John Zizioulas, John Polkinghorne developed a project on 'Relational Ontology', which reached out to Greek Orthodox contexts and traditions. I organised a project on the topic 'The Spirit in Creation and New Creation: Science and Theology in the Orthodox and Western Realms', which primarily engaged colleagues from the Russian Orthodox traditions. Under the topic 'Love and Law: The Science and Theology Discourse in China and the West', we dealt with love and law as key concepts of the Confucian and neo-Confucian traditions. We did this in order to gain new perspectives on concepts that are also central in Jewish and Christian thought.

Finally, over recent years we have cooperated in an international and interdisciplinary project entitled: 'Concepts of Law in Science, Legal Studies and

[22]   John Polkinghorne, 'The Hidden Spirit and the Cosmos', in *The Work of the Spirit*, 169–82.

[23]   John Polkinghorne, 'Anthropology in an Evolutionary Context', and Michael Welker, 'Theological Anthropology Versus Anthropological Reductionism', in E.K. Soulen and L. Woodhead (eds), *God and Human Dignity*, Eerdmans: Grand Rapids, MI, 2006, 89–103 and 317–42; John Polkinghorne, 'An Integrated Anthropology', and Michael Welker, 'Flesh–Body–Heart–Soul–Spirit: Paul's Anthropology as an Interdisciplinary Theory', in M. Welker (ed.), *The Depth of the Human Person*, Eerdmans, MI: Grand Rapids, forthcoming.

[24]   Michael Welker, 'Kommunikatives, kollektives, kulturelles und kanonisches Gedächtnis', in *Jahrbuch für Biblische Theologie, Bd. 22: Die Macht der Erinnerung*, Neukirchener: Neukirchen-Vluyn, 2008, 321–31.

Theology'. It was not at all easy to relate the science-and-theology discourse to the well-established law-and-religion research and to the historians connected with it. We were also faced with philosophical positions that questioned whether there were indeed 'laws' in the natural and social realms – in other words, whether 'law' is a concept realistically applicable within those areas. John Polkinghorne concluded his contribution on 'The Character of the Laws of Nature' as follows:

> Science is more than a Baconian accumulation and classification of particular instances. It involves creative imagination leading to overarching schemes of understanding within which regularities of behaviour may be interpreted as consequences of intrinsic properties, rather than their being mere constant conjunctions. The concept of laws of nature provides a fitting metaphysical foundation for the scientific enterprise. However, our knowledge of these natural laws is fragmentary and the connection between different physical regimes (such as between quantum theory and classical mechanics) is often problematic.

This tension between deep intellectual satisfaction and the experience of the fragmented character of our knowledge creates spaces for truth-seeking communities both in science and theology, but also in the church.

The results of the last projects I mentioned will be published in the course of the next year. The relations between Spirit, love and law will most likely remain foci of common interest in the science-and-theology discourse, and will hopefully be the basis of further cooperation. Different international configurations, and different interdisciplinary constellations, will offer new challenges to the search for truth, but they will also shed new light on topics and issues worth the effort of intensive reflection. Let me conclude by summing up just some of the strategic, methodological and particularly topical insights that developed out of these discourses, and were greatly stimulated not only by John Polkinghorne's thoughts and writings but also by his unique ability to help his colleagues with catalytic insights during complicated phases of the science-and-theology discourse.

'Topicality is crucial!' Twenty years ago this was not a guiding principle in the discourse. Instead, we saw rather a lot of engagements driven primarily by metaphysical, transcendental, existentialist, methodological and metatheoretical concerns. In contrast, our cooperation over recent years has been accompanied and shaped by a concentration on topicality together with a process of reducing theoretical and topical complexity in order to find convergences or helpful contrasts in areas of discovery and modes of thought. A second step focussed on delicately balancing the topic-centred reduction of complexity on the one hand with the enhancement of complexity by the inclusion of symbol systems from biblical studies on the other. The participation of biblical scholars, together with a few contributions from literary studies, as well as the more recent attempt to connect with the 'law-and-religion discourse' and with the Chinese and Orthodox thought worlds presented us with such challenges.

On the basis of some projects that we felt had been successful in their topicality, John Polkinghorne encouraged us to question not only naturalistic and scientistic reductionisms but also popular religious, philosophical and common-sense modes of thought that have blocked the interaction between scientific and theological areas of thought and discovery. He offered a typology, imagined as 'Opening (specific) Windows onto Reality', and supported many attempts to clarify and describe the epistemological processes characteristic of 'truth-seeking communities'.

In terms of topical insights, John Polkinghorne really caused a breakthrough in the exploration of topics in eschatology. Old styles of dichotomised thinking – such as 'immanence and transcendence', 'present and future' – had mostly navigated these issues using the 'dialectic of unity and difference'. By replacing this mode of thought with the figure of 'continuity and discontinuity', we were able to invite realism into the eschatological discourse and to reflect with critical realism on topics such as 'the coming realm of God' and 'the presence of the Resurrected in the Spirit', and to do so in terms of processes of emergence.

John Polkinghorne helped us to gain insights into the nature and the working of the Holy Spirit by his exploration of the hidden and emergent working of the Spirit in natural creation. He helped us with his proposal to understand the personhood of the Spirit with respect to its context-sensitivity. We reinvested some of these observations and insights into the areas of anthropology, with well-supported proposals to replace naturalistic, mentalistic and dualistic approaches with more sophisticated frameworks.[25] There are many good reasons for the academic community in general and the theological community in particular to be deeply grateful for John Polkinghorne's continuous challenge to engage in the science-and-theology discourse, to engage in bottom-up approaches of thought, and to embrace a critical and self-critical realism in order to provide interdisciplinary inspiration in our common search for truth.

---

[25]   Cf. note 23 and Michael Welker, 'Science and Theology: Their Relation at the Beginning of the Third Millennium', in P. Clayton and Z. Simpson (eds), *The Oxford Handbook of Religion and Science*, Oxford University Press: Oxford, 2006, 551–61.

Chapter 16

Some Responses

John Polkinghorne

I was touched by, and grateful for, the degree of interest and generosity shown in relation to my work by speakers at the Conference at Oxford in 2010, which was associated with my 80th birthday. At the time I was only able to make some brief comments at the end of each lecture and I welcome this opportunity to expand my responses a little, although inevitably there will remain points of detail for which there is not space to address here.

The first serious book on theology and science that I ever read was Ian Barbour's *Issues in Science and Religion*, and I was very glad that he was willing to make a long journey to speak at the Conference. In his contribution, Ian surveys, in the clear and fair-minded way that has consistently characterised his writing, the work of three scientist–theologians, Arthur Peacocke, Ian Barbour himself and myself. One of the most important commonalities between us is our endorsement of the concept of critical realism in both science and theology, a stance that Barbour pioneered. The quest for truthful understanding attained through motivated belief has been central to my own intellectual life. A key theological concept for me has been the idea of a divine kenosis in the act of creation in bringing into being a world in which creatures are allowed to be themselves and 'to make themselves' through the evolutionary exploration of potentiality. Like Peacocke, I see this divine self-limitation as a voluntary act of love, rather than the metaphysical necessity that Barbour's adherence to process theology leads him to suppose. Barbour has always been willing to revise the thought of A.N. Whitehead where he deems it necessary, and I was interested to read that he now thinks that there is 'considerable validity' in my criticism that process theology offers an account of divine power that falls short of an adequate basis for ultimate hope.

Another important commonality among the three of us is belief in a dipolarity of eternity/time in the divine nature, although we understand the details of this in somewhat different ways. Dipolarity is certainly a concept that has been strongly asserted in process thinking, but I do not think it requires commitment to other aspects of the process metaphysical account.

A critical difference between the three of us lies in our attitudes to inherited theological tradition, which I sought to indicate in the characterisations labelled 'theistic', revisionary' and 'developmental' that are referred to by Barbour. I do not doubt that there is a continuing need for interaction between theology and contemporary thinking, not least in the case of scientific insight, but I believe that the scheme set out in the terse phrases of the Nicene Creed still provides the framework within which to shape theological discourse. For me, Incarnational and Trinitarian thinking provides a rich and illuminating context within which to pursue the quest for theological truth. I believe that the saving power of Christ requires that both humanity and divinity were present in Jesus and that the Christian myth of the Word made flesh derives its supreme power and significance from the fact that it is an *enacted* myth, fusing the power of symbol with the power of historical reality. Although I acknowledge that classical theology failed to do justice to the immanence of God, I believe that it is important to sustain a clear separation between Creator and creatures, a distinction that I find blurred by panentheism.

I am grateful to Pat Bennet for a careful and sympathetic account of my thinking. A point I would like to emphasise is a distinction, which over time I have come to acknowledge more clearly, between two modes of theological discourse. One is systematic theology, a first-order discipline that evaluates experiential evidence and analytical argument relating to issues such as the motivations for belief in the existence and nature of God. The other mode is philosophical theology, a second-order discipline presenting a metaphysical overview based on the premise of theism. In my understanding, the concept of critical realism is to be invoked in relation to systematic theology's encounter with spiritual reality, in analogy with science's encounter with physical reality. I see a cousinly relationship between these two first-order disciplines (in the way of a kind of Wittgensteinian family resemblance), although one must also acknowledge the differences that arise from one being an investigation into an impersonal level of reality, which in consequence is open to experimental repetition, and the other concerned with personal and transpersonal levels of reality in which every occasion is in some degree unique and unrepeatable. I often summarise the distinction between these two regimes by saying that, in moving from one to the other, testing has to give way to trusting. Furthermore, one must heed the warnings of apophaticism concerning the limited access finite minds can have to divine Infinite Reality. Theology is much more difficult than science, since we transcend the physical world but God transcends us. Yet apophatic caution should not induce total intellectual paralysis.

Any second-order metaphysical scheme has to be based on a non-negotiable foundational belief on which it builds its edifice of understanding. It is in this sense that I have spoken of my commitment to Trinitarian theology. I certainly agree with Wentzel van Huyssteen that human knowledge requires assent to what goes beyond the simply certain. The main difference between us lies, I believe, in the role we assign to evolutionary epistemology. I do not doubt that it offers helpful insights, but I have argued that the physico-biological context of conventional evolutionary thinking is insufficient to explain certain human abilities, such as being able to discover the deep truths of mathematics. I believe the latter capacity is most persuasively understood if it arises from encounter with a noetic realm of mathematical reality.[1]

---

[1]   J.C. Polkinghorne, *Exploring Reality*, London, SPCK and New Haven, CT, Yale University Press, 2005, 54–8.

I am grateful to Nicholas Saunders for his clear account of classical chaos and his sympathetic treatment of my ideas on its relevance to the consideration of metaphysical issues of causality. Of course, we know that the mathematical equations of classical dynamics can only be approximations to actual physical reality. The future behaviour of a chaotic system soon comes to depend formally on details of its initial conditions that lie below the limits of Heisenberg uncertainty. Attempts to fuse classical chaos theory and quantum theory are frustrated by their mutual incompatibility – the one formally scale-free in its fractal in character, the other with a scale set by Planck's constant. The actual causal structure of the physical world is something more subtle and complex than current thinking is able to describe. My conjectured appeal to 'downward emergence' is an attempt to express something of this subtlety.

Nancy Cartwright and Eric Martin draw our attention to the complex character of our actual encounter with the physical world. I agree that our current understanding is 'dappled', not only in the sense of the difficulties presented by attempts at the detailed analysis of really complex systems, but also because, while we can give good accounts within well-defined domains, the relationship between different domains is often problematic and ill-understood. The paradigm example of the latter fact is provided by the presently unanswered questions about how the apparently clear and orderly world of everyday process emerges from its cloudy and fitful quantum substrate. The intrinsic unpredictabilities encountered in contemporary physics (quantum theory, chaos theory) are certainly metaphysically compatible with a world whose behaviour is not wholly determined by laws expressed in terms of the exchange of energy between constituents. The discoveries of the emerging infant science of complexity theory, investigating the astonishing self-organising powers of complex systems, are suggestive that there may be hitherto undiscovered holistic laws of nature that complement constituent accounts. Martin is right in saying that I regard the contemporary somewhat confused state of affairs as largely a temporary stage in the development of physical science, rather than it being intrinsic to science in the manner suggested by Cartwright.

Philip Clayton reflects on kenotic theology which, like him, I regard as one of the most important developments in twentieth-century theology. Of course it represents a significant departure from classical theology, but I believe that it can fully find a place within the Trinitarian envelope of understanding that I wish to affirm. Clayton's five-step programme laid out a progression from one selected first-order discipline (science) to the eventual construction of a metaphysical world-view. I think the problem with the programme was its privileging of a single selected starting point. In metaphysical endeavour all first-order disciplines (including, of course, systematic theology) should participate on an equal basis from the start. It is attractive that a kenotic approach to science and religion, as proposed by Clayton, encourages respect for the positions held by others and a recognition that one is not infallible. The problem of drawing on the insights of all faith traditions is important and challenging and one to which Clayton himself has made significant contributions. Part of the reason for the present numerical dominance of Christians in the science and theology discourse is, I believe, due to the fact that Christianity is the most intellectually obsessed of the world faith traditions. When we were forming ISSR, we initially thought of calling it the International Society for Science and Theology, but it was pointed out to us that 'theology' is not a highly important term for some of the world faiths.

Daniel Darg explores a conceptual scheme in which the analogy of physical process to a computer program is saved from mere reductionism by the operation of if-clauses in appropriately complex circumstances. Although I believe that physical reality is too subtle and too supple to be represented properly in computational terms, Darg's work is an interesting thought experiment. I do not think, however, that it illuminates radical miracles such as the Resurrection. I believe the latter to be a seminal event in which God began to bring into being a genuinely new creation, brought about through the divine transformation of the old creation.

I am grateful to Junghyung Kim for his careful account of my eschatological thinking and his analysis of its relationship with that of Jürgen Moltmann. Moltmann is the contemporary theologian who has been the greatest influence on me in my own theological thinking. I think that Kim is right in identifying our different conceptions of eschatological 'time' as being the principal source of a degree of divergence between us over eschatology. I also think he is right to associate this divergence partly with the difference between the top-down thought natural to a systematic theologian and the bottom-up thought natural to a scientist–theologian. These are deep matters and all of us in our eschatological thinking are to some extent playing with the speculative toys of thought when we seek to say something about the life to come. I absolutely agree that this is an area of theological exploration that will benefit from work from a variety of perspectives.

Russell Manning characterises my work in terms of a liberal 'modesty' that aims for motivated insight rather than the attainment of certain proof. I suppose this could be seen as a pale counterpart of the Dionysian apophatic restriction on speech about God. I fact, I think that virtually all human knowledge has this modest character (including scientific belief), a conclusion in which I am influenced by the philosophy of Michael Polanyi. Manning refers to the distinction I make between theology as a first-order discipline (systematic theology) and as a second-order-discipline (philosophical theology). He feels that he finds in my thinking some confusion about the role of natural theology. In response, I would like to point to the important distinction commonly made by scientist–theologians between natural theology and a theology of nature. In the former, the flow of the argument is from some aspect of general experience (such as science's discovery of the deep intelligibility of the universe) to the claim that this supports belief in the existence of God (a divine Mind behind cosmic order). Natural theology is clearly part of the first-order project of systematic theology, where it is conjoined with revealed theology in the manner described, for example, by Thomas Torrance. It is at this level of theological discourse that the concept of critical realism applies most directly. In a theology of nature, the flow of the argument is reversed, from the *assumed* existence of God to an enhanced understanding of some aspect of science's account of the physical world. A theology of nature is therefore part of the second-order project of a theistic metaphysics. Its explanatory scope is wider than that of natural theology proper. For example, it can interpret the deep relationality discovered in the physical world, exemplified by quantum entanglement, as a pale reflection of the character of that world's triune Creator, but it would be absurd to try to argue in the reverse direction as if quantum theory somehow implied the Trinity. I look forward to reading *The Oxford Handbook of Natural Theology*.

I certainly share with Bob Russell a conviction of the importance to theology of the concept of flowing time and I am grateful for his careful discussion of how this relates to special relativity. I think that his emphasis on the relational character of tensed properties is helpful. I note that he considers that a 'supertemporal' concept of eternity and belief in a divine drawing power from the future resolve problems about divine knowledge of the future because 'the future is potentially real and not simply not real'. I have to confess that I do not fully understand this, but I shall keep thinking.

I am very grateful to Keith Ward for his challenging and penetrating discussion, which deserves a fuller consideration than I can give here. The quest for a theory of dual-aspect monism is inspired by the desire to find an account of the human person that lies between the extremes of physical reductionism (mind is a mere epiphenomenon of the brain) and a substance dualism (even if the substances are welded together in a Cartesian way). Dual-aspect monism seeks to speak of one 'stuff', experienced in the complementary aspects that we label mind and matter. In my stuttering attempts to participate in this ambitious project, I have frequently invoked Thomas Nagel's well-known judgement that the best we can attain at present is 'pre-socratic flailings around'. In my own flailings I have drawn attention to a duality between the concepts of 'energy' and what I call 'information' or dynamical pattern, which seems to be emerging as science begins to engage holistically with the properties of complex systems. Of course, if these concepts are to be of any relevance to thinking about human nature, 'information' would require generalisation and complexification far beyond the banalities of, say, encodings in DNA. The one absolute duality that I believe is theologically essential to preserve is that between Creator (disembodied Spirit) and creatures (beings in a world of mind/matter complementarity). I see human psychosomatic unity as realised through information/matter complementarity, without denying the possibility of extremes of pure matter (stones) and pure mind (the truths of mathematics; angels?).

James Watkins rightly identifies the debt I owe to W.H. Vanstone for his discussion of an analogy between the nature of human creativity and the character of divine creation. In thinking of the latter, I seek to steer a path between the extremes of deistic detachment and tyrannical control. A kenotic account of creation seems to me to attain this objective. I believe that all attempts by finite human beings to speak of the infinite reality of God have to make extensive use of appropriate analogies. Artistic creativity is so deep a human capacity that I believe it to be particularly fruitful in this respect. I value Vanstone's emphasis on the significance of relationship and risk.

Fraser Watts has been a valued friend and colleague in Cambridge over many years. I shall try to respond to a few of the points he has made. In our present state of knowledge and given the unobservability of those hypothesised other worlds, I see the multiverse as being as metaphysical a concept as that of a divine Creator. However, I agree that theology could live with a multiverse if necessary. It is not for us to limit the creative generosity of God, although personally I believe that the Creator would only be likely to bring into being worlds selected from the small subset of possible universes that would be capable of a significantly fruitful history. I agree that Purpose/Freedom is a more comprehensive concept than Necessity/Chance. When I use the latter I have in mind partly its widespread usage and partly its suitability in relation to the level of physical process that I myself most frequently engage with. I do *not* think that information is 'the fundamental stuff' of the universe but simply that it is one pole of that stuff, together with energy in their complementary relationship. I personally do not find persuasive the idea of a gradual spiritualisation of matter in a Teilhardian fashion. Science's present account is not final because finality belongs to the Creator, who I believe wills a destiny beyond futility brought about by the radically novel divine act of the new creation. Much of my discussion of eschatological matters centres on an attempt to understand this radical novelty in a way that does not produce so great a discontinuity between the new and old creations as to make the latter seem ultimately irrelevant.

I have certainly been blunt in expressing my reservations about the classical notion of primary causality. Yet I am only too aware that over the centuries it has been a concept affirmed by a large number of theologians of the highest intellectual power and integrity. Terry Wright's careful analysis of the issues involved is a helpful contribution. I see a clear distinction between primary causality and the idea of special providential action exercised through active information operating within the open grain of nature. The latter is surely in strong contrast both to the intrinsically divine act of holding creation in being and to the idea of the existence of primary causality underlying all forms of secondary causality. My concept of the nature of special providential action is also in acknowledged contrast to radically new forms of divine action (miracles), such as the Resurrection. As Wright notes, I have come to believe that the divine kenosis involved in creation includes a willingness on the part of the Creator to condescend to act as a cause among causes. Two points require clarification. One is that, in referring to the Spirit in relation to the input of pure information, I have in mind the *work* of the Spirit rather than the essential nature of the Spirit. The other point is that, in the course of continuing reflection, I have modified my initial almost exclusive emphasis on the role of chaotic processes as furnishing the necessary causal joint for divine providential action. Agency, whether human or divine, is a highly complex matter and it surely operates at and through a variety of interlocking levels of physical process. I see the extensive work in the science and theology community in the 1990s on divine action, with its appeals made by a variety of people to a variety of kinds of putative causal joints, as achieving, not a total explanation but, in the wise words of Ernan McMullin, 'the defeat of the defeaters'. The enterprise was able to show that one could take what physics really implies with all due seriousness, without being driven to deny the reality of human or providential agency. Certainly, an honest science has not established the causal closure of the world on its own terms alone.

Michael Welker has been my closest theological friend and I have benefitted greatly from participation in the many interactive occasions that he describes. The context provided by an interdisciplinary group of scholars in sustained interaction over a number of meetings, ultimately culminating in the production of a jointly authored book, has proved to be an exceptionally stimulating and fruitful experience. I am glad that Michael began his paper with a reference to my work on what I perceive to be the cousinly relationship between truthful exploration and discovery in quantum physics and in theology. My academic life has been spent working in these two truth-seeking communities and my conviction of their kinship arises from that experience. As befits a self-confessed bottom-up thinker, I believe that their relationship has to be explored by analysis of actual occasions of enhanced understanding, rather than simply relying on a top-down discourse on generalised methodological issues.

The quest for truth in science and the quest for truth in theology are two of the most significant intellectual activities of our time. It has been an enormous privilege to be part of the community that is seeking to understand their mutual interaction. I believe that science and religion are truly friends and not foes. I like to say that I am 'two-eyed', looking at reality though the eye of science and through the eye of religion, and I believe that such binocular vision enables me to see further and deeper than either eye would achieve on its own.

A Selected Bibliography of Works on the Science–Theology Dialogue

Books

The Way the World Is (Triangle, 1983; Eerdmans, 1984; Warminster John Knox, 2007; Japanese and Polish translations).

Creation and the Structure of the Physical World – the 1985 Drawbridge Lecture (The Christian Evidence Society, 1986).

One World – the Interaction of Science and Theology (SPCK, 1986; Princeton University Press, 1987; 2nd edn. Templeton Foundation Press, 2007; Italian, Hungarian, Slovak and Danish translations).

Science and Creation – The Search for Understanding (SPCK, 1988; New Science Library, 1989; 2nd edn. Templeton Foundation Press, 2006)

Science and Providence – God's Interaction with the World (SPCK, 1989; New Science Library, 1989; Italian translation; 2nd edn. Templeton Foundation Press, 2005).

Reason and Reality – The Relationship Between Science and Theology (SPCK/ Trinity Press International, 1991).

Quarks, Chaos and Christianity: Questions to Science and Religion (Triangle, 1994, 2005; Crossroads, 1996, 2006; Italian, Japanese, Romanian and Dutch translations).

Science and Christian Belief – Theological Reflections of a Bottom-up Thinker (SPCK, 1994; Princeton University Press, 1994; Fortress, 1996 as *The Faith of a Physicist*).

Serious Talk – Science and Religion in Dialogue (Trinity Press International, 1995; SCM Press, 1996).

Scientists as Theologians: A Comparison of the Writings of Ian Barbour, Arthur Peacocke and John Polkinghorne (SPCK, 1996).

Beyond Science: The Wider Human Context (Cambridge University Press, 1996; Greek, Korean, Polish, Portugese and Turkish translations).

Searching for Truth: A Scientist looks at the Bible (The Bible Reading Fellowship/ Crossroad, 1996; Lent Book for 1997; Portugese translation).

Belief in God in an Age of Science (Yale University Press, 1998; German, Italian, Korean and Japanese translations).

Science and Theology: An Introduction (SPCK, 1998; Fortress, 1998; Chinese, Czech, German, Japanese, Russian, and Spanish translations).

Faith, Science and Understanding (SPCK, 2000; Yale University Press, 2000; Korean translation).

Traffic in Truth (Canterbury Press, 2000; Fortress, 2002).

(With Michael Welker) *Faith in the Living God: A Dialogue* (SPCK, 2001; Fortress, 2001; Chinese, German and Korean translations).

The God of Hope and the End of the World (SPCK, 2002; Yale University Press, 2002; Chinese, Italian and Spanish translations).

Living with Hope (SPCK, 2003; Westminster John Knox, 2003).

The Archbishop's School of Christianity and Science (York Courses, 2003).

Science and the Trinity (SPCK/Yale University Press, 2004).

Exploring Reality (SPCK/Yale University Press, 2005; French, Spanish and Portugese translations).

Quantum Physics and Theology (SPCK/Yale University Press, 2007; Korean translation).

From Physicist to Priest (SPCK, 2007; Cascade 2008).

Theology in the Context of Science (SPCK, 2008; Yale UP, 2009).

(With N. Beale) *Questions of Truth* (WJK, 2009).

Encountering Scripture (SPCK, 2010).

The Polkinghorne Reader, ed. T.J. Oort (SPCK/Templeton Press, 2010).

Science and Religion in Quest of Truth (SPCK/Yale University Press, 2011).

Journal Papers, Book Chapters, etc.

'The Quantum World', in *Physics, Philosophy and Theology*, ed. R.J. Russell et al. (Vatican Observatory, 1988).

'A Revived Natural Theology', in *Science and Religion*, ed. J. Fenemma and I. Paul (University of Twente and Kluwer Academic Publishing, 1990).

'A Scientist's View of Religion', *Science and Christian Belief*, 2 (1990), 83.

'The Interaction of Science and Theology', in *Fundamentalism and Tolerance*, ed. A. Linzey and P. Wexler (Bellew Publishing, 1991).

'The Spirit and Creation' (anonymously), in *We Believe in the Holy Spirit* (Church House Publishing, for the Doctrine Commission of the Church of England, 1991).

'Reckonings in Science and Religion', *The Anglican Theological Review*, 74 (1992), 376.

'Spiritual Growth and the Scientific Quest', *The Way* (October 1992).

'Temporal Origin and Ontological Origin', in *Cosmaos, Bios, Theos*, ed. Henry Margenau and Roy A. Varghese (Open Court, 1992).

'The Mind of God?', *The Cambridge Review*, 113 (March 1992).

'Chaos and Cosmos: A Theological Approach', in *Chaos: The New Science*, ed. John Holte (University Press of America, 1993).

'Physical Science and Christian Thought', in *Modern Christian Thought*, ed. A.E. McGrath (Blackwell, 1993).

'Science and Religion – recent writing', *Epworth Review* 20 (1993), 92.

'The Debate over the Block Universe' (with C.J. Isham), in *Quantum Cosmology and the Laws of Nature*, ed. R.J. Russell, N. Murphy and C.J. Isham (Vatican Observatory, 1993).

'The Laws of Nature and the Laws of Physics', in *Quantum Cosmology and the Laws of Nature*, ed. R.J. Russell, N. Murphy and C.J. Isham (Vatican Observatory, 1993).

'A Potent Universe', in *Evidence of Purpose: Scientists Discover the Creator*, ed. J.M. Templeton (Continuum, 1994), 105–15.

'Can a Scientist Pray?', *Colloquium*, 26 (1994), 2–10.

'Personal Experience' (108–10) in *Glimpses of God*, ed. D. Cohn-Sherbok (Duckworth, 1994).

'Theological Notions of Creation and Divine Causality', in *Science and Theology: Questions at the interface*, ed. M. Rae, H. Regan and J. Stenhouse (T&T Clark, 1994).

'The New Natural Theology', *Studies in World Christianity*, 1 (1995), 41–50.

'A Scientist's Approach to Belief', *Sewanee Theological Review*, 39 (1995), 12–50.

'Contemporary Interactions between Science and Theology', *Modern Believing*, 36 (1995), 33.

'*Creatio Continua* and Divine Action', *Science and Christian Belief*, 7 (1995), 101.

'Creation and the Structure of the Physical World', in *Readings in Modern Theology*, ed. R. Gill (SPCK, 1995), 25–42.

'The Metaphysics of Divine Action', in *Chaos and Complexity*, ed. R.J. Russell et al. (Vatican Observatory, 1995), 146–56.

'The Modern Interaction of Science and Theology', in *The Great Ideas Today, 1995* (Encyclopaedia Brittanica Inc., 1995).

'From Physicist to Priest', in *My Journey, Your Journey* (Lion, 1996), 127–38.

'From Physicist to Priest', *Dialogue* (Spring, 1996).

'The Theological Significance of Cosmological Theories of Origin', in *Scienza, Filosofia e Teologia di Fronte alla Nascita dell' Universo*, ed. Padre Eligio et al. (Edizioni New Press, 1997), 199–207.

Contributions (98–9, 140, 144, 157–8) in *Inspired*, ed. J. Laufer and K.S. Lewis (Doubleday, 1998).

'From Physicist to Priest', in *Science and Theology*, ed. T. Peters (Westview, 1998), 56–64.

'Natural Science, Temporality and Divine Action', *Theology Today* (October, 1998), 329–43.

'Natural Theology Today', *The Anglican* (April 1998).

'Physicist and Priest', in *Spiritual Evolution*, ed. J.S. Templeton and K.S. Giniger (Templeton Foundation Press, 1998), 113–20.

'Public Ethics and Religious Belief', *International Journal of Bioethics*, 9 (1998), 27–30.

'Wolfhart Pannenbergs Engagement with the Natural Sciences', *Zygon*, 34 (1999), 151–8.

'God in Relation to Nature', in *Perspectives* (CTI, Spring 1999).

'Science and Religion are Complementary', in *Healing Through Prayer*, ed. L. Dossey et al. (Anglican Book Centre, 1999), 15–27.

'So Finely Tuned a Universe', in *Commonweal Confronts the Century*, ed. P. Jordan and P. Baumann (Touchstone, 1999), 311–23.

'The Spirit-Wrestler' (interview with Chris Floyd), *Science and Spirit* (November/December 1999), 16f.

'Cloning: After Dolly', in *Christians and Bioethics*, ed. F. Watts (SPCK, 2000), 13–20.

'Eschatology: Some Questions and Some Insights from Science', in *The End of the World and the Ends of God*, ed. J.C. Polkinghorne and M. Welker (Trinity Press International, 2000; Chinese and German translations).

'The Nature of Physical Reality' [reprinted]; 'Science and Theology in the Twentyfirst Century'; 'The Life and Works of a Bottom-up Thinker'; 'Twenty Years in the Science and Theology Alpine Climbing Club', *Zygon* 35 (2000), 927–40; 941–54; 955–62; 985–88.

'The Truth is out There' (interview with Roger Penrose), *Third Way* (January 2000), 17f.

'Christian Faith in the Academy: The Role of Physics', in *Higher Learning and Catholic Traditions*, ed. R.E. Sullivan (University of Notre Dame Press, 2001), 39–59.

'Evolution and Information: The Context', *Currents in Mission and Theology* (2001) [Festschrift volume for Philip Hefner].

'Kenotic Creation and Divine Action', in *The Work of Love*, ed. J.C. Polkinghorne (SPCK, 2001; Eerdmans 2001), 90–106.

'Opening Windows onto Reality', *Theology Today*, 58 (2001), 145–54.

'Prayer and Science', in *Perspectives on Prayer*, ed. F. Watts (SPCK, 2001), 27–38.

'Therapeutic Uses of Cell Nuclear Replacements', *Zeitschrift fur Evangelische Ethik*, 45 (2001), 149–52.

'Understanding the Universe', in *Cosmic Questions*, ed. J.B. Miller (New York Academy of Science, 2001), 175–82.

'Does God exist ?', in *Big Questions in Science*, ed. H. Swain (Jonathan Cape, 2002), 6–10.

'Eschatological Credibility: Emergent and Teleological Processes', in *Resurrection: Theological and Scientific Assessments*, ed. T. Peters, R.J. Russell and M. Welker (Eerdmans, 2002), 43–55.

'Physical Process, Quantum Events and Divine Agency', in *Quantum Mechanics: Scientific Perspectives on Divine Action*, ed. R.J. Russell, P. Clayton, K. Wegter-McNelly and J.C. Polkinghorne (Vatican Observatory, 2002), 181–90.

'The Credibility of the Miraculous', *Zygon*, 37 (2002), 751–7.

'Christian Scholarship and the Practice of Science', in *Christian Scholarship …for What?*, ed. S.M. Felch (Calvin College, 2003).

'God, Science and Philosophy', in *Comparative Theology*, ed. T.W. Bartel (SPCK, 2003).

'Is There a Destiny Beyond Death?', *St George's Cathedral Lecture* 10 (2003), Perth, Western Australia.

'Physics and Metaphysics in a Trinitarian Perspective', *Theology and Science*, 1 (2003), 33–50.

'Progress in Religion? Interfaith Opportunities', *Theology*, 106 (2003), 188–91.

'A Scientist Looks at Theological Inquiry', in *Loving God with Our Minds*, ed. M. Welker and C.A. Jarvis (Eerdmans, 2004), 91–7.

'Science and Religion', in *The Oxford Companion to the Mind*, 2nd edn. ed. R.L. Gregory (Oxford University Press, 2004), 824–5.

'The Inbuilt Potentiality of Creation', in *Debating Design*, ed. W.A. Dembski and M. Ruse (Cambridge University Press, 2004), 246–60.

'The Person, the Soul, and Genetic Engineering', *Journal of Medical Ethics*, 30 (2004), 593–7.

'Universal Values in Science and Technology', in *Universal Values*, ed. L.C. Christophorou and G. Contopoulos (Academy of Athens, 2004), 129ff.

'Comments on Sanborn Brown's "Can Physics Contribute to Theology?"', *Zygon*, 40 (2005), 513–15.

'Star Warrior' (an interview with Martin Rees), *Third Way* (April 2005).

'The Continuing Interaction of Science and Religion', *Zygon* 40 (2005), 43–50.

'Time in Physics and Theology', in *What God Knows*, ed. H.L. Poe and J.S. Matson (Baylor University Press, 2005), 61–74.

'Anthropology in an Evolutionary Context', in *God and Human Dignity*, ed. H.K. Soulen and L. Woodhead (Eerdmans 2006), 89–103.

'Christian Interdisciplinarity', in *Christianity and the Soul of the University*, ed. D.V. Henry and M.D. Beaty (Baylor University Press, 2006), 49–64.

'Christianity and Science', in *The Oxford Handbook of Religion and Science*, ed. P. Clayton (Oxford University Press, 2006), 57–70.

'Does "Science and Religion" Matter?' and 'Science and Religion: Where Have We Come From and Where Are We Going?', in *Why the Science and Religion Dialogue Matters*, ed. F. Watts and K. Dutton (Templeton Foundation Press, 2006), 27–32 and 41–52.

'Quantum Theology', in *God's Action in the World*, ed. T. Peters and N. Hallanger (Ashgate, 2006), 137–45.

'Rich Reality', *Science and Christian Belief*, 18 (2006), 31–4.

'Space, Time and Causality', *Zygon*, 41 (2006), 975–83.

'The Church is Marked by Openness to Science', in *The Many Marks of the Church*, ed. W. Madges and M.J. Daley (Twenty-Third Publications, 2006), 171–4.

'The Hidden Spirit and the Cosmos', in *The Work of the Spirit*, ed. M. Welker (Eerdmans, 2006), 169–82.

'Where is Natural Theology Today?', *Science and Christian Belief*, 18 (2006), 169–79.

'More than is Dreamt of in Your Theologies', in *The Life of Meaning*, ed. B. Abernethy and W. Bole (Seven Stories Press, 2007), 33–4.

'Science and Religion: Bottom-Up Style, Interfaith Context', *Zygon*, 42 (2007), 573–6.

'Science and Values', in *Science, Technology and Human Values*, ed. L.C. Christophorou and C. Drakatos (Academy of Athens, 2007), 39–50.

'The Universe as Creation', in *Intelligent Design*, ed. R.B. Stewart (Fortress, 2007), 166–78.

'An Evolving Creation and its Future', in *Evolution: Woher und Wohin*, ed. H.A. Muller (Vandenhoeck & Ruprecht, 2008), 17–25.

'The Nature of Time', in *On Space and Time*, ed. Shan Majid (Cambridge University Press, 2008), 278–83.

'A Scientist Looks at the Epistle to the Hebrews', in *The Epistle to the Hebrews and Christian Theology*, R. Bauckham et al. (Eerdmans, 2009), 113–21.

'Christian Belief in Creation and the Attitude of Moral Responsibility', *Journal of Law, Philosophy and Culture*, 3 (2009), 137–47.

'Evolution and Providence: A Response to Thomas Tracy', *Theology and Science*, 7 (2009), 317–22.

'God and Physics', in *God is Great, God is Good*, ed. W.L. Craig and C. Meister (IVP, 2009), 65–77.

'The Corporate Christ', in *Who is Jesus Christ for us Today?*, ed. A. Schuele and G. Thomas (Westminster John Knox, 2009), 103–111.

'The Demise of Democritus', in *The Trinity and the Entangled World*, ed. J. Polkinghorne (Eerdmans 2010), 1–14.

'Mathematical Reality', in *Meaning in Mathematics*, ed. J. Polkinghorne (Oxford University Press, 2011), 27–40.

'The Incompleteness of Science', *International Studies in Catholic Education*, 3 (2011), 136–144.

'Some Light from Physics', in *Light from Light*, ed. M.A. Meyers and G. O'Collins (Eerdmans, 2012).

Index

Dennet, D.C. 114
determinism 24, 54, 60, 64
Di Bucchianico, Marilena 70
discipline, science-theology study as 253–5
divine action 9–10, 33–50, 228–34, 248–9
    see also causal joint
Dixon, Thomas 150
Drees, Willem 28
dual-aspect idealism 130–1
dual-aspect monism 15, 41, 130, 147, 271
dualism 11, 15, 20, 41–2, 128–33, 141,
    146–7, 184, 271
Duhem, Pierre 68

Earman, John 54
Edwards, Denis 234
Einstein, Albert *see* relativity
Ellis, George 109–10, 145, 252–3
Elsasser, Walter 100
emergence 14–15, 27, 58–62, 130
empiricism 67–73
epiphany philosophers 149
epistemology 9–10, 58–65, 72–4, 85–6,
    175–96
eschatology 11, 22, 90, 139, 144–9,
    153–74, 261–2, 266, 272
Evans, Stephen 248
evil, natural *see* natural evil
evolution 8–9, 15

faith 3
fine tuning *see* anthropic fine tuning
Foster, Michael 231
foundational events 5
fractal 57
Fraser, Nancy 236
fundamentalism 5

Galison, Peter 70
Gaut, Berys 240
gene 15
Genesis, creation account in 5, 15
Gleick, James 53
Goldsworthy, Andy 238
Gregersen, Niels Henrik 192
Gregory of Nazianzus 26
Griffin, David 20
Gunton, Colin 231–2

Harré, Rom 150
Hartshorne, Charles 16, 20–1,30, 77, 235
Hitchens, Christopher 246
Hogan, Edward 203–4
holism 14
Holy Spirit 28, 43–4, 46–9, 263, 266, 272
human nature 15

idealism 127–37
if-statements 93–125
immanence, divine 20, 33, 49
incarnation 27 *see also* Jesus Christ
indeterminacy *see* determinism
information, information-bearing patterns
    11, 24, 33–50, 61–4, 108, 131–6,
    139, 147–8, 159, 184, 230–1, 271
intelligent design (ID) hypothesis 120–1,
    246–7
intelligibility of natural world 2–3, 7,
    141–2, 178
interfaith dialogue 5–6, 31, 255
interiority 20–1
International Society for Science and
    Religion 6, 255

Jaeger, Lydia 71
James, William 54, 57, 64
Jantzen, Grace 226
Jesus Christ 26–8, 46–8, 107, 243–8, 254

Kauffman, Stuart 146
kenosis, divine 9, 16–17, 39, 46–8, 107,
    140–1, 182–3, 217–42, 243–56,
    263, 267, 269, 272
Kim, Junghyung ix–x, 270
    chapter by 153–74
Kingsley, Charles 8
Koselleck, Reinhard 259

Lakatos, Imre 244
Lampe, Geoffrey 28
laws of nature 21–2, 74, 133, 265
liberal theology 197–215
Lieber, Theodore 53
Lonergan, Bernard 3
Lorenz, Edward 55–8
Losch, Andrew 181
Luhmann, Niklas 259